Refugee Protection
A European Challenge

To those who have had to flee
in order to seek international protection in another country
among them
my mother and father
Aurelio
Alex
and Javad

Vigdis Vevstad

Refugee Protection
A European Challenge

Tano Aschehoug

All rights reserved. No part of this work covered by the copyright may be reproduced in any form or by any means – graphic, electronic or mechanical, including photocopying, taping, or information storage and retrieval systems – without the written permission of the publisher.

© Vigdis Vevstad og Tano Aschehoug 1998
Omslag: Sigrid M. Jansen
Omslagsillustrasjon: Pjotr Sapegin
Sats: Tano Aschehoug
Trykk og innbinding: AiT Enger AS, Otta

Boken er satt med: AGaramond 11/13 pkt.
Papir: Carat 100 g

ISBN 82-518-3630-1

Acknowledgements

The ideas presented in this book have their origins in my research work leading to the degree of Docteur en Droit at the University of Strasbourg in 1995. The jury, headed by my inspiring adviser professor Alexandre Kiss, first encouraged me to have the thesis published.

Immediate and sustained support was given by my husband and most exacting critic, Arild Isegg. A seemingly endless patience and love as well as sound advice given while the original manuscript was being updated and changed, made the project feasible.

While working for the Norwegian Refugee Council (NRC) as legal adviser in 1996–1997, the necessary leeway and practical support to work on the book was given.

The Norwegian Scientific Council, the Norwegian Ministry of Justice and the Norwegian Directorate of Immigration provided the necessary funding which enabled publication.

The original manuscript was written in French. Cecilia Bailliet, Research Fellow at the University of Oslo Faculty of Law undertook the initial English translation and gave assistance with the updating. Sara Gaunt and Richard White, both interns at the Brussels office of the Euoropean Council on Refugees and Exiles (ECRE), finalized the English translation and contributed immensely through discussions on both form and substance.

With a background of working with refugee law and policies from various perspectives, governmental and non-governmental, national and international, I have had the privilege of discussing many of the ideas contained in this book with colleagues and friends in the various camps and many have given assistance in the research. I owe appreciation to many. Nevertheless, the responsibility for the opinions expressed in the book is mine.

A special thank you to Antonio Fortin, Senior Legal Adviser for Western and Northern Europe, UNHCR, Geneva, Johannes van der Klaauw, Senior European Affairs Officer, UNHCR, Brussels, Torill Myhren, Adviser to the Norwegian Directorate of Immigration and Pascal Steller, Administrator at the European Commission.

There are also those whose acclaim, criticism and advice I particularly cherish, as they took the time and trouble to read and comment on the manuscript in whole or in part, among these, Trygve G. Nordby former Secretary General of NRC, now City Manager, who also initiated cooperation between

NRC and the publisher Tano Aschehoug and gave me the «go ahead», Eirik Berg, Assistant Director General, Norwegian Ministry of Justice and Helga Fastrup Ervik, Legal Adviser of NRC.

To all the persons and institutions who have contributed in different ways to the making of the book:

Thank you.

Foreword

International protection of refugees consists in allowing them to enjoy fundamental human rights necessary for survival in safety and dignity. The right of refugees to such security is recognized in international law, but existing international instruments do not provide sufficient guarantees to all in need of international protection such as victims of war, civil war, international unrest and massive violations of human rights. The challenge posed by today's refugee problems is a daunting one, not least due to the approximately one hundred wars and civil wars over the last decade of the 20th century. Solutions can only be found through international cooperation. Political willingness to adhere to already existing obligations as well as willingness to think along new lines are both necessary prerequisites for improvement.

The book provides a welcome input to a necessary debate about how to come to grips with today's refugee situation in the European regional context. The realities of the modern refugee phenomenon might justify a re-evaluation of issues and definitions.

European States have remained in the forefront in assuring a regional protection system for human rights. Similar efforts should be encouraged for the protection of refugees in order to enhance refugee protection while taking the interests of refugees as well as the interests of States into consideration.

Vigdis Vevstad's innovative approach in calling upon European States to rethink their refugee policy is an important contribution to the European refugee debate and deserves a careful hearing.

Thorvald Stoltenberg

Contents

Introduction 13

Chapter 1 Historical background 17
    1.1 Origins of refugee protection 17
    1.2 Development of refugee protection in the 20th century 18
    1.3 Refugee protection since 1980 26

Chapter 2 Sources of international refugee law 33
    2.1 Treaty law 33
    2.2 Customary law 36
    2.3 Other sources, including «soft law» 37

Chapter 3 1951 Convention refugee status and its criteria 43
    3.1 Who is a refugee? 43
    3.2 Limitations to the application of the 1951 Convention 47
        Time limitation 47
        Geographical limitation 49
        A refugee must be outside the country of his nationality ... 51
        Refugee «sur place» 53
        Internal flight alternative 54
    3.3 Well-founded fear of persecution 55
        «Well-founded fear» 58
            Subjective and objective elements of fear 58
            The time when fear must have manifested itself 60
            Burden of proof 61
            Refugee status determination interviews 62
        «Persecution» 63
            Agents of persecution 65
            Persecution in relation to human rights principles 67
            Specific criteria referred to in the definition 72
            «Race» 72
            «Religion» 73
            «Nationality» 74
            «Membership of a particular social group» 74
            «Political opinion» 77

New trends – gender related persecution 78
The debate in the context of international organizations ...83
3.4 Cessation and exclusion of refugee status 86
«Cessation clauses» 86
«Exclusion clauses» 89

Chapter 4 Evolution of the refugee concept 95
4.1 Development of UNHCR's mandate 96
4.2 The refugee concept at a regional level 103
The OAU Convention 103
The Cartagena Declaration 107
4.3 The «de facto» refugee concept – a European perspective 109
Current understanding of the «de facto» refugee concept 112
State practice on «de facto» refugees 115
The debate in the context of international organizations.117
UNHCR 117
The Council of Europe 120
The Parliamentary Assembly 120
The Committee of Ministers 122
The European Union 123
4.4 Existing ideas for an expanded refugee definition 124
Broad interpretation of the 1951 Convention 125
Expansion of the 1951 Convention 126
4.5 Proposal in part for a new European convention on
refugee protection 127

**Chapter 5 International protection and the principle
of non-refoulement** 136
5.1 Various forms of protection 137
Residence permits for humanitarian reasons 138
Diplomatic asylum 139
Asylum requests presented to embassies or international
organizations 142
Internationally protected areas 143
5.2 Legal basis of the principle of non-refoulement 146
At the universal level 146
At a regional level 149
Africa and Asia 149
The Americas 149
Europe 151
The Council of Europe approach 151

   Article 3 of the European Convention on Human Rights. 153
   The European Union approach 156
  5.3 Legal developments of the principle of non-refoulement. 157
   From treaty law to customary law 157
  5.4 Particular aspects related to the non-refoulement
   principle 161
   Non-rejection at the border 161
   Non-expulsion and non-extradition 163
   Exceptions to the principle of non-refoulement 164
  5.5 Proposal in part for a new European convention
   on refugee protection 166

Chapter 6 Asylum 169
  6.1 Asylum at the universal level 171
   Article 14 of the Universal Declaration of Human Rights 172
   The UN Declaration on Territorial Asylum of 1967 173
   Conclusions on Asylum adopted by UNHCR's
   Executive Committee 175
   The failure of creating a Universal Convention on
   Territorial Asylum in 1977 176
  6.2 Asylum at a regional level 179
   European approaches 180
    The Council of Europe 181
    The European Union 186
  6.3 Temporary protection 191
   Legal developments of temporary protection 194
    UNHCR 194
    The European Union 199
    The Council of Europe 205
  6.4 Proposal in part for a new European convention on
   refugee protection 206
   The right to asylum and its duration 209
   Solutions if temporary asylum is lifted 214
   International solidarity and burden sharing 216
   Beneficiaries of asylum 219
   Treatment of refugees 221

Chapter 7 State responsibility for asylum requests 224
  7.1 «First country of asylum»/ «safe third country» concept .. 229
  7.2 Determination of responsibility 236
   Criteria 241

Right to choose an asylum country 242
Links to a particular State 243
Transit and «en route» 244
«Protection elsewhere» and «safe country» concept 246
7.3 Consequences of application of the «first country of
asylum»/«safe third country» concept 250
Refugees «in orbit»/danger of refoulement 250
Lack of international solidarity 251
7.4 Harmonization experience in the European context 253
The «Dublin/Schengen regime» 253
Examination by at least one State 257
Criteria according to the «Dublin/Schengen regime» .. 260
The London Resolutions 262
Present day practice 267
Readmission agreements 270
7.5 Proposal in part for a new European convention
on refugee protection 273
Safety of the asylum seeker 274
«Protection elsewhere» 276
Transit 277
Burden sharing and international solidarity 278
An international refugee tribunal 283

Chapter 8 Proposal for a new European convention
              on refugee protection 285

Appendix 1
Convention relating to the status of Refugees of 28 july 1951 292

Appendix 2
Protocol relating to the Status of Refugees of 31 january 1967 309

Bibliography 313

Index 334

Introduction

European countries are at a crossroads in their refugee policies. Half measures and national «ad hoc» solutions no longer suffice if Europe is to come to grips with the problems currently confronting it.

Almost half a century has passed since the international community, in response to the horrific events of the Second World War, introduced an international refugee protection regime. The Office of the United Nations High Commissioner for Refugees (UNHCR) was created by the adoption of the Statute of the Office of the United Nations High Commissioner for Refugees.[1] With the adoption of the Convention relating to the Status of Refugees of 28 July 1951,[2] which was later expanded by the adoption of the Protocol relating to the Status of Refugees of 31 January 1967,[3] the fundamental legal basis for refugee protection was established.

This refugee regime established international responsibility for the protection of victims of persecution. Since then changing circumstances have given rise to new groups of refugees in need of protection. Therefore, fifty years on, it is necessary to make a thorough evaluation of existing instruments in the light of today's requirements. The purpose of such an evaluation is twofold. Firstly, it should promote further consolidation of the 1951 Convention through insistence on a respectful and generous interpretation of this most significant universal instrument of refugee law. Secondly, it should identify the legal gaps from which refugee protection is suffering and propose an appropriate development of refugee law.

The main purpose of this book is to suggest a way of filling these gaps through the proposal of a new legal instrument: a European refugee convention.

States, although recognizing that refugee matters are international in character, do not easily accept legal harmonization because it implies relinquishment of sovereignty in an area in which complete control tends to overshadow all other considerations. As a consequence, international refugee law

---

1. General Assembly Resolution 428(V) of 14 December 1950.
2. The Convention often referred to as the Geneva Convention or the 1951 Convention, was adopted by the United Nations Conference of Plenipotentiaries on the Status of Refugees and Stateless Persons, held at Geneva from 2 to 25 July 1951.
3. Entry into force on 4 October 1967, hereafter called the 1967 Protocol.

is largely fragmented. Many questions are left pending in the international legal sphere.

In the absence of a comprehensive legal framework for refugee protection, States resort to «ad hoc» solutions when refugee crises occur rather than undertaking legal commitments which would contribute to consistent State practice. Without commitment to the rule of law, refugee protection depends solely on the political will of States.

The fact that international law is of marginal value unless States have a self interest in ensuring its implementation, should not inhibit furtherance of international cooperation as the crucial guarantee of refugee protection. To take international cooperation a step further, several questions need to be addressed. Firstly, is the timing right for proposing increased legal commitments? Secondly, should the proposal be universal or regional in character? Thirdly, what kind of legal instrument would be appropriate and under which auspices should it be negotiated? Finally, and more specifically, which elements should be included in such a legal instrument?

Whether or not the timing is appropriate, must be considered in view of the present necessity to find solutions for new groups of refugees in need of international protection. Claiming that «the time is not ripe» is the perennial excuse for evading unpleasant and challenging issues; the recipe for inaction. While the international community is watching and waiting, hundreds of thousands of persons are forced to flee their home country for reasons of war, civil strife and upheaval, massive violations of human rights and other kinds of generalized violence. These are people who are not necessarily covered by the criteria of the 1951 Convention. In Europe they are called «de facto» refugees. Their life and security as well as their rights, while in exile, depend entirely on the discretion of each State. Therefore, acknowledgement of international responsibility for these vast groups should no longer be postponed.

The objective to strive for should be a universal improvement of refugee protection. This ultimate goal would be best achieved through gradual regional developments, like those already witnessed in Africa and Latin-America. Success at a regional level could pave the way, towards a global approach. In terms of regional approaches, Europe stands out as a natural entity, due to its region-specific problems and because a harmonization of refugee and asylum law is, to a certain extent, taking place. However, that ongoing process concerns directly only the member countries of the European Union. Indirectly, the other countries in Europe and countries outside are affected by the policies adopted by the Member States of the European Union and therefore negotiations relating to these issues should be conducted in a much broader European context. Furthermore, it is time that negotiations, and hopefully results, reflect the interests of refugees as well as the interests of States.

As far as legal instruments are concerned, the sensible course of action, is to aim at establishing a new regional convention to supplement the 1951 Convention. Such a European convention should be negotiated under the auspices of the only pan-European organization suited for this purpose, the Council of Europe. With its forty member States, the Council of Europe is the most representative regional organization, it is founded on human rights principles and it has competence to adopt mandatory legally binding instruments.

The elements which should be included in a new legal instrument derive from that which is needed to fill the present legal gaps, i.a. a legally binding recognition of a supplementary refugee definition, a legally binding obligation for States to acknowledge refugees' right to protection and an equitable division of responsibility for the examination of asylum requests.

The book is divided into eight chapters:

Chapter 1 contains a brief historical background to the present state of development of international refugee law.

Chapter 2 presents the sources pertaining to refugee law.

Chapter 3 examines who is a refugee. Firstly, it discusses the refugee concept from a traditional refugee law perspective, the refugee definition contained in the 1951 Convention, and secondly, it expands on the need to interpret its criteria generously and thereby in accordance with its intention, notably to offer protection to the persecuted.

Chapter 4 deals firstly with the expansion of the refugee definition so far; the evolution of UNHCR's mandate and the African and Latin American refugee definitions. It describes various suggestions related to the harmonization of the concept of «de facto» refugee at a European level and gives examples of the variable practice of European States in the present day. Furthermore, the chapter discusses possible international solutions concluding with a proposal for a new European refugee definition which broadens the 1951 Convention definition to cover other persons in need of international protection.

Chapter 5 explores the meaning of international protection and the main emphasis is placed on State responsibility. This chapter focuses on the status of the fundamental principle of protection in international law, the non-refoulement principle, which prohibits return of a person to an area where his life or security would be in danger. A number of questions relating to the standing of the non-refoulement principle in customary international law, or relating to its scope, for example the issue of non-admission at the border, are still unresolved and are therefore addressed in this chapter. A clarifying article on non-refoulement is proposed as part of a new European refugee convention.

Chapter 6 examines the institution of asylum and other forms of protection. This includes States' right to grant asylum and refugees' right to seek it. Furthermore, this chapter contains a description of various international attempts at securing refugees' right to asylum. A discussion of alternative ways of according protection includes the need to institutionalize temporary protection in international law. Articles on the right to asylum and State obligations pertaining to treatment of refugees are proposed to be included in a new European refugee convention.

Chapter 7 deals with how States divide responsibility among themselves for the examination of asylum requests based on the «first country of asylum»/«safe third country» concept, which indicates the first country in which an asylum seeker has or could have sought asylum as the country responsible for the examination of the asylum request. The chapter also describes the consequences of returning asylum seekers to countries through which they had travelled prior to their arrival in the country of final destination. The purpose of the suggested new international rules in this area, is to ensure legal safeguards for refugees and to ensure State practice which, instead of creating legal barriers for refugees, establishes an equitable system of burden sharing based on the principle of international solidarity.

Chapter 8 brings together the individual proposals in the preceding chapters and presents the text for a new European refugee convention in its entirety. The draft convention reflects the purpose and content of this book The reader would, therefore, be well advised to begin by reading the draft convention first.

Many obstacles have to be overcome in order to bring to fruition a new European refugee convention. This fact alone should not prevent the contribution of ideas and the generation of discussion to arrive at an improved refugee protection regime. The need is unquestionable, the international community has the opportunity and the means to act, it only remains to take up the challenge.

Chapter 1
Historical background

1.1 Origins of refugee protection

Throughout history movements of people have occurred repeatedly. There has rarely been a civilization that has not experienced an exodus of persons in search of sanctuary and protection as a consequence of warfare or other reasons seriously threatening life and security. The institution of asylum developed during the age of antiquity and became an established and known concept within the philosophy and practice of the time. The term asylum is derived from the Greek word «asylon» which, translated literally, means «without capture, without violence, without devastation».

During antiquity, places of worship were considered to be inviolable and therefore natural places of asylum. During the Middle Ages, the link between religious institutions and asylum was further established by inclusion in the canon law of the Catholic Church.[4] In modern times, this link remains in cases in which persons seek sanctuary in churches. The inviolability of churches is still largely respected in spite of the fact that refugee status may have been denied by the State. Nevertheless, as far as secular law is concerned, the granting of such protection by the Church constitutes civil disobedience. The sanctuary movement in the U.S. and «church asylum» practice in European countries like France, Germany, Denmark and Norway, have revived the tradition of the Middle Ages. In France, police intervention against the three hundred so called «sans-papiers» who had taken refuge in a Parisian church in 1996, caused an outcry by the French public at large. In line with a longstanding human rights activist tradition in France, pressure against government policy was led by intellectuals who protested deportation orders. In Norway, a government appointed advisory committee to the Ministry of Justice, recently presented its recommendations on how to handle deportation cases involving children in «church asylum». According to this committee, the cases involving children should, as stipulated in the 1989 Convention on the Rights of the Child, take the interest of the child into consideration. The Ministry was advised to grant them a residence permit on humanitarian grounds and complied with the request in most of the cases.

---

4. Waldo Villalpando, «L'asile dans l'histoire», in Quaderni, published by UNHCR, 1991, p. 36.

As early as the Middle Ages, great movements of peoples took place in Europe. The more modern secular form of asylum began to develop after the birth of the feudal system, but did not fully mature until the development of the concept of the sovereign State. Before the French Revolution, although States took it upon themselves to grant or deny asylum, as for example, in the case of Protestant countries granting refuge to Huguenots in the 17th century, political refugees still risked extradition. The French Revolution, however, brought a fundamental change to the concept of a refugee and recognized the rights of asylum in the Constitution of 1793. Ironically however, the Revolution itself provoked a significant flow of political refugees from France.

1.2 Development of refugee protection in the 20th century

The theory and practical procedures for dealing with refugees and asylum have developed throughout the centuries. Not until the present century, however, have legally binding rules concerning refugees been adopted at an international level. This century has also witnessed the creation of international organizations given particular responsibility to assist and protect refugees.

The League of Nations was the first such organization to assume responsibility for dealing with a mass exodus of refugees. In the 1920s, approximately 800,000 Russians fled the consecutive political and military upheavals in their country beginning with the Revolution in 1917, following the defeat of the White armies in 1919-1920, the famine in 1921 and the final downfall of the counter-revolution in Siberia in 1922. The League of Nations High Commissioner for Refugees was established in June 1921. Dr. Fridtjof Nansen, a Norwegian scientist, explorer and politician, was the first person to hold the position of High Commissioner. He received the Nobel Peace Prize in 1922 for his work on behalf of refugees. During the 1920s and 1930s, the League of Nations initiated a number of instruments pertaining to refugees.

The first international instruments on the subject of individuals having been deprived of the protection of their country of origin were drawn up specifically to deal with the consequences of political events outlined above. The Arrangement of 5 July 1922 provided identity certificates for Russian refugees and was followed by the Accord of 31 May 1924 which extended «Nansen passports» to Armenian refugees fleeing from similar circumstances in search of protection. On 12 May 1926 these two separate agreements were combined in one legal instrument [5] providing a refugee definition by category and thereby awarding Armenian and Russian refugees the right to settle in a receiving country.[6] According to the definition contained in this instrument, a Russian refugee was any person of Russian origin who did not enjoy the protection of the government of the U.S.S.R. and who had not acquired another nationality. Similarly, an Armenian refugee was any person of Armenian origin, previously a subject of the Ottoman Empire, who did not enjoy the protection of the Turkish government and who had not acquired another nationality.

In 1928 these arrangements were extended[7] to Assyrian and Assyro-Chaldean refugees, as well as certain Turkish refugees. In 1935, they were further extended to political and religious dissidents from the Saar.[8] In these successive instruments, refugees were defined according to their national origin, or according to the territory they had left and the lack of protection on the part of their country of origin. This type of definition by category provides for a straightforward interpretation and allows an easy determination of the refugee status, as there is no conditional requirement of individual persecution in order for international protection to be accorded – a condition which appears in instruments adopted later. However, as so called pragmatic definitions which responded to specific circumstances, these arrangements were shown to be inadequate when overtaken by other events, for example, excluding all other refugees and displaced persons from international protection during the Second World War.

During the 1930s and 1940s, the persecution of Jews in Europe provoked a new wave of refugees. In 1933, when the situation was for the first time brought to the attention of the League of Nations, the result was the signing of the Convention on the International Status of Refugees, (28 October 1933).[9]

The establishment of various offices to deal with refugees originating from Germany turned out to be an inadequate display of international cooperation. In 1935, a disappointed High Commissioner, J. McDonald, the person charged with the international responsibility of the protection of the persecuted, resigned. In his letter of resignation, he directed strong criticism not

---

5. Arrangement of 12 Mai 1926. (League of Nations Treaty Series, No. 2004, Vol. LXXXIX (89), p.47).
6. M. Iogna-Prat, «L'évolution du concept de réfugié: Pratiques contemporaines en France», p. 16.
7. Arrangement of 30 June 1928 (League of Nations Treaty Series, No. 2006, Vol. LXXXIX (89), p. 63).
8. Resolution of the Council of the League of Nations No. 3593, of 24 May 1935 (Official Journal of the League of Nations, June 1935, p. 633).
9. League of Nations Treaty Series, No. 3663, Vol. CLIX (159), p.199.

only at Germany, but also at the League of Nations which he declared should not merely concern itself with dealing with the exodus as such, but should also address the source of the problem by exerting pressure on the German Nazi government.[10] The debate regarding the behaviour of States of origin in refugee crises, and the pressure which should be applied on these by the international community, States and organizations alike, is an ongoing and controversial one. McDonald's example of speaking out is one which others should follow.

A further Convention, pertaining to refugees originating from Germany, was signed on 10 February 1938.[11] Article 1 of this Convention contained an exclusion clause for those persons who left Germany for reasons of personal convenience. The article was in fact a forerunner to the concept of «persecution»,[12] subsequently developed and incorporated in the universal instruments which established that each case should be examined on an individual basis.

This latter, like the earlier Conventions, failed to keep up with the scale and nature of events as they unfolded. The Second World War provoked mass flights not only among the populations in the direct line of advancing troops, but also among «pre-war» refugees who had fled the fascist regime of Italy, the Spanish civil war, and the Nazi occupation of the Saar, Austria and Sudetenland, during the 1930s, and once again found themselves in danger. An estimated 30 million people were uprooted by the war and it was this experience which exerted a powerful influence over the international community.

The creation of the United Nations (UN) in 1945 marked an important progression in international cooperation and in refugee law. The UN brought

---

10. See G.J.L. Coles, «Solutions to the Problem of Refugees and the Protection of Refugees», Study presented at a Round Table organized by UNHCR and the International Institute of Humanitarian Law, 1989, p.33-36.
11. League of Nations Treaty Series, No. 4461, Vol, CXCII (192), p.59. As a consequence of World War II two additional international instruments were adopted: the Resolution of the Council of the League of Nations No. 4119 on January 17, 1939 (Official Journal of the League of Nations, February 1939, p.72) on the refugees of the territory of the Sudetens (which concerns the refugees who possessed Czechoslovak nationality, but who, after the incorporation to the Sudetenland found themselves to be without either the protection of the German government or the Czechoslovak government) and the Protocol of September 14, 1939 on the Austrian victims of the Nazi persecution (Treaty Collection, League of Nation, No. 4643, Vol.CXCVIII (198), p.141.
12. See G. Melander, «Further Development of International Refugee Law» in «The Refugee Problem on Universal, Regional, and National Level», Institute of International Public Law and International Relations, Tessaloniki, 1987 p.475.

to bear the wishes of the victors of the war, their principal expressed goal being to maintain international peace and collective security. A first step in this direction was the signing of the Charter of the United Nations on 26 June 1945 in San Francisco. The Charter of the United Nations lays down the rights and duties of Member States – the majority of States in the world. It establishes the organs which make up the organization, among which the most important are: the General Assembly, the Security Council, the Economic and Social Council (ECOSOC), and the International Court of Justice (ICJ).

Although the Charter itself does not directly include references to refugee or asylum problems, the General Assembly and the Security Council have both played a primordial role in the development of refugee law. The Charter serves as the basis from which the organization created special agencies, including UNHCR. Moreover, contributing to successive developments within the domain of human rights and refugee law is entirely in keeping with the Charter's proclaimed goals: «To achieve international cooperation in solving international problems of an economic, social, cultural or humanitarian character, and in promoting and encouraging respect for human rights and for fundamental freedoms for all without distinction as to race, sex, language, or religion». The inclusion of a commitment to the protection of human rights in the Charter was again a particular lesson learnt from the Second World War, inspired by the recognition of the need to restrain the authority of a State over its nationals.[13]

Preceeding UNHCR, various specialized organizations were established in order to address the problems of refugees and displaced persons immediately after the war. The United Nations Relief and Reconstruction Administration (UNRRA)[14] worked with allied military authorities to help the millions of civilian nationals of the allied countries and displaced persons in liberated countries. UNRRA also assisted in the repatriation and return of prisoners of war. Its mandate included the protection of refugees who had been denied fundamental civil and political rights, but the organization was, in principle, not authorised to resettle the displaced or to find solutions for refugees.

UNRRA was succeeded in 1946 by the International Refugee Organization (IRO) whose Constitution defined the terms «refugee» and «displaced person».[15] The definition of «refugee» applied to, among others: victims of Nazi and Fascist regimes, Quisling regimes, Spanish Republicans and per-

---

13. See the Preamble and Articles 55 and 56 in particular.
14. Established in November 1943.
15. Constitution of the International Refugee Organization, Annex I, concerning refugees and displaced persons as understood in the Resolution adopted on 16 February 1946 by the UN Economic and Social Council.

sons who had been considered to be refugees before the outbreak of the Second World War. Furthermore, IRO applied the Convention to all other refugees: «de jure» or «de facto» stateless persons, who had qualified as refugees before the war.

The definition of a «displaced person» applied to all those who, as a result of actions by the authorities of the Nazi and Fascist regimes, had been deported i.a. because of their race, religion, or political opinions; or had been compelled to forced labor. The term «displaced person» reappeared in 1975, when UNHCR accorded its assistance to refugees and displaced persons from Indochina.[16] The application of the term in contemporary times refers, for example, to persons who are not considered covered by the classical mandate of UNHCR in terms of the Statute of 1950, but who nevertheless are in need of international protection accorded to them by way of an extended mandate.

The IRO Constitution was also the first international instrument to make reference to the term «persecution» where the criteria of persecution were enumerated. In legal literature, the IRO definition has been described as an «ad hoc definition» which was aimed at protecting refugees from Communist countries,[17] thereby implying that persecution was a concept elaborated in the political context of the Cold War.[18] The Western bloc's assistance to refugees escaping from communist countries was considered provocative by the Communist bloc and therefore a political victory by the West.

In spite of the tension of the Cold War, the Office of the United Nations High Commissioner for Refugees was established on 1 January 1951[19] and the Convention relating to the Status of Refugees was signed on 28 July 1951.[20] UNHCR's initial mandate was for a period of three years, but it has since been extended regularly, each time for a duration of five years.[21] The function of the High Commissioner is defined in the Statute and in various resolutions subsequently adopted by the General Assembly of the UN.

When UNHCR began its work at the beginning of 1951, European refugees originated above all from Central and Eastern Europe. The largest exodus which Europe faced in the years immediately following the organization's inception, was that of approximately 200,000 Hungarian refugees in 1956.

---

16. See G.Goodwin-Gill, «The Refugee in International Law», p.8.
17. G. Melander, «Further Development of International Refugee Law», p.476.
18. See also F. Tiberghien, «La Protection des Réfugiés en France», 2nd edition, Economica, 1988, p.15; and J.C.Hathaway, «A Reconsideration of the Underlying Premise of Refugee Law», p.142 -143, and p.148-151.
19. The decision to establish the Office of the High Commissioner for Refugees is contained in Resolution 319 IV of the General Assembly, adopted on 3 December 1949.

This occurred at a time when the refugee problem in Europe was considered to have been more or less solved. However, from then onwards the need for UNHCR in other parts of the globe has increased enormously, as Africa, Asia and Latin-America have become the scenes of large scale displacements due to wars of independence, revolutions and coups. For example, in Algeria thousands were displaced by the battle for independence from French rule which began in 1954; in Asia, the civil war in Pakistan forced ten million persons into exile in India in 1971, and the Soviet occupation of Afghanistan in 1979 forced approximately six million Afghans to seek protection in Pakistan and Iran. The exodus of Vietnamese refugees started in 1975 with the fall of Saigon. Since then more than one million Vietnamese have become refugees. The response of the international community to these and other situations of population displacement has been mixed. For example, in the case of Vietnamese refugees an agreement was gradually reached among the «first countries of asylum». These countries agreed to grant «the boat people» temporary asylum, on condition that they would receive financial aid from the West to do so, and that the refugees would eventually be settled elsewhere. This approach marked the beginning of what is known as the refugee quota system. Under this system Western governments have proved to be generous in their willingness to resettle quota refugees from Indo-China. The U.S. alone has received more than 400,000 people.

The way in which UNHCR responds to the protection needs of refugees in various parts of the world is determined by its mandate. UNHCR's basic

---

20. In conformity with Resolution 429 (V), adopted by the General Assembly on 14 July 1950, a Conference of Plenipotentiaries on the Status of Refugees and Stateless persons, was convened in Geneva from 2 to 25 July 1951 in order to negotiate the convention on refugees. With the exception of the draft preamble and draft Article 1 on the refugee concept, the Conference used as a working base, the project on the Convention relating to the Status of Refugees and the project on Protocols regarding the Status on Stateless Persons prepared by the «Ad hoc» Committee on Refugees and Stateless Persons (the «Ad hoc Committee»), which was drafted during its second session held in Geneva from 14 to 25 August 1950. The text of the draft preamble was that which ECOSOC had adopted in its resolution 319B II on 11 August 1950 and the text of draft Article 1, was that which the General Assembly had annexed to Resolution 429 (V) of 14 December 1950. In order to ensure a universal representation of the new convention, participation in the Conference of Plenipotentiaries, included not only the member States of the UN, but also non-member States. The Convention was unanimously adopted on 28 July 1951 (the vote count was 24-0, with no abstentions). The 1951 Convention entered into force on 22 April 1954.
21. According to UN General Assembly Resolution 47/104 of 16th December 1993, the present five year term expires on 31 December 1998.

mandate emanates from the Statute of 1950 which authorizes the agency to decide who can receive its protection and assistance. Moreover, the Statute of 1950 serves as a legal foundation for activities carried out in countries which have not adhered to the 1951 Convention or which have done so with reservations because the Statute is universal in scope and application.

UNHCR was given an explicit protection mandate to defend the rights and interests of refugees, and the responsibility to search for solutions to their problems. In addition to the Statute of 1950, the legal foundation of UNHCR's protection efforts is based on conventional law such as refugee law instruments, human rights and humanitarian law instruments and on customary law. The whole range of «soft law» instruments and the evolution of UNHCR's mandate through the General Assembly and the Economic and Social Council resolutions contribute to the whole, as do the Executive Committee Conclusions[22]. Legal principles resulting from established practice, principles of humanity and requirements pertaining to public conscience equally play a role in this regard.[23]

The essential responsibilities which are thereby attributed to UNHCR include: supervision of the application of international conventions for the protection of refugees, and promotion, conclusion and ratification of such instruments. It is also UNHCR's task to improve the situation of refugees and to reduce the number of persons in need of international protection. Furthermore, while working for solutions to refugee problems, whether by enhancing local integration, resettlement or repatriation, UNHCR must always ensure that due consideration is given to protection guarantees.

In order to be effective, international protection depends on effective cooperation between States in the application of the principles of solidarity, and international responsibility and burden sharing. It depends equally on effective cooperation between UNHCR and States and other cooperative partners: governmental and non-governmental organizations (international and local). Flexibility, dynamism and courage are other prerequisites for UNHCR to be able to carry out its protection function.

UNHCR is subordinate to the UN and is therefore required to implement

---

22. G. Goodwin-Gill, «Refugees: The Functions and Limits of the Existing Protection System», in «Human Rights and the Protection of Refugees under International Law», Canadian Human Rights Foundation, 1988, p.157 in which, in reference to Veuthey, he arrives at an interpretation analogous to that of the protection function of the International Committee of the Red Cross consolidated by the 1949 Geneva Conventions and the 1977 Protocols, and in particular, the right to take humanitarian initiative and action which the wording of the conventions do not foresee but which are necessary for the protection of the victims.
23. D. Turpin, «Aspects Politico-Juridiques Internes de la Situation des Réfugiés en Afrique», p.103.

directives emanating from the General Assembly or ECOSOC.[24] UNHCR also has the duty to engage « ... in such additional activities ... as the General Assembly may determine ... »,[25] a base from which many of UNHCR's activities derive. For example, UNHCR acted as the lead UN humanitarian agency in former Yugoslavia and has frequently been called upon by specific governments, the Secretary General of the UN, and ECOSOC to assist not only refugees who have crossed an international border, but also internally displaced persons (IDPs).

The Executive Committee of UNHCR,[26] responsible for approving and controlling the material assistance programmes of the High Commissioner, also advises the High Commissioner on the accomplishment of her protection functions. At each annual meeting, the Executive Committee adopts Conclusions on important policy issues regarding refugee protection. The High Commissioner then reports to the General Assembly through ECOSOC to gain endorsement.

In 1995, the Executive Committee decided to reconstitute its annual cycle of meetings to comprise one annual plenary session and a number of inter-sessional meetings of a Standing Committee of the Whole, which meets four times a year, to deal with financial issues and focus on questions related to international protection.[27]

The number of member States of the Executive Committee has increased since it was first established, ensuring the widest possible geographic representation, including that of «refugee receiving» countries and «refugee producing» countries.[28] The annual meetings of the Executive Committee are open to observers: non-member States and international organizations, governmental and non-governmental alike. The Standing Committee meetings, however, ex-

---

24. See Article 3 of the Statute of 1950. UNHCR was established as a subsidiary organ within the terms of Article 22 of the UN Charter.
25. See Article 9 of the Statute of 1950.
26. In Resolution 393 (XIII) of 10 September 1951, ECOSOC created an advisory committee on refugees which was later transformed into the UN Refugee Fund (UNREF) in ECOSOC Resolution 565 (XIX) of 31 March 1955, adopted following Resolution 832 (IX) of the General Assembly of 21 October 1954. The latter was replaced in 1958 by the Executive Committee of the High Commissioner's Programme (Resolution 1166 (XII) of the General Assembly of 26 November 1957 and Resolution 672 (XXV) of the Economic and Social Committee of 30 April 1958.
27. The Standing Committee created in 1995 replaced the former Sub-Committee of the Whole on International Protection, the Sub-Committee on Administrative and Financial Matters and the Informal Meetings of the Executive Committee.
28. The number of member States is at present 53. The Standing Committee is made up of the same member States.

cluded the NGO-community and others from observer-status when they were established. This meant that NGOs did not have access to information and documents during the preparatory stages, which are often crucial to the outcome of plenary meeting decisions. The possibility for NGOs of acting effectively to influence the outcome of important protection policy questions therefore diminished. NGO observer status has since been established and access has been given to draft documents before adoption. This is of crucial importance for UNHCR's implementing partners in the field and policy partners to be heard in the international debate and thereby exercise some influence. The Oslo Declaration should always be kept in mind.[29]

The difficulties experienced by actors outside the realm of States and governmental organizations in gaining access and representation in the UNHCR fora are indicative of a more hostile and restrictive climate which currently exists in the world of international refugee protection. Whereas in the post war era an impressive amount of international instruments were adopted so as to ensure the inherent dignity of man and States' responsibility to help realize the goals set forth by the world community, today, States seem preoccupied with protecting themselves rather than offering protection to those in need. The very philosophy of human rights which guided States to adopt the 1951 Convention and establish an agency charged with the international responsibility of refugee protection, is increasingly being overtaken by the imperative of States' self-interest.

1.3 Refugee protection since 1980

Since the early 1980s, approximately five million[30] persons have sought asylum in Western Europe, and growing numbers are now making their way into Eastern and Central Europe as well.

The dramatic increase in arrivals of asylum seekers in the last two decades has been spurred by the accessibility of traveling by air which has trans-

---

29. A Conference taking place in Oslo 6–9 June 1994, organized by the Norwegian Refugee Council, marked the culmination of a year-long series of consultations and regional meetings (UNHCR and NGO PARinAC (Partnership in Action conferences) in Africa, Asia, Latin America, the Middle Eeast and Europe as well as consultations in Canada, Japan, and the U.S., to discuss the operational and policy related relationship between UNHCR and NGOs. The Oslo meeting was the most comprehensive meeting of its kind and it culminated with a so called Oslo Declaration and Plan of Action defining the agenda for future NGO/UNHCR humanitarian action.
30. UNHCR estimate, July 1997.

formed the possibilities for those fleeing persecution and violence. In the past, people would flee across a border and seek refuge in a neighbouring country; now they are increasingly arriving in the West by air from developing countries, giving rise to the expression «jet age refugees».[31] Some people arriving at western borders to claim asylum are economic migrants in search of a better future and some are in search of necessary protection from persecution and other forms of violence. As the borders of most Western countries are closed to immigration, one of the few alternative means of gaining entry to a European country is to apply for asylum. This has presented the countries concerned with a new challenge: the difficult task of separating those in need of protection from those abusing the institution of asylum.

An additional complicating factor for European countries receiving asylum seekers, is the uneven burden placed on those countries which are perceived by asylum seekers as being more likely to accept their applications. For example, out of approximately 679,400 asylum applications in Western-Europe in 1992, 438,191 were presented in Germany. This had a direct influence on the attitude of the German government in the drafting of new more restrictive legislation on asylum in 1993 as the government sought to counter the traditional image of Germany as the most generous asylum country in Western Europe.[32]

From the beginning of the 1980s the combination of a growing number of asylum applications in the Member States of the European Union and the realization of the goal of free movement of persons [33] inspired intensified intergovernmental cooperation in the area of refugee and asylum law. Governments of the Member States moved to counter fears that abuse of the asylum institution, coupled with ease of transit from one Member State to another, would lead to a dramatic rise in immigration throughout the Union.[34] The introduction of more rigorous external border controls as a security against unwanted immigration has inevitably had considerable repercussions on asylum policy in Europe.

---

31. See Michiel den Hond, «The new Asylum Seekers», Refugee Law in the 1980s, p. 49.
32. In 1993, there was a total of 322,599 applications in Germany, whereas, after the legislative change, it was down to 127,210 in 1994 and 127,937 in 1995. Source: The German Ministry of Interior, The Reuter European Community Report of 9 January 1996.
33. The European Single Act, signed on 28 February 1986 and entered into force on 1 July 1987.
34. See W. De Lobkowicz, «L'Union européene et le droit d'asile», Report presented to the colloquy «Evolutions récentes du droit des réfugiés en Europe», Toulouse, 25 March 1993, p. 8.

The Treaty of the European Union (the TEU or the Maastricht Treaty) [35] aims at a harmonized policy on asylum and refugees within the terms of its Title VI, the so called Third Pillar. According to Article K1 of the Maastricht Treaty, asylum issues are defined as «matters of common interest». The institutionalization of asylum issues under the Third pillar is perceived by some as a significant shift from earlier policy which made cooperation dependent on the goodwill of States.[36] However, asylum and immigration issues were not, at the outset, transferred to organs with supranational competence, although Title VI does give the Commission, along with Member States, the right of initiative.[37] Title VI also stipulates that the European Parliament should be «informed» and «consulted» regularly. However, in repeated declarations concerning issues of asylum and refugee policy, the Parliament has criticized the secrecy and withholding of information and documents and therefore the lack of parliamentary control.

In June 1997, the European Council revised the Treaty of Maastricht by the adoption of the Treaty of Amsterdam on 17 June 1997. [38] The new Treaty resulted from negotiations within the Intergovernmental Conference which had started in March 1996. Amendments have been made in the field

---

35. The forerunner to the European Union (EU), the European Community, was created by the adoption of the Treaty of the European Economic Community (Treaty of Rome), signed on 25 March 1957 and entered into force on 1 November 1958. (The term «European Community» will be used to signify the period previous to the entry into force of the Treaty of the European Union (Maastricht Treaty or TEU) which institutionalized the European Union). The annexes and the final act of the Maastricht Treaty were signed on 7 February 1992. The Treaty is the result of negotiations during an inter-governmental conference, which started in Rome on 17 December 1990 and was concluded in Maastricht on 11 December 1991.The Treaty entered into force on 1 November 1993.
36. W. Lobkowicz, «L'Union européene et le droit d'asile», p. 21.
37. Within the terms of article K.9, the TEU allows Article 100 C of the EC Treaty to be applied to areas under Article K.1, (1–6). Article K.9, called «the bridge», allows transfer of jurisdiction to community organs. The European Commission concluded in its Report to the Council that, notwithstanding the advantages offered by Article 100 C, the moment had not yet arrived for proposing the application of Article K.9, (Doc. SEC (93) 1687 final of 4 November 1993, p. 6). The Commission felt that an eventual application of article K.9 should be reexamined in the light of experience. It was, as expected, done during the Intergovernmental Conference on the revision of the TEU.
38. The Intergovernmental Conference came to a conclusion on 16 and 17 June 1997 in Amsterdam and the Revised Treaty on the European Union (the Treaty of Amsterdam) was published on 19 June 1997 in Document CONF/4001/97). The Treaty of Amsterdam was signed formally on 2 October 1997 and it is not expected to enter into force until 1999.

of asylum and immigration.[39] The asylum related provisions are to be found in the First Pillar (Treaty on the European Community) in Title IV «on visa, asylum, migration and other policies linked to free movement of persons».[40]

However, before the respective EU institutions of Council, Commission, Parliament and the Court of Justice are granted the competence in this area in the same way in which they enjoy them in other areas which fall under the First Pillar[41] there will be a «transitional period» of five years. During this transitional period following the entry into force of the Amsterdam Treaty, both the Commission and Member States will retain the joint right to initiate proposals to the Council, and the Council will continue to take decisions by voting in unanimity. At the end of this transitional period (presumably in 2004), the Commission will be given the sole right of initiative in asylum matters. At the same time, the Council will take a unanimous decision as to whether it will take decisions by qualified majority voting and as to whether the Parliament will be given further powers so that it can veto Community legislation in the area of asylum and immigration[42]. If these latter two decisions are unanimously approved by the Council, it is hoped that the present system of consensus voting which tends to lead inevitably to the adoption of asylum legislation based on the lowest common standards, will at least be replaced by a more democratic decision making procedure among the Member States which is in turn more likely to ensure the introduction of better legal safeguards for asylum seekers entering the Union. It is nevertheless regrettable that no changes will be made for another six to seven years.

Measures taken in the field of asylum and refugees in the period of European Union cooperation leading up to the institutional changes contained in the Treaty of Amsterdam have been developed in changing political fora. The

---

39. See more specifically on this, Johannes van der Klaauw, «The provisions on human rights and asylum in the revised Treaty on European Union», Netherlands Quarterly on Human Rights, 15/3, 1997, p. 365-369.
40. See, the Treaty of Amsterdam, Consolidated version, reviewed by legal linguists after its adoption on 2 October 1997.
41. The Treaty of Amsterdam has kept its three pillar structure: The First Pillar (Treaty of the European Community) is part of the three-pillar structure of the Treaty on European Union. The Second Pillar concerns Common Foreign and Security Policy and, the Third Pillar concerns Judicial and Police Cooperation.
42. Exceptions relating to visa policy are stated under Article G3. The list of nationals requiring visas and the format of visas will be decided by qualified majority voting procedures as soon as the Treaty enters into force. After five years, the issues under visa policy will be handled under procedures of co-decision with the Parliament. See ECRE, «Analysis of the Treaty of Amsterdam in so far as it relates to asylum policy», (Bo4/02/97), 16 July 1997.

«Ad Hoc Immigration Group» which pre dated the Maastricht Treaty and consisted of Ministers of the Member States responsible for immigration was succeeded in 1993 by the Council of Ministers of Justice and Internal Affairs and its sub-organs in which the substance of policy is developed in various working groups.[43] It was this latter forum which on 10 December 1993, adopted a programme of action[44] which, i.a., specified that harmonizing the application of the 1951 Convention refugee definition, was an area of «common interest». This eventually led to the adoption by the European Council, on 4 March 1996, of the Joint Position on a harmonized application of the definition of the term «refugee» in Article 1 of the Geneva Convention of 28 July 1951 relating to the Status of Refugees.[45]

Taking the decisions which were made on an intergovernmental level during the pre -Maastricht period, the 1980s and the 1990s can be characterized as decades of attempted cooperation between the Member States aimed at controlling and minimizing the number of asylum seekers arriving on the territory of the Union. A common approach, although in practice executed on a unilateral basis as each Member State was required to adopt legislation on a national level in order to bring legal effect to bear on intergovernmental measures, has led to the adoption of various restrictive measures to prevent uncontrolled flight and entry for the purpose of preventing what is perceived as abusive asylum claims. Visa obligations, carrier sanctions, strict interpretation of the 1951 Convention and resort to the concept of «first country of asylum» are among these.[46] Such measures have led to a general decrease in asylum applications in Western Europe. There are, however, already speculations regarding a corresponding increase in clandestine immigration. Un-

---

43. See in this regard, the Report by the Ministers of Immigration at the Maastricht meeting of the European Council on immigration and asylum policy (SN 4038/91), (WG1 930) approved on 3 December 1991 as the Maastricht work programme in which it was equally affirmed that immigration policy is restrictive, but that refugee policy, the policy of family reunification, and the policy of access to the territory for humanitarian reasons constitute important exceptions to the restrictions. It also notes that the European tradition is founded on principles of social justice and respect for human rights, such as they are defined in the European Convention on Human Rights. The Maastricht work programme included, i.a.: the establishment of a harmonized interpretation of the refugee definition of the 1951 Convention, the establishment of an information exchange system, the creation of an Information Center for analysis and discussion of asylum matters. Priority was also to be given to the ratification by all member States of the Dublin Convention.
44. See Communication of the Commission to the Council and to the European Parliament, COM (94) 23 final, Brussels on February 23, 1994, p.10.
45. See below, p. 66–67.
46. See below, Chapter 7.

official estimates are into the millions. Such a development is detrimental not only to States, but also implies a risk that persons in need of protection do not present themselves to the authorities of an asylum State out of fear of deportation and therefore remain without assistance of any kind.

The adoption of restrictive measures does not solve either the problem of abusive asylum claims, nor more importantly the problems surrounding the protection of refugees. Rather they create new problems for States and place unnecessary obstacles in the way of those seeking refuge in Europe from persecution. Restrictive measures aimed primarily at combating illegal immigration are implemented on a non-discriminatory basis, and therefore they effect not only those who are not in need of protection, but also «bona fide» refugees, for example, those who are prevented from fleeing their country of origin because they are unable to obtain the necessary travel documents to gain entry to the territory of the EU. The implications for international refugee law are grave. The right to seek asylum as it was incorporated in the Universal Declaration on Human Rights is being undermined; so is the aim and purpose of the 1951 Convention itself, in which States took it upon themselves to extend their protection to refugees. The principle of protection, the right to seek asylum included, has no value if the same States which guaranteed they would uphold it are, by the measures they are adopting on a European and national level, actively preventing refugees from seeking protection in the first place.

The Parliamentary Assembly of the Council of Europe, commenting on the restrictive asylum policy of the EU countries in Recommendation 1236 of 12 April 1994, suggests that, instead of the bilateral and multilateral agreements which flourish in the European context at present, European countries should strive for a broader pan-European cooperation. Such calls were being made as early as 1992. The Conference of Ministers which addressed the issue of the movement of persons coming from Central and Eastern Europe, in which all the Member States of the Council of Europe participated, in addition to Australia, the Soviet Union, the United States and Canada, issued a final communiqué[47] advocating a much broader international cooperation in the future, which was not restricted to the fifteen Member States of the European Union.

Protection issues undoubtedly need to be put back on the agenda, and the context of discussion must be broad enough to cover the whole European region. It therefore would seem appropriate to bring the discussions back into the sphere of the Council of Europe which has its foundation on principles

---

47. Annexed to the 1992 Report of the Council of Europe on Europe and the refugee policies, Doc. 6413 (Rapporteur Sir John Hunt), p.15 and following.

of human rights. The EU Member States, which are equally members of the Council of Europe, will obviously play an important role. There can be no valid reason why they should not be willing to bring the discussions forward in this appropriate forum.

If the international community really wants its human rights policy, in general, and refugee policy, in particular, to be carried out successfully, it is feasible. The opportunities now exist as they have never done before for pressure to be exerted on those States which do not honour their human rights obligations, be it towards their own citizens or towards refugees residing within their territory. Many factors are in place: accessibility to information, economic means, education and expertise, universal and regional mechanisms adopted particularly for the protection of human rights, (although often poorly used), and the option for humanitarian intervention to be carried out on an equitable basis not determined by particular economic and other interests.

However, the development of a coherent international refugee policy which brings protection guarantees up to date with changing requirements and circumstances, does require a change in attitude, and not only on the part of States jealously guarding the integrity of their territorial borders. A change of attitude is required on the part of UNHCR as well which needs to prioritize its unique protection mandate rather than divert its attention to too many areas better left to other organizations.[48] Finally, better efforts at cooperation are also necessary in the NGO community. Globally and regionally it is possible to act. There is an opportunity to reverse the present negative trend, provided that all actors cooperate in order to achieve a comprehensive refugee policy in which refugee protection is the main focus.

---

48. See Trygve G. Nordby and Vigdis Vevstad, Aftenposten, Article of 10 November 1996. See equally, G. Goodwin-Gill, «Refugee Identity and the Fading Prospect of International Protection», Human Rights Law Centre, University of Nottingham, Conference on Refugee Rights and Realities of 30 November 1996.

CHAPTER 2
Sources of international refugee law

The sources of law pertaining to refugees are international in character and are to be found mainly in three sets of international rules: refugee law, human rights law and humanitarian law. Refugee law is also national in character in the sense that international public law is transformed into national law in order for it to be applicable in the national context. International law is sometimes, as in the case of fundamental non-derogatory principles of human rights, directly applicable in national law, and sometimes it is transformed into national law by way of incorporation of the international text into an existing piece of national legislation. The latter pertains in the case of the 1951 Convention (the principal international instrument for refugee protection), which has been incorporated in this way into many national legislations. International law may also assume national applicability by way of reference to the international text in the national legislation. On occasion, national law goes further than international law, for example, in rights pertaining to asylum, which can be found in some States' national constitutions and in other domestic legislation.[49]

2.1 Treaty law

A logical point of departure for the definition of the sources of international law which are relevant is Article 38(1) of the Statute of the International Court of Justice. In the Statute the traditional sources on which refugee law is founded are defined as: international conventions, international customary law sanctioned by general usage, general principles of law, judicial decisions and doctrine. Traditionally, the first three are considered «principal sources» of international law, whereas the latter two are considered to be «subsidiary sources». National legislation, and moreover, national court decisions, are also indicators of the present state of affairs of international law, but cannot be considered as sources of international law as such.

---

49. France and Germany have rights pertaining to asylum in their constitutions, whereas other Member States of the European Union and Norway are examples of countries which deal with this issue in domestic legislation.

Within refugee law, States have been particularly hesitant to adopt conventions which would entail legal, mandatory obligations and which would restrict their sovereignty. This is why no universal convention has been adopted in order to regulate the issue of asylum. Another example which reflects this hesitation by States, is the lack of international harmonization of the concept of «de facto» refugees, that is, refugees in need of international protection, but who are not considered as 1951 Convention refugees.

Therefore, rather than sign up to conventions to deal with questions pertaining to refugees, States tend to make use of «ad-hoc» solutions. Nevertheless, they have also contributed to the development of refugee law within international organizations through the adoption of important policy declarations in resolutions, recommendations etc. Although as a starting point, such declarations are not legally binding in the way that conventional law is, they can contribute to legal development, as «soft law» instruments. In spite of the fact that the principle of sovereignty excludes the existence of a central international legislative power, it does not preclude the formation of norms within the international order. The authority of «soft law» instruments depending on the interest and follow-up by States, can attain a legal bearing. In other words, all norms of international law do not have the same origin and legal value. Legal obligations are sometimes created exclusively by States, sometimes international organizations play an important role.[50] The UN General Assembly, ECOSOC and UNHCR are, in this regard, primarily responsible for the development of the refugee concept and for developments regarding international responsibility for refugee protection.

In spite of the differing authoritative value which the term «instrument of international law» can have in different contexts, it will be used in the following paragraphs, both when dealing with an instrument of conventional, mandatory legally binding law as, for example, the 1951 Convention; or when referring to an instrument derived from an international organization which, at least as a point of departure, if not mandatory, has moral and political value.

Norms which derive from international treaties could be compared to «legislative norms», while those which result from customary law should be considered as the «unwritten rules». Together, these norms form what has been called «the hard core of international law» and constitute legal sources which have mandatory binding validity. However, treaties – whether bilateral or multilateral – are undeniably the pre-eminent source of international law.

The link between refugee protection and human rights law cannot be em-

---

50. H. Thierry et. Al., «Droit International Public», Editions Montchrestien 1984, p.8.

phasized enough. Violations of human rights principles constitute the foundation on which the criteria of the 1951 Refugee Convention are based, and the international instruments pertaining to the protection of human rights are therefore indispensable for the interpretation of the refugee protection instruments. The foundation stone of these international instruments pertaining to human rights protection is the 1948 Universal Declaration of Human Rights. This was followed in 1966 by the International Covenants on Civil and Political Rights[51] and on Economic, Social and Cultural Rights[52] which, as conventions, have legally binding mandatory validity. Furthermore, the UN Convention on the Elimination of all Forms of Racial Discrimination was adopted in 1965[53] and was followed-up by a «lex specialis» instrument, the International Convention on the Suppression and Punishment of Apartheid in 1973.[54] The Convention for the Repression of the Crime of Genocide entered into force in 1951.[55]

In 1984, the UN adopted an instrument which is of particular relevance and importance to the interpretation of human rights instruments for the protection of refugees: the UN Convention against Torture and other Cruel, Inhuman or Degrading Treatment or Punishment.[56] This Convention has a significant bearing on an individual's claim for refugee status in relation to an evaluation of whether or not a return to another country would constitute a violation of the non-refoulement principle, which implies that no one may be returned to an area where his life or security would be threatened. Other human rights instruments which are important in relation to particular refugee groups are the Convention on the Elimination of All Forms of Discrimination against Women of 1979 [57] and the Convention on the Rights of the Child of 1989.[58]

In the adoption of instruments for the protection of human rights at a regional level, Europe has led the way. The European Convention for the Protection of Human Rights and Fundamental Freedoms (hereafter called the European Convention on Human Rights) was adopted as early as 1950.[59] Regional instruments in other parts of the world were adopted much later: the American Convention on Human Rights was only adopted in 1969,

---

51. Entry into force on 23 March 1976.
52. Entry into force on 3 January 1976.
53. Entry into force on 4 January 1969.
54. Entry into force on 18 July 1976.
55. Approved and submitted for signature and ratification or adhesion by the UN General Assembly in Resolution 260 A (III) on 9 December 1948.
56. Entry into force on 26 June 1987.
57. Entry into force on 3 September 1981.
58. Entry into force on 2 September 1990.
59. Entry into force on 3 September 1953.

(Pact of San José de Costa Rica),[60] whereas the African Charter on Human and Peoples' Rights was adopted in 1981.[61]

However, Europe has lagged behind when compared to other regions of the world in the further development of international instruments directly relating to the protection of refugees. The only convention adopted to date which contains provisions on an expanded refugee concept has come from Africa. The OAU[62] Convention governing the specific aspects of refugee problems in Africa (hereafter called the OAU Convention) was adopted on 10 September 1969.[63] This Convention was drawn up in response to refugee problems experienced in Africa, and stands out on the world stage as an exceptional regional instrument. An important contribution to the development of refugee law in Latin America, which again goes beyond anything so far adopted on a European level, is the Cartagena Declaration on Refugees of 1984.[64] Although this instrument had no direct legally binding applicability on States, it has since been incorporated into the national legislation of several countries in the region, for example, in Ecuador, Bolivia, Mexico and Colombia, and the principles contained therein are referred to as regional customary law.

The reluctance on the part of sovereign States, in particular European States, to sign up to universal instruments which develop the refugee concept beyond that which is contained in the 1951 Convention is one anomaly which has left us with a refugee protection regime which does not guarantee protection for all refugees. Another is the fact that the 1951 Convention itself does not explicitly regulate the question of asylum, and therefore the most important universal refugee instrument in international law leaves the grant of asylum entirely to the discretion of States. Nevertheless, the criteria contained in the 1951 Convention pertaining to its application, have become the criteria by which States grant asylum as laid down in their national legislation.

2.2 Customary law

Customary law is an unwritten, but mandatory legally binding source of law. Two conditions need to be met in order for a customary norm to become

---

60. Entry into force on 18 July 1978.
61. Entry into force on 1 October 1986.
62. Organization of African Unity.
63. Entry into force on 20 June 1974.
64. This Declaration was adopted on 22 November 1984 by ten Latin American governments (Belize, Colombia, Costa Rica, Guatemala, El Salvador, Honduras, Mexico, Nicaragua, Panama and Venezuela).

mandatory, legally binding. Firstly, the customary norm has to be reflected in consistent practice of States and secondly, all concerned States must consider it to be legally binding («opinio juris»). It is evident that today, with often opposing interests among different States, an evolution of customary law of universal application is more difficult than at a regional level.

The cornerstone of international refugee protection, the «non-refoulement» principle, prohibiting return to an area where life or security would be threatened, is an example of customary law. This principle is firstly a conventional rule, in view of its incorporation as Article 33 of the 1951 Convention, and has become a universally accepted customary norm in cases in which the person concerned risks being subjected to torture upon return. The scope of the principle as regards other violations of human rights is, as will be discussed later, disputed.

2.3 Other sources, including «soft law»

The other traditional sources to be taken into consideration, are, as previously indicated, «general principles of law», judicial decisions and doctrine.

With regard to the general principles, it has been debated whether the principles mentioned in Article 38 (1) of ICJ's Statute, concern only fundamental international principles, such as «pacta sunt servanda» and the principle of good faith, or also principles emanating from various national laws.[65] There is no reason why international law cannot derive in part from rules originating in national law.[66]

As for doctrine and judicial decisions, Article 38 clearly states that these are «subsidiary» sources. It is evident that doctrine can not in any context attain the same value as conventional or customary law. Judicial decisions of the International Court of Justice, on the other hand, have great importance because they contribute to the recognition of «soft law» principles as legally binding.

The creation of a judiciary organ specializing in refugee and asylum matters to which individuals could have recourse, has been discussed in different expert and NGO fora. States have not yet accepted the idea let alone begun to develop it, either at a universal level, or at a regional level. However, this does not mean that the idea should not be pursued. NGOs have often referred to the importance of increased judicial and democratic control in the

---

65. See, K.A. Fleischer, «Folkerett» («International Public Law»), Universitetsforlaget, 6th edition, 1994, p.31 and H.Thierry et. al., «Droit international public», 1984, p.132-36.
66. H. Thierry et. al., «Droit international public», 1984, p.134.

EU-context as the asylum practice of the Member States has been shown to suffer from their absence.

It is interesting to note that the Dutch Parliament refused, for a long time, to ratify the Convention Determining the State Responsible for Examining Applications Lodged in one of the Member States of the European Communities (hereafter called the Dublin Convention),[67] precisely because it does not make reference to a judicial organ, but rather, to a committee composed of a governmental representative from each Member State «... in charge of examining, upon the request of one or several member states, any question of general order relative to the application and interpretation of the present convention».[68]

As explained above, the fact that a centralized international legislative organ does not exist, does not preclude the creation of normative refugee law by norms of soft law. These norms are created by virtue of the fact that international organizations have the competence to adopt resolutions which recommend definite behaviour and, in consequence, have a normative bearing. The formation of international law is therefore affected by the role of international organizations. Depending on the quality of resolutions, these may, in other words, contribute to the expression or elaboration of customary norms, and thus to the formation of international law.[69] However, States disagree regarding the «law-generating effect» of «soft law» norms, i.e. at what point the content of resolutions emanating from, for example, the UN General Assembly can be seen as constituting norms of customary law and not merely politically and morally binding norms.

«Soft law» resolutions, recommendations, etc., form a unity of provisions which can be used with flexibility and freedom of action if circumstances so require. Not only does this ensemble of provisions have a regulatory effect, but it also contributes to the development of law, for example, human rights law derived from the Universal Declaration of Human Rights of 1948.[70] The concept of «soft law» is, however, difficult to define and its effect is difficult to measure,[71] but it should be kept in mind that in international relations,

---

67. Adopted on 15 June 1990 and entered into force on 1 September 1997.
68. Article 18 of the Dublin Convention.
69. H. Thierry et.al., «Droit international public», 1984, p.9. See also, S.M. Schwebel, «The Effect of Resolutions of the UN General Assembly on Customary International Law», American Society of International Law, Proceedings of the 73 Annual Meeting, Washington D.C., 1979, p.301.
70. C.M. Chinkin, «The Challenge of Soft Law: Development and Change in International Law», International and Comparative Law Quarterly, Vol.38, Part 4, October 1989, p.853.
71. B. Sloan, «General Assembly Resolutions Revisited (Forty Years Later)», 1987, p.107.

there is not always a big difference between the effect of the mandatory, legally binding instruments and the effect of «soft law» instruments.

The fact that States choose to adopt norms through the intermediary of the General Assembly of the UN, a non-legislative power, is a paradox. In principle, this prevents the norms from having an immediate legal effect, yet, on the other hand, these non-legal norms may, as has already been stated, acquire a binding character over time.[72] It can be argued that consistent State practice, in harmony with the content and intent of a resolution, is proof of transformation into law. In the same way, when international principles of «soft law» are incorporated or transformed into national law, this could constitute a demonstration of «opinio juris».

One characteristic of «soft law» is that it is written law. Another characteristic which is of particular relevance to refugee protection, is that the authority of different resolutions vary. However, two principles should inform any interpretation and assessment of the authority of a «soft law» instrument: international cooperation and interpretation in «good faith»[73]. It would thus be legitimate to expect that a State, after having consented to a rule, would respect it even if it is not legally binding in the strictest sense.[74]

The authority of a resolution can be evaluated through an assessment of various factors: its nature, content and intent. The nature and intent of a resolution shows in whether it is a «declaring» or «recommending» resolution. If, for example, a resolution is adopted unanimously, that in itself constitutes an element which reinforces its authority. Positions taken by States during the deliberation process, and of course, subsequent State practice, should also be taken into consideration.[75] The pertinence of a resolution, in comparison with other sources of international law, and the political implication of its content, must also be considered. The resolutions of a limited scope from those more widely recognized. Repetition also in-

---

72. C.M. Chinkin, «The Challenge of Soft Law: Development and Change in International Law», 1989, p.856.
73. The principle of interpretation in «good faith» is implicitly a part of the principle «pacta sunt servanda». It is furthermore an explicit obligation of international law according to Article 2 (2) of the Charter of the United Nations and in Article 26 of the Vienna Convention on the Law of Treaties of 1969. See B. Sloan, «General Assembly Resolutions Revisited (Forty Years Later)», 1989, p.121.
74. W. Kälin, «Protection from Forcible Return for De Facto Refugees: Approaches and Principles in International Law», ELENA (European Legal Network on Asylum) Seminar, «The Legal Status of De Facto Refugees and Rejected Asylum Seekers», February 12–14, 1988, p.128.
75. See B. Sloan, «General Assembly Resolutions Revisited (Forty Years Later), 1989, p. 125.

creases the value of the resolution as precedent and confirms a persistent practice.[76]

The Universal Declaration of Human Rights is an interesting example in the discussion on the degree to which «soft law» instruments have a law generating effect. Some claim that the Declaration is merely a political statement, whereas others maintain that it has acquired the effect of a legally binding instrument of international law. However, there can be no doubt that the Declaration does contain universally accepted principles of human rights, of which some are non-derogable, and that it has influenced the creation of international conventions pertaining to the protection of human rights.

Another important declaration emanating from the UN General Assembly concerning refugees is the UN Declaration on Territorial Asylum of 1967. The intention of the UN was to create an instrument of legally binding authority, namely a convention on territorial asylum. The attempt having failed, the declaration must nevertheless be considered as an instrument containing moral and political validity, but not in itself as a legally binding instrument although its principles have contributed to the development of international customary law, including States' right to grant asylum.

In the fifty years following the adoption of the 1951 Convention and the Statute of 1950, the refugee concept has developed due to repeated resolutions adopted by the UN General Assembly and ECOSOC. The question is whether these resolutions have resulted in State obligations or whether they are merely instructions on assistance and protection of refugees to UNHCR, being a subordinate organ to the General Assembly and ECOSOC. No one disputes, at this point, that the resolutions have expanded UNHCR's mandate to cover both victims of persecution and victims of other man made disasters. However, States would reject claims that they thereby have assumed legal responsibility vis-à-vis «de facto» refugees.

UNHCR plays an active role in the development of international refugee law through advice given by its Executive Committee[77] in resolutions (Conclusions) on refugee protection.

---

76. For further discussion on the law generating effect of «soft law» instruments, see C.M. Chinkin, «The Challenge of Soft Law: Development and Change in International Law», 1989, p. 857; S.M. Schwebel, «The Effect of Resolutions of the General Assembly on Customary International law», American Society of International Law, Proceedings of the 73rd Annual Meeting, Washington D.C., 1979, p. 302; B. Sloan, «General Assembly Resolutions (Forty Years Later)», p. 132.
77. M. Moussalli, Introduction, Collection of Conclusions on the International Protection of Refugees, adopted by the Executive Committee of UNHCR, Geneva 1990.

The clearest manifestation of the importance of the Conclusions, is when States incorporate them into their legislation and respect them in their practice. The same applies when reference is made to the Conclusions in other international instruments. The Member States of the European Union made reference to Conclusion No. 58 (XL) of UNHCR's Executive Committee, for example, in their 1992 Resolution on a Harmonized approach to questions concerning host third countries.[78]

UNHCR's Executive Committee Conclusions are not imposed on States. Nevertheless, the fact that they are adopted within the agency responsible for international protection of refugees gives them an exceptional value also at the political and moral level. Moreover, the Conclusions are of importance for the interpretation of refugee law and they contribute to assuring, or attempting to assure, international harmonization for refugee protection.

Another useful, although not binding tool, for the interpretation of international law is UNHCR's Handbook on Procedures and Criteria for Determining Refugee Status which was produced at the request of the Executive Committee. The Handbook gives States useful guidance on refugee status determination according to Article 1(A) of the 1951 Convention. It also ensures, if followed, a harmonized interpretation of the refugee definition.[79] According to Article 8 of the Statute of 1950, UNHCR is given the duty to provide the protection of refugees by i.a. supervising the application of international conventions for the protection of refugees. Article 35 of the 1951 Convention obliges contracting States to cooperate with UNHCR by i.a. facilitating UNHCR's duty of supervising the application of the provisions of the 1951 Convention. These provisions clearly indicate the importance of UNHCR's involvement in the interpretation of the 1951 Convention and this argument is further strengthened by the fact that UNHCR is the international body which has a global overview of questions pertaining to refugees and their need for protection. It is also worth noting that, each year, UNHCR presents its views and discusses current issues relating to international protection in its «Note on International Protection» which is presented for consideration to the annual meeting of the Executive Committee.

At a regional level, the Council of Europe adopts both conventions, of an unquestionable mandatory legal nature, such as the European Convention

---

78. Adopted on 30 November 1992, see below, p. 262–267.
79. This view is supported by the European Parliament which, recognizing the difficulties linked to the interpretation of various elements of the 1951 Convention definition, such as the concepts of «well-founded fear» and «persecution», suggested to take recourse of the UNHCR Handbook to resolve interpretation problems and reach a harmonized interpretation, See Official Journal, C337, Vol. 35 of 21 December 1992.

on Human Rights, and resolutions which, as a starting point, have a more political and moral value. Instruments on refugee and asylum law are for instance normally adopted by the Parliamentary Assembly and the Committee of Ministers.[80] Although the recommendations and resolutions emanating from these organs are, initially not legally binding, they do express the political opinion of European politicians and governments and should therefore not be disregarded. For example, the Council of Europe has contributed to the development of the «non-refoulement» principle as a regional principle of customary international law. This has resulted from the application of the Human Rights Convention and the adoption of various recommendations and resolutions, of which Resolution 14 (1967)[81] on asylum to persons in danger of persecution, is the most significant. These developments have influenced European State practice and «opinio juris».

The international legal order within which international instruments relating to refugees are made is in a state of evolution. The process is a slow one, making refugees in need of international protection also victims of protracted discussions in various international political fora. It remains difficult to establish unequivocally when and how the effect of «soft law», which accounts for most of international refugee law, becomes customary law by which individual States are bound. In order to accelerate legal developments which will be of concrete and direct benefit to refugees, the international community should adopt conventions containing mandatory legal norms. Moral and political standards are not always enough to ensure adequate refugee protection – especially as there is scarce agreement on the authority pertaining to such norms. The proposal for a new European refugee Convention seeks to incorporate norms which, at present, are to be found in Treaty law instruments, such as the 1951 Convention, as well as norms presently found in «soft law» instruments or deducted from positive State practice.[82]

---

80. The Parliamentary Assembly recommendations are expressions of European political attitudes whereas the recommendations by the Committee of Ministers reflect what governments are willing to commit themselves to. This accounts for the Parliamentary Assembly often showing a more generous approach in matters of refugees and asylum, and it would be desirable if the Committee of Ministers to a greater extent than is the case now, would take the lead from the parliamentarians' recommendations.
81. Adopted on the 29 June 1967 by the Committee of Ministers.
82. Full text of the proposed convention, see below, Chapter 8.

CHAPTER 3
1951 Convention refugee status and its criteria

3.1 Who is a refugee?

The historical development of refugee protection has been gradual and has centered on the creation of international institutions to take responsibility for refugee issues and the adoption of legal instruments aimed at defining the legal status of refugees and guaranteeing their basic rights. It is important to note that the creation of refugee law instruments should be seen as a development of «lex specialis» human rights law. On the one hand, violations of human rights principles create refugees. On the other hand, it is by means of human rights principles that the international community seeks to compensate for the evasion of responsibility by some States towards those who have been forced to flee persecution and other forms of violence. There are many difficulties involved in defining and ensuring international responsibility for refugee protection. The first concerns criteria defining who should be protected.

Prior to the adoption of the 1951 Convention, which aims at both revising and codifying previous agreements and extending the scope of State responsibility, refugee instruments defined refugees according to specific categories which were pragmatic and reflected the historical circumstance of the time. For example, the legal status of those fleeing the political upheavals in the former Russian and Ottoman Empires in the 1920s was defined simply by reference to «Russian refugees», and «Armenian refugees». These definitions were arrived at by taking three elements into consideration: national or ethnic origin, lack of protection by country of origin, and non-acquisition of a new nationality. Although such definitions were considered pragmatic and responded to particular recognized situations of need, they did thereby exclude all other refugees from international protection.

A quite different consideration informs the refugee concept as elaborated in the 1951 Convention. A refugee is defined according to the reasons why he would be required to flee his country or why he cannot return to his country. According to the 1951 Convention definition, a refugee is a person outside the country of his nationality and who is unable or unwilling to avail himself of the protection of that country or to return there because he has a well-founded fear of being persecuted for reasons of race, religion, nationality, membership of a particular social group or political opinion.

A multitude of potential situations are thus encompassed their essential characteristic being that individuals or groups of persons are being specifically targeted for persecution. Consequently, the legal basis of refugee protection is ideological: the protection of human rights. This essential point of departure for defining who is a refugee is also evident in the Preamble of the 1951 Convention, in which reference is made to the Charter of the United Nations and to the Universal Declaration of Human Rights.

These references serve to highlight that refugee protection must be seen as an integral part of human rights protection, both regarding civil and political rights and economic, social, and cultural rights. All international and national efforts for refugees should therefore be evaluated with regard to obligations, to which States have adhered through the adoption of human rights instruments. Even if this point of view is difficult to contest in theory, it is not always taken into consideration in practice. This interpretative approach will, however, be used as the touchstone in the following analysis of the refugee concept, against which both the classical, more limited definition as contained in the Statute of 1950 and the 1951 Convention and a broadened refugee concept will be measured.[83]

The 1951 Convention and its Protocol relating to the Status of Refugees of 31 January 1967,[84] establishes the universal legal standards for refugee protection. By signing these instruments, a government binds itself to the legal obligations contained in the documents.

Until the adoption of the 1967 Protocol, the 1951 Convention applied solely to persons who became refugees before 1 January 1951. An optional geographical limitation attached to the Convention also permitted States to limit their obligations to events occurring in Europe. However, the Statute of 1950

---

83. Extensive legal literature exists on the interpretation of the 1951 Convention refugee concept, of which the following are outstanding examples: P. Weis, «Le Concept de réfugié en droit international», Journal du Droit International, No.1, 1960; A. Grahl-Madsen, «The Status of Refugees in International Law», Vol. I & II, Sijthoff-Leyden, 1966 and 1972; G. Goodwin-Gill, «The Refugee in International Law», Clarendon Press, 1983 and 1996; J.C. Hathaway, «The Law of Refugee Status», Butterworths, 1991; and F. Tiberghien, «La Protection des Réfugiés en France», Economica, 2nd edition, 1988.
84. The Protocol relating to the Status of Refugees was adopted by the UN General Assembly through Resolution 2198 (XXI) on 16 December 1966 and signed by the President of the General Assembly and by the Secretary General on 31 January 1967. The project of a Protocol originated in the Executive Committee of UNHCR. Henceforth, reference to the 1951 Convention covers both the Convention and the Protocol, unless otherwise indicated.

does not contain any time or geographical limitation. Today, both the 1951 Convention and the Statute of 1950 are considered «universal», with the adhesion of 132 States to the Convention and/or the Protocol of 1967.[85]

Whereas the 1951 Convention governs States' obligations, the Statute of 1950 constitutes the foundation of UNHCR's mandate. The definitions of the refugee concept of the two instruments have several similarities, but the definition in the Statute does not, for instance, contain the category «membership of a particular social group».[86] The differences are otherwise primarily due to the different objectives of the two instruments. The lapse of time, seven months, between the signing of the two also contributed, no doubt, to some changes.

The main difference between the Statue of 1950 and the Convention of 1951 is that determination of refugee status according to the 1951 Convention rests with the contracting States, whereas the interpretation of the Statute rests with UNHCR. The Statute is applied, and refugee status accorded by UNHCR in countries which have not adhered to the 1951 Convention. This is a necessary prerequisite before UNHCR can submit quota refugee cases from countries which have not adhered to the Convention, or which have maintained a geographical limitation to resettlement countries.

Already shortly after its adoption, UNHCR's mandate as contained in the Statute of 1950 was considered too limited with respect to the organization's assistance and protection responsibilities. This is why in 1957, the General Assembly of the UN had to specifically ask UNHCR to use its «good offices» and give all possible assistance with a view to alleviating the distress of the Chinese refugees in Hong Kong. On this occasion UNHCR's mandate was thereby extended beyond the Statute. Numerous similar examples have followed and UNHCR's mandate is no longer considered to be limited to the definition which is contained in the Statute.

Nevertheless, the classical refugee definition as contained in the 1950 Statute and the 1951 Convention could not be extended far enough to respond to the perceived protection needs in regions of the world which have witnessed major political, social and economic upheavals in the last fifty or so years. In Africa and Latin America, as already mentioned, regional instruments have been adopted which contain additional enlarged refugee definitions. In Europe the issue of whether there is a need for a harmonized, supplementary refugee definition to the 1951 Convention has been on the

---

85. UNHCR, Documentation Center, Geneva, October 1996.
86. For a detailed analysis of the similarities and differences between the definitions contained in the Convention of 1951 and the Statute of 1950, see A. Grahl-Madsen, «The Status of Refugees in International Law», Vol. I, 1966, p.102-122 and p.305-309.

agenda in different fora – both governmental and non-governmental, but so far no substantive discussion has taken place. There is little doubt that a supplementary definition would imply increased protection to those in need, but who fall outside the scope of the 1951 Convention, a fact which constitutes the decisive argument in favour of a broadened definition. However, States have so far demonstrated a reluctance to address this issue with the serious intent and commitment it deserves. Therefore, it is of the utmost importance that States are now not only reminded of their human rights and humanitarian obligations under international law, but also are persuaded of the real benefits which such a development would bring. Convincing States that the main advantage of a harmonized regional refugee regime would be the contribution it would make to a more fair and equitable burden sharing between States would seem to be an essential step on the way to realizing the development of a new European refugee convention.

In order to develop refugee law and draw up a new European refugee convention, it is necessary to first analyze the 1951 Convention «de lege lata» and assess its potential and its limitations. A new approach, «de lege ferenda», depends on such an analysis and can only be a supplement to this already existing universal instrument of refugee protection. Furthermore, it is important to stress that a new approach does not diminish the necessity of applying the 1951 Convention according to its maximum intent. The refugee definition contained in Article 1 of the 1951 Convention is the cornerstone of the Convention, and consequently of international refugee law. It should be noted, however, that this definition, approximately fifty years after its coming into being, now covers fewer and fewer of the total number of persons in need of international protection. Regardless of the gravity of the reasons an asylum seeker may invoke, he is not recognized as a refugee and given Convention status, unless the motivating circumstances of his request can be linked to the specific criteria of the definition. One reason for fewer conventional refugees is caused by the present trend of restrictive interpretative approach. Another reason is that more and more persons are fleeing not only for reasons of persecution as defined in the 1951 Convention, but for other reasons which threaten their life and security, but which are not covered by the Convention.

The Convention establishes two groups of refugees:
– «Statutory refugees» are persons who were granted refugee status according to an instrument prior to the adoption of the 1951 Convention and to whom the 1951 Convention also applies.[87] However, it is no longer very

---

87. Article 1(A)(1).

likely that persons envisioned by the instruments prior to the 1951 Convention will request formal recognition of their refugee status today.
– «Conventional refugees» are persons who are granted refugee status according to the 1951 Convention; that is persons who fear persecution due to their race, religion, nationality, membership of a particular social group, or political opinion. [88]

The applicability of the Convention is ruled by several conditions. Some of these conditions describe the necessary criteria for obtaining Convention Status, the so called «inclusion clauses», whereas others indicate under which circumstances refugee status may be withdrawn, the so called «cessation clauses». Finally, «exclusion clauses» indicate under which circumstances refugee status should not be granted at all.

At the time of adoption of the 1951 Convention, it was thought that the problem of refugees would be solved within a short period and therefore its authors introduced a dual limitation in the definition; one on time, «ratione tempore», and one (optional) on geography, «ratione loci».[89] This dual limitation quickly revealed itself to be a major obstacle to the recognition of refugee status for individuals persecuted after 1 January 1951 and/or outside of Europe. In order to overcome the problems created by these limitations, the 1967 Protocol was adopted.

3.2 Limitations to the application of the 1951 Convention

Time limitation

The time limitation introduced to the 1951 Convention delimited the granting of refugee status to asylum seekers who feared being persecuted « … as a result of events occurring before 1 January 1951 … ». The purpose of the inclusion of such a time limitation was to preclude the responsibility of the contracting States extending beyond already existing refugees.

According to the «Ad hoc» Committee which had negotiated the text of the Convention, contracting States could not give a «carte blanche» for the future, since it was impossible to estimate the numbers of refugees for whom

---

88. Article 1(A)(2).
89. For a more complete discussion on the limitations of the 1951 Convention, see A. Colella, «Les réserves à la Convention de Genève (28 juillet 1951) et au Protocole de New York (31 janvier 1967) sur le statut des réfugiés», A.F.D.I., 1989, p.446–475.

the States would thereby be called upon to assume responsibility.[90] The time limitation, therefore, enabled States to determine the extent of their obligations. The date of 1 January 1951 was chosen because it coincided with that of the creation of UNHCR.[91]

The term «events» is not defined in the Convention, but it is understood to refer to events provoking fear of persecution. The «Ad hoc» Committee defined the term «events» as «happenings» of major importance involving territorial or profound political changes as well as the systematic programmes of persecution (in this period) which are after-effects of earlier changes».[92]

Reflecting on this interpretation with the benefit of hindsight of events which have given rise to refugee flows and with contemporary situations in mind, it would seem that the «Ad hoc» Committee's definition of «events» is too narrow. For example, a government may persecute a religious or racial minority, without this event resulting in «profound political changes». As noted by N. Robinson, it would be more in harmony with the objectives of the Convention to interpret «events» as happenings under which a group of persons become victims of racial, religious, national, social, or political persecution.[93]

The phrase «after-effects» was also interpreted in relation to the time frame governing the term «events». In other words, persons becoming refugees after 1 January 1951 have been recognized as Convention refugees provided that their flight was caused by events which had taken place before this date.

Within the restrictions of this interpretation, the «Ad hoc» Committee did forsee circumstances which on first assessment might otherwise have been considered to fall outside the logic of the interpretation as described.[94] For example, in the case of the Hungarian refugees who sought the protection of the international community in 1956, Convention status was granted because the cause of their flight, the Soviet invasion of Hungary in 1956, was

---

90. See, P. Weis, «Legal Aspects of the Convention of 25 July 1951 Relating to the Status of Refugees», B.Y.I.L., 1953, p. 479; see also, ECOSOC, Doc. ONU E/1618, February 1950, p.38 and I. Jackson, «The 1951 Convention relating to the Status of Refugees: A Universal Basis for Protection», International Journal of Refugee Law, Vol. 3, No. 3, 1991, p.406.
91. See N. Robinson, «Convention Relating to the Status of Refugees. Its History, Contents, and Interpretations», The Institute of Jewish Affairs, New York, 1953, p.52 and A. Grahl-Madsen, «The Status of Refugees in International Law», Vol. I, 1966, p.171.
92. See Report of the Committee on Statelessness and Related Problems to ECOSOC's 11th session, February 1950, UN Document E/1618. See also N. Robinson, Ibid., p. 45.
93. Ibid., p. 46.
94. Ibid.

considered to be the consequence of events dating back to the Second World War.

Another means by which countries have had recourse to protect refugees after 1 January 1951, has been to make reference to Recommendation E of the Final Act of the Conference of Plenipotentiaries, which solicited the contracting States not to limit their protection to those refugees who were strictly covered by the definition in the 1951 Convention. It was in order to counterbalance the time limitation, that the Conference of Plenipotentiaries adopted this Recommendation.[95]

Nevertheless, political events outside Europe after the 1950s persuaded the contracting States of the need to abolish the time limitation. This explains the adoption of the 1967 Protocol which rendered the substantive provisions of the 1951 Convention applicable to those becoming refugees after 1 January 1951.

Geographical limitation

The Convention also established an optional limitation for individual contracting States on the geographical scope of the Convention. According to article 1(B)(a), a contracting State may limit its responsibility by declaring that the Convention is not applicable except to persons coming from Europe («events occurring in Europe … »). On the other hand, Article 1(B)(b) extends responsibility to cover «events occurring in Europe or elsewhere … ». Each state, at the moment of signature, ratification, or adhesion, was supposed to make a precise declaration concerning which of the two alternatives it would choose. Moreover, according to article 1(B)(2), all States adopting formula (a) may, at any moment, extend its obligations by adopting formula (b).

When the 1967 Protocol was adopted, the aim was, in this regard, to extend the refugee definition in conformity with the reality of events by making the 1951 Convention equally applicable to non-Europeans.

Article 1(3) of the 1967 Protocol states that «The present Protocol shall be applied by the State Parties hereto without any geographic limitation». Contracting States to the 1951 Convention, however, were not forced to abolish the reservations they had already formulated in reference to a geographical limitation. This explains article 1(3) of the 1967 Protocol which, as far as the declarations already made in reference to article 1(B)(a) of the 1951 Convention are concerned, establishes that they «shall, unless extended under article

---

95. I. Jackson, «The 1951 Convention relating to the Status of Refugees», 1991, p.406.

1B(2) thereof, apply also under the present Protocol». In other words, the contracting States are not obliged to abolish the geographical limitation even if that is the intention of the 1967 Protocol.[96]

In practice the continued existence of an optional geographical limitation means that, even within Europe, a person who has fled his or her country following events occurring outside Europe, would not be consistently considered a refugee by all countries that have adopted the 1951 Convention. For example, Turkey, which has maintained a geographical limitation, has allowed itself to disregard many refugees in need of international protection who arrive from neighbouring countries. This restrictive policy has had serious consequences for many refugees.

The desire of some contracting States to maintain a geographical limitation is perhaps understandable from a domestic political point of view in countries which border refugee producing areas. In the absence of the development of a proactive policy to improve the distribution of the costs and responsibility of refugee protection, countries who by tradition have proved generous in the reception and recognition of refugees are beginning to act in an increasingly restrictive manner. Problems of this kind could be solved through improved international cooperation and burden sharing, which would be one of the aims of the proposed new European refugee convention which, in its approach seeks to take first asylum countries' problems into consideration.[97]

A significant blow was dealt to the purpose of the 1951 Convention and the 1967 Protocol in the European context when EU Member States adopted a Protocol to the Treaty on European Union on 17 June 1997, which denies an EU citizen the right to apply for asylum in any other Member State of the Union. The background to the adoption of this Protocol which was originally proposed by Spain, (hence reference to the «Spanish proposal»), was the granting of protection to Basque separatists in some other European countries. Not only is the EU Protocol contrary to the 1951 Convention guarantees on unqualified access to seeking refugee status and thereby protection, but it introduces a geographical limitation of the kind which the 1967 Protocol sought to eliminate, and which weakens the universality of the instrument. According to UNHCR, this geographical restriction to the right of access to asylum is not consistent with the international responsibilities assumed by States which have ratified the Convention.[98] However, neither a

---

96. States which have made the declaration of geographic limitation are: The Congo, Hungary, Madagascar, Malta, Monaco and Turkey. (Italy extended its obligations by removing its reservation as late as in 1990.)
97. See below, Chapter 8.
98. UNHCR Press Release, 23 June 1997.

statement by UNHCR making this argument, nor the principled and legal objections of the international NGO community proved able to deter the adoption by the fifteen Member States of the European Union of the Protocol. One consolation, although poor, is that one of the Member States, Belgium, has declared that it intends to receive and consider all asylum applications, according to the criteria laid down in the 1951 Convention, irrespective of the country of origin.

As a final remark on this most recent development in the policy of the European Union, it would be fair to characterize the adoption of the EU Protocol as a step backwards for refugee protection in Europe. Furthermore, it sets an unfortunate example to the rest of the world, and represents therefore a serious set back for refugee protection in general. The Protocol touches at the very essence of refugee protection, i.e. the right to seek and to enjoy in other countries asylum from persecution.

A refugee must be outside the country of his nationality

In order to qualify as a convention refugee, the person who asks for international protection must be outside of his country of nationality. The act of having crossed an international border is therefore considered one of the general conditions for obtaining refugee status according to the 1951 Convention. However, although this condition implies that internally displaced persons are not covered by the definition, it does not also imply that the international community does not regard persons fleeing internally as being in a refugee like situation in need of international protection and assistance.

The criteria that the refugee must be outside of his country in order to enjoy refugee status was evidently added in order to protect State sovereignty. The granting of diplomatic asylum, where people remain in their country, but seek protection on the diplomatic premises of a foreign State, an embassy or a consulate, is an exception to the rule. This is a practice which has its roots in Latin America and is regulated in regional Treaty law.[99]

It should also be kept in mind, that since the adoption of the 1951 Convention, the philosophy and practice in the arena of human rights protection has developed. Strict orthodoxy which maintained that State sovereignty has greater authority than principles pertaining to protecting human lives is no longer accepted by the international community. For example, humanitarian intervention used to be considered an interference in the internal affairs of a sovereign State, but this no longer obtains to quite the same degree. The doctrine of humanitarian intervention has been characterized as the first expres-

---

99. On diplomatic asylum, see below, p. 139–141.

sion of the idea that there are limits to the liberty of States to treat their subjects as they see fit.[100] Accordingly the UN has, on many occasions since 1951, invoked the principle of humanitarian intervention and the need for the use of force to put an end to human rights violations.[101] In his «Agenda for Peace» of June 1992, the then Secretary General of the UN, Boutros-Boutros-Ghali, reiterated the necessity of respecting the fundamental sovereignty of States in order to promote international progress. However at the same time, and more importantly, he also stated that the time of absolute and exclusive sovereignty is over.[102] This signifies that although, according to the 1951 Convention a refugee must have crossed an international border, the international awareness of the plight of IDPs who are forced to flee their home and often have difficulty returning, is increasingly being raised.

According to UNHCR, the term «nationality» indicates «citizenship» that is, the link between an individual and a specific State. The phrase «is outside the country of his nationality» relates to persons who have a nationality, as distinct from stateless persons. In most cases, refugees retain their nationality.[103]

The criteria determining whether the asylum seeker fears persecution is also judged in relation to the country of nationality which is also often referred to as «country of origin». If the asylum seeker's fear relates to a country other than his country of nationality, he could request to be protected by the latter and would therefore not need international protection. However, if the asylum seeker's fear relates to both the country in which he is currently resident and his country of origin as has been the case, for example, for many refugees residing in Turkey in the 1980-90s, international protection would be merited.

For a person with several nationalities, the expression «country of nationality» includes each of the countries of which he is a national. This is explicitly stated in the 1951 Convention.[104] The reason for this clause is that a person may normally claim the protection of one of the countries.

---

100. T. Buergenthal/A. Kiss, «La Protection Internationale des Droits de l'Homme», Précis, Editions Engel Verlag, 1991, p.3.
101. See for example Security Council Resolution 688 of 5 April 1991, in which the Council insisted that Iraq authorize immediate access for international organizations in order to provide humanitarian aid to all persons in need on its territory. A «humanitarian protection» zone was created. Later on, the UN General Assembly adopted Resolution 46/182 in December 1991 in which it was decided that humanitarian assistance could be accorded with the consent of the country in question, but without it having requested it.
102. Quoted in «Les Réfugiés dans le monde», UNHCR, 1993, p.74.
103. UNHCR handbook, paragraph 87, p.22.
104. Article 1(A)(2), paragraph 2.

Refugee «sur place»

The situation to which «outside of his country» refers, does not necessarily mean that the asylum seeker must have left his country illegally or even that he must have left it on account of well-founded fear of persecution. Some persons request asylum due to reasons of fear which arise while they are abroad. The term which has evolved to describe such refugees is refugee «sur place».

Various kinds of situations create a refugee «sur place». The first arises when events take place or escalate in a person's country of origin after he has left it which preclude his return for reasons of fear of persecution as a consequence of those events, as is the case when a diplomat refuses to cooperate with the new regime in his country after a revolution has taken place. In such cases the claim would be considered as an «objective sur place» refugee claim. There is broad agreement that persons making such claims are covered by the 1951 Convention. If the person in question started his political activities in his country of origin before fleeing and has continued being politically active in the receiving country, he is also likely to be considered for conventional status.

«Subjective sur place» refugee claims concern people whose activities have given rise to persecution since leaving their country. For example, when the person in question works politically against the interest of the regime in his country and fears that this will come to the knowledge of the authorities at home, his refugee claim would be considered a «subjective sur place» claim.

In instances of «subjective sur place» refugee claims, host countries are less disposed to grant asylum because they consider that the person in question is somehow to blame. Such policy is usually directly linked to the political imperative of the asylum country wishing to avoid playing host to political activities of foreign dissidents which may prove embarrassing in their relations with the country of origin. It is also a way of minimizing numbers of refugees accorded conventional status and thus asylum. Restrictive practice diminishes «the pull factor» of asylum applications from persons already on the territory. In other words, if it were easy to obtain refugee status by engaging in political activities abroad, authorities of receiving countries fear that this method would be used extensively.[105] Such motives for not granting refugee status should not be considered valid, and would in fact be contrary to the

---

105. This point of view has also been incorporated into the EU member countries' Joint position on Article 1(A), but these guidelines also state that refusal of refugee status in these instances, must not prejudice the right not to return to a country where the person's life, physical integrity or freedom would be in danger (the «non-refoulement» principle).

1951 Convention which does not allow for the exclusion of a claimant on the basis of where and when his views have been expressed.[106] At the same time it must be acknowledged that some people may exploit the possibility of applying for asylum in this way. The difficulty for an asylum State lies in making an appropriate assessment of whether the political interest is genuine and whether the risk to the person expressing it is a real one.

Although State practice shows unwillingness to grant asylum to the «subjective sur place» refugees, the fear of persecution may very well be real. This is why, in order not to risk violating the principle of non-refoulement, States tend to grant other kinds of status such as «tolerated stay», «B-status», etc. Refugees «sur place» would therefore often be considered as «de facto» refugees who, for a variety of reasons, are unable or unwilling to obtain conventional status, but who cannot return to their country of origin. Their need of international protection is in this way acknowledged and provided for.[107]

According to UNHCR's Handbook the question of refugees «sur place» must be evaluated in the light of whether actions creating such a situation, are sufficient to justify a well-founded fear of persecution. A careful examination of the circumstances must take place. It also says that regard should be paid to whether such actions have come to the notice of the authorities of the country of origin and how they are likely to be viewed by those authorities.[108]

Internal flight alternative

The question of whether persecution linked only to one region of a country could be considered covered by the definition in the 1951 Convention, is not answered by the «travaux préparatoires» of the Convention. According to UNHCR, however, fear of persecution need not always extend to the whole territory of the refugee's home country. Thus, in ethnic clashes or in the case of grave disturbances involving civil war conditions, persecution of a specific ethnic or national group may occur in only one part of the country. In such a situation, a person should not be excluded from refugee status merely because he could have sought refuge in another part of the same country, if under all the circumstances it would not have been reasonable to expect him to do so.[109]

---

106. Regarding at what point in time the fear of persecution must have manifested itself, see further under Chapter 2. 2.
107. See below, p. 112 and following.
108. UNHCR Handbook, paragraph 96, p. 24.
109. UNHCR Handbook, paragraph 91, p.23

At a distance it is often difficult to evaluate the day to day situation in a civil war or in circumstances of internal strife. It is therefore not easy to know if, in the case of a peace accord, for example, peace will last long enough to refuse refugee status to a person and to impose return without a risk of violating the non-refoulement principle. As always, the evaluation of the situation in such a case should be made after a careful examination of all circumstances. When international «protected areas» were first established, refusal of refugee status and return to such regions was considered to be a practicable solution. However, in such a situation, a prerequisite must be that durable security is provided in the protected area. Failure to do so, for example in Bosnia, has strengthened arguments against this so called internal flight alternative.

In State practice, the internal flight alternative has been invoked by several European countries who have denied refugee status to Tamils from Sri Lanka. While Northern and Eastern parts of Sri Lanka have been and still are regarded as dangerous by European States, the Southern part of the country is generally considered to be safe. Consequently, against the advice of many human rights organizations, Tamils at present, find themselves refused refugee status and in many cases returned to Southern Sri Lanka. Returnees who encounter serious problems are particularly those who do not have any links to the South. Moreover, a country returning asylum seekers to a region other than from where they originate, contributes to the creation of internal displacement.

The fact that the practice of receiving countries differs in such cases, in itself illustrates the difficulty in determining the risks associated to returning a person to a certain area and knowing whether forced return would be contrary to the principle of «non-refoulement». A careful assessment of all available reports and sources in the governmental and non-governmental environment is called for in situations in which the internal flight alternative presents itself to receiving countries as an option. The chief role of UNHCR should not be principally that of helping States return rejected asylum seekers. Rather, in situations in which the question of whether protection is necessary is as controversial as that of returning Tamils, UNHCR should be directly called upon to provide an «expert» and informed opinion. The organization's acceptance in recent times of returns of rejected asylum seekers to parts of Sri Lanka is in this light questionable.

3.3 Well-founded fear of persecution

A 1951 Convention refugee is a person who is either unable or unwilling to return home, due to fear of persecution, on account of one of the reasons enumerated in the definition. The criteria «unwilling» relates to the refugee who refuses to accept the protection of his country of origin whereas the criteria «is unable to» refers to the fear of persecution. Reasons based on personal convenience and economic motivation are not covered by the definition of the 1951 Convention. Normally, the granting of refugee status is made according to an evaluation of each individual case and the criteria of persecution normally relates to an individually targeted person or groups of persons. There are cases in which whole groups have been displaced in circumstances which indicate that each member of the group is at risk of persecution and therefore could individually be considered to be a refugee. For example, during the Nazi persecution of the Jews throughout the 1930s and up until the end of the second World War, each Jew in Germany or in occupied territory would rightly have had a well-founded fear of persecution in the sense of the 1951 Convention. An example from our own time of the treatment of groups of people which rendered each individual of that group at risk of persecution is the Serb persecution of Bosnian Muslims as a way of ethnic cleansing in the former Yugoslavia.

In such situations in which a case by case determination of refugee status cannot be made for practical reasons, often because of a mass exodus in which there is also an element of urgency, the refugee determination according to the criteria of fear of persecution can be made on a collective basis. This implies that each member of a group is considered a refugee without having to go through the individual determination procedure to establish whether they have a well-founded fear of persecution. The expression applied to an individual considered to be a refugee according to this notion of group evaluation is «prima facie» refugee.[110]

The first time group determination of this kind took place, was in 1956, after the revolution in Hungary. Material assistance had to be provided before anyone could even begin to think of evaluating refugee status of the Hungarian refugees in relation to the 1951 Convention. Those fleeing the political situation in Hungary were seen as collectively qualifying as refugees.

The «prima facie» practice has since been used several times, mainly in situations of mass exodus. Again, to use the former Yugoslavia as an example, various countries have granted protection on a temporary basis to refugees from Bosnia, not using «prima facie» as such, but according protection on a collective basis and postponing an examination of individual asylum requests.

The term «well-founded fear of persecution» constitutes the key element of the definition and hence of the refugee concept as such. The two elements

---

110. UNHCR Handbook, paragraph 44, p.13.

of the phrase, the «well-founded fear» on the one hand and «persecution», on the other, need to be considered separately in order to arrive at a clearer understanding of the difficulties surrounding interpretation of the definition. The definition itself does not give much indication regarding its interpretation and not much was explained by the authors of the Convention either. Generally accepted international principles of interpretation of treaties in good faith and according to their purpose and content, should therefore be adhered to. In this context, it should always be kept in mind that the main focus of the 1951 Convention is protection of refugees and that determination of refugee status can be a matter of life or death for the person concerned.

The risk is reduced if protection is granted on other grounds, such as when «de facto» refugee status is granted. However, not to grant Convention status when this is merited entails an evasion by States of their international obligations and is to the detriment of the refugee. For example, being granted «de facto» status, implies that he cannot necessarily benefit from the rights which should pertain to the status of a refugee according to the 1951 Convention. While some States provide more or less equal rights for both conventional and «de facto» refugees, the fact that State practice varies is an inequity which needs to be addressed. [111]

The existing tendency of States to assume that granting of protection as opposed to convention status is sufficient can be illustrated by a decision of the Norwegian Supreme Court of 1991. In the so called «Abdi Case,»[112] the Supreme Court disregards the necessity of granting Convention status since the applicant is given protection on analogous grounds.

The term «fear of persecution» refers to persons who have already suffered persecution, but the main problem of interpretation concerns potential persecution because this means having to assess future risks. Taking future events into consideration is one of the major difficulties when evaluating the validity of a claimant's fear of persecution. The risk of future persecution must be evaluated in the light of persecution or threats of persecution already experienced, either by the applicant himself, or by relatives, or other members of, for example, the same ethnic or racial group.

---

111. See, therefore, below, Chapter 8 on the proposal for a new European refugee convention.
112. See, Decision by the Norwegian Supreme Court (Høyesterett) of 30 May 1991, (No. 1, 74/1991, No. 245/1989), Abdi, a Somali refugee who had engaged in political activities in Quatar, after having left Somalia had continues in Norway. He was considered a «sur place» refugee and granted a residence permit on humanitarian grounds by the Ministry of Justice. Abdi appealed the decision, wishing to be granted 1951 Convention status.

The fundamental consideration should always be whether persecution would take place upon return and whether life in the country of origin would, as a result of that persecution or the fear of persecution, be intolerable. It should also be acknowledged that, in some cases, the risk of future persecution may be minimal or non-existent, but that past experience of an atrocious character, leaves no other option than to accord protection to the person concerned.

«Well-founded fear»

The term «well-founded fear» was described by the authors of the 1951 Convention as meaning that a person has been a victim of persecution or that he can give good reasons why he fears persecution.[113] Nevertheless, the interpretation of the concept has proved problematic, as both theoretical works on the subject and State practice demonstrate. At the heart of the difficulties surrounding interpretation of the term is the question of whether the subjective element of fear or the objective element of fear should prevail in the evaluation of whether a person who is seeking refugee status, has a well-founded fear of persecution.

Subjective and objective elements of fear

The subjective element of fear is not difficult to demonstrate, but the emphasis that should be placed on the subjective as opposed to the objective facts surrounding the fear, is problematic. The condition of objectivity, means that imaginary or simulated fear of persecution can on no grounds be considered a sufficient reason for the granting of refugee status. Neither can a general feeling of insecurity alone be grounds for a well-founded fear of persecution. The danger of persecution must, objectively speaking, be plausible – the fear must be «well-founded» – which, in turn, assumes the existence of a danger threatening the life or liberty of the person concerned. This danger can only be assessed through thorough knowledge of the situation and conditions in the country of origin of the asylum applicant. Once the objective facts of persecution have been established, the relationship between the subjective and the objective elements must then be analysed.

In order to evaluate a person's fear in a just and fair manner, it is also necessary to take into account the individual circumstances and background of the person concerned.[114] The element of «fear» refers to the mental state of

---

113. P. Weis, «Le concept de réfugié en droit international», 1960, p.971 cf. UN Document E/1618.
114. P. Weis, «Le concept de réfugié en droit international», p.971.

the person and the propensity for fear will inevitably vary from one person to another, according to different circumstances. A person's psychological attitude and sensitivity towards his environment are only valid reasons for a well-founded fear in cases in which the factual events can be shown to substantiate the feeling of fear. An exception to this balanced approach concerns asylum requests by children or mentally ill persons. In such cases it is particularly difficult to evaluate the degree of fear compared to persons expected to be more rational. This is why, in such cases, if the objective facts are not as convincing as they should be, due consideration should be given to the subjective fact that they feel fear.

It has been said that the state of mind of the person concerned can hardly be taken into account in the evaluation of «well-founded fear», because all persons claiming refugee status experience a feeling of fear, regardless of their personal circumstances and character, because the greater fear of one person has no more merit than the lesser fear of another.[115] This assessment leads to the conclusion that in order to guarantee a wholly reliable determination of well-founded fear it is necessary to focus principally on external facts and thereby eliminate the influence of the particular state of mind of the person concerned.

However, although difficult, it is necessary to evaluate the state of mind of the person concerned because the factual circumstances do not always sufficiently enlighten the situation. The subjective element needs to be assessed through the statements made in connection with the asylum request, the personal and family background of the applicant, his membership in a particular racial, religious, national, social, or political group and his own interpretation of the situation.

The applicant's fear should be considered well-founded if he can establish, to a reasonable degree, that his continued stay in his country of origin had become intolerable to him, for one or more of the reasons stated in the definition of persecution in the 1951 Convention, or would, for the same reasons, be intolerable if he were to return there.[116] If an applicant has already been a victim of persecution in the past, the presumption that the fear be «reasonable» is even more well-founded.

Nevertheless, improvements within a country since the moment of the person's flight should also be assessed. If it is evident that the person, even if he has experienced a previous persecution, has no longer anything to fear on objective grounds, he should not necessarily be considered as being in need

---

115. See, A. Grahl-Madsen, «The Status of Refugees in International Law», Vol. I, p.174.
116. UNHCR Handbook, paragraph 42, p.13.

of international protection. The «cessation clauses» of the Convention could be considered in such cases.[117] The «cessation clauses» are the grounds which are listed in the Convention allowing an asylum country to withdraw refugee status for specific reasons of which changed circumstances in the home country is one.

An analysis of State practice of evaluation of claims of persecution indicates that, in their interpretation of the concept, States tend to give priority to the objective element of fear. This would seem partly to be guided by the policy pursued by asylum receiving countries of restricting the flow of refugees since the 1980s. Depending on whether a country weights its evaluation procedure in favour of the subjective element or the objective element, this emphasis has a direct influence on the number of applicants accorded refugee status. However, in spite of such evidence that is certainly persuasive for those asylum receiving countries wishing to actively restrict the numbers of applicants who are granted refugee status, it must be emphasised that to favour the objective element to the extent that the subjective element of fear of an applicant is disregarded, would be contrary to the purpose of the 1951 Convention.

While the approach to the evaluation of well-founded fear of persecution, as described above, leads to fewer asylum applicants gaining Convention refugee status, it tends on the other hand to result in an increase in the number of «de facto» refugees. The use by States of a restrictive interpretation which focuses on the objective element of fear does not therefore have the effect of diminishing the overall total number of persons in need of protection who are permitted to stay in the refugee receiving country, whether it is for a shorter or longer period of time. As the 1951 Convention contains certain rights which are attached to the status of Convention refugees, States obviously have an interest in limiting the number of asylum applicants who are granted Convention status in order to escape obligations.

The time when fear must have manifested itself

Another consideration which tends to be interpreted in a restrictive light by States in the evaluation of well-founded fear is the analysis of the point in time at which the fear of the asylum applicant must have manifested itself, in order for his claim to be credible. Should fear have manifested itself at the moment of flight, at the moment of determination of refugee status, or at the moment of eventual return to the country of origin? This question is not dealt with in the text of the Convention, although other situations which are foreseen give an indication of the interpretation which would be in keeping

---

117. Article 1(C) of the 1951 Convention, see below, p. 86 and following.

with the spirit of the Convention. There is no legitimate reason for States to demand that asylum applicants must have feared persecution at the moment of departure from their country of origin.[118]

However, in practice this interpretation is not always shared by States. State practice in the evaluation of this part of the asylum procedure is determined by internal legislation. For example, Switzerland, for a long time, followed a particularly restrictive interpretation of this point. The Swiss authorities did not accept that fear was sufficiently well-founded unless it was held at the moment of flight. However, since 1989, refugees «sur place» have been considered as convention refugees by the Swiss authorities. In view of the fact that return to the country of origin could constitute a violation of the «non-refoulement» principle, the authorities took the pragmatic decision to grant temporary residence permits instead of asylum. Such a decision which in effect awards a lesser means of protection purely on the condition of the timing of the experience of fear can be justified by no logical legal argument.

In France, asylum has been granted to «subjective sur place refugees». According to traditional French practice, it is the moment at which the decision on eligibility for refugee status is taken by the authorities, which is the decisive factor in the overall evaluation: i.e does the asylum seeker at this point have a well-founded fear of persecution. The reasoning which is at the root of this practice, is that the 1951 Convention allows for taking future threats to the asylum applicant into consideration.[119]

In a case where a person, for no plausible reason, postponed his flight although he claims that he feared persecution, the authorities examining an asylum application will find it difficult to believe the gravity of the alleged risk and the well-founded nature of the invoked fear of persecution.

Burden of proof

In all instances, it is the applicant who bears the burden of proof in order to establish that his fear may be considered «well-founded». Given the circumstances of flight, lack of identification documents occurs frequently. For this and other reasons proof, in the traditional sense of law, may be difficult to provide. For the asylum applicant, it is essential that in the absence of such proof, the authorities of the receiving country place a degree of faith in his statement which, considered in the light of the known objective facts, render the claim of well-founded fear plausible. The principle of being granted the benefit of the doubt («in dubio pro reo») should be present in the mind of the immigration official conducting the interview with the asylum applicant.

---

118. See above on refugees «sur place», p. 53.
119. F. Tiberghien, «La Protection des Réfugiés en France», 1988, p.91.

However, in practice this principle does not always prevail. According to State practice, the claimant must be able to demonstrate that there is a reasonable degree of likelihood of persecution. In other words, «well-founded fear» presupposes that fear exists and that there is good reason for it. This presupposes that the claimant must be able to substantiate his reasoning through the evidence he can present.

Refugee status determination interviews
The assessment of the immigration authorities inevitably takes into consideration the manner in which the applicant conveys his fear in his statement and the presentation of supporting evidence. The psychological reactions of the applicant, coherence and absence of contradictions in his statement, all contribute to the credibility upon which the claim of well-founded fear rests. In this regard, it is therefore essential as far as the procedural aspect of an evaluation is concerned, to pay special attention to the use of interpreters. It can be safely assumed that no asylum seeker would be inclined to risk telling the truth about his political activities and thereby risk jeopardizing the life of his peers and family, unless he has confidence in the interpreter.[120]

Another element which must be equally considered is the factor of distrust and even fear which may be provoked in the asylum applicant when confronted with officials or men in uniform, given the fact that he may have escaped persecution directly enacted by or consented by representatives of his government in uniform. Immigration officials may therefore find it difficult to persuade an asylum applicant to speak of his reasons for seeking protection.

On the other hand, it is the responsibility of the immigration officials to advise the asylum applicant that if he does not tell the truth he risks being denied the protection he requires. The asylum seeker should also be informed that indications of what is regarded as «abuse of the asylum system», for example, lies about forged documents, etc. will be taken into consideration to the detriment of his case. However, at the same time it can not be excluded that the asylum seeker himself does not actually know why he was the object of persecution or why he was threatened by measures of persecution. This should not in itself prevent the person from being recognized as a refugee.[121]

---

120. Women asylum seekers also deserve special attention for gender-related reasons, see, below, p. 78 and following.
121. P. Weis, op. cit. p. 971. See also UNHCR's Handbook, paragraphs 66, p. 17; and J.C. Hathaway, «The Law of Refugee Status», p. 137.

«Persecution»

The concept of «persecution», as such, is not defined in the 1951 Convention or in any other international instrument. The term had been used, prior to the drafting of the Convention, in the 1938 Convention on the Status of Refugees which covered refugees originating from Germany. The aims and objectives of the 1938 Convention were to protect the victims of Nazi persecution, to procure them relief, and to exclude those who left their country for reasons of personal convenience. The term was also used in the Constitution of the International Refugee Organization (IRO), adopted in 1946. However, an explanation of the term «persecution» was not offered by the authors of the IRO Constitution.

The lack of precision in the 1951 Convention was, for political reasons, intentional, as a way of ensuring a flexible legal concept which would allow States to apply «persecution» in a manner compatible with political and policy developments after the adoption of the Convention. However, this flexibility has been misused by States which interpret the Convention either generously or restrictively, depending on their own political interest. For example, US practice clearly varies according to the political imperative of time; while refugees from Cuba have traditionally been granted refugee status, those fleeing Haiti have traditionally been refused refugee status. Western practice of making a «political statement» when granting Convention status to persons fleeing the former Soviet bloc during the Cold War, whether persecuted or not, is another example.

The refusal of States to grant refugee status for reasons of foreign policy is one of the problems of international law in making refugee protection both effective and consistent in its application. While the authors of the 1951 Convention lacked precision in their definition of the term persecution, they can not have intended that internal or external political interest would come to dominate the determination of refugee status with consequences which are so clearly contrary to the aims and objectives of the Convention to ensure that refugee protection be granted to those in need of it. The political nature of a regime and the nature of a relationship between States are, therefore, criteria which must be disregarded when the refugee definition is interpreted, if States are to honour the commitments implied by their signature to the Convention.

No clear definition of the term persecution is contained in the Convention, nor has there evolved a coherent interpretation in legal literature. An important interpretative statement has been made by I. Jackson, formerly Deputy Director of UNHCR's Division of International Protection, with which there is every reason to agree, that the concept of persecution was definitely not introduced in order to restrict the refugee concept.[122] Two schools of thought on the subject exist. One can be described as the «restrictive school» in that it limits the concept of persecution to the most serious violations of human rights, such as taking of life and restricting physical liberty; and the other, referred to as the «liberal school», which considers that persecution equally includes other attacks on human dignity. However, even within these schools of thought there are seeming inconsistencies which provide further illustration of the problematic nature of interpreting the term persecution. For example, Grahl-Madsen, who is relatively liberal in his approach to the subject, defines a person as having a well-founded fear of persecution if he finds himself «…faced with the likelihood of losing his life or physical freedom for more than a «negligible» period of time, if he should return to his home country, or is likewise threatened with other measures which, in his particular case and his special circumstances, appear as more severe than a short-term imprisonment…».[123] On the other hand, and without explanation, he considers that violations of the freedom of belief, conscience, and religion, falls outside the concept of persecution.[124]

It is evident that normally showing simple disagreement or simple opposition to a government would not be considered a cause for fear of persecution. However, in some cases this may indeed prove sufficient for the authorities in a given country to take disproportionate measures amounting to persecution against the person concerned. Therefore, the premise must always be that as long as there is a serious risk that the person in question may experience a disproportionate prejudice, or indeed harm, due to the reasons enumerated in the definition, this should be considered as persecution. It must also be kept in mind that sometimes different types of harassment occur together and that the combination of events each of which, taken separately, does not constitute persecution may, depending on the circumstances, amount to persecution.

Another aspect which needs to be taken into consideration concerns the existence or otherwise of effective remedies which can put an end to the circumstances amounting to persecution within the framework of national law. International protection is, however, necessary in cases where no redress exists or where the person concerned is deprived of the opportunity of having

---

122. I. Jackson, «The 1951 Convention Relating to the Status of Refugees», p. 405-406. P. Weis, who participated in the drafting of the 1951 Convention, has the same non-restrictive inclination, see P. Weis, «Convention Refugees and De Facto Refugees», «African Refugees and the Law», Scandinavian Institute of African Studies, Uppsala, 1978, p.15.
123. Atle Grahl-Madsen, «The Status of Refugees in International law», Vol. I, p. 216.
124. Ibid.

access to the national protection available. This consideration is expressed by the EU member countries in their Joint Position on Article 1(A) of the 1951 Convention. According to the principle of sovereignty, it is the duty and right of States to accord protection to their citizens. When a State neglects this duty to such a point that its citizens fear persecution and flee their country, the responsibility of the international community to guarantee protection under the terms of the 1951 Convention, must be exercised.

Agents of persecution
A further complicating factor which was not foreseen by the 1951 Convention is the question of the agent of persecution. Persecution is normally understood to be an act committed by the authorities of the country of origin, e.g. by the police or by military personnel. If this is the case, then national protection clearly does not exist, and the likelihood of a risk of persecution is therefore not difficult to establish. On other occasions, the persecutors are persons or private groups to which the authorities of the country close their eyes, thereby consenting in the human rights violations being perpetrated. National protection evidently does not exist in such cases either, and therefore, the persons against whom the violations are perpetrated should also in these cases be considered victims of persecution.

The 1951 Convention and its «travaux préparatoires» are mute in this regard and therefore provide no guidance as to how the issue of agent of persecution should be interpreted. However, UNHCR's Handbook, states that where serious discriminatory or other offensive acts are committed by the local populace, these can be considered as persecution if they are knowingly tolerated by the authorities. The same interpretation also applies if the authorities refuse or prove unable to offer effective protection.[125]

In the practice of several countries, a distinction has been made between situations in which the authorities are «unwilling» to protect their nationals and situations in which they are «unable». Several States consider that as long as the authorities are incapable of assuring their protection, that country is not responsible and the acts committed therefore do not constitute persecution. The decision is thus made dependent on whether the official authorities' failure to act to protect their citizens is shown to be deliberate or not.

The interpretation of the 1951 Convention with regard to the issue of

---

125. UNHCR Handbook, paragraph 65, p.18 and 19. See also Grahl-Madsen, «The Status of Refugees in International Law», Vol. I, p.189-192; J. Van der Veen, «Does persecution by fellow-citizens in certain regions of a state fall within the definition of 'persecution' in the convention relating to the status of refugees of 1951? Some comments based on Dutch judicial decisions», p. 170-172.

agents of persecution, constituted a major problem in the harmonization efforts of the members of the European Union. Contrary to the European Parliament's recommendation[126], the EU member countries adopted a Joint Position on the harmonized application of the definition of the term «refugee» of the 1951 Convention according to which, States can, when interpreting the definition of persecution carried out by «non-State agents», make a distinction between different authors of persecution. This creates a situation in which someone targeted by the government in a civil conflict could gain asylum abroad, but not an equally innocent civilian persecuted by the opposition. People fleeing persecution by rebel groups are thus barred from Convention status.[127] The consequences of this interpretation are witnessed in Algeria where fundamentalist Islamic forces are fighting a civil war against the Algerian government and where liberals, intellectuals and other members of the civilian population are targeted. The victims of persecution perpetrated by these «non-State agents», risk not obtaining refugee status in European Union countries if these States are faithful to the interpretation they signed up to in the Joint Position.

This restrictive approach, which has the effect of narrowing down the definition of victims of persecution to whom the international community has a responsibility to grant protection, was adopted by the European Union in order to conform with restrictive policies currently practiced by a minority of countries, which included France, Germany, Italy, and Sweden. Switzerland and Norway are not EU members, but have had a similar practice.[128] The Joint Position was thus established on the basis of the lowest common denominator, a fact which was regretted, not only by UNHCR which stated that «EU undermines refugee rights»[129] and the NGO community, but equally by the EU Commissioner responsible for asylum and immigration issues.[130]

Sweden has, for example, been criticized by Human Rights Watch for its narrow interpretation of the 1951 Convention on this point, denying refugee status to Algerians persecuted by the insurgent Armed Islamic Group, Peruvians targeted by Shining Path guerillas and Bosnian Muslims under attack by

---

126. Plenary session of the European Parliament of the 29 September 1995.
127. This Joint Position was endorsed by the European Council on 4 March 1996.
128. Norway has recently reviewed its interpretation of the refugee definition in this regard and has introduced a liberalization.
129. The Reuter European Community Report of 24 November 1995, p. 24 and 25.
130. Commissioner Anita Gradin made a comment to this effect after the Justice and Home Affairs Council had adopted its proposal (November 1995), Reuter Textline Agence Europe of 28 November 1995.

Bosnian Serbs.[131] According to new Swedish legislation, however, refugee status may be granted in cases where the authorities of the State concerned are unable to protect their citizens.[132] In France persons having escaped persecution by FIS («Front islamique du salut») in Algeria, have not been granted Convention status.[133] Similarly, Somali refugees having fled a country ruled by anarchy where clans and sub-clans try to gain power over certain territories, are also not regarded as conventional refugees since they have escaped persecution by warlords and no central government can be held responsible for lack of protection.[134] However, France is in the process of adapting its legislation in order to accommodate victims of non-state agents in its protection regime. The legislative proposal introduces new categories of refugees, according to which «freedom fighters» could be considered in need of protection and therefore be granted asylum.

Invasion or occupation of a country by a foreign power also gives rise to persecution which results from the incapacity of national authorities to grant adequate protection. Normally, war refugees are not considered as Convention refugees in the sense that victims of war usually suffer because of the general violence which prevails, but not because they are targeted for persecution on an individual or on a group basis. This must never preclude determination of refugee status on an individual or on a «prima facie» basis, however, because there are of course many victims of war who also fulfil the criteria laid down in the 1951 Convention.

There can be no doubt that refusing refugee status to persons who are subjected to or who fear persecution by non-state agents is contrary to the spirit of the Convention. An interpretation which distinguishes between «state» and «non-state agents» can only be seen as «protectionism» on the part of the receiving State. The main purpose of the Convention which is to offer protection to refugees is thereby undermined.

Persecution in relation to human rights principles
Refugee law forms an integral part of human rights law. Violations of principles contained in human rights instruments first necessitated the creation of refugee law. Therefore it follows logically that human rights principles «a priori» form part of refugee law and vice versa, that refugee law principles «a priori» form part of human rights law. This does not mean that they overlap en-

---

131. The Reuter European Community report, 18 October 1996, p. 31.
132. Alien's law adopted by the Swedish parliament on 10 December 1996.
133. See for example, Commission des recours des réfugiés, Sections des recours (Refugee Appeals Commission), Case no. 258992 of 5 May 1995.
134. See Commission des recours des réfugiés, Sections réunies (Refugee Appeals Commission), case No. 264373 of 28 February 1995.

tirely in terms of protection. However, the link between the two is essential because together they form part of people's perception of morality and justice.

This link has developed consistently, albeit gradually, over the past decades and the majority of current legal writers now consider that serious violations of human rights do constitute persecution which in turn forms a ground for refugee status.[135] In this context, a definition of persecution which has been suggested refers to the sustained or systematic violation of basic human rights demonstrative of a failure of State protection.[136] Although this definition has its merits, it does not solve the problem of knowing exactly which human rights violations should be considered as falling within the scope of persecution.

An essential part of human rights law is protection of the individual from fear. This is i.a. confirmed by the reference to the UN Declaration of Human Rights of 1948 in the Preamble of the 1951 Convention. The preamble proclaims that one of the highest aspirations of man is that human beings should enjoy «freedom from fear». This aspiration was later reiterated in the International Covenant on Civil and Political Rights of 1966 which declared as ideals that free human beings should enjoy civil and political freedom and «freedom from fear».

The development of the link in question can be seen in national and international application of human rights instruments and pronouncements from human rights bodies, for example the European Court of Human Rights or the UN Committee against Torture. Therefore, giving due regard to these would be one way of learning how refugee law should be interpreted and implemented in relation to violations of human rights principles. One example of the way in which national practice can inform the development of the international legal order, is the evolution of the concept of gender related persecution.[137]

Human rights principles must always be at the forefront when refugee determination is carried out. The difficulty is to determine and define which violations should constitute persecution. And this difficulty is compounded by the fact that each refugee case must be assessed on an individual basis even when taking into account general established principles. However, not every violation

---

135. See UNHCR Handbook, paragraph 51, p.15, G.Goodwin-Gill, «The Refugee in International Law», p.38 and following, P.Weis, «Le concept de réfugié en droit international», p.971, J.C. Hathaway, «The Law of Refugee Status», p.108, M. Chemille-Gendreau, «Le concept de réfugié en droit international et ses limites», Pluriel No. 28, 1981, p.9; and G. Stenberg, «Non-expulsion and Non-Refoulement», p.65-67.
136. Hathaway, «The Law of Refugee Status», p.104–105.
137. See, below, p. 78 and following.

of human rights would amount to persecution. The human rights principles which are being violated must, in principle, be of a fundamental character.

In order to assess which human rights principles amount to persecution, the starting point would be to distinguish between rights to which no derogation is permitted and rights to which derogation is permitted, for example, in case of public emergency.[138] The rights from which no derogation is permitted concern the right to life and integrity of a person: no one shall be arbitrarily deprived of his life,[139] no one shall be subjected to torture or other cruel, inhuman, or degrading punishments and treatments,[140] and no one shall be the subject of slavery or servitude.[141] A violation, or fear of violation, of these norms protecting life[142] and liberty[143] of the person and the right not to be subjected to torture and other cruel treatment, sexual violence included,[144] amount to persecution.

Other rights from which no derogation is allowed, are norms which aim to

---

138. See, for example the International Covenant on Civil and Political Rights of 1966, Article 4.
139. Ibid, Article 6.
140. See, for example, Article 5 of the Universal Declaration on Human Rights; Article 7 of the Convention against Torture and other Cruel, Inhuman, or Degrading Punishments or Treatments; Article 7 of the International Covenant on Civil and Political Rights; Article 3 the European Convention on Human Rights and Article 5 of the «San José Pact».
141. See, the Universal Declaration on Human Rights, Article 4; the European Convention on Human Rights, Article 4 and the «San José Pact», Article 6. According to G. Goodwin-Gill in «The Refugee in International Law», p. 39, the Barcelona Traction case of 1970 of the ICJ, allows for the interpretation that a violation or risk of violation of these norms should be considered as persecution as the Court recognized the notion of an «erga omnes» obligation of States regarding the prohibition in international law of genocide, slavery, and racial discrimination (ICJ Reports, 1970, p. 32). In this regard, cf. also the International Convention on the Elimination of all Forms of Racial Discrimination of 21 December 1965, Articles 2 and 3.
142. For example a violation of the following provisions: Article 3 of the Universal Declaration, Article 6 of the International Covenant on Civil and Political Rights of 1966, Article 2 of the European Convention on Human Rights of 1950.
143. For example, Article 15 of the International Covenant on Civil and Political Rights: «No one shall be held guilty of any criminal offense on account of any act or omission which did not constitute a criminal offense, under national or international law, at the time when it was committed» and Article 16 which states that «Everyone shall have the right to recognition everywhere as a person before the law».
144. See UN Document, A/AC.96/622/Corr.1 of October 19, 1993 on certain aspects of sexual violence against refugee women, p.29. See below, p., «New trends – gender related persecution».

protect the right to freedom of belief, conscience, and religion.[145] There can be no doubt as to the importance of these principles seeking to protect the personal convictions of a person.[146] However, in current State practice there seems to be some difficulty in accepting that a violation of these norms should be considered as amounting to persecution. Another way of looking at this is to acknowledge the difficulty, for the refugee, as it would be for anyone, to give sufficient proof of his convictions whilst undergoing a refugee determination interview. This may therefore indicate that the burden of proof is set too high in cases pertaining to, for example, religious persecution.[147]

Provisions from which derogation is permitted, in case of public danger, also include norms relating to fundamental rights, such as, the principle of freedom against arbitrary arrest or detention[148] and the protection against arbitrary or unlawful interference with one's private life.[149] In spite of the fact that they are derogable rights, it could be argued that a violation would nevertheless constitute persecution because they are fundamental in character.

However, violations of other derogable rights which are less fundamental in character, for example, the right to freedom of peaceful assembly and association,[150] would not necessarily amount to persecution. This also applies to other rights pertaining to education, health, work, etc. Violation of several of these rights may amount to persecution in cases where they are shown to be cumulative. For example, incidents of harassment, seemingly of minor importance in isolation, may constitute persecution when they are assessed together. Such would be the case if the harassment is repeated and inflicts serious harm on the person's everyday life and feeling of security. It is often difficult to determine when «harassment» becomes «persecution», and is therefore one area in which States tend to set a too high threshold on the interpretation of what constitutes persecution.

A penalty incurred for an infraction of common law would neither be a

---

145. See the Universal Declaration of Human Rights, Article 18, the International Covenant on Civil and Political Rights of 1966, article 18, the European Convention on Human Rights, Article 9, «The San José Pact», Article 12, etc.
146. See J.C Hathaway, «The Law of Refugee Status», p. 109 and G.Goodwin-Gill, «The Refugee in International Law», p.39. In contrast, as stated previously, A.Grahl-Madsen considers that such a violation is outside of the concept of persecution, see «The Status of Refugees in International Law», Vol. I, p.195.
147. See also below on religious persecution, p. 73–74.
148. See Article 9 of the Universal Declaration of Human Rights, Article 9 of the International Covenant on Civil and Political Rights of 1966; Article 5 of the European Human Rights Convention, Article 7 of the «San José Pact», etc.
149. See, for example, the International Covenant on Civil and Political Rights, Article 17.
150. Article 20 of the Universal Declaration on Human Rights.

human rights violation nor constitute persecution except in cases where the penal sanction is disproportionate to the infraction. In order to determine whether prosecution for a particular crime amounts to persecution, one must refer to the laws of the country in question. It could be the case that the law itself may not conform with human rights norms. More often, however, it is the implementation of the law rather than the actual law which will be important to analyse in the evaluation of whether persecution exists.

A final category of human rights concerns economic rights and the norms set forth in the UN Declaration of Human Rights of 1948 and further developed in the International Covenant on Economic, Social, and Cultural Rights of 1966. The recognition of the right of everyone to the enjoyment of just and favorable conditions of work is contained in both of these international instruments.[151] The Covenant of 1966 lays down the right to gradual development of these rights and States are given time to ensure them. This means that the lack of respect for economic rights as contained in these instruments of international law, or the inability of signatory States to uphold their obligation in this regard, would not normally constitute persecution.

However, in the case of negligence whereby a State fails in its duties regarding socio-economic rights for its citizens, a situation equal to cruel, inhuman, and degrading treatment may be created which may amount to persecution. Violation of economic and social rights may also occur on cumulative grounds with civil and political rights. For example, if a person is refused work because of his membership in a particular ethnic group the combination of these two elements could be evaluated to constitute persecution.

Even if the norms relative to economic and social rights have legal bearing, and a failure to uphold economic responsibilities should be considered a violation of human rights, economic oppression vis-à-vis an individual or a group is rarely considered to be persecution unless there is a cumulative effect where the violation of one or several civil and political rights is also established. A contemporary example of such a situation would be State practice vis-à-vis Albanian asylum seekers from Kosovo who, in their request for asylum, in addition to alleging, for example, arbitrary arrests, also list economic motives for their flight. It is a known fact that Albanians are being discriminated against by the Serb minority in Kosovo, and that their possibility of keeping their jobs is often uncertain. However, in keeping with a general climate of restrictive asylum policies in western Europe there is a demonstrable reluctance to grant refugee status to Kosovo-Albanians on the grounds that the difficulties described do not adhere as strictly as they might to the persecution criteria.

---

151. Article 23 of the Universal Declaration on Human Rights and Article 7 of the International Covenant on Economic, Social, and Cultural Rights of 1966.

A regrettable confusion, in both national and international debates, has emerged over the concepts of «refugee» and «economic migrant». Since the majority of Western States are not countries of open immigration, one way persons in search of a better life can hope to enter a country, is by claiming they are refugees and presenting an asylum request. The consequences of abuse in this area have been serious, specifically resulting in asylum States introducing restrictive measures to combat illegal immigration and thereby effecting not only potential immigrants, but also persons in need of international protection.[152]

Specific criteria referred to in the definition
Notwithstanding, the need for development in the interpretation of the concept of persecution, in principle, the refugee status is determined on the basis of at least one of the enumerated criteria listed in the 1951 Convention, which are: race, religion, nationality, membership of a particular social group or political opinion.[153] Whether the persecution is initiated because of only one or several of these reasons is irrelevant. Often, as has been seen, the reasons for persecution overlap, for instance, in the case of a person who fears persecution because he belongs to an ethnic group and practices a prohibited religion.

«*Race*»
According to UNHCR, «race» has to be understood in its widest sense to include all kinds of ethnic groups that are referred to as «race» in common usage. Frequently it will also entail membership of a particular social group of common descent forming a minority within a larger population. Discrimination for reason of race has found world-wide condemnation as one of the most striking violations of human rights. Racial discrimination, therefore, represents an important element in determining the existence of persecution.[154]

The term «race» largely refers to a social prejudice. It is applicable each time a person is persecuted due to his ethnic origin.[155] Membership of a particular racial group alone does not suffice to obtain refugee status, except under particular circumstances. Such a claim must be supported by precise facts

---

152. See, below, Chapter 7.
153. Given the fact that many studies have already been made on the interpretation of these grounds for persecution, this analysis will contain an outline which refers to some of these works specifically. For a broader analysis, three major works should be consulted: A. Grahl-Madsen, «The Status of Refugees in International Law», Vol. I; G. Goodwin-Gill, «The Refugee in International Law» and J. Hathaway, «The Law of Refugee Status». The UNHCR Handbook should equally be consulted.
154. UNHCR Handbook, paragraph 68, p.18.
155. A. Grahl-Madsen, «The Status of Refugees in International Law», Vol I, p. 218.

on how the person himself or his relatives, for example, have been effected, by their membership of a particular racial group.[156]

According to the definition of the International Convention on the Elimination of All Forms of Racial Discrimination,[157] «racial discrimination» means any distinction, exclusion, restriction, or preference based on race, colour, descent, or national or ethnic origin. This definition should be applied in order to suitably interpret the criteria «race». After thirty years of legal developments in human rights law, in which the protection against racial discrimination has always been considered particularly important, this would seem logical in reference to modern international usage.[158] State practice shows, on the other hand, that «race» is one of the criteria hardly ever used as a reason for granting refugee status on the grounds of well-founded fear of persecution.

«Religion»
In reality religion has long constituted one of the major reasons for persecution, although it does not thereby follow that refugee status on these grounds is easy to obtain. Existing instruments of international law in this regard, seek to protect not only the right to freedom of belief, conscience, and religion, but also the right of the person to bear witness to his religion and convictions, for example by practicing the religion in public.[159]

In terms of the 1951 Convention, the interpretation of «religion», should

---

156. M. Bauwens, «La définition du réfugié à la lumière de la jurisprudence du Commissariat General aux Réfugiés et aux Apatrides», p.10. See also UNHCR Handbook, paragraph 70, p.19.
157. Adopted by Resolution 2106 A (XX) by the UN General Assembly on December 21, 1965, entered into force on January 4, 1969 in conformity with Article 19. Text: UN Treaty Doc. No. 9464, Vol. 660, p.195.
158. The authors belonging to this school of large interpretation, see J.C. Hathaway, «The Law of Refugee Status», p.142; G. Goodwin-Gill, «The Refugee in International Law», 1983, p.27; A. Grahl-Madsen, «The Status of Refugees in International Law», Vol. I, p. 218. See also UNHCR Handbook, paragraph 68, p.18.
159. See the Universal Declaration of Human Rights, Article 18: «Everyone has the right to freedom of thought, conscience, and religion; this right includes freedom to change his religion or belief, and freedom, either alone or in community with others and in public or private, to manifest his religion or belief in teaching, practice in teaching, practice, worship, and observance.» The content of this article has been repeated in other international instruments, universal and regional, for example: the International Covenant on Civil and Political Rights of 1966, Article 18; the European Convention for the Protection of Human Rights of 1950, Article 9; the American Convention on Human Rights «San José Pact of Costa Rica» of 1969, Article 12; and the Declaration for the Elimination of All Forms of Intolerance and Discrimination Based on Religion or Conviction, Resolution 36/55 of the UN General Assembly, adopted on November, 25, 1981.

take into consideration, that persecution for this motive may take diverse forms, for example: a prohibition on being part of a religious community, a prohibition on practicing religion in public or in private, a prohibition on giving or receiving religious instruction, etc.[160] Furthermore, the right of a person not to belong to a religion or not to be a believer should also be respected and upheld.

Membership of a religious community alone is, in principle, not sufficient to benefit from refugee status unless a particular religious group is specifically targeted such as the Bahaii in Iran. In order to be granted refugee status on this basis, there must be a real risk of persecution or a serious discriminatory measure against those who practice such a prohibited religion or who belong to a given religious community.[161]

«Nationality»
«Nationality», is the legal bond linking an individual to a State through citizenship. This criteria can also be seen as designating membership in an ethnic or linguistic group.[162] Persecution for reasons of nationality consists of adverse attitudes and measures directed against a national (ethnic/linguistic) minority. In certain circumstances the fact of belonging to such a minority may in itself give rise to well-founded fear of persecution.[163] Members of the Kurdish minority in Iraq and Turkey and Muslims in the former Yugoslavia could be seen as covered by this category. Persecution for reasons of nationality is also interpreted as including persecution for lack of nationality, i.e. persecution of stateless persons,[164] and lack of full citizenship.[165]

«Membership of a particular social group»
The element «membership of a particular social group» was added to the definition in the 1951 Convention through a Swedish proposal. It had not been incoporated in the definition of the Statute of 1950. The «travaux préparatoires» of the 1951 Convention contain little further information or elaboration on this criteria, and problems of interpretation have duly arisen since.

Fear of persecution due to «membership of a particular social group» often overlaps or is confused in part with fear of persecution due to other reasons,

---

160. UNHCR Handbook, paragraph 72, p.19.
161. M. Bauwens, «La définition du réfugié à la lumière de la jurisprudence du Commissariat General aux Réfugiés et aux Apatrides», p.10.
162. UNHCR Handbook, paragraph 74, p.19; A. Grahl-Madsen, «The Status of Refugees in International Law», Vol. I, p.218 and 219; G. Goodwin-Gill, «The Refugee in International Law», p.29 and J.C. Hathaway, «The Law of Refugee Status», p.145.
163. UNHCR Handbook, paragraph 74, p.19.
164. A. Grahl-Madsen, «The Refugee in International Law», Vol. I, p.219.
165. J.C. Hathaway, «The Law of Refugee Status», p.1991, p.144.

such as race, religion, or nationality. It has been stated that this is not an independent criteria compared with the others enumerated in the definition.[166] However, the danger of suggesting such a limitation is to undermine the value of this criteria and, by implication, risk weakening the others which are frequently associated with it. In fact, the real value of the social group criteria lies in the allowance that its subtle character provides for a more flexible interpretation of the grounds on which well-founded fear of persecution is acknowledged to exist

According to a traditional interpretation, the persons envisioned by the element «social group», may be persons of a «common denominator», i.e. those who have the same lifestyle or the same social status: nobility, capitalists, businessmen, workers, liberal professions, artists, etc. ... [167] During the first few years after the entry into force of the Convention, this criteria was applied above all to persons belonging to the bourgeoisie coming from countries where revolutions had taken place.

In practice, the interpretation has evolved and so has legal writing on the subject. In his analysis on the subject, Hathaway refers to the principle «ejusdem generis» («of the same kind»), to describe the groups of persons covered by the criteria. This would seem to be a wholly persuasive interpretation of the criteria as it allows for an evolution of the concept according to need.[168]

As with the other criteria, membership of a particular social group alone does not normally suffice to justify a recognition of Convention status, except under particular circumstances.[169] The person in question must himself be the object of persecution, and the discrimination must be of a serious kind, e.g. serious restrictions on his right to earn his livelihood, his right to practice his religion, or his access to normally available educational facilities.[170]

North-American and European jurisprudence concerning the interpretation and independence of the concept of «social group» has evolved, a phenomenon which has been described as an «evolution of mentality».[171] The concept of «social group» is not only tied to a social class or to political or

---

166. See, for example, M. Iogna-Prat, «The Notion of membership of a Particular Social Group»: A European Perspective», Asylum Law & Practice in Europe and North America, Federal Publications, 1992, p. 73.
167. See A. Grahl-Madsen, «The Refugee in International Law», Vol. I, p.220 who is in favour of a rather expanded interpretation of «social group»; see also G. Goodwin-Gill, «The Refugee in International Law», p.30.
168. J.C. Hathaway, «The Law of Refugee Status», p. 160 and 161 where he considers the golden mean as the proper interpretation.
169. UNHCR's Handbook, paragraph 79, p. 20.
170. UNHCR Handbook, paragraph 54, p. 15.
171. M. Iogna-Prat, «The Notion of Membership of a Particular Social Group». A European Perspective, p. 78.

economic factors. As State practice shows, «social group» also characterizes a group of persons who have the same values or behaviors which distinguish them from other members of the society to which they belong. Homosexuality and gender-related persecution are two issues which, in later years, have also contributed to the discussion of the meaning of this criteria.

Consequently, there has been a rise over the past few years in the numbers seeking refugee status by claiming persecution on account of their membership in a particular social group and a growing number of countries have granted refugee status and asylum to lesbians and gay men persecuted in their country of origin.[172] This is not surprising considering the fact of criminalization of homosexuality in many countries: as many as sixty-seven countries criminalize sex between men and, at least twenty-seven criminalize sex between women.[173] Penal codes and their implementation vary – ranging from death sentence, in some countries to dormant laws in others.

In 1997 a Russian woman won an asylum plea in the U.S.[174] She claimed having been persecuted in Russia because of her lesbianism. She had been arrested, assaulted, expelled from medical school and given electric-shock treat-

---

172. In an article written by E. Vagelos in 1993, she refers to courts in the Netherlands, Germany and Australia as already at that time having recognized that homosexuals constitute a particular social group, see «The social group that dare not speak its name: should homosexuals constitute a particular social group for purposes of obtaining refugee status? Comment on Re: Inaudi, Fordham International Law Journal, 1993, p. 622. She also referred to US Administrative decisions which had taken the same stand. Ibid.

In 1992, the Canadian Immigration and refugee Board granted asylum to an Argentinian gay man, recognizing homosexuals as a particular social group. The person concerned, Inaudi, had been repeatedly detained, threatened and tortured by Argentinian police. (In Colombia and Costa Rica, hundreds of gay men and tranvestites have been reported murdered or missing resulting from police brutality and death squads which are claimed to be State sponsored). See S. Minter, «Sodomy and Public Morality Offenses Under U.S. Immigration Law: Penalizing Lesbian and Gay Identity», Cornell International Law Journal, 1993, p. 607 and E. Vagelos, op. cit. p. 624. In Sweden, three somewhat similar cases, in that they concerned Iranian women claiming to be lesbian, were all rejected by the Swedish Alien's Appeals Board in the summer of 1996. The peculiartity of the cases is not so much the fact that the Alien's Appeals Board did not find the claims credible, but the fact that it considered that the «sole fact of being homosexual cannot establish a right to asylum in Sweden». Flogging or imprisonment are evidently not sufficient grounds for Swedish authorities to accord neither Convention status nor «de facto» status.

173. Ibid, p. 600.
174. Reported in The Times, 27 June 1997. See Unites States Court of Appeals for the ninth circuit, California 24 June 1997.

ment in Russia because of her sexuality. Her shop in Moscow had also been burned down by Russian mafia for the same reason. The U.S. Immigration Board had rejected her asylum claim, referring i.a. to the involuntary psychiatric treatment she had been submitted as not constituting persecution because the intention of the psychiatric institution had been «to cure her». A panel of appeals court judges ruled that her case must be reviewed.

In another case, homosexuality was recognized as a valid reason for fearing persecution.[175] A Cuban citizen who had been informed by the police that because of his homosexuality he would either have to spend four years in prison in Cuba or leave and go to the U.S. He chose to seek asylum in the U.S.[176]

«Political opinion»
The criteria «political opinion» has given the name «political refugees» to refugees within the terms of the 1951 Convention, and constitutes the base from which most refugees are granted their status. It should obviously be interpreted in the light of existing international instruments on human rights relating to political opinions and expressions.[177] A typical «political refugee» is one who is persecuted due to his opinions, which are considered to be threatening to the State or its institutions.[178]

Merely to have political opinions which are contrary to the policy of a government cannot normally be regarded as sufficient grounds for well-founded fear of persecution. It must be shown, that the political thoughts of the applicant are not tolerated by the government and that he risks repercussions for having, for example, criticized the policy and the methods of those in power. This presupposes that the authorities know of his political opinions because they have been openly expressed or that they have otherwise learned about them.

The opinions of a writer or a professor are, naturally, better known and more threatening to a totalitarian regime than those of a more anonymous person. But due consideration should also be given to less exposed persons, for instance, someone in hiding who opposes his government and sooner or

---

175. Matter of Toboso-Alfonso in Exclusion Proceedings No. A-23220644 Interim Decision 3222 Department of Justice, Board of Immigration Appeals. (March 12, 1990).
176. Although the claimant was not granted asylum because of drug possession he was not deported. This case marks an important precedence in American practice regarding homosexuality and refugee protection.
177. See the Universal Declaration of Human Rights, Article 19; the International Covenant on Civil and Political Rights of 1966, Article 19; the International Convention on the Elimination of All Forms of Racial Discrimination, Article 4 and the European Convention on Human Rights, Article 10.
178. G. Goodwin-Gill, «The Refugee in International Law», p.31.

later risks being discovered. For more anonymous persons, the risk of persecution begins when their membership in a political group, for example, becomes known.

An argument often used, that a person could remain quiet and not express his political beliefs, runs counter to the right of freedom of opinion and expression which are human rights principles protected by international law. Hathaway's argument that a practice that denies refugee status to persons who courageously manifest their political opinions, is not in harmony with international human rights principles is a persuasive one.[179]

Nevertheless, it is necessary to distinguish between politically motivated «opinions» and «acts». The definition of the 1951 Convention uses the term «opinion» which covers a broader range than the term «act». Thus, a person must not necessarily have committed a political act before flight. The political opinions which he professes could be sufficient in order to establish that risk of persecution is well-founded.

On the other hand, when a person is prosecuted for acts perpetrated for political motives, and if the penalty which he encounters is in conformity with that which is foreseen by the law of the country, the fear in itself cannot give grounds for refugee status. Only if the sanction exceeds the law of the land through its severity or appears manifestly disproportionate compared with the acts committed, should the fear be considered justified with respect to persecution.[180]

New trends – gender related persecution

One of the most visible and positive developments in refugee law is the increasing acknowledgement of gender related violence as a form of persecution. Changing attitudes towards gender related issues, and in particular violence against women,[181] have resulted in an increasing acceptance that gender related violence forms an integral part of the concept of persecution. Gender related persecution is now widely recognized at various international fora and legal literature on the subject is developing.[182] Furthermore, the emergence of positive and progressive jurisprudence on the subject is beginning to influence State practice.

Women become refugees for the same reasons as men, namely, fear of persecution because of race, nationality, political activity, religious conviction

---

179. J.C. Hathaway, «The Law of Refugee Status», p.160.
180. UNHCR Handbook, paragraphs 84 and 85, p.21.
181. See J. Fitzpatrick, «Revitalizing the 1951 Refugee Convention», Harvard Human Rights Journal, Spring 1996, p. 180. See also L. Holck, «Gi asyl til kvinder der forfølges på grund av deres køn» («Give asylum to women who are persecuted because of their sex»), Berlingske Tidende, 27 June 1997.

and membership of a particular social group as well as for reasons of generalized violence, war, civil war and so on. In addition, however, women are more likely to face persecution for reasons directly related to their gender, for example, rape, female genital mutilation, forced marriage, forced sterilization or forced abortion[183] and for reasons related to behavioural norms in society, for example, homosexuality.[184]

Against such a background, women asylum seekers face two sets of problems: procedural and substantive.[185] Procedural problems arise out of the fact that women are, more often than not, unable to file a claim for asylum because they are accompanying male members of the family and are therefore often not heard on an individual basis. Substantive problems are related to difficulties women face in stating the grounds for an asylum request. For example, this is often the case when persecution takes the form of sexual abuse and the woman concerned is too ashamed to talk about it, «in casu» to a male interviewer. In other instances it is the male head of the family, whether husband, son or father, who, when applying for asylum on behalf of his family, is too ashamed to talk about the rape of his wife, daughter, mother or sister.

---

182. In legal literature substantive doctrine has developed over the last years. To mention but a few: Susan Forbes Martin, «Refugee Women», Zed Books Ltd., London, 1992; Heaven Crawley, «Women As Asylum Seekers: A Legal Handbook», Immigration Law Practitioner's Association (ILPA), 1997; Joan Fitzpatrick, «Revitalizing the 1951 Convention», Harvard Human Rights Journal, Spring 1996; Bernadette Passade Cisse, «International Law Sources Applicable to Female Genital Mutilation», Colombia Journal of Transnational Law, 1997, Kristine M. Fox, «Gender Persecution: Canadian Guidelines Offer a Model for Refugee determination in the United States», Arizona Journal of International and Comparative Law», Spring 1994; Maryellen Fullerton, «A Comparative Look at Refugee Status Based on Persecution due to Membership in a Particular Social Group», Cornell International Law Journal, 1993 and Lauren Gilbert, «The Impact of Reproductive Subordination on Women's Health: Rights, Refugee Women and Reproductive Health», The American University Law Review, Spring, 1995.
183. See Marit Kohonen, «Vold mot kvinder» («Violence against women»), article in «Politiken», 19 July 1997, in which she refers to the rape of approximately 12,000 women in Bosnia in 1992 (estimated total figures of rape victims from the war in ex-Yugoslavia amount to between 20,000 and 50,000 women); the disappearance of approximately 30 million «missing» women in India or 38 million «missing» women in China – «missing» because sons are preferred, because of sex-related abortions, killings and malnutrition; and 2 million girls undergoing female genital mutilation in Africa every year.
184. Men also risk persecution on these grounds.
185. See S. Forbes Martin, «Refugee Women», Zed Books Ltd, London, 1992, p. 23. See also Remarks by Karin Landgren, «Gender-Related Persecution» at a Symposium on Women and Asylum, Copenhagen, 3 March 1997.

Shame related to sexual abuse is known in all societies, but in some cultures sexual abuse has more negative connotations than in others.

Recourse to national protection can also be particularly problematic in cases of gender related persecution. For example, it is often extremely difficult, if not impossible, for women who fear sexual persecution to seek the protection of their national authorities, because they would be forced to expose their shame. Often, women face extreme difficulties in securing protection against members of their own family[186] or the family of their husband,[187] from male police officers who do not necessarily have much regard for women's rights.

Gender related violations of human rights against women take many forms. Rape is a particularly complex one. For example, during the war in Former Yugoslavia, Serb soldiers raped Muslim women in order to humiliate them, to make them pregnant with Serb children and to make it difficult for them, as «good Muslim women» to have children later, or for the unmarried to get married. In other words they were targeted for rape because of their reproductive capacity as Muslim women. Under the terms of the 1951 Convention, these women could equally be regarded under the «social group» or «nationality» category. The persecution could, in other words, be regarded as a direct result of their gender, but just as appropriately because they belonged to a social group, had religious affiliation to Islam, or because they belonged to an ethnic group of Bosnian Muslims. Various convention criteria could therefore be applied.

In some instances, persecution of women is linked to political or religious criteria. Those responsible for making decisions regarding refugee status should bear in mind the fact that women's political expressions may not always be the same as those of men. For example, refusal by Iranian women to wear the chador in Iran, an action which could carry a penalty of flogging or even a stoning to death, may be seen as a demonstration of disagreement against the gender politics and values of the Iranian society and State. Not following the appropriate dress code could therefore be seen as an expression of political disobedience. It could equally be seen as defiance of religious norms. It is essential that alternative categories of persecution criteria listed in the 1951 Convention, other than that of «social group», should be used more often in relation to women. Today it is often the case that those responsible for making decisions regarding refugee status tend to define men within the political context of persecution more easily than women.

---

186. Female genital mutilation is, for example, forbidden by law in many countries, but remains a custom to which authorities close their eyes.
187. Bride burning in India, for example, although forbidden by law, is not unusual in cases where the husband's family is dissatisfied with the dowry.

Female genital mutilation is another violation of human rights which is sometimes referred to as a ground for persecution. For example, in 1994, a Somali woman and her ten year old daughter were granted asylum in Canada because the mother feared that forced genital mutilation would be carried out on her child.[188] In 1985, in the Acosta case,[189] the United States Board of Immigration Appeals had pronounced its understanding of the term «social group» to reflect a common, immutable characteristic, i.e. a characteristic which is beyond the power of the individual to change, or which is so fundamental to individual identity or conscience that changing it should not be required. This application of the «ejusdem generis» rule implies an element of «open-endedness potentially capable of expansion of a variety of different classes susceptible to persecution.[190] It was also found that persecution could result from the infliction of harm or suffering by a government, or by persons a government is unwilling or unable to control, for reasons that are designed to overcome a characteristic of a person. Gender was found to be one such «common, immutable characteristic».

In 1996, in a case concerning a young woman from Togo, Fauziya Kasinga, the United States Board of Immigration Appeals found that female genital mutilation was a form of persecution.[191] Often, acts committed in such cases involve a subjective intent to punish the victims, but, according to the legal reasoning in the Kasinga case, subjective «punitive» or «malignant» intent was not required for harm to constitute persecution. Kasinga's relatives, on her father's side, had wanted her to marry well, and had therefore sought to have her circumsized, a decision which resulted in her flight. Further grounds for persecution in the Kasinga case were deemed to be her membership of a «particular social group», which, as practice has shown, is defined by «common characteristics that members of the group either cannot change, or should not be required to change because such characteristics are fundamental to their individual identities».[192] The characteristics of being a «young woman» and a «member of the Tchamba-Kunsuntu Tribe» could not, according to the Appeals Board, be changed, but the characteristic of having intact genitalia is one that is so fundamental to the individual identity of a young woman that she should not be required to change it.

---

188. Immigration and refugee Board, Refugee Division, Toronto, Canada, Case of Khadra Hassan Farah, Mahad Dahir Buraleh and Hodan Dahir Buraleh of 13 July 1994 (T93-12198, T93-12199, T93-12197).
189. Matter of Acosta, 19 I&N Dec. 211,222-23, BIA 1985.
190. See G. Goodwin-Gill, «The Refugee in International Law», 1996, p. 46 and 47.
191. Department of Justice, Board of Immigration Appeals, Decision in re Fauziya Kasinga, on 13 June 1996.
192. Cf. the Acosta case.

In some States, an increasing number of gender related asylum applications, concerning cases of forced sterilization and abortion, concern Chinese parents who have fled China because of its «one child» policy. For example, in 1994, an Australian Federal Court granted asylum to a Chinese couple, having found that forced sterilization was indeed «a clear violation of human rights» and moreover local practices condoned by the Chinese central government represented persecution in the context of the 1951 Convention.[193] However, the following year, the same Federal Court reached a contradictory decision. Having found that forced sterilization did constitute grounds for persecution, the couple concerned were denied asylum because the Court found that they did not to fulfill the necessary criteria of being members of a «particular social group».[194] This interpretation of the 1951 Convention excludes, in other words, a violation of basic human rights from being regarded as persecution and therefore warranting refugee status and protection. One could argue that whether or not the case fits the criteria «social group» this should not be decisive. If it is deemed necessary to link the assessment of persecution to one of the criteria enumerated in the 1951 Convention, the act of protesting against the Chinese «one child» policy could, for example, be regarded as covered by the criteria of persecution on political grounds.

In 1996, the Canadian Supreme Court rejected an asylum claim by a Chinese woman, who already had two children and who feared forced sterilization. The Court found that forced sterilization could constitute persecution. Nevertheless, it ruled that there was a lack of evidence in this case because not all local authorities in China apply forced sterilization to breaches of the «one child policy». In addition, the Court held that a general fear of victimization does not in itself fulfil the criteria of persecution on the grounds of a particular social group. Furthermore, the Court found that opposition to forced sterilization was not regarded as being a political statement and the applicant was therefore not found to have a well-founded fear of persecution on political grounds either.[195] Even so, the Court did, at least, assess the criteria of persecution for political reasons, albeit with a negative outcome. The fact that the political assessment was made must be acknowledged as a positive case example.

---

193. Minister for Immigration and ethnic affairs v. respondent A, respondent B and Janet Wood, the refugee review tribunal, No. NG327 of 1994; FED No. 1024/94 in the Federal Court of Australia, New South Wales District, Sydney, 15 November 1994, (6 December 1994).
194. Minister for Immigration and ethnic affairs v respondent «A», respondent «B» and Janet Wood, the refugee review tribunal, No. NG887 of 1994; FED No. 401/95 in the Federal Court of Australia, New South Wales District, Sydney, 15 May 1995, (16 June 1995).
195. Supreme Court Judgment in Chan v. Minister of Employment and Immigration, et al., 19 October 1996.

The debate in the context of international organizations
In 1985, the UNHCR Executive Committee Conclusion on «Women Refugees and International protection»,[196] stated that States were free to «…adopt the interpretation that women asylum seekers who face harsh or inhuman treatment due to their having transgressed the social mores of the society in which they live may be considered as a «particular social group» within the meaning of Article 1(A)…».

Following the 1985 UNHCR Executive Committee Conclusion on «Women Refugees and International protection» the UNHCR Executive Committee, with the endorsement of the UN General Assembly, has reiterated its concern for women refugees on several occasions.[197] In 1990, the 41st Session of the Executive Committee Meeting marked a turning point and helped focus attention on refugee women by adopting Conclusion No. 64 on Refugee Women and International Protection,[198] which stressed that «…all action taken on behalf of women who are refugees must be guided by the relevant international instruments relating to the status of refugees as well as other applicable human rights instruments, in particular, for States parties hereto, the UN Convention on the Elimination of All Forms of Discrimination Against Women».

In the wake of the 1990 Executive Committee Meeting, it was decided that comprehensive guidelines on the protection of refugee women needed to be developed as a matter of urgency.[199] In 1991, guidelines were submitted to the 42nd Session of the Executive Committee which, in its Conclusion on Refugee Women,[200] not only welcomed the guidelines but also reiterated that gender related persecution should be considered as covered by the 1951 Convention. The Conclusion also requested that the Guidelines be made an integral part of all UNHCR protection and assistance activities and that

---

196. Conclusion No. 39 (XXXVI), adopted during the 36th Session of the Executive Committee.
197. For example, in Conclusion No. 54 (XXXIX), adopted at the 39th Session of the Executive Committee in 1988 and in Resolution 43/117 of 8 December 1988 by the UN General Assembly; Conclusion No. 60 (XL), adopted at the 40th Session of the Executive Committee in 1989.
198. Adopted during the 41st Session of the Executive Committee in 1990 (later approved by Resolution 45/140 by the UN General Assembly on 14 December 1990), reiterated, i.a. Conclusion No. 54 (XXXIX) on Refugee Women of 1988.
199. See Doc. EC/SCP/67 of 22 July 1991, Information Note on UNHCR's Guidelines on the Protection of Refugee Women (submitted by the High Commissioner).
200. UNHCR Executive Committee, 42nd Session, 1991, (Doc. A/AC.96/783, paragraph 24(b))

UNHCR should evaluate and report on the progress achieved in implementing the Guidelines.

In the 1993 Conclusion of the Executive Committee on Refugee Protection and Sexual Violence,[201] the Executive Committee strongly condemned persecution through sexual violence and called it, not only a gross violation of human rights, but equally, when committed in the context of armed conflict, a grave breach of humanitarian law and a serious offense to human dignity.[202] The Executive Committee equally supported the recognition as refugees of persons whose claim to refugee status is based upon a well-founded fear of persecution, through sexual violence.

These developments aside, persecution of women did not come into real focus until the horrendous, mass-scale sexual abuse that took place during the conflicts in Bosnia and Rwanda in the beginning of the 1990s. Since these conflicts, gender related issues have been a developing area in refugee law, principally linked to the criteria of «social group». States have, however, been slow to follow up international recommendations in this regard. So far, only three States, the United States, Canada and Australia, have issued particular guidelines concerning refugee women and the interpretation of the 1951 Convention. Their example needs to be followed by other States .

The issue of gender related persecution has been raised at a regional level in Europe, but thus far has not been developed. In 1984, the European Parliament adopted a resolution calling on European Member States to grant refugee status «to women who suffer cruel and inhuman treatment because they have violated the moral or ethical rules of their society».[203] According to the Resolution, women should be included within the criteria of a «particular social group». [204] In September 1995, the European Parliament called on the European Commission to draw up a proposal, with a view to having oppression and sexual violence against women accepted as legitimate reasons for requesting asylum.[205] Action on this matter has yet to be taken. In April 1995,

---

201. Conclusion No. 73 (XLIV), adopted at the 44th session of the Executive Committee in 1993.
202. Rape and cruelties during the war in former Yugoslavia were condemned as war crime and crime against humanity in UN General Assembly Resolution 48/143 of 20 December 1993 which makes reference to Resolution 3074 (XXVIII) of 3 December 1973, in which member States of the UN are invited to arrest, extradite and punish persons guilty of having committed war crimes and crimes against humanity.
203. Resolution of 14 may 1984 (Official Journal of the European Communities C127).
204. Resolution of April 13, 1984 (Official Journal of the European Community C 127/137).
205. Reuter Textline Agence Europe, 30 September 1995.

the Parliamentary Assembly of the Council of Europe proposed that European Member States should assess gender-related discrimination of women, and consider whether, for example, the obligation to wear a veil, the prohibition of practicing certain professions or pursuing education, should not be considered as grounds of persecution.[206]

However, in spite of these efforts, the concept of gender related persecution has rarely been recognized in European practice.[207] In most cases involving gender, women have traditionally been accorded «de facto» status and not Convention refugee status. NGO communities across Europe are currently working to redress the issue of gender-related persecution.[208] Hopefully the new trends in the U.S., Canada and Australia will help influence developments in Europe.[209]

The importance of always interpreting the 1951 Convention in relation to human rights principles needs to be reiterated in the context of persecution of women.[210] On the one hand, governments should be encouraged to view persecution of women in the context of the criteria of «social group», but, on the other hand, such policy should not prevent women from being recognized as 1951 Convention refugees under other criteria. There is no reason why women's manifestations should not be viewed as political, as expressions of religious belief and non-belief or other fundamental convictions which could lead to persecution.

---

206. ESMV, List of Events, No. 4, April 1995, p. 9.
207. In «Women As Asylum Seekers», H. Crawley gives advice on how women's claims should be handled by national immigration authorities.
208. Both British and Danish NGOs have taken specific initiatives in this regard and policy on refugee women is equally on the agenda of ECRE. It is surprising that the Scandinavian countries, with their alleged standards of equality between the sexes and emancipation of women have not taken initiatives also on a governmental level. By tradition, refugee women are rarely granted asylum in these countries, but they are often considered as persons in need of international protection and therefore granted «de facto» status. See for example ECRE's position paper on women as Asylum Seekers and Refugees, 1997.
209. The Swedish example of placing gender-related persecution outside the realm of the 1951 Convention in its new legislation on aliens is unfortunate because this form of persecution also belongs in the context of the 1951 Convention and not in a sub group.
210. See the 1995 Declaration from the Women's Conference in Beijing that «women's rights are human rights» should be kept in mind and equally the Beijing Platform E, paragraph 136. (UN Doc. A/CONF.177/20).

3.4 Cessation and exclusion of refugee status

The refugee concept enshrined in Article 1 of the 1951 Convention provides for a refugee definition that contains not only «inclusive» elements, which delineate the criteria by which refugee status is granted, but also contains elements which regulate the loss of refugee status, otherwise referred to as «cessation clauses», and elements which regulate the exclusion of refugee status, otherwise referred to as «exclusion clauses». The termination or refusal of refugee status has profound consequences for refugee protection and the interpretation of these causes should therefore be prudent.

«Cessation clauses»

There are six «cessation clauses», Article 1(C)(1-6), which delineate the criteria according to which a person ceases to be a refugee. The reason behind the inclusion of such clauses is that international protection should be limited to real needs. According to UNHCR, international protection is created as an «intermediary measure» in order to bridge a gap between the moment when a refugee is forced to leave his country and the moment when he may again enjoy national protection, be it by his country of origin, through repatriation, or country of asylum, through naturalization. Refugee status is not meant to be permanent, but temporary. In general, UNHCR is extremely prudent, and rightly so, when giving advice to governments on the use of the cessation clauses.

The first four «cessation clauses» (Article 1(C) (Clauses 1-4) concern changes under the refugee's control, in that he himself has taken an initiative which may have consequences for his refugee status.

The first «cessation clause», Article 1(C)(1), applies to a person who has «voluntarily re-availed himself of the protection of the country of his nationality». For example, a refugee who returns to his country of origin for a visit is demonstrating that his fear of persecution has disappeared. According to UNHCR, recourse to this clause presupposes three conditions. Firstly, that the refugee has acted voluntarily, secondly, that he has the intention of again reclaiming the protection of his country and thirdly, that that protection will be accorded. It is necessary, therefore, to distinguish between the reclaiming of national protection and an occasional contact. For example, if a refugee asks for a national passport or for the renewal of a passport, it would not be unjust to assume, in the absence of proof to the contrary, that the refugee wants to reclaim full rights, including protection, as a citizen of his country of origin. On the other hand, a request to an embassy for a birth certificate should be considered an «occasional contact».[211]

The second «cessation clause», Article 1 (C)(2), applies to a person who, «having lost his nationality, he has voluntarily re-acquired it». Only if a nationality previously lost is regained, does a person risk having his refugee status withdrawn. A person does not automatically lose his nationality upon recognition of refugee status by a receiving State.

The third «cessation clause», Article 1(C)(3), applies to a person who «has acquired a new nationality, and enjoys the protection of the country of his new nationality». When a refugee acquires another nationality, for example in his country of residence, international protection is no longer needed.

The fourth «cessation clause», Article 1(C)(4), applies to a person who has «voluntarily re-established himself in the country which he left or outside which he remained owing to fear of persecution». This clause refers to refugees for whom the first and second clauses are not applicable. The term «voluntarily re-established» should be understood as return to the country of nationality or of former habitual residence with a view to permanently residing there.[212]

The fifth «cessation clause», Article 1(C)(5) applies to a person who «can no longer, because the circumstances in connection with which he has been recognized as a refugee have ceased to exist, continue to refuse to avail himself of the protection of the country of his nationality; Provided that this paragraph shall not apply to a refugee falling under Section A(1) of this Article who is able to invoke compelling reasons arising out of previous persecution for refusing to avail himself of the protection of the country of nationality».

The sixth «cessation clause», Article 1(C)(6) applies to a person who «being a person who has no nationality he is, because the circumstances in connection with which he has been recognized as a refugee have ceased to exist, able to return to the country of his former habitual residence; Provided that this paragraph shall not apply to a refugee falling under Section A(1) of this Article who is able to invoke compelling reasons arising out of previous persecution for refusing to avail himself of the protection of the country of his former habitual residence».

These two final «cessation clauses», Article 1(C)(5/6), refer to situations where the need for international protection is no longer required because circumstances have changed in the country where a refugee fears persecution. However, the circumstances which have ceased to exist, must be seen as implying that changes are fundamental, stable and of a durable character.[213]

Accordingly, UNHCR's Executive Committee has underlined «... the

---

211. UNHCR Handbook, paragraph 121, p. 30.
212. UNHCR Handbook, paragraph 134, p.33.
213. UNHCR, Handbook, paragraph 135, p.34.

possibility of use of the cessation clauses of the 1951 Convention in situations where a change of circumstances in a country is of such a profound and enduring nature that refugees from that country no longer require international protection, and can no longer continue to refuse to avail themselves of the protection of their country, ... ».[214] State practice has shown that the interpretation of «change of circumstances» in individual cases includes those in which an amnesty has been offered to a person or a group of persons in the country of origin whereby they will not be prosecuted for the political offence for which they fled. There is a risk that in such cases no consideration is given to whether the general circumstances in the country of origin have changed or not.

The second part of these two final «cessation clauses», Article 1(C)(5/6), provides an important limitation. It is important that a refugee is not forced to return to his country of origin if a well-founded fear of persecution remains. This humanitarian principle should come into play in all cases and not only for «statutory refugees», to whom the 1951 Convention makes explicit reference. The explanation of this reference is that the 1951 Convention was created at a time when the majority of refugees had fled Nazi atrocities during the Second World War. A forced return to a country where the refugee had been submitted to such treatment, was considered «inhumane» at the time. Atrocities today should lead to the same assessment. This is why, in 1991, UNHCR's Executive Committee also reiterated the need to take into consideration compelling reasons why the cessation clauses should not apply.[215]

In 1992, the Sub-Committee of the Whole on International Protection underlined the possibility of using the cessation clauses on change of circumstances, reiterating the Executive Committee Conclusion of the previous year. However, the Sub-Committee went further, recommending that similar considerations should be had to persons who have lived for a long time in the country of asylum and have established family, social, and economic links there.[216]

Application of the «cessation clauses» in the 1951 Convention rests exclusively with the contracting States. States must, however, « ... carefully assess the fundamental character of the changes in the country of nationality or origin, including the general human rights situation, as well as the particular cause of fear of persecution, in order to make sure in an objective and verifia-

---

214. Conclusion No. 65 (XLII) adopted by the Executive Committee of UNHCR in 1991.
215. Ibid.
216. Report by the Sub-Committee of the Whole on Protection, UN Document A/AC.96/802 of October 6, 1992, p.13.

ble way that the situation which justified the granting of refugee status has ceased to exist».[217] In this context the risk of violating the non-refoulement principle must always be taken into consideration.

States should be guided by humanitarian principles and pay due consideration to the particular circumstances in each case. Moreover, in order to ensure the development of more coherent and harmonized international practice, States should follow the advice of UNHCR before applying the «cessation clauses».

The need for international harmonization, was most recently demonstrated in connection with «cessation» of temporary protection to refugees from the Former Yugoslavia. Although the «cessation clauses» were not applied directly to refugees given temporary protection on a collective basis, the same philosophy as that governing the «cessation clauses» was presumably applied on the discussion concerning the lifting of temporary protection. However, opposing views and lack of coordination between European States manifested itself with regard to the return home of Bosnian refugees following the signing of the Dayton Peace Accord. Some States, like Germany and Switzerland, began returning refugees to Bosnia first, whereas other States showed themselves more hesitant. To conclude, in spite of each State having the exclusive right to decide whether or not to apply the «exclusion clauses» directly or by analogy, there are good reasons in favour of international harmonization in this field. Such reasons are to the benefit of States and refugees. [218]

«Exclusion clauses»

There are three «exclusion clauses», Article 1(D) (E) and (F), which delineate the criteria according to which a person may be excluded from refugee status, even if he complies with the enumerated conditions of the «inclusion» clauses. The main purpose of the authors of the Convention was to exclude certain persons from refugee status, for example, war criminals and individuals who might endanger the internal security of asylum countries.[219]

Article 1 (D) excludes «persons who are at present receiving from organs or agencies of the United Nations other than the United Nations High Commissioner protection or assistance». For example, Palestinian refugees, who receive assistance and protection from the United Nations Relief and Works

---

217. Ibid.
218. See below, Chapter 6 and 8 on temporary protection, European practice in this regard and proposals for harmonization.
219. J.C. Hathaway, «The Law of Refugee Status», 1991, p.214.

Agency for Palestine Refugees in the Near East (UNRWA), are therefore excluded from Convention refugee status. The objective is to avoid an overlap between the competencies of UNHCR and those of UNRWA.

Article 1(E) excludes «a person who is recognized by the competent authorities of the country in which he has taken residence as having the rights and obligations which are attached to the possession of the nationality of that country». The motive for this clause was the wish to exclude refugees and expelled persons of German ethnicity, who in terms of German legislation were considered «Germans». The text of this paragraph is general in its phraseology and therefore would include other nationals in similar situations.

Article 1(F) excludes « any person with respect to whom there are serious reasons for considering that: (a) he has committed a crime against peace, a war crime, or a crime against humanity, as defined in the international instruments drawn up to make provision in respect of such crimes; (b) he has committed a serious non-political crime outside the country of refuge prior to his admission to that country as a refugee; (c) he has been guilty of acts contrary to the purposes and principles of the United Nations». This clause represents a pragmatic form of «international morality», which recognizes the right of any States to refuse «undesirables» access to their territory.

Article 1(F)(a) was, in part, influenced by the vivid memories in the minds of the authors of the 1951 Convention, of the Second World War and the trials against war criminals. The Article also refers to international instruments for determining what constitutes a crime against peace, a war crime, or a crime against humanity. The traditional interpretation of «a crime against peace» includes preparation and participation in an illegal war, whereas «a war crime» includes violations of humanitarian law, mistreatment of civil populations and war prisoners included. «A crime against humanity» includes behaviour fundamentally contrary to humanitarian and human rights principles, such as genocide, slavery, torture, and apartheid.[220]

In 1993, the UN Security Council established an «ad hoc» War Tribunal in the Hague, in charge of prosecuting persons presumed responsible for serious violations of international humanitarian law, committed during the war in Former Yugoslavia.[221] The UN General Assembly also condemned the practice of «ethnic cleansing», carried out during the Bosnian conflict, and stated that such practices constituted genocide and were thus to be consid-

---

220. J.C. Hathaway, op. cit., p.217. See also A Grahl-Madsen, «The Status of Refugees in International Law», Vol. I, p. 276 and G. Goodwin-Gill, «The Refugees in International Law», p.60.
221. Resolution 808 of the Security Council, adopted unanimously on 22 February 1993. The last tribunals of this type were the Nüremberg Tribunal and the Tokyo Tribunal after the Second World War.

ered as crimes against humanity.[222] In 1994, the UN General Assembly reiterated this point in relation to the massacres in Rwanda. A new «ad hoc» Tribunal was established with the mandate to prosecute those responsible for genocide and other serious violations of international humanitarian law committed in Rwanda. The need for the establishment of a permanent war crimes Tribunal is an issue which is presently being discussed in the context of the UN.

Article 1(F)(b) was included in order to protect States from criminals who might jeopardize national security. In other words, persons who have committed a serious non-political crime cannot take refuge in another State in order to escape a lawsuit. This in itself is understandable, but what is not understandable, is that a person who has committed a crime and has served his punishment before becoming a refugee, is excluded from international protection. Such practice runs counter to the generally accepted principle of penal law, according to which, a person should not incur further sanctions for the same offense.[223]

In 1977, during the UN negotiations on a Convention on Territorial Asylum, the delegates agreed that Article 1(F)(b) should only apply to those persons who remained susceptible to being prosecuted and punished for a crime of common law.[224] This was an important interpretation which States should take into consideration, despite the fact that the Convention was never adopted.[225]

Moreover, Article 1(F)(b) only concerns crimes committed outside of the country in which the person is requesting asylum and furthermore concerns «serious crime». UNHCR has described «serious crime» as a crime implicating serious violence, such as homicide, rape, arson, drug trafficking, and armed robbery.

Article 1(F)(c) excludes persons who have acted contrary to the purposes and principles of the UN from refugee status.[226] This «exclusion clause» overlaps in part with Article 1(F)(a), concerning crime against peace, war crime, or crime against humanity. The Preamble and Articles 1 and 2 of the UN Charter enumerate the fundamental principles of the UN. These provisions govern the conduct of UN Member States. In order to apply this «exclusion clause», the person in question must be one who exercises power in a

---

222. Resolution 47/121 of the UN General Assembly, later confirmed in Resolution 48/153 on 20 December, 1993.
223. P. Weis, «Le concept de réfugié en droit international», p. 987.
224. A. Grahl-Madsen, «Territorial Asylum», p. 209.
225. See below, Chapter 6, p. 176–179.
226. A similar reference is reflected in Article 14, second paragraph of the Universal Declaration of Human Rights.

UN Member State and who has contributed to the violation of the principles in question. A sensible interpretation of this «exclusion clause» is that it is intended to enable States to « ... avoid tarnishing refugee status by the admission to protection of those who have exploited their political authority to jeopardize the well-being of individuals, their nation, or the world community».[227]

Guy Goodwin-Gill contends that Article 1(F)(c) was included in order to counter such acts as hostage taking, hijacking and apartheid and also in general to promote human rights.[228] Perpetrators of these types of crime risk being excluded from refugee status. In interpreting the clause expansively, he makes an important point regarding refugee law, as well as international law as a whole, namely, that it develops and that it should do so. In this particular regard, the development is to the detriment of a potential asylum seeker who, as for instance a highjacker, risks not being granted refugee status. On the other hand, this same person would be protected, according to the «non-refoulement» principle if he risks being subjected to violations of basic, non-derogable human rights principles as contained in, for example, the Torture Convention of 1984. This shows that in spite of being excluded from the 1951 Convention status, a person may, if necessary, be protected by the use of human rights instruments.

The responsibility for determining whether serious reasons exist to refuse refugee status under the «exclusion clauses», rests with the contracting States, in which an asylum request has been filed. To date, States have been prudent with regard to the utilization of «exclusion clauses» and, as a consequence, they have not been used excessively in State practice. On the other hand, States have every right to be firm towards representatives of regimes and other persons who would be covered by Article 1(F), if they in turn have to flee their country. The use of «exclusion clauses» must ultimately rest with a decision based on individual responsibility and the acts committed. This position is evidently adhered to by UNHCR, which has recommended the application of the exclusion clause, 1(F)(a) on war criminals from Rwanda.

In conclusion, the 1951 Convention does not provide any explicit instructions with respect to its interpretation and the task of interpretation is therefore the responsibility of contracting States. Interpretation of the 1951 Convention refugee definition varies not only from one State to another, but also from one era to another, according to political and economic fluctuations. If States interpret the Convention in a restrictive manner when it suits their interest, they risk doing so to the detriment of the protection needs of refugees

---

227. J.C. Hathaway, «The Law of Refugee Status», p.229.
228. G. Goodwin-Gill, «The Refugee in International Law», 1983, p.65.

which is contrary to the purpose of the 1951 Convention. As a rule, interpretation of the 1951 Convention should be guided by human rights and humanitarian principles as well as other principles of international law.

In recent years, EU Member States have been working towards a common approach to the interpretation of Article 1(A) of the 1951 Convention. Harmonization of the interpretation of the 1951 Convention is indeed important, but not if the common aim is to minimize the concept of a Convention refugee. The regional approach of the EU Member States Joint Position on Article 1(A) which has had precisely this effect is not therefore an example to follow. On the contrary, it should be kept in mind, that the task of supervising the application of international conventions for the protection of refugees, was given to UNHCR, in order to ensure a common universal interpretation of the Convention. If States were, for example, to refer more often and more faithfully to UNHCR's Handbook, a more objective and internationally harmonized interpretation of the 1951 Convention could emerge, to the benefit of both refugees and States.

The international agenda of «refugee protection» is turning into an agenda of «State protection». States adopt restrictive measures, ostensibly to combat abusive asylum applications. The need to react against such abuses should be acknowledged, not only by States, but also by all those involved in refugee policy matters, such as humanitarian NGOs and intergovernmental organizations, because the effect of misuse is to the detriment of the refugees themselves. However, illegal immigration should not be fought at the expense of the 1951 Convention. State policy designed to counter illegal immigration has clearly resulted in the creation of technical obstacles which render flight next to impossible, by imposing barriers such as visa requirements, carrier sanctions, etc.[229] The result is, that persons who would qualify for refugee status under the 1951 Convention and others who are in real need of international protection, are not guaranteed access to refugee status determination procedures. Furthermore, even if these persons do manage to get access to determination procedures, they are not necessarily granted refugee status because States apply a restrictive interpretation of the 1951 Convention. States often fear the so called «pull factor», meaning that a liberal policy, regarding the interpretation of the 1951 Convention and regarding social benefits to refugees, may attract asylum seekers. The «pull factor» is, however, overrated and it is becoming increasingly difficult for an asylum seeker to reach a specific asylum country of his choice.[230]

The integrity of the 1951 Convention must be protected. In order to do

---

229. On the impositions of legal barriers, see below, Chapter 7.
230. Ibid.

so, the Convention must be applied conscientiously. This would not only set an example to States which do not have a tradition of applying the 1951 Convention, such as Central and Eastern European States, but would also deter negative developments taking place in other parts of the world, and especially in States which have been mimicking less than laudable European practices. For example, in recent years around one percent of the total number of asylum seekers in Norway, have been granted Convention refugee status whereas approximately forty percent have been granted residence permit on humanitarian grounds. Although the Norwegian government has recently reviewed its refugee policy, it is far from being the only government that ought to chart a new course. In France, for example, recognition rates fell from sixty percent in 1983, to approximately thirty-four percent in 1988, and to twenty percent in 1992.[231]

---

231. On statistical material, see J. Fitzpatrick, «Revitalizing the 1951 Refugee Convention», Harvard Human Rights Journal, Spring 1996, p. 184.

CHAPTER 4
Evolution of the refugee concept

The evolution of the refugee concept, since the adoption of the 1951 Convention and the Statute of 1950, has not been consistent. At a universal level, the expansion of the refugee concept has first and foremost been of relevance to the High Commissioner's assistance and protection work. Over the years, UNHCR's mandate has been expanded through the adoption of numerous UN General Assembly resolutions, instructing UNHCR to care for, not only victims of persecution, but also victims of war, internal strife and other situations of general violence.

At a regional level, the 1951 Convention, not proving sufficiently adequate as a protection instrument in Africa and Latin-America, has been supplemented, as has been seen, by the adoption of the OAU Convention and the Cartagena Declaration. The need for a similar regional approach is present elsewhere, not least because of mass-exoduses in recent years from, for example, Afghanistan, Bosnia, Albania, Iraq and Haiti.

With regard to Europe, the refugee definition of the 1951 Convention still constitutes the international legal base which European States refer to when determining refugee status, and it should, due to its universality, remain the principal international instrument for the protection of refugees. Nonetheless, there is an urgent need to make a legal adjustment to the European refugee regime, in order to cover the vast majority of refugees who are now subject to national administrative and legislative «ad hoc» solutions. The next logical step for European States to undertake would, therefore, be a harmonized approach to the challenge of protecting «de facto» refugees. This would ultimately mean the creation of a European regional instrument designed to supplement the refugee definition of the 1951 Convention, and, in keeping with reality, expand the refugee concept in Europe to include «de facto» refugees. The ultimate aim of such an additional regional instrument would be the development of a new universal instrument.

In order to arrive at a concrete proposal for a new European refugee convention in which an expanded refugee definition is an important element, it is necessary to examine the evolution which has already taken place at a universal and at a regional level. Furthermore, it is necessary to assess the present status of «de facto» refugees more closely and suggestions which have already been put forward in the international debate on this issue.

4.1 Development of UNHCR's mandate

Refugee law, with regard to refugee determination and protection, has developed as a result of international efforts to find adequate solutions to humanitarian needs. Pragmatic initiatives to extend assistance and protection to persons falling outside the scope of the Statute of 1950, have gradually expanded UNHCR's mandate to cover victims of man made disasters such as victims of massive violations of human rights and victims of war. In order to achieve this, UNHCR has been instructed through numerous UN General Assembly resolutions, to render its «good offices» to the benefit of various categories of displaced persons.

The need to go beyond UNHCR's statutory refugee definition, as defined in the Statute of 1950, first became apparent in the 1950s, but manifested itself more strongly in the 1960s, as a result of decolonialization and wars of independence in Africa. When the additional Protocol to the 1951 Convention was adopted in 1967, there were already close to half a million displaced persons throughout the African continent. To political observers it was obvious that the number of displaced persons was increasing exponentially and that the reasons for flight of the vast majority of African refugees did not correspond to the refugee definition of the 1951 Convention.[232]

This would have been a perfect time to introduce an additional protocol to the 1951 Convention, which would not only have eliminated its geographical and time limitations, but would also have extended its rather narrow refugee definition beyond individually targeted persons or groups of persons, to include other displaced persons. However, the international community pursued another path, which had already been chosen in the 1950s, shortly after the adoption of both the 1951 Convention and the Statute of 1950. Through the UNHCR «good offices» procedure[233] a flexible practice was established, allowing for an expanded refugee concept to include groups of persons, who would otherwise not be considered as refugees but who were nonetheless in need of assistance.

Initially, the expanded mandate only covered particular assistance responsibilities placed upon UNHCR. The «good offices» procedure was used in specific cases as the need arose, hence the denomination «geographic resolutions».[234] The adoption of Resolution 1167 (XII) in 1957, concerning

---

232. J. Oloka-Onyango, «Human Rights, the OAU Convention and the Refugee Crisis in Africa: Forty Years After Geneva», International Journal of Refugee Law, Vol. 3, 1991, p.454.
233. For the antecedents of the UN «good offices» procedure, see B.G. Ramcharan, «The Good Offices of the United Nations Secretary General in the Field of Human Rights», The American Journal of International Law, Vol. 76, 1982, p.130-141.

Chinese refugees in Hong Kong, created a precedent that allowed UNHCR to provide assistance to refugees not strictly covered by its mandate.

It was not until 1960, that the practice of «good offices» was definitively established through the adoption of Resolution 1388 (XIV) of 1959 on UNHCR's Report to the General Assembly in which the General Assembly «…authorizes UNHCR, in respect of refugees who do not come within the competence of the UN, to use his good offices in the transmission of contributions designed to provide assistance to these refugees» and Resolution 1499 (XV) on UNHCR's Report to the General Assembly in which the General Assembly invites Member States of the UN to continue to consult with UNHCR «…in respect of measures of assistance to groups of refugees who do not come within the competence of the Unites Nations». It is worth noting, that at the time, these developments were not considered of great importance,[235] and it was only through subsequent events that the true value of these resolutions was confirmed. Since then, the practice of «good offices» has constituted a base for the extension of UNHCR's competence, to accord assistance and protection to persons not covered by its original mandate.

During the decolonization era of the 1960s, a series of resolutions aimed at enlarging UNHCR's competence were adopted by the UN General Assembly. Resolution 1673 (XVI) of 18 December 1961 on UNHCR's Report to the General Assembly, in which the General Assembly asks UNHCR to «…pursue his activities on behalf of the refugees within his mandate or those for whom he extends his good offices…» is considered a turning point. From this point on, UNHCR's broadened competence to accord assistance to groups outside of the traditional mandate, was well established. In 1962, the UNHCR Executive Committee confirmed the development of the «good

---

234. Resolution 1129 (xi) of 21 November 1956 on Hungarian refugees was the first «geographic resolution». Later ones include i.a. Resolutions 1389 (XIV) of 20 November 1959, 1500 (XV) of 5 December 1960 and 1672 (XVI) of 18 December 1961 on refugees coming from Algeria, Morocco, and Tunisia; Resolution 1671 (XVI) of 18 December 1961 on Angolan refugees to the Congo; Resolution 1784 (XVII) of 7 December 1962 on the Chinese refugees to Hong Kong; Resolution 2040 (XX) of 7 December 1965 on refugees in Africa; Resolution 2958 (XXVII) of 12 December 1972 on the Sudanese refugees returning from abroad; Resolution 3143 (XXVIII) of 14 December 1973 on the report of the High Commissioner for Refugees; Resolution 3454 (XXX) of 9 December 1975 on humanitarian assistance to displaced persons coming from Indo-China. See also the Resolutions of the Economic and Social Council: 1655 (LII) of 1 June 1972; 1741 (LV) of 4 May 1973; 1799 (LV) of 30 July 1973; 1877 (LVII) of 16 July 1974 and 2011 (LXI) of 2 August 1976.
235. G. Melander, «Further Development of International Refugee Law», p.481.

offices» procedure by referring to it as part of UNHCR's normal activities, describing it as a procedure which had introduced an element of flexibility and dynamism to the UNHCR mandate, whilst at the same time responding to the needs of the situation at the time.[236] The evolution of the procedure in a pragmatic and humanitarian rather than legalistic way, allowed for the development of a «prima facie» collective refugee determination, far removed from the individual concept contained in the Statute of 1950.[237]

In 1965 the UN General Assembly gave a fundamental confirmation of UNHCR's extended mandate. Resolution 2039(XX) of 7 December 1965, instructed the High Commissioner to «... pursue his efforts with a view to ensuring an adequate international protection of refugees and to providing satisfactory permanent solutions to the problems affecting the various groups of refugees within his competence ...», leaving no doubt as to the expansion of UNHCR's competence.[238] Hereafter, terms such as «... protection to refugees who are his concern, within the limits of his competence ...», began to be used.[239] Later, reference was also made to previous resolutions.[240] In 1974, the General Assembly instructed UNHCR to continue his activities «... on behalf of those of concern to his Office ...».[241]

From the beginning of the 1970s, the resolutions refer to «refugees and displaced persons».[242] Initially, the UN General Assembly specified to which displaced population it was referring, for example, to displaced women and children in Africa. However, from 1975 onwards, the UN General Assembly

---

236. UNHCR Report to the General Assembly, 17th Session, 1962.
237. S. Aga Khan, «Refugees and Displaced Persons», Sijthoff-Leyden, 1977, p.341.
238. Resolution 2039 (XX) of 7 December 1965. In this resolution, the General Assembly also invited member States and the special agencies to increase their support of UNHCR's humanitarian action and to continue to collaborate with UNHCR in this respect. In later resolutions, the General Assembly requested UNHCR to continue to ensure international protection of refugees who «are his concern», and to promote permanent solutions to their problems, for example Resolution 2197 (XXI) of 16 December 1966.
239. For example Resolution 2197 (XX) of 16 December 1966.
240. For example Resolution 2594 (XXIV) of 16 December 1969, Resolution 2650 (XXV) of 30 November 1970, Resolution 2789 (XXVI) of 6 December 1971 and Resolution 2956 (XXVII) of 12 December 1972. In Resolution 3143 (XXVIII) of 14 December 1973, the General Assembly asks UNHCR to «...continue his assistance and protection activities in favour of refugees within his mandate as well as for those to whom he extends his good offices or is called upon to assist in accordance with relevant resolutions of the General Assembly». Here again, different refugee groups are mentioned separately as they had been in the beginning of the 1960s.
241. Resolution 3271 (XXIX) of 10 December 1974.

began to make a general reference to «refugees and displaced persons», without specifying which category of displacement it had in mind.[243] Thus UNHCR's mandate was extended to cover large unspecified groups of displaced persons. The status of displaced persons had therefore become analogous to that of refugees.[244] By the beginning of the 1980s, displaced persons had come to be regarded as being part of UNHCR's regular activities.[245]

The cumulative effect of all the resolutions on UNHCR's competence throughout the 1960s and 1970s, was to erase the distinction between «good offices» refugees and refugees covered by the Statute of 1950, and in so doing, both categories of refugees became recognized as «refugees within the mandate of UNHCR».

In 1976, the UN General Assembly, recognizing the need to continuously improve international protection for refugees, endorsed a resolution adopted by ECOSOC, asking UNHCR to provide assistance not only to refugees but also to persons displaced because of «man-made disasters» and to whom humanitarian aid was urgently needed.[246]

The notion of «man-made disasters» has not been defined in international law, but it may be deduced from an analysis of UN General Assembly resolutions. In 1981, the UN General Assembly [247] established a Governmental Group of Experts on International Cooperation to Prevent New Flows of Refugees, and in doing so, reaffirmed its condemnation of the policies and practices of racist and oppressive regimes, such as aggression, colonialism, apartheid, foreign domination, intervention, and occupation, which were

---

242. For example Resolution 2958 (XXVII) of 12 December 1972, Resolution 3454 (XXX) of 9 December 1975, Resolution 31/35 of 30 November 1976, Resolution 32/67 of 8 December 1977, Resolution 33/26 of 29 November 1978, Resolution 34/60 of 29 November 1979, Resolution 35/41 of 25 November 1980 and Resolution 35/ 187 of 15 December 1980.
243. Resolutions 2958 (XXVII) of 12 December 1972 and 3454 (XXX) of 9 December 1975. See also Resolution 31/35 of 30 November 1976, Resolution 32/67 of 8 December 1977, Resolution 33/26 of 29 November 1978, Resolution 34/60 of 29 November 1979, Resolution 35/41 of 25 November 1980, Resolution 35/135 of 11 December 1980 and Resolution 35/187 of 15 December 1980.
244. D. Hull, «Displaced Persons: The New Refugees», 1983, p. 768.
245. D. McNamara, «Determination of the Status of Refugees – Evolution of the Definition», Symposium on the Promotion, Dissemination and Teaching of Fundamental Human Rights», Tokyo, from 7 to 11 December 1981, UNHCR, Geneva, 1982, p. 77.
246. Resolution by the Economic and Social Council 2011 (LXI) of 2 August, 1976, approved by the General Assembly in Resolution 31/35 of 30 November, 1976.
247. Resolution 36/148 of 16 December, 1981.

considered as the primary causes of refugee movements. In the Group of Experts' Report of 1986, reference was made to natural, political, and socio-economic factors forcing persons to flee for fear for their life, freedom and security. Wars, armed conflict and other human rights violations were confirmed as being the principal causes of flight.[248]

In 1984, authorization had been given to UNHCR by the UN Secretary General, to accord its assistance to persons in Ethiopia displaced by a combination of «man-made disaster» and «natural disaster». In Ethiopia, making a distinction between displacement due to «man-made disasters» and «natural disasters» would have been absurd, as the number of refugees was growing, the country's economic resources were dwindling and there was a drought.[249] The humanitarian need was the same for all categories of displaced persons. Since 1984, the UN General Assembly has continued to take both kinds of disasters into consideration when it asks UNHCR to act on behalf of both refugees and displaced persons.[250] The definition of «displaced persons» covers persons who are internally as well as externally displaced.[251] However, in order for internally displaced persons to fall within UNHCR's competence, the UN Secretary General must have instructed UNHCR to

---

248. UN Document A/41/324 (13 May, 1986), see p. 10. The principles of the report were adopted by the UN General Assembly in December 1986 (Resolution 41/124).
249. See UN Document A/Res./40/135 of the Executive Committee, Geneva, 9–11 July, 1984 in which the UNHCR asked to be authorized by the Secretary General.
250. See Resolution 40/133 of 13 December 1985 on displaced persons in Ethiopia; Resolution 42/107 of 7 December 1987 on assistance to refugees in Africa in general; Resolution 43/141 of 8 December 1988 on the situation of refugees in the Sudan; Resolution 44/176 of December 1989 on the special economic assistance to refugees and displaced persons in Africa; and Resolution 47/107 of 16 December 1992 on refugees and displaced persons in Africa.
251. For example, Resolution 2958 (XXVII) of 12 December 1972 on Assistance to the Sudanese refugees returning from abroad which speaks of assisting the government of Sudan in the relief, rehabilitation and resettlement of «Sudanese refugees coming from abroad and other displaced persons». In Resolution 32/67 of 8 December 1977, the General Assembly refers to UNHCR's responsibilities in the different regions of the world (mentioning Africa, Asia and Latin America in particular) and a growing number of refugees and displaced persons. The resolution asks States to contribute so that UNHCR can «intensify his efforts» to assist refugees and displaced persons of concern to his Office, for example in Resolution 33/26 of 29 November 1978, Resolution 35/41 of 25 November 1980 and Resolution 40/118 of 13 December 1985 in which States are called upon to contribute generously to UNHCR so that he may «assist refugees, returnees and displaced persons of concern to the High Commissioner...».

undertake the task and the State, within which internal displacement has taken place, must have given its consent.

Following major, complex emergency situations around the globe, and a turbulent period within UNHCR culminating with the entry into office of a new High Commissioner, Thorvald Stoltenberg, an open-ended Working Group on Durable Solutions and Protection was established in 1990.[252] The purpose of the Working Group was to analyze protection and solutions in a coherent and comprehensive manner, whilst bearing in mind the mandate of the High Commissioner, existing refugee law and doctrine and human rights principles. The following categories of refugees were assessed: (1) persons covered by the 1951 Convention; (2) persons covered by the OAU Convention and the Cartagena Declaration; (3) other persons forced to leave or prevented from returning because of man-made disasters; (4) persons forced to leave or prevented from returning because of natural or ecological disasters or extreme poverty; (5) persons who apply to be treated as category one or, when applicable, category two, but who are found not to be in these categories; (6) internally displaced persons; and (7) stateless persons.[253]

In 1992, the recommendations of the Working Group were approved by the 43rd Session of UNHCR's Executive Committee,[254] and confirm that UNHCR's competence extends to persons fleeing armed conflict, internal disorder or serious and generalized violence, regardless of their status under the 1951 Convention. Furthermore, it was agreed that it is the displacement and the need for protection which must determine the basis of UNHCR's competence and the extent of UNHCR's engagement.[255] The Working Group proposed a similar interpretation for situations involving internally

---

252. The initiative was taken by UNHCR's Executive Committee in 1989 and adopted by General Assembly Resolution 44/137 of 15 December 1989. Originally, the idea of creating a working group had been debated during informal discussions during a Round Table in San Remo in July 1989 examining the link between protection of and effective solutions to refugee problems. The topic was chosen because of fundamental changes in the characteristics of asylum applicants since the adoption of the 1951 Convention, which necessitated an analysis of who should fall within the competence of UNHCR. (See UN Doc. EC/SCP/64 of 12 August 1991),
253. See the Report by the Working Group, (EC/SCP/64) of 12 August 1991, p. 3, which contains an analysis of the different categories.
254. The recommendations of the Working Group are contained in the Note on Protection presented to the UNHCR's Executive Committee at its 43rd session in 1992. The approval by the Executive Committee of the Working Group's conclusions are found in the Report of the 43rd Session of the Executive Committee. The endorsement by the UN General Assembly during its 47th Session is incorporated in Resolution 47/105.
255. UN Document A/AC.96/799 of 25 August 1992, paragraph 15, p. 5.

displaced persons. However, many States do not accept that UNHCR's protection mandate extends to internally displaced persons.

Furthermore, the Working Group recognized the need for international cooperation on material assistance despite the fact that in principle, persons who have fled on account of natural or ecological disasters are not considered to fall under UNHCR's protection mandate. However, although flight due to extreme poverty was recognized as being a fundamental issue, it was considered beyond the competence of the Working Group and therefore beyond the competence of UNHCR.

In spite of the open-ended nature of this debate, the points of view expressed are not necessarily acceptable to all UN Member States. It must also be kept in mind that each time UNHCR's Executive Committee speaks of groups of persons or highlights important subjects to examine, it does not necessarily imply a change or extension of its mandate. The Executive Committee has a consultative function, its proposals must be approved by the UN General Assembly.[256]

However, in conclusion to the discussion on the evolution of UNHCR's mandate, it can be stated that persons considered as being within the mandate of UNHCR are covered by several categories. Firstly, those who have left their country on account of fear of persecution for the reasons enumerated in Article 6 of the Statute of 1950. Secondly, those who left their country for an analogous reason, for example, due to man-made disasters, international and civil armed conflicts, general social and political instability, human rights violations and so on. Thirdly, persons who have left their country for multiple reasons, for example, civil war and famine. Finally, it must be noted, that in an increasing number of cases, UNHCR is also mandated to assist internally displaced persons.

UNHCR's principal function, that of protection, ultimately depends on the will and the cooperation of States. If UNHCR's protection role is to be upheld, there must be further international developments to this end. Firstly, it is necessary to establish a universally harmonized understanding of the refugee concept in terms of UNHCR's competence. Secondly, it is necessary to bridge the gap between a universal refugee concept and the refugee concept according to which States are bound, as defined in the 1951 Convention. The following example illustrates this point. UNHCR gave protection to refugees fleeing Rwanda due to the massacres in 1994. These persons were equally considered refugees within the terms of the expanded refugee definition of the OAU Convention of 1969. However, if one of these refugees were to leave Africa and seek asylum in Europe, the determination of refugee status would be strictly linked

---

256. Cf. Article 9 of the Statute of 1950.

to the criteria of the 1951 Convention. For example, in June 1994, a Tutsi woman was denied asylum in France, as the situation of generalized violence in Rwanda did not, according to French authorities, constitute a threat to her as an individual. In other words, a person obtaining refugee status in Africa, within the terms of the OAU Convention, and who would also be covered by UNHCR's mandate, would not be granted refugee status in Europe unless that person was considered individually targeted for persecution, either as an individual or as member of a targeted group.

4.2 The refugee concept at a regional level

Regional approaches to the refugee concept are inspired by unique regional situations, reflecting regional concerns and diversities, and thus vary considerably. For example, in Asia, only a few States have adhered to the 1951 Convention and although mass exoduses on this continent are far from unknown, a regional approach to a broadened refugee definition does not exist. In Europe, harmonization efforts regarding asylum law have so far appeared not to be heading in the direction of an enlarged refugee concept. European countries remain attached to the 1951 Convention and have only adopted unilateral measures to give protection to those who fall outside the scope of this Convention, but who nevertheless are in need of international protection. In contrast, both Africa and Central America, through the OAU Convention and the Cartagena Declaration respectively, recognize that States have not only humanitarian, but also legal obligations to those who are forced to flee due to involuntary or uncontrollable circumstances not covered by the 1951 Convention. Both the OAU Convention and the Cartagena Declaration provide working models of regional instruments, an analysis of which provides ideas for an expanded refugee concept.

The OAU Convention

Against the background of decolonization and wars, the Organization of African Unity adopted the OAU Convention in 1969 which was designed to address specific refugee problems in Africa. The OAU Convention is complementary to the 1951 Convention, in so far as its Article 1(1) reiterates the conditions of the 1951 Convention. However, Article 1(2) extends protection to other persons not covered by the 1951 Convention. These are people who have fled their country across an international border due to other man-made disasters which do not target individually but which create victims of generalized violence. Article 2 states:

«The term «refugee» shall also apply to every person who, owing to external aggression, occupation, foreign domination or events seriously disturbing public order in either part or the whole of his country of origin or nationality, is compelled to leave his place of habitual residence in order to seek refuge in another place outside his country of origin or nationality».

By reiterating the definition contained in the 1951 Convention and by adapting it to the particular needs of the African continent, where mass exodus is more common, the refugee definition of the OAU Convention represents a significant development in international refugee law, through the introduction of a group eligibility concept.

The extension clause applies, first of all, to situations in which protection is lacking against persecution and violent acts perpetrated by a State against its population, or provoked by civil wars. It equally applies in cases of external aggression, occupation or foreign domination, which means that flight on account of aggression committed by a foreign power, is considered to be as valid as flight resulting from aggression inflicted by national authorities. In erasing this distinction the OAU Convention allows for the adoption of a more realistic position with regard to the realities faced by refugees. To a refugee, whose primary concern is the life and liberty of himself and his family, it does not matter whether his life and that of his family is being threatened by national authorities or by a foreign power. Furthermore, the OAU definition goes on to establish that aggression, occupation and events disrupting public order, are threats that do not necessarily address themselves to an individually targeted person or group of persons. This expanded refugee definition recognizes that generalized danger caused by war, coups or internal upheavals constitute valid reasons for flight. The refugees are, in these instances, victims of unintentional violence.

The OAU definition extends protection to persons who, for previously mentioned reasons, were «compelled» to leave and in doing so recognizes that it is the individual himself who is the judge of the circumstances seriously disrupting public order. The definition also permits a person to flee abroad regardless of the possibility of first seeking protection in another part of the country. In other words, international protection is afforded on the basis of individual judgment.

The Convention has been interpreted as implicitly including protection of guerrilla fighters.[257] It did not, however, aim at extending protection to those who fight against their own country from a neighbouring state.[258] In effect,

---

257. G. Melander, «Further Development of International Refugee Law», p. 485.
258. J. Oloka-Onyango, «Human Rights, The OAU Convention and the Refugee Crisis in Africa: Forty Years After Geneva», p. 456.

Article III of the Convention prohibits all subversive activities, as does Article 23 of the African Charter on Human and Peoples' Rights,[259] which presupposes that all persons enjoying the right of asylum should abstain from undertaking a subversive activity directed against his country of origin or another state party to the Charter.[260]

However, in reality this does not prevent the policies of certain recipient States from being largely a function of diplomatic, economic, and military considerations. For example, Tigray and Eritrean refugees from Ethiopia were received and armed in the Sudan. Ethiopia acted likewise with Somali refugees. In practice, the OAU Convention has been interpreted as including refugee guerrillas who fought against South-African apartheid. In contrast, these same persons could not, however, benefit from the assistance of UNHCR because of the apolitical and humanitarian mandate of the agency.[261]

D. Turpin has stated that the principles codified in the OAU Convention would be applicable even outside the explicit OAU context, because it is based on: the principle of respect for life and moral and physical integrity, the principle of non-discrimination (based on race, religion, opinions, etc.), the principle of security (which prohibits reprisals, collective penalties, deportation, etc.), and principles applicable to victims of armed conflict (meaning that humanitarian assistance must never be seen as constituting interference in a conflict or in the affairs of a State).[262] However, these viewpoints do not exclude the need for specfic instruments in other regions in order to better guarantee protection to a wider category of persons.

In spite of the generosity of the supplementary refugee definition established by the OAU Convention, it must also be acknowledged that the criteria of the definition do not cover all instances of flight in Africa.[263] The African refugee concept only addresses man-made disasters and does not

---

259. Adopted by the Organization of African States on 26 June 1981 and entry into force on 21 October 1986.
260. M. Keba M'Baye, «Les mouvements de population et les organes des droits de l'homme», Annuaire de l'Institut du Droit Humanitaire, 1984, p. 39.
261. E. Arboleda, «Refugee Definition in Africa and Latin America: The Lessons of Pragmatism», p.196.
262. D. Turpin, «Aspects Politico-Juridiques Internes de la Situation des Réfugiés en Afrique», Les réfugiés en Afrique – Situation et problémes actuels, Les Cahiers du Droit Public, Institut Français de Droit Humanitaire et des Droits de L'Homme, 1986, p. 103.
263. For an examination of typologies of African refugees, «sur place» refugees, «ecological» refugees, «expelled» and «evacuated» persons, etc. See J. Rogge, «Some comments on definitions and typologies of Africa's refugees», Zambian Geographical Journal, 33–34, 1978–79, p.53–59.

address natural and economic disasters, moreover, it does not address the problem of internally displaced persons, who total several millions in Africa alone,[264] and to whom international humanitarian organizations, both governmental and non-governmental, provide assistance and, to some extent, protection. In principle, internally displaced persons are covered by human rights law and, in case of conflict, by humanitarian law, but this is not worth much unless the principles contained in such instruments, are respected. In reality, internally displaced persons are often particularly vulnerable precisely because they have not been able to escape across an international border and their home country fails to protect them. There are no special international agencies dedicated to assist the internally displaced and no special principles concerning them have been adopted. Assistance and protection efforts undertaken by the international community to assist internally displaced persons, suffer from being «ad hoc» arrangements and from a lack of coordination and planning between agencies involved in the field.

The main merit of the OAU Convention is, however, that it has helped develop international refugee law, through encompassing persons in need of international protection within a legal framework which was previously non-existent. It has also influenced discussion regarding the adoption of other regional accords, of which the Cartagena Declaration is the most striking example. Within Europe, it has also inspired efforts within the Council of Europe regarding «de facto» refugees. In 1977, during the attempt by the UN to establish a Convention on Territorial Asylum, which will be discussed below, the refugee concept discussed and agreed upon during deliberations was based on an extended concept similar to that of the OAU Convention. UNHCR's competence and responsibility in Africa has also been formally harmonized with the OAU-definition.[265]

African States have demonstrated great generosity, not only by adopting an expanded legal framework for extended refugee protection, but also by ensuring its implementation in practice. African States now have a long tradition of hosting countless millions of refugees from neighbouring States. Yet, there are some very serious problems facing the effective protection of refugees in Africa. Firstly, the lack of internal legislation, in conformity

---

264. No precise statistics on internally displaced persons exist, because no internationally recognized definition on internally displaced persons has been adopted. On a world wide basis, however, the Representative of the UN Secretary General on Internally Displaced Persons has estimated a total of 25 to 30 million. The Norwegian Refugee Council is at present preparing an annual publication on internally displaced The first edition of the Annual Survey on Internally Displaced persons is expected in 1998.

with the 1951 Convention and the OAU Convention, and the intentions of the international instruments on refugee protection not always being respected by the Contracting States. They seem to be increasinlgy under the influence of the restrictive refugee and asylum measures of industrialized States.[266] Recent examples included the situation of the Liberian «boat people» who were refused entry in one country after another in West Africa. Another example is that of Tanzania which has begun to apply the concept of «first country of asylum», which will be examined below.[267] The treatment of Rwandan refugees in The Republic of Congo is yet another sad example of a State not respecting its obligations either under refugee law or under other principles of international law, human rights law, and humanitarian law.

The Cartagena Declaration

In Latin America, a number of instruments on refugees, political and diplomatic asylum and non-extradition have been adopted. These instruments, however, do not contain any reference to a refugee concept which would oblige States to grant protection to persons fleeing because of generalized violence. The 1984 Cartagena Declaration, which contains an expanded refugee definition, was developed during the first half of the 1980s, in the wake of a period of great confusion and violence in many Latin American States, which had forced millions of persons to flee their homes. To date, the principles of the Cartagena Declaration have been generally respected and adhered to by States throughout the region and may even be considered principles of regional customary law, a point which is confirmed by their incorporation into the domestic legislation of many Latin Ameri-

---

265. See Resolution 34/61 on the situation of African refugees, adopted by the UN General Assembly on 29 November 1979 which adheres to proposals made during the Conference on the Situation of Refugees in Africa, which was held in Arusha in Tanzania and addressed the application of the OAU Convention. In Recommendation 7, it was suggested that, being a regional instrument complementary to the Convention of 1951, the OAU Convention should be applied by the UN and all of its subsidiary organs, as well as by the NGOs dealing with refugee problems in Africa. (quoted by D. Hull, «Displaced Persons: 'The New Refugees'», The Georgia Journal of International and Comparative Law, Vol. 13, No. 3, 1983, p. 769.) See also, Conclusion No. 14 (XXX) of the UNHCR Executive Committee, adopted during its 30th Session in 1979.
266. See J. Oloka-Onyango, who cites as an example the existence of bilateral agreements on the expulsion of refugees in «Human Rights, The OAU Convention and the Refugee Crisis in Africa: Forty Years After Geneva», 1991, p.458-460.
267. See below, Chapter 7.

can States.[268] The principles of the the Cartagena Declaration have also been endorsed in several international contexts, by the UNHCR Executive Committee, by the Organization of American States, the OAS, and by the Parliamentary Assembly of the Council of Europe.[269]

As far as the refugee concept is concerned, the Cartagena Declaration refers to the experience gained from having to cope with massive flows of refugees in Central America, and therefore, in its Conclusion No. 3, it states that «…it is necessary to consider enlarging the concept of a refugee, bearing in mind, as far as appropriate and in the light of the situation prevailing in the region, the precedent of the OAU Convention Article 1(2) and the doctrine employed in the reports of the Inter-American Commission on Human Rights. Hence the definition or concept of a refugee to be recommended for use in the region is one which, in addition to containing the elements of the 1951 Convention and the 1967 Protocol, includes among the refugees persons who have fled their country because their lives, safety or freedom have been threatened by generalized violence, foreign aggression, internal conflicts, massive violation of human rights or other circumstances which have seriously disturbed public order».

As will be noticed, the refugee definition of the Cartagena Declaration was inspired by the OAU Convention, a fact which explains the similarities in the expanded refugee concept of both instruments. Even though the wording of the two instruments seems to differ somewhat, the differences are largely cosmetic.[270] However, the OAU Convention does contain two elements which do not figure in the Cartagena Declaration, namely, «occupation» and «foreign domination», whereas the Cartagena Declaration contains three elements which are not in the OAU Convention, namely «generalized violence», «internal conflicts», and «massive violations of human rights». In practice, the

---

268. E. Arboleda, «Refugee Definition in Africa and Latin America: The Lessons of Pragmatism», International Journal of Refugee Law, Vol. 3, No. 2, 1991, p. 185. See also E. Arboleda, «The Cartagena Declaration of 1984 and its similarities to the 1969 OAU Convention - a Comparative Study», International Journal of Refugee law, Special Issue, July 1995, p. 87–101. What was originally a political Central American declaration, gained significance and became the example for aliens' legislation throughout Latin-America in countries like Argentina, Bolivia, Ecuador, Colombia and even Mexico, which has not adhered to the 1951 Convention, has incorporated the principles of the Cartagena Declaration in its national legislation.
269. See, for example, Conclusion No. 37 (XXXVI) on refugees in Central America and the Cartagena Declaration, adopted during the 36th Session of UNHCR's Executive Committee in 1985.
270. UNHCR's Sub-Committee of the Whole on International Protection, UN Document, EC/1992/SCP/CRP.5, 2 April 1992, p. 6.

interpretation of these elements do not create differences. Indeed, both definitions adhere to the 1951 Convention definition and both definitions extend the refugee concept to cover victims of generalized violence.

It is noteworthy that, as regards ensuring harmonized standards of treatment of refugees in the region, the Cartagena Declaration refers to other international instruments such as the 1951 Convention, the American Convention on Human Rights, and «soft law» instruments such as UNHCR's Executive Committee Conclusion No. 22[271] on the protection of asylum seekers in situations of large scale-influx.[272] Unlike the OAU Convention, it also refers to the particular situation pertaining to internally displaced persons and calls on national authorities and international organizations to offer protection and assistance to them.[273]

The key characteristic of the Cartagena Declaration definition of the «refugee» concept is its pragmatism. The concept of persecution is maintained in relation to the 1951 Convention, but is otherwise not a condition for refugee status. Nevertheless, the situations which merit international protection are well defined in a humanitarian context in the «expansion clause». In other words, although the person in question is not required to prove fear of individual persecution, he must be able to show that his «life, safety or freedom» has been threatened. This is in contrast to the OAU Convention, which simply requests that the person in question has a perception of danger without being required to «justify» that perception.

4.3 The «de facto» refugee concept – a European perspective

The above examination of international responses to the dramatic refugee situations in different parts of the world in the last fifty years, provides an indication of the gaps that exist in international law with regard to displaced persons who are not covered by the 1951 Convention, but who nonetheless are in need of international protection.

In the European context, the concept of «de facto» refugees was gradually developed. At the same time it suited States to limit the number of refugees recognized as 1951 Convention refugees by interpreting the Convention in an increasingly restrictive manner. National legislation and European State

---

271. Adopted during the 32nd Session of UNHCR's Executive Committee in 1981.
272. Conclusion No. 8 of the Declaration.
273. Conclusion No. 9 of the Declaration.

practice both refer to «de facto» refugees or use other terms such as «B-status refugees», persons granted residence permits for humanitarian reasons, or persons granted «exceptional leave to remain». Hereafter the term «de facto» refugee will be used to refer to all these categories of refugees except for those who need assistance for reasons of health or for other valid reasons of a more personal character.[274] The introduction of a system whereby the concept of «de facto» refugees is applied has merit in that as a broader concept it allows for protection to be granted to a larger number of people. However, at the same time it contains the insecurity of being an «ad hoc» mechanism used at a national level which has not reached the level of international harmonization. It could be stated that rather than work towards harmonization of a broadened refugee concept, Western European States have instead demonstrated their unity in a reluctance to call «de facto» refugees «refugees».[275] Nevertheless, attempts in the context of the Council of Europe, to reach an agreement on a broader understanding of the refugee concept should not be ignored when examining developments at a regional level.[276]

Initially, during the «Cold War» era, the majority of asylum seekers to Western Europe came from European countries under communist regimes. In general they were therefore granted 1951 Convention status in the West even if many of these persons did not leave their country for fear of persecution on account of being individually targeted.[277] In cases where refugee status was not granted, Western States often refused to return the persons to their country of origin,[278] qualifying them as «de facto» refugees. This remained the case up until the 1980s, when hundreds of thousands of Poles left their country and were welcomed in the West.[279]

However, as the characteristics of the asylum applicants to Western Europe changed considerably, so did State practice. Not only did the dimensions of refugee flows grow dramatically throughout the 1980s but the new asylum-

---

274. Note, however, that the distinction between «de facto» refugees and «humanitarian cases» sometimes is blurred and confusion is created because of usage of common legislation for the two categories which should be kept separate since their reasons for being aliens have nothing in common.
275. P. Nobel, «De Facto-Flyktingebegreppet i Norden» in «Asyl i Norden» («The Refugee Concept in the Nordic Countries» in «Asylum and the Nordic Countries»), Danish Refugee Council, 1990, p. 104.
276. See for example, Parliamentary Assembly Recommendations 773 (1976) and 1088 (1988). See below, p.
277. J. Cels, «Responses of European States to De Facto Refugees», p.189 and E. Lapenna, «Les réfugiés de facto – un nouveau problème pour l'Europe», AWR Bulletin, No. 2–3, 1981, p.61
278. S. Bodart, «Les autres réfugiés: Le statut des réfugiés «de facto» en Europe.», p. 21.

seekers came from the Third World.[280] Initial generosity shown by States concerning the application of the «de facto» refugee concept thus diminished during the 1980s and 1990s,[281] and instead European States began to introduce requirements which made access to determination procedures for refugee status more difficult.

This may explain why, that in spite of international debates and several attempts within international organizations to promote the creation of international instruments, the will of States to renounce some of their sovereignty in this domain has not yet manifested itself. Increasing international concern for refugees, coupled with inadequate national «ad hoc» responses, demonstrate the need for an international harmonization reinforced by legally binding international rules. The question remains as to what would be an appropriate form of harmonization and what would be the most constructive strategy for its development. There is no doubt, that the lack of international harmonization of the «de facto» refugee concept, remains one of the very serious gaps in international refugee law which needs to be filled. The destiny of the

---

279. Between 1980–1988, approximately 800,000 persons left Poland, of which about half headed to Germany. See A. Sakson, «Hintergründe der polischen Massenemigration – die De-Facto-Flüchtlinge aus Polen», AWR Bulletin, No. 3, 1990, p.109. He states that political asylum was accorded to the majority of those who requested it between 1982 and 1984. With the increase of asylum seekers in Germany since 1985, the percentage of acceptances diminished gradually, from 19% in 1985 to 2,9% in 1988 and 0% in 1989.

280. The total number of asylum seekers increased significantly at the time. In 1983, approximately 70,000 persons requested asylum in Europe as compared with 700,000 in 1992. The total figures between 1983 and 1992 are approximately 3 million asylum applicants in Europe (more than half, 1.7 million throughout the latter years of 1989–1992), see «Les réfugiés dans le monde», 1993, p.157. According to T. Einarsen in «The European Convention on Human Rights and the Notion of an Implied Right to «de facto» Asylum», International Journal of Refugee Law», Vol. 2. No. 3, 1990, p. 362 , in 1990 there were, however, approximately 14 million refugees in the world, of which 90% remained in their region.

281. According to J. Cels in «Responses of European States to De Facto Refugees», 1989, p. 191, the majority of refugees in the 1970s were accepted in Europe through the refugee quota systems, adopted for refugees from Latin America and Indo-China. Humanitarian considerations replaced the restrictive interpretation of the 1951 Convention as long as their «prima facie» status had been accepted. In the 1980s, in contrast, asylum applicants arrived to escape civil wars, natural disasters, external aggressions and economic declines. Their arrival, often undocumented, also rendered the application of the 1951 Convention difficult. This, in turn, resulted in irregular movements and also the creation of refugees «in orbit». See W. Kälin «Protection from forcible return for de facto refugees: Approaches and principles in international law», p.1.

vast majority of today's asylum seekers and refugees remains entirely the responsibility of national State practice. This situation is unfortunate because it puts protection at stake, both with regard to the principles of international refugee law and with regard to other principles of human rights. «De facto» refugees often find themselves even without the most basic rights to food and accommodation[282] and without an assurance that they will be protected. Such a lack of rights in so called civilized nations is unacceptable.

Current understanding of the «de facto» refugee concept

The definition of «de facto» refugee encompasses many elements. One way in which to define the concept of «de facto» refugee is through a negative deduction of the 1951 Convention definition. In other words, a person who is not considered to be a refugee within the framework of the 1951 Convention, but who nevertheless is in need of international protection, is a «de facto» refugee. This would therefore include, for example, a person who meets the objective criteria of the 1951 Convention, but who is not granted Convention status because those responsible for the assessment of the asylum claim apply a restrictive interpretation. An example of this would be the interpretation of persecution by «non state agents».[283]

This general definition of the «de facto» refugee concept also includes persons who have not been targeted in an individual manner and therefore fall outside the scope of the 1951 Convention, but who cannot be returned home because of the situation in the country of origin. This would, for example, be the case for a war refugee who has fled from his country of origin in order to save his life from generalized violence. The person's life or security would be endangered if he were to be returned home and he is therefore allowed to remain.

In other cases, the «de facto» refugee concept concerns persons who in principle are covered by the 1951 Convention, but who have not been granted refugee status within the terms of the 1951 Convention for special reasons, for example, because they fear reprisals against family members who are still living in the country of origin.

It may also be the case that the authorities responsible for refugee status determination procedure simply do not believe the applicant and therefore take recourse to a restrictive interpretation of the 1951 Convention. For example, women, who have been subject to «gender related persecution», are

---

282. In some western countries «de facto» refugees live on the street and survive as best they can.
283. See above, p. 65–66.

more often than not, refused Convention status. Women often find status determination interviews difficult and consequently do not tell the truth about their experiences because of shame and cultural pressure.[284] Similarly an asylum applicant may fail to adequately explain his case and as a consequence may fail to convince the authorities responsible for refugee status determination. However, for reasons of safety, it may be that the asylum seeker is given the «benefit of the doubt» and is, therefore, granted «de facto» status.

Yet another example is that of «sur place» refugees. As a general rule, «subjective sur place refugees» are not granted status under the 1951 Convention.[285] In principle, however, they are not sent back to their country of origin. For example, several States did not return Chinese students who were abroad during the turmoil following the student demonstrations for democratization in China in 1989, but instead offered them temporary protection as «de facto» refugees.

Conscientious objectors and deserters are often regarded as «de facto» refugees. In States where military service is compulsory the authorities hesitate to grant Convention refugee status to deserters and draft-evaders, because failure to perform this duty is considered a criminal offense.[286] Penalties for failure to perform these duties are not normally regarded as persecution. Under these circumstances, a person is not granted refugee status if the only reason given for desertion or draft evasion, is a dislike of military service or fear of combat.[287] An asylum seeker could, however, be considered a refugee if, for example, he has fled in order to avoid participating in conflict situations which involve actions that are contrary to human rights and humanitarian principles.

In practice, many States consider deserters and draft evaders to be «de facto» refugees. For example, throughout the 1960s and 1970s, some European States accepted young Americans, who had fled in order not to participate in the Vietnam war, as temporary «de facto» refugees. Similarly, «de facto» refugee status was also granted to Portuguese and Spanish draft-evaders, who refused to participate in the wars conducted by their totalitarian governments against colonial populations fighting for independence. More recently, there were discussions in Europe concerning conscientious objectors and deserters from Former Yugoslavia. In Norway, for example, the authorities made a distinction between Serbs from Bosnia and Serbs from other parts of Former Yugoslavia. Serbs from Bosnia were considered «de facto» refugees and were accorded temporary protection, but this was not necessarily the case

---

284. See above, p. 78–79.
285. See above, p. 53–54.
286. UNHCR Handbook, paragraph 167, p. 39-40.
287. UNHCR Handbook, paragraph 168, p. 40.

for Serbs from other regions. The NGO community, however, considered that both groups should be treated equally, given the risk that they might be forced to fight in the war in Bosnia.[288]

Another group of persons who must be regarded as «de facto» refugees are asylum seekers themselves. Asylum seekers are potential refugees, who while they are waiting for a decision by the immigration authorities concerning their eligibility under the 1951 Convention, must also be given due protection.

Persons who do not wish to be granted refugee status, for example, because they do not want to turn in their national passport, are also, at times, given «de facto» status. For example, family members of Convention refugees sometimes take this position, as has been the case with many Latin American refugees who have traditionally been considered as «exiles», and who do not want to be considered as refugees within the terms of the 1951 Convention.[289]

However, there are limits to the «de facto» refugee concept. For example, persons who flee their country for strictly humanitarian reasons, such as economic deprivation or ecological disaster or on account of age, health, family links, etc., may be granted temporary residence permits because their general well being is at stake. Nevertheless, understandable as such reasons for flight are, they do not warrant refugee status. Persons who are granted a residence permit for such reasons should therefore not be confused with «de facto» refugees. Confusion often stems from the fact, that in national legislation, the same provisions are applied to both categories.

The consequences of mixing the concepts is first of all, the risk of weakening necessary response mechanisms pertaining to each separate group, the poor, the sick, or other humanitarian groups, on the one hand and the refugees on the other hand. The latter are not only in need of assistance, but also of protection – protection of human rights the international community has undertaken specific legal obligations to uphold. By blurring all groups of people in need into one, international responsibility is weakened. Secondly, the mixing of concepts creates internal political difficulties for the country receiving refugees because the public at large becomes confused as to the application of the refugee concept and the duties pertaining to it. Besides understanding that legal obligations must be respected, populations in most democratic societies, also have an understanding of and sympathy for the need to assist and protect those who have fled persecution and wars. The same is not necessarily the case concerning assistance to foreigners who are poor or who

---

288. J. Borgen, Aftenposten, 18 May 1994.
289. P. Weis, «Convention Refugees and De Facto Refugees», p. 17.

strive to make a better life for themselves and their family. When the obligation to offer protection and assistance to refugees becomes linked to political agreement or disagreement on aid and assistance to the poor, this may have serious repercussions on refugees in host countries. The worst case scenario is that refugees are put at risk of becoming victim of extremist xenophobia, racial discrimination, and violence.

State practice on «de facto» refugees

There is, as already indicated, no uniform European practice for the determination of refugee status. The lack of a harmonized European approach has not only contributed to the creation of the notion of «de facto» refugees, but at the same time, provoked discrepancies between European States with regard to the application of Convention status on the one hand, and «de facto» status on the other. The same applies to the treatment afforded to the two categories in European States. «De facto» refugees are often seen as second class refugees and face problems obtaining rights to housing, work, employment, education and so on, rights which must, according to the 1951 Convention be accorded to Convention status refugees. Moreover, Convention refugees are presented and seen by the public at large as deserving refugees, whereas «de facto» refugees are described and perceived in a less favourable light and are sometimes regarded as completely undeserving of the benefits which may have been bestowed upon them.

In some States, for example, in the Scandinavian countries, permanent or temporary stay is, according to national legislation, granted to «de facto» refugees for humanitarian reasons. In other States, there is no specific legislation at all, with regard to «de facto» refugees. However, the presence of «non-status refugees» is tolerated, sometimes even after an asylum request is rejected, because there are compelling and valid reasons why a person cannot return home. Such practice exists, for example, in Belgium where, largely as a consequnce, there are an estimated 150,000 illegals.

According to the European Council on Refugees and Exiles (ECRE), [290] the practice of European States may be classified in four categories (which often overlap):

The first category concerns countries whose national constitution recognizes a refugee concept which differs from that of the 1951 Convention, but which is not effectively applied to the benefit of «de facto» refugees, for example Italy and Portugal.

---

290. ECRE, «The Need for a Supplementary Refugee Definition», p.2-3.

The second category concerns countries which have specific legislation on «de facto» status, for example the Nordic countries and the Netherlands. In Norway, the vast majority of persons granted protection belong to the category of «de facto» refugees, although this term is not used in the legislation. The Netherlands has applied «B status» since 1974 when an American deserter was given protection. Following this case, «B-status» was used for other asylum applicants, and temporary stays were accorded for specific humanitarian reasons.[291] In some countries, for example, the Netherlands and Scandinavian countries, the civil rights accorded to «de facto» refugees are almost the same as those accorded to refugees under the terms of the 1951 Convention.

The third category concerns countries which do not have specific legislation on «de facto» status, but which, through legislation or administrative practice, grant protection against forced removal from the territory so as not to violate the «non-refoulement» principle, be it for humanitarian reasons or for reasons of human rights. In the United Kingdom, for example, «exceptional leave to remain» was introduced in 1974, after the influx of Greek Cypriots following the Turkish invasion. Although the distinction between «de jure» and «de facto» refugees was officially abolished, the trend in the United Kingdom has been to interpret the 1951 Convention in an increasingly restrictive manner and even to refuse the large majority of asylum seekers the right to stay at all. Those who are allowed to stay, are predominantly offered the right to temporary stay, on the grounds of «exceptional leave to remain».[292]

The fourth category concerns countries where «de facto» refugees live in a legal «limbo» because there is no official recognition of the concept of «de facto» refugees. In Belgium, France and Greece, for example, refugee status is granted according to the 1951 Convention and is generally interpreted more generously than in most other countries. However, if a person is not granted Convention status, then he has no status at all. This is not the same as saying he would in all instances be deported. For example, Belgium may in exceptional cases or circumstances respect the non-refoulement principle, but would only grant minimal, if any, civil rights to such persons. In France, protection against refoulement may be granted up until such time as the situation in the country of origin has improved, but this is a rare exception.[293]

---

291. J. Cels, «Responses of European States to 'de facto' refugees», p. 194.
292. See H. Lambert, «Seeking Asylum – Comparative Law and Practice in Selected European Countries», Martinus Nijhoff Publishers, 1995, p. 138 and p. 140.
293. Ibid, p. 143.

The debate in the context of international organizations
UNHCR
In 1991, UNHCR's Working Group on Solutions and Protection found that a large number of persons who had crossed national borders, and were in need of international protection, but who were outside the 1951 Convention, were receiving some form of protection and assistance from the international community through UNHCR, and, on an «ad hoc» basis, from individual States. These «ad hoc» measures may not always be sufficient to meet the needs of all those requiring international protection and assistance. Therefore, the Working Group concluded that there was further scope for considering the possibility of a new global refugee definition which would be applicable to persons not protected by the 1951 Convention and the 1967 Protocol or by regional instruments such as the OAU Convention and the Cartagena Declaration.[294]

In 1992, the High Commissioner, in his Note on International protection, concluded that the time was not yet appropriate for UNHCR to promote new universal instruments for the protection of refugees by States, outside of the 1951 Convention and the 1967 Protocol. Nevertheless, it was stated that this option should be further explored.[295] The challenge is to bridge the gap between the broadened refugee concept of the UNHCR mandate and of regional instruments, and the 1951 Convention refugee concept, which is applied on a discretionary basis by individual States.[296]

In spite of the fact that there is no general agreement among States on a strategy, let alone a need, for establishing a universal refugee definition, which embraces both the Convention and the «de facto» refugee concept, at the same time there is no disagreement as to the need for international protection for persons who are not considered 1951 Convention refugees.[297]

---

294. See Report of the Working Group on Solutions and Protection, UN Doc. EC/SCP/64 of 12 August 1991 in which a universalization of the OAU Convention and the Cartagena Declaration are referred to as possible solutions. It proposed to add an additional protocol to the 1951 Convention or, as a first step, to adopt a UN General Assembly resolution annexing a declaration to this effect.
295. Note on International protection, (A/AC.96/799), 25 August 1992, p. 7.
296. Doc. EC/1992/SCP/CRP.5 of 2 April 1992.The complexity of population movements and, as a result, the lack of clarity about the protection responsibility of States, the proper role of UNHCR and the appropriate solutions to pursue, had already been discussed in the Executive Committee meeting in 1991 (See Note on International protection Doc. A/AC.96/777 of 9 September 1991).
297. Ibid.

The following example illustrates the problem. In the 1980s, UNHCR declared its discontent with the practice of deporting Tamils from Europe back to Sri Lanka, an issue which remains hot. Some States maintained that even if these persons, due to UNHCR's «good offices» procedure, were covered by UNHCR's mandate, UNHCR's intervention on their behalf could be seen as interference by an international organization in the affairs of sovereign States. The persons concerned were not seen as 1951 Convention refugees and States therefore maintained that they did not have an obligation to accord protection.[298] This claim is not valid because the persons concerned were under UNHCR's mandate and UNHCR is the organization charged with the duty to uphold the rights of refugees. This example therefore also serves to underline the need for a coherent international approach to «de facto» refugees which would eliminate the ambiguity surrounding the obligations of both States and UNHCR as far as refugee protection is concerned.

The major difficulty which remains, however, is in delineating groups of persons to be covered by an expanded refugee concept and in defining the content and duration of the protection to be provided. It is States themselves, which must first agree on the need for a new instrument and decide on the way forward. At the beginning of the 1990s, it was commonly held that rather than moving to negotiate a binding, globally applicable instrument, it would be preferable to strengthen protection accorded to Convention refugees, by ensuring that national legislation and practice reflect agreed universal or regional standards. Reference to regional instruments and «soft law» instruments were seen as particularly relevant for this process. Indeed, regional instruments were even referred to as potential examples upon which States could draw, when developing national legislation. In 1992 UNHCR stated that «steps at the national and regional levels would be progress towards a universal regime»,[299] clearly implying that in order to achieve a broadened universal refugee definition, it would be necessary to start at a national level, continue at a regional level and then move on to the universal level.

The proposal for a regional approach contained in this book is therefore not contrary to UNHCR's stated objectives as regards the need for a supplementary refugee definition. However, there are a number of aspects in this regard which cause difficulties apart from these two basic starting points.

---

298. On this «conflict», see R. McDowell, «Co-ordination of Refugee Policy in Europe» in «Refugees and International Relations», Oxford University Press, 1989, p.189 and J. Cels, «Responses of European States to De Facto Refugees», 1989, p.203-209.

299. See «Protection of persons of concern to UNHCR who fall outside the 1951 Convention: a discussion Note», (Doc. EC/1992/SCP/CRP.5), 2 April 1992.

One aspect concerns what was already mentioned in 1992, in UNHCR's Note on International protection,[300] that the timing may not right. In this regard it should be pointed out that UNHCR's comment in 1992 concerned a universal approach. The timing may not have been right then as it may not be right now, to undertake negotiations at a universal level for a broadened refugee definition, of which an additional protocol to the 1951 Convention would be one way of achieving this. However, as far as «timing» is concerned for a regional approach, it should be noted that this was in fact referred to as a way of going about eventually reaching the goal of a universally broadened refugee definition.[301] In more general terms, the political climate which is influenced by so called compassion fatigue, must not be allowed to be a decisive factor preventing a necessary process from being initiated. In this regard there has been no improvement since 1992 and it is not likely that there will be any in years to come. It is the need for appropriate legal safeguards pertaining to «de facto» refugees which must determine whether action is taken. «De facto» refugees are, at present, in a legal limbo in Europe and they need a protection instrument now.

Another aspect relates to a legitimate concern that a new European set of rules would only reflect minimum standards of protection. This has its background in the examples set by the Member States of the EU which, in their endeavours to harmonize refugee and asylum policy, have taken positions and adopted instruments which demonstrate agreement only on the lowest common denominator. In relation to this issue, it must be kept in mind that all the States in question are signatories to the 1951 Convention and must therefore, in principle, respect its content in the spirit in which it was intended. Furthermore, it could be argued that the harmonization of a restrictive interpretation of the Joint Position on Article 1(A), [302] adopted by the EU Member States, in fact reinforces the necessity for the development of an instrument for those in need of protection who fall outside the 1951 Convention. This restrictive interpretation means that even more refugees are left without protection by any international legal instrument. The purpose of a supplementary refugee instrument is, in principle, to expand the refugee definition beyond the scope of the 1951 Convention so as to cover «de facto» refugees. In practice, it will also inevitably encompass those who should be covered by the 1951 Convention but who are neglected by current State practice.[303]

---

300. Ibid.
301. Ibid.
302. See above, p.
303. See below, Chapter 8 for a broadened refugee definition contained in the proposal for a new European refugee convention.

The Council of Europe

As has already been indicated, Europe has not been blind to the need of extending refugee protection to persons who are not covered by the refugee definition of the 1951 Convention. Both governmental and non-governmental international organizations as well as States themselves, have recognized such a need.

The Council of Europe has traditionally played an important regional role with respect to refugees and has taken several initiatives on the issue, since recognizing the legal weakness of the status of «de facto» refugees as early as the 1970s.

The Parliamentary Assembly

On 26 January 1976, the Parliamentary Assembly adopted Recommendation 773, concerning the situation of «de facto» refugees. This Recommendation had the elaboration of an international instrument for the protection of «de facto» refugees as its primary aim. Furthermore, it recommended that Member States should harmonize their treatment of «de facto» refugees, with regard to such practices as granting of residence and work permits and also recommended the similar application of the 1951 Convention regarding, for example, the right relating to wage earning employment (Article 17), public relief (Article 23), labour legislation, and social security (Article 24), as well as the provisions concerning refugees unlawfully in the country of refuge (Article 31), expulsion (Article 32) and, especially, prohibition of expulsion or return (Article 33). The recommendation went on to call for adequate housing, recognition of professional qualifications, language and vocational training and the issuance of travel documents for «de facto» refugees. It is also worth noting that Recommendation 773 invited Member States to apply the 1951 Convention definition «liberally».

On 16 September 1976, the Parliamentary Assembly adopted Recommendation 787, concerning the harmonization of eligibility practice for refugees under the 1951 Convention. Given the fact that not all European States had established a formal procedure for the examination of refugee applications and furthermore that existing procedures did not conform to a single pattern, Recommendation 787 sought to suggest the most appropriate ways in which to reach cooperation within the area of refugee status determination. It was also of concern to the Council of Europe that refugee status granted in one State was not necessarily recognized by other Member States. An «ad hoc» Committee of Experts on Legal Aspects of Territorial Asylum, Refugees and Stateless Persons (CAHAR), was established and charged with the responsibility of examining the harmonization of eligibility practice and to undertake further work relating to refugee law.

Some member States have, on a unilateral basis adhered to some of the suggestions contained in Recommendation 773, but overall, the picture remains bleak. Treatment of «de facto» refugees has hardly improved and States certainly do not interpret the 1951 Convention liberally. With regard to working out an appropriate instrument on «de facto» refugees, so far nothing has been done.

In October 1988, as a follow up to Recommendation 773, the Parliamentary Assembly adopted recommendation 1088, which recommended that CAHAR «examine the possibility of preparing a European convention, including the establishment of a consultative body, dealing with people falling outside the scope of the Geneva Convention, but requiring protection, and on whose fate the Council of Europe, under the term «de facto refugees», has been proposing concrete measures for many years». [304] However, this recommendation was never carried through and only two years later, CAHAR concluded, after having had the topic on its agenda for many years, that the time was not ripe for a definition of the «de facto» refugee concept.[305]

This did not discourage the Parliamentary Assembly from addressing the issue again in 1991, at the same time as UNHCR's Working Group on Solutions and Protection was addressing the same issue in Geneva.[306] On 23 April 1991, the Parliamentary Assembly adopted Recommendation 1149, concerning the asylum policy of the European countries, which recommended that Member States, in cooperation with UNHCR, should examine how to solve the problem of «de facto» refugees. In 1994, a Parliamentary Assembly Report on the Right of Asylum, described it as «very desirable» that the Council of Europe draw up a legal instrument for the protection of «de facto» refugees.[307] This proposal was followed-up by Recommendation 1236 of 12 April 1994 in which the Parliamentary Assembly recommends Member States to «… draw up a legal instrument for the protection of de facto refugees who – in international law – are not even afforded the basic refugee protection secured through the 1951 Geneva Convention and the 1967 New York Protocol».

Even though this Recommendation also did not lead to any concrete initiative, at least it may have contributed to the enthusiasm with which Recommendation 1324 was adopted by the Parliamentary Assembly in April 1997. Recommendation 1324 recommends that Heads of State and Government of the Council of Europe Member States draw up a European

---

304. Recommendation 1088 (1988), adopted on 7 October, 1988.
305. CAHAR, (90), of September 3, 1990, «Réfugiés de facto.»
306. See above, p. 117.
307. Report on the Right of Asylum (Rapporteur: Mr. Franck, Sweden), Doc. 7052 of 23 March 1994, p. 17.

Convention on the protection and rights of refugees and asylum seekers.[308]

The Committee of Ministers
In January 1984, the Committee of Ministers of the Council of Europe adopted Recommendation R(84)1, which recommended that protection should be accorded to persons who satisfy the criteria in the 1951 Convention but who are not formally recognized as refugees.[309] Making reference to the European Convention on Human Rights, and in particular Article 3, the Recommendation advises Member States to adhere to the non-refoulement principle according to which «...no person should be subjected to refusal of admission at the frontier, rejection, expulsion or any other measure which would have the result of compelling him to return to, or remain in, a territory where he has well-founded fear of persecution. . .». The Recommendation continues by saying that this provision should be applied regardless of whether or not a person has been recognized as a refugee under the 1951 Convention. In the European context, this represents an important step towards affording equal protection to both «de facto» refugees and Convention refugees. However, the Committee of Ministers has, until now, not followed-up on the various proposals made by the Parliamentary Assembly to negotiate a new refugee protection instrument in which the «de facto» refugee concept forms an important part.

In conclusion, it must be acknowledged that owing to the nature of the proposal for a new European refugee convention,[310] it is inevitable that certain governments will be unwilling to see the discussion brought back into the sphere of the Council of Europe. However, it is important to remember that not only is this organization founded on principles of human rights, but it is also the only pan-European organization and thus the only representative regional organization. It should also be kept in mind that at the Second Summit of Heads of State and Government of the Council of Europe in Strasbourg in October 1997, it was recognized that «...social cohesion is one of the foremost needs of the wider Europe and should be pursued as an essential complement to the promotion of human rights and dignity». The Heads of State and Government therefore stressed «... the importance of a common and balanced approach, based on international solidarity, to questions relating to refugees and asylum seekers,...».[311] At the subsequent meeting of the

---

308. Doc. 7786 3 April 1997.
309. Recommendation No. R(84)1, adopted by the Committee of Ministers of the Council of Europe on 25 January, 1984 during its 36th meeting of the Delegates of Ministers. See also Exposition of Motives, Strasbourg, 1984.
310. See below, Chapter 8, on the proposal for a new convention.

Committee of Ministers in November 1997, the Norwegian Deputy Minister for Foreign Affairs reiterated that the objective of the Committee of Ministers should be to elaborate a European convention on the protection and rights of refugees and asylum seekers.[312] This means that the proposal has once again been brought to the attention of the Committee of Ministers and Member States cannot continue to avoid addressing this issue.

The European Union
Despite the fact that the «de facto» refugee issue has never been discussed in depth in the EU context, the European Parliament has pronounced itself clearly on behalf of «de facto» refugees. In June 1987, the European Parliament adopted a Recommendation,[313] which recommends that European Community Member States base their eligibility decisions on a refugee concept like that of the OAU Convention. In the same recommendation, it was also suggested that during their stay in Europe, «de facto» refugees should be treated in the same way as Convention refugees.[314] In 1994, the Committee on Civil Liberties and Internal Affairs of the European Parliament, prepared a draft resolution calling on Member States to adopt «…a common approach to providing protection to the many refugees who are not covered by the 1951 Geneva Convention».

The European Commission Communications of October 1991 and February 1994, proposed European harmonization concerning «de facto» refugees,[315] but so far with no results. With its joint right of initiative under the Maastricht Treaty, the Commission could have been expected to play a more active role on this issue.

When the formal framework for intergovernmental cooperation under the «Third Pillar» of the Maastricht Treaty came into being, the intergovernmental cooperation continued the process of EU harmonization, through adopt-

---

311. Final Declaration , Strasbourg 10–11 October 1997, Doc. SUM(97)PV2.
312. Based on i.a. ideas contained in this book, the Norwegian Parliament and Government had been lobbied extensively by the Norwegian Refugee Council in order to take a regional initiative in this regard. In May 1997, the majority of the Norwegian Parliament voted for taking an initiative for a new European refugee convention (Innst. S. Nr. 229 – 1996–97) and the government followed suit.
313. Resolution adopted on 18 June 1987, (Official Journal of the Europen Communities C 190).
314. W. Kälin, «Protection from forcible return for de facto refugees: Approaches and principles in international law», p.126.
315. Communications of the Commission to the Council and the European Parliament on Immigration and Asylum Policies, Doc.of 23 October 1991 and Doc.of 23 February 1994.

ing joint measures in the field of immigration and asylum. One of the priority issues Member States have discussed, is that of «subsidiary protection», specified as «de facto protection», and «humanitarian residence permits».[316] In relation to such discussions, it is known that one Member State, Denmark, has presented a proposal for discussion on «de facto» refugees and the Commission is preparing a comparative study of European practice vis-à-vis «de facto» refugees. Documents are classified and not publicly available and it is not known whether the study will eventually be developed into a formal proposal.

The war in former Yugoslavia created a significant influx of refugees in Europe and had profound consequences for protection issues in European States. UNHCR called not only for international cooperation, but also for the granting of temporary protection for persons fleeing former Yugoslavia as a result of the conflict. In response, EU Member States adopted a Resolution in June 1993, on the admission of particularly vulnerable groups among displaced persons from the former Yugoslavia. In September 1995, a more general Resolution on burden-sharing was adopted, with regard to the admission and residence of displaced persons on a temporary basis. Furthermore, a decision for an urgency and alert procedure to implement the elements of this resolution was adopted by the EU in November 1995.

Nevertheless, the response by European States was unilateral, each State created specific programmes to receive ex-prisoners of war, wounded refugees and others, through the adoption of specific legislation or administrative directives on temporary protection.

However, an initiative which may prove more important than the resolutions mentioned, is a proposal by the European Commission to the Council, for a Joint Action on temporary protection of displaced persons.[317]

4.4 Existing ideas for an expanded refugee definition

In legal literature as well as in international debates, three different solutions have been proposed to regulate the issue of «de facto» refugees in international law. The first solution proposes a broad interpretation of the 1951

---

316. European Council Resolution of 14 October 1996 on establishment of priorities for the cooperation on judicial and internal affairs for the period from 1 July 1996 until 30 June 1998, (Official Journal 96/C 319/01, p. 2.).
317. Based on Article K.3 paragraph 2(b) of the TEU. See more on this proposal, below, p. 201–205.

Convention in conformity with Recommendation E of the Conference of Plenipotentiaries. The second solution proposes an enlargement of the 1951 Convention. The third solution proposes the adoption of a new instrument of international law, either at a universal or at a regional level.

Broad interpretation of the 1951 Convention

At the time of the adoption of the 1951 Convention, the international community was already aware of the fact that the refugee concept contained in the 1951 Convention was rather limited, due to the emphasis that was placed on the need to establish that persecution was individually targeted. Concern for this limitation is reflected in the Recommendations adopted by the Conference of Plenipotentiaries, which are annexed to the 1951 Convention. According to Recommendation E, it was the hope of the Conference, that the Convention would «...have value as an example exceeding its contractual scope and that all nations be guided by it in granting so far as possible to persons in their territory as refugees and who would not be covered by the terms of the Convention, the treatment for which it provides».

With reference, though not always explicit, to Recommendation E of the Conference of Plenipotentiaries, States have, in practice, granted humanitarian protection in situations where the 1951 Convention did not seem applicable, in particular before the 1967 Protocol was adopted.[318]

It is widely held that the definition of the 1951 Convention itself, includes the possibility of covering many refugees who are presently, according to State practice, considered as «de facto» refugees.[319] Whilst the 1951 Convention definition is often interpreted in an increasingly restrictive manner, it should, in line with existing international law, be interpreted in accordance with its spirit and purpose and thus in a more liberal manner. A liberalization of the interpretation of the 1951 Convention would, to a large extent, solve the problem of «de facto» refugees. However, it should also be understood that this may not suffice.

It is important to stress that a broad interpretation of the 1951 Conven-

---

318. For example, the treatment of Hungarian refugees, see above, p. 48–49.
319. See G. Goodwin-Gill, «Refuge, De Facto Refugees and Rejected Applicants», seminar organized by the European Legal Network on Asylum (ELENA), «Le statut juridique des réfugiés de facto et des demandeurs d'asile rejetés», 1988, p. 99; T. Einarsen, «The European Convention on Human Rights», p. 363; G. Jaeger, «A Succinct Evaluation of the 1951 Convention and the 1967 Protocol relating to the status of refugees», p. 13. See also, S. Bodart, «Les autres réfugiés: le statut des réfugiés 'de facto' en Europe», p.34; and G. Melander, «Further Development of International Refugee Law», p.488 and 489.

tion, based on human rights principles should always be the basis of application, so that threats to human rights, as embodied in other human rights instruments are taken into consideration.[320] As J. Hathaway rightly comments when describing the dominant view on this in legal literature, «...refugee law ought to concern itself with actions which deny human dignity in any key way, and that the sustained or systematic denial of core human rights is the appropriate standard». [321]

Expansion of the 1951 Convention

Even if a generous interpretation were to become the rule, not all categories of «de facto» refugees could claim to fall under the 1951 Convention. One example would be persons who flee situations of generalized violence, such as war. In the majority of cases, such persons cannot prove fear of individual persecution because they are not individually targeted nor are they always targeted because they belong to, for example, a particular ethnic group. However, persons fleeing a war in fear for their life, have no less valid a reason for flight than persons who are specifically targeted and the need for protection therefore exists in both cases.

With this in mind, it should be recalled that another solution proposed, in the course of the discussions in UNHCR's Working Group on Protection and Solutions in 1992,[322] is the enlargement of the 1951 Convention through the addition of a protocol to cover the «de facto» refugees. The reason for adding to the 1951 Convention is that the Convention is already established and is universally applicable. Furthermore, an addition to such an instrument would establish a legal tie between «de jure» refugees and «de facto» refugees at a universal level.

However, analyses by prominent refugee law specialists demonstrate just how problematic this proposal is. The need for a supplementary definition, its timing and legal framework are all contested issues. For example, according to P. Weis, the best solution would be to adopt an instrument which extends the 1951 Convention to cover «de facto» refugees.[323] On the other hand, in 1980, G. Jaeger, claimed that given the developments in international law on the concept of refugee, both within the UN and regional instruments, war refugees and other displaced persons should normally be seen as refugees covered by the existing definition of the 1951 Conven-

---

320. On persecution in relation to human rights, see above, p. 67 and following.
321. J. Hathaway, «The Law of Refugee Status», p. 108.
322. See above, p. 101–102.
323. P. Weis, «Convention Refugees and De Facto Refugees», 1978, p.22.

tion.³²⁴ In any case, an enlargement of the definition does not, in Jaeger's view, seem possible.³²⁵ Ten years on, in 1990, P. Nobel stated that political conditions were such that States would not agree to extend the definition of the 1951 Convention.³²⁶ Arguments along the same lines are still prevailing, even in quarters where a more proactive stance ought to be expected.

In 1992, UNHCR's Sub-Committee of the Whole on International Protection alluded to the danger of opening a debate on the content of the 1951 Convention. The fear is that States, in a climate insensitive to the refugee problem as a whole, would try to weaken the 1951 Convention rather than strengthen it. This is also why the Sub-Committee recommended developing the concept of protection of «de facto» refugees on regional and national levels first,³²⁷ before progressing towards a universal regime.

4.5 Proposal in part for a new European convention on refugee protection

In the preceding pages, it has been established that there is a need to develop a harmonized international approach to «de facto» refugees and to ensure that they are accorded appropriate international protection. The problems concern when and how proposals should be taken forward rather than on the fact that something ought to be done. The question that needs to be answered is why, so far, has so little been done in the context of international law. The reason is that consensus has broken down on a range of issues that must be addressed if the international community is to get beyond declarations of good intent.

In order for further progress to be made, further discussions must address five fundamental questions: Firstly, is it the right time to undertake such a project? Secondly, what are the consequences, if any, to the application of the 1951 Convention? Thirdly, which would be the most adequate international forum to undertake this work? Fourthly, who would be the beneficiaries of such an instrument? And, finally, what kind of instrument is needed for a new international refugee regime?

The first question concerns the timing of a new initiative. There is indeed a real risk that the timing may never be right, especially from the perspective

---

324. G. Jaeger, «A Succinct Evaluation of the 1951 Convention and the 1967 Protocol relating to the Status of Refugees», p. 9.
325. Ibid., p.11.
326. P. Nobel, «De facto-flyktningbegreppet i Norden», p.107.
327. UN Document, EC/1992/SCP/CRP.5, April 2, 1992.

of States. States tend to focus negatively on the broadening of responsibility which such an undertaking would entail, ignoring the advantages that would be derived from an international harmonization of the interpretation of the 1951 Convention and of the «de facto» refugee concept. From the perspective of refugee lawyers and others the timing may not seem right because of the fear that opening up a discussion, may in itself induce even more restrictive State practices. However, it is difficult to believe that the so called «political climate» will change for the better unless something is actively done in order to bring about such change. Silence and postponement certainly do not bring pending protection issues into focus. Misgivings about «timing», are therefore an invalid argument.

The second question concerns consequences, if any, to the application of the 1951 Convention. It could be feared that whatever comes out of an attempt to create a new instrument, it may impair already existing practice with regard to refugee protection, which, according to most, is already poor. One argument made is that any attempt to create a new instrument on refugee protection could endanger the application of the 1951 Convention. However, the adoption of a regional instrument does not diminish the importance of the 1951 Convention, the existence of the OAU Convention and the Cartagena Declaration testify to this. Moreover, both the OAU Convention and the Cartagena Declaration refer to the 1951 Convention, with regard to refugees who are victims of individualized persecution, and, in addition, they both make a complementary, expanded refugee definition, to include refugees who are victims of generalized violence such as war and massive violations of human rights. This means that the 1951 Convention refugee concept and the «de facto» refugee concept are merged into one, simply the concept of «refugee». This example should be followed by European States.

There can be no doubt about the importance attached to the 1951 Convention in European countries. Along with the European Convention on Human Rights, the 1951 Convention is the instrument to which EU Member States, for example, refer when adopting instruments on refugee and asylum law in the EU context. A new European instrument would therefore compliment the 1951 Convention. The fact that we are at present witnessing a period of restrictive interpretation of the 1951 Convention, has led to concern that efforts to codify a definition of «de facto» refugees might land Convention refugees in the «de facto» category. This is, regrettably, exactly what is happening now.[328] For example, the EU Joint Position on the application of Article 1(A) limits the scope of the concept of persecution to that committed by «state agents». Another example, at a national level, is the newly adopted Swedish alien's legislation which does not categorize gender related persecution or persecution for reasons of homosexuality as being covered by the

1951 Convention. Given these circumstances, a substantive international debate on the refugee concept as a whole, seems conducive to safeguarding the interests of those who definitely lack adequate protection today, namely, «de facto» refugees, as well as 1951 Convention refugees whose rights are threatened.

One category of refugees in need of protection should never be emphasized to the detriment of another. This is often forgotten by those who advocate the need to protect 1951 Convention refugees only instead of being willing to think along new lines in order to work for increased protection of all refugees. Reluctance by States to assume binding protection responsibility is used as an explanation and an excuse for doing nothing.

The third question concerns which would be the most adequate international forum within which to undertake this work. As already indicated in the previous discussion, the Council of Europe would be the most appropriate international body to deal with refugee matters on a European regional level. First of all, because it has forty Member States, including those in Eastern and Central Europe, and as such is truly an inclusive pan-European organization. Secondly, it has a long tradition as a coordinator on refugee and asylum issues and has already discussed the issue of elaborating an instrument which includes «de facto» refugees in various organs.[329] Thirdly, it is founded on the tradition of human rights and is the regional human rights organization.[330] And finally, it is an organization in which legal, mandatory international instruments can be adopted.

The fourth question concerns the beneficiaries of a new instrument. This question relates to how the «de facto» concept should be defined for the purposes of international harmonization in a supplementary refugee definition. The pertinent question is: Who is in need of international protection. Once identified, according to given criteria, these persons would be refugees. Thus,

---

328. As long as systems of two separate categories of refugees are being upheld, those who are covered by the 1951 Convention should definitely be granted convention status. This is of course of particular importance in cases where there is a difference between rights accorded to convention refugees as opposed to those accorded to «de facto» refugees. But, even in a country like Denmark, where convention refugees and «de facto» refugees are placed on an equal footing as far as rights are concerned, the appropriate status nomination should be upheld until, hopefully, the distinctions are made to disappear through the adoption of a regional European instrument which merges the different refugee concepts into one broad definition.
329. See above, p. 120–123.
330. Some of the most significant developments of refugee law have taken place in Strasbourg under the application of Article 3 by the European Human Rights Commission and Court.

another aim would be achieved, that of erasing the unfair distinction made between «Convention refugees» who are seen as «first class refugees» and «de facto» refugees who are seen as «second class refugees». Moreover, there should be no difference in the rights accorded to them, be it civil and political rights or economic, social, and cultural rights.[331]

Many have tried to give suggestions on who should be legally defined as refugees in addition to Convention refugees, but always, it seems, with a certain reservation. In 1976, during a Council of Europe conference, P. Weis attempted a definition of «de facto» refugees which is widely held to be one of the best.[332] He defines «de facto» refugees as «...persons who are not recognized as refugees within the meaning of Article 1 of the Convention relating to the Status of Refugees of 28 July 1951 as amended by the Protocol of 10 January 1967 relating to the Status of Refugees and who are unable or, for reasons recognized as valid, unwilling to return to their country of nationality or, if they have no nationality, to the country of their habitual residence». As valid reasons Weis lists:

a. The reasonable belief of a person that he/she will be:
(i) seriously prejudiced in the exercise of his human rights as proclaimed in the European Convention of Human Rights and Fundamental Freedoms of 30 November 1950 and Protocol No.1, thereto, in particular discriminated against for reasons of race, religion, ethnic or tribal origin, membership of a particular social group or political opinion;
(ii) compelled to act in a manner incompatible with his conscience.

b. War or warlike conditions, occupation by a foreign or colonial power, events seriously disturbing public order in either part or the whole of the person's country of nationality, or, if he has no nationality, the country of his habitual residence.[333]

In an interpretation of his own proposed definition, P. Weis emphasized, that the term «seriously prejudiced» should not indicate that all violations of human rights would entitle someone to «de facto» refugee status.[334] The reference to the European Convention on Human Rights must, however, be seen in the light of the discussions within the Council of Europe at that time, and should not be seen as precluding victims of violations of other principles

---

331. See below, p. 221–223.
332. See, G. Jaeger, «A succinct evaluation of the 1951 Convention and the 1967 Protocol relating to the Status of refugees.», 1980, p.12.
333. P. Weis, «Convention Refugees and De Facto Refugees», p.18 and 19.
334. Ibid., p.19.

of human rights contained in other instruments, from constituting a «de facto» refugee.

The terms «seriously prejudiced», «discriminated against», and «compelled to act in a manner incompatible with his conscience» not only replace the concept of «persecution» defined in the definition of the 1951 Convention but go further than the Convention. On the other hand, it is worth noting that the terms do not include economic motives for flight.[335] Focus is on the need of protection for reasons of massive human rights violations and for reasons of generalized violence, such as war.

The 1951 Convention's term «well-founded fear» has been replaced by the term «reasonable belief», which better emphasizes the victim's subjective fear. The proposal provides for a better description of victims in need of international protection than that of the 1951 Convention in general. The intention seems to have been to enlarge the refugee concept in a manner covering all civil and political human rights, but linked to the five criteria enumerated in the 1951 Convention. To conclude on Weis' proposal, there is no doubt that it would be an interesting starting point for debate. However, there are good reasons why a «de facto» definition should be even more general.

Representing more than sixty NGOs, ECRE has also proposed a definition[336] of «de facto» refugees which, as a point of departure, uses the enlarged refugee concept of the Cartagena Declaration[337] and adds further elements to cover post-flight reasons and refugees «sur place». ECRE's proposal is that the refugee definition include the following:

«a. persons who have fled their country, or are unable or unwilling to return there, because their lives, safety, or freedom are threatened by generalized violence, foreign aggression, internal conflicts, massive violation of human rights, or other circumstances which have seriously disturbed public order.
b. persons who have fled their country, or who are unwilling to return there, owing to well-founded fear of being tortured or of being subjected to inhuman or degrading treatment or punishment or violations of other fundamental human rights.»

Some authors believe that a definition of «de facto» refugees is impossible, given the complex and multifarious reasons invoked by persons claiming a

---

335. J. Cels, «Responses of European States to de facto Refugees», p.202.
336. ECRE, «Working Paper on the need for a supplementary refugee definition, p. 5.
337. Whereas V. Muntarbhorn had proposed the incorporation of the enlarged definition of the OAU Convention, in «Determination of the Status of Refugees: Definition in Context.», 1981, p.88.

need for protection and who are not 1951 Convention refugees. With this in mind, E. Lapenna defines a «de facto» refugee as «…a foreigner in special circumstances which qualify him to obtain asylum in the country which shelters him».[338] G. Goodwin-Gill, maintains that a formal list of causes and beneficiaries would not be necessary.[339] In his proposal for an Additional Protocol to the European Convention on Human Rights, Goodwin-Gill defines a refugee by referring to the 1951 Convention and the 1967 Protocol and as regards a broadened refugee definition, he limits himself to the wording «…other refugees who have valid reasons for not being required to return to their country of origin».[340]

In conclusion, despite all of the arguments concerning the timeliness or feasibility of attempting to define a «de facto» refugee and the proposals which already exist to this end, the bottom line is that it could and should be done. Furthermore, a supplementary definition needs to be flexible and therefore should not be too detailed. National laws, which generally refer to «situations analogous to those of Convention refugees», may serve as examples.[341]

The most important consideration is that «de facto» refugees should be guaranteed adequate protection and treatment, in line with the rights accorded to Convention refugees, according to the 1951 Convention. Recommendation 773 adopted by the Parliamentary Assembly of the Council of Europe in 1976, refers to the need for work, housing, travel documents, and so on, to be accorded to «de facto» refugees and also gives good guidance on principles of required treatment. Conclusion No. 22 of UNHCR's Executive Committee on Protection of Asylum Seekers in Situations of Large Scale Influx, also adresses the issue by setting international minimum standards. Although the latter specifically speaks of large-scale influx, it should be used as a model for minimum treatment of «de facto» refugees now while waiting for

---

338. E. Lapenna, «Les réfugiés de facto – un nouveau problème pour l'Europe», p. 64. See also, S. Bodert, «Les autres réfugiés: Le statut des réfugiés «de facto» en Europe», p. 23.
339. G. Goodwin-Gill, «The Principles of Refuge: An Outline» 1988, p. 98 and 99.
340. G. Goodwin-Gill, «The Refugee in International Law», 1996, p. 527.
341. The Danish Alien's Act (Consolidated act No. 562 of 30 June 1995) is an excellent example: Its section 7(1) reads: «Upon application a residence permit will also be issued to an alien who does not fall within the provisions of the Convention relating to the Status of Refugees, 28 July 1951», followed by section 7(2) which reads: «Upon application a residence permit will also be issued to an alien who does not fall within the provisions of the Convention relating to the Status of Refugees, 28 July 1951, but for reasons similar to those listed in the Convention or for other weighty reasons, ought not to be required to return to his country of origin».

a more adequate regional instrument to be instituted.[342] Conclusion No. 22 stresses the importance that the non-refoulement principle be scrupulously observed, non-rejection at the border included. Other rights of importance are, of course, the internationally recognized civil rights, in particular those set out in the Universal Declaration of Human Rights. Conclusion No. 22 also refers to necessary assistance, including food, shelter and health facilities, family unity, and so on.

The final question which needs to be assessed in relation to a new European refugee regime, relates to form. The most appropriate form an instrument could take would be that of a new European refugee convention which would be an independent instrument. First of all, it is important that the convention creates a harmonized, mandatory, and legally binding refugee regime for European States. Secondly, it should be independent in order to highlight the importance of refugee law and the rights and duties this area of law entails. It has been suggested that an additional protocol to the European Convention on Human Rights could be a good solution because it would place the right of asylum and the refugee concept in the general framework of human rights.[343] This is indeed an interesting proposal but one which would not emphasise sufficiently the importance of the development of international refugee law as an intrinsic, but nevertheless independent part of human rights law.

The concrete proposal for a refugee definition in a new European refugee convention reads as follows: [344]

Draft Article 1 REFUGEE DEFINITION

Within the terms of the present Convention, a refugee, to whom international protection shall be accorded, is a displaced person (or a group of persons) who has fled his country or who cannot or will not return there, due to well-founded fear of persecution within the terms of the Convention relating to the Status of Refugees of 28 July 1951 and the Protocol relating to the Status of Refugees of 31 January 1967, or a displaced person (or a group of persons) who cannot or will not return for analogous reasons.

---

342. See below, Chapter 8.
343. See ECRE, «Working paper on the need for a supplementary refugee definition», in which it is confirmed that this might have its advantages. On the other hand, the document concludes by referring the discussion to the debate within the EU context. See also, G. Goodwin-Gill, «The Refugee in International Law», 1996, p. 527–533.
344. Note, this proposal constitutes Article 1 of a proposed European refugee convention which concludes this book, see Chapter 8.

Analogous reasons could include: when life, liberty and security are threatened by violations of fundamental human rights principles or principles of humanitarian law, or by generalized violence, foreign aggression, internal conflict or other circumstances seriously disturbing public order.

It follows from the discussion above that reference must be made to the 1951 Convention. Thus the first paragraph places 1951 Convention refugees and «de facto» refugees on an equal footing, thereby eliminating the distinction between a «de jure» and a «de facto» refugee. Both categories are regarded as «de jure» refugees. The persons concerned are «refugees» due to their need for «international protection» which States undertake to give them, thus the wording, «shall be accorded». The term «international protection» is incorporated in order to underscore that the proposed convention addresses situations in which national protection is absent, but most importantly, in order to emphasize State responsibility. State protection, as will be seen from the analysis which will follow, concerns non-violation of the principle of «non-refoulement», the granting of asylum, and the treatment afforded by the asylum State.[345]

Reference to «life, liberty and security» in the second paragraph of the proposition is modeled on Article 3 of the Universal Declaration of Human Rights. This reference is made to show that the threats in question, directed against one or several persons, must be of a certain gravity, a point reaffirmed by the addition «violations of fundamental human rights principles». This wording covers all fundamental principles of human rights contained in different international instruments. Reference is also made to «principles of humanitarian» law in order to underline these particular sets of rules, which are relevant in case of armed conflict.[346]

The proposed definition makes reference to a person «or a group of persons» so as to leave no doubt that its scope encompasses individually targeted persons or groups of persons covered by the 1951 Convention, as well as groups fleeing war and similar situations.

It should be noted that the list of analogous reasons should not be considered exhaustive. This is of fundamental importance. A refugee definition including the «de facto» concept needs to contain flexibility.

The aim of this exercise is to contribute to the evolution of international refugee law. It goes without saying that refugees would benefit from a new regional instrument. States would also benefit for several reasons. First of all,

---

345. On these protection elements, see below, Chapter 5 and 6.
346. The interpretation should be in accordance with the 1949 Geneva Conventions and the 1977 Protocols.

because such an instrument, defining persons in need of protection on a mandatory legal level in Europe, would in itself ensure an improved burden sharing among European States. Specific provisions on burden sharing and responsibility sharing would also have to be included. [347] The term «international solidarity» need not be a term of empty words and no substance. In cases of mass influx, this would be of particular importance.

Secondly, increased harmonization would ensure equality among European States. For the same reasons that EU Member States thought it necessary to harmonize their interpretation of Article 1 (A) of the 1951 Convention, so is it necessary to harmonize the «de facto» concept. Otherwise, States with a more liberal approach, and States offering «de facto» refugees more or less the same rights as Convention refugees, would risk attracting more asylum seekers than other States.[348] Another important aspect is the «learning» effect such harmonization would have upon the States of Eastern and Central Europe, with regard to rights and duties of States to accord protection to those in need.

Due regard should be given to the harmonization process which is otherwise taking place in Europe, for example, the entry into force of the Dublin Convention in September 1997 and the possible development of a parallel convention to the Dublin Convention by associated States. This development presupposes that the contracting States have faith in each other's refugee and asylum policy, as responsibility for an asylum request is transferred from one State to another. In order not to risk violating the «non-refoulement» principle, harmonization is therefore crucial both as regards 1951 Convention refugees and «de facto» refugees.

Yet another reason why States should be interested in developing a consistent approach is that, for fear of deportation, an increasing number of asylum seekers do not approach the police or immigration authorities to request asylum, although their reasons for flight are valid. This causes increased clandestine immigration which has the negative consequence of encouraging trafficking in human beings, forced labour and other crimes, all of which imply a lack of State control, which in turn breeds racism and xenophobia.

Finally, is it too far fetched to presume that European States would want to maintain or regain their reputation as protectors of, not only human rights principles, but equally of the persons those principles were meant to protect?

---

347. See below, Chapter 8, draft Article 6.
348. This relates to different welfare systems, political and social rights, possibility of eventually obtaining citizenship, etc.

CHAPTER 5

International protection and the principle of non-refoulement

In principle, each State is responsible for the protection of its citizens. However, when States are unable or unwilling to fulfill their protection responsibilities and citizens flee their countries in fear of their lives or security, the responsibility for protection becomes a matter for the international community. The responsibility, as such, for providing international protection for refugees, has never been legally defined in an instrument of international law. Nevertheless, there is general recognition that the term «protection» must be seen as having both a legal and a political dimension, as well as a dimension of care.[349]

States have undertaken a number of obligations in treaty law which are of importance in connection with refugee protection, the most essential of which are the 1951 Convention and various human rights and humanitarian law instruments. International protection responsibility is also derived from customary law and humanitarian principles, for example, various «soft law» instruments, UN resolutions and UNHCR Executive Committee Conclusions. State practice also provides an important indication of present and future international protection responsibilities and, if this does not always entail legal obligations, it does entail political and moral obligations.

International protection responsibility is undertaken by different international actors of which States and intergovernmental organizations are predominant. Among the intergovernmental organizations, UNHCR is, with its particular protection mandate, the essential actor. NGOs play a supplementary role, often as implementing partners to the intergovernmental organizations and as watchdogs monitoring and reporting on violations of human rights. Notwithstanding a certain division of labour among the international actors, the protection of refugees rests first and foremost with States. Sometimes the international community as a whole, acts in unity while making efforts to provide necessary protection on an «ad hoc» basis. For example, this

---

349. G.J.L. Coles, «Solutions to the problem of refugees and the protection of refugees», Study presented to a Round Table, UNHCR and the International Institute of Humanitarian Law, 1989, p. 3.

is the case when so called UN «safe havens» or «protected areas» are established in order to protect civilian populations against persecution or against more generalized violence, or when International Plans of Action are created, in order to facilitate resettlement or repatriation of refugees.

However, at the level of individual State practice, protection manifests itself principally in two areas: by respecting the principle of non-refoulement and by granting asylum. As the aim of this book is to propose a new European refugee convention pertaining to protection, these two issues need to be examined more closely.

The non-refoulement principle entails that States may not return a refugee to an area where his life or security would be endangered.[350] As a principle of international law, non-refoulement originates from the aftermath of the Second World War[351] and it is often described as «the corner stone of refugee protection». However, notwithstanding its importance, there are questions related to its scope and applicability, both within and outside treaty law which still need to be clarified. In view of refugees' right to seek asylum and States' right to grant asylum, the fact that there exists no obligation to grant asylum, can only be seen as a missing link in international refugee law. A new European refugee convention must therefore contain a provision on asylum, which, according to need, insists on the duty to grant asylum on a permanent basis or on a temporary basis. The issue of asylum will be examined under a separate chapter.[352]

5.1 Various forms of protection

Territorial asylum, permanent or otherwise, is not the only form of international protection accorded to refugees or potential refugees. On the contrary, protection of refugees manifests itself in various ways. The institution of «extra-territorial asylum» which includes the granting of protection aboard a ship, in embassies or consulates are further examples of the different forms which international protection takes. Beyond the provision of protection outside the country of origin of the person in need, the international community has also shown itself willing to intervene in internal conflicts, for ex-

---

350. For a thorough examination of the non-refoulement principle in international law, see G. Goodwin-Gill, «The Refugee in International law», 1996, p. 117-170. See also G. Stenberg, «Non-Expulsion and Non-Refoulement», 1989.
351. See G. Stenberg, «Non-expulsion and Non-Refoulement», p.172; G. Goodwin-Gill, «The Refugee in International Law», p. 69 and G. Fourlanos, «Sovereignty and the Ingress of Aliens», p.147.
352. See below, Chapter 6.

ample by creating «protected areas» for the civilian population and thereby preventing flight from the country or region concerned.

As territorial asylum in the Western world is traditionally granted to 1951 Convention refugees, there is a clear need to elaborate forms of protection for «de facto» refugees who do not meet the necessary criteria to qualify for Convention status, but who are nevertheless in need of protection. In practice, the international response to «de facto» refugees is often the granting of a permanent residence permit for humanitarian or for analogous reasons. Another response is the granting of «temporary protection» which implies that the country of «asylum» offers protection while necessary.[353]

«Sanctuary» is yet another form of protection which involves individual citizens performing civil disobedience, for example, by hiding asylum seekers whose asylum requests have been rejected and who are in the process of being expelled. Church asylum is the classical example. This form of protection has been recognized under the name of sanctuary since the Middle Ages, a time when asylum in general was considered to be a religious institution.[354]

Residence permits for humanitarian reasons

On a unilateral basis, States have created national protection schemes (legislative or administrative practices) for «de facto» refugees. One of these pragmatic solutions which involves the issuing of a residence permit on humanitarian grounds or for reasons similar to those pertaining to 1951 Convention refugees, has not been codified in international law, and a significant gap therefore exists. It is of crucial importance to find a solution to today's crisis pertaining to the asylum institution given the fact that the majority of today's refugees belong to the category of «de facto» refugees. Although they do not necessarily warrant refugee status under the 1951 Convention, they certainly warrant protection.[355] Rather than depend on a variety of national protection schemes such as «B-status» and residence permits on humanitar-

---

353. On temporary protection, see below, p. 191 and following.
354. See above, p. 17.
355. The Norwegian example illustrates this point. In 1996, the Norwegian government granted 1951 Convention status and asylum to six persons (0,4% of the total number of 1,778 asylum-applications, which was an increase in the number of asylum seekers of 21 % compared to 1995) and issued residence permits for humanitarian reasons to 610 persons. 788 persons were granted asylum as quota refugees whose cases had been presented by UNHCR. Until June 1997, ten persons had been granted refugee status and asylum. Statistics provided from «Refugee 1997» issued by the Norwegian Refugee Council, p.20.

ian grounds in the Scandinavian countries, «exceptional leave to stay» in Great Britain, protection must be harmonized at an international level. Such a strategy would cover all refugees in need of international protection and would render the unilateral protection systems currently applied by individual States in an inconsistent and ineffective way, superfluous. Only when such a strategy has been developed will the due emphasis intended by the 1951 Convention be placed on the protection needs of refugees.

A harmonization of the asylum institution would also serve to clarify the concept of «humanitarian reasons» which is often used in domestic asylum legislation as grounds for granting refugee status when a person in need is considered not to meet the Convention criteria. However, confusion arises in the interpretation of the concept as it is also utilized to refer to the protection granted in the form of a temporary residence permit to people fleeing their home country for reasons of economic misery, against a background of international short term humanitarian assistance or longer term development aid. The same terminology is also used to refer to persons who go to other countries and are permitted to stay for among others, reasons of health or family reunification. The application of the one term, «humanitarian», to refer to so many different situations blurs the picture and causes mistakes by politicians, pressure groups of various kinds and others, in confusing the two quite different concepts of «refugee» and «economic migrant». For the refugee, any misunderstanding of the reasons for his flight caused by such a confusion can have a detrimental effect on the determination procedure at a national level. Furthermore, the use by national governments of the term humanitarian reasons as a general «catch all» term for those who are perceived to be in need, but to whom they are reluctant to commit themselves to the provision of any longer term protection, amounts to an easy evasion by States of the obligations entailed in the interpretation of the Convention in the generous spirit intended. In this context, it is therefore essential that the protection needs of persons who have fled for reasons of persecution or other reasons pertaining to their life or security, be clearly assessed, understood and respected, with acknowledgement and consideration of the need for dignity as well as protection.

Diplomatic asylum

Diplomatic asylum developed from the creation and establishment of permanent embassies in the XVth century and the immunity which was granted to the ambassador and his premises. Charles V authorized «that the houses of ambassadors should serve as places of inviolable asylum, as previously did the temples of the gods.»[356] Diplomatic asylum, gradually developed to supersede the concept and practice of religious asylum and, in the modern era of nation States, diplomatic asylum has in turn been increasingly overtaken by the development of the concept of territorial asylum.

Diplomatic asylum is the most well-known type of extra-territorial asylum and it has enjoyed a long tradition in Latin America where it is considered a legal concept, codified in the Caracas Convention on Diplomatic Asylum of 1954[357] and used in practice in certain notable situations. In 1950, in the Asylum case,[358] the International Court of Justice declared, in contradiction to the customary law of diplomatic asylum of the region, that diplomatic asylum constituted an intervention in State affairs. However, in 1951, the Court «corrected itself» in the Haya de la Torre Case.[359] On this occasion, the ICJ interpreted the Havana Convention of 1928 on Asylum, which applied to the two parties to the conflict which formed the framework of the case, Colombia and Peru. The Havana Convention allows for the grant of asylum in embassies for persons accused or convicted of political crimes.

In 1988, the Peruvian embassy in Havana was invaded by approximately 3,000 Cubans seeking diplomatic asylum[360] and in 1994, 114 Cubans stormed the entrance of the Belgian Embassy in Havana for the same purpose. The latter were not granted diplomatic asylum, but the Belgian authorities requested guarantees for their security before they were expelled from the Embassy. After this, the Cuban authorities declared that they would not grant exit visas to persons who forcefully penetrated the embassies in the country.[361]

There have also been examples of diplomatic asylum[362] in other parts of the world. In 1989 persons sought by the Chinese authorities following events in Tienanmen Square in Peking received diplomatic asylum at the US

---

356. J.Y. Carlier, «L'état du droit international», p. 49 and 50.
357. See Article 1 which affirms that «Asylum granted in legations, war vessels, and military camps or aircraft, to persons being sought for political reasons or offenses shall be respected by the territorial state ...» The second paragraph defines the content of the term «legation» as «... any seat of a regular diplomatic mission, the residence of chiefs of mission, and the premises provided by them for the dwelling places of asylees when the number of the latter exceeds the normal capacity of the buildings.»
358. ICJ Collection 1950, p. 83, Judgment of 27 November 1950.
359. ICJ Collection 1951, Judgment of 13 June 1951.
360. A. Suhrke, «Mer styring med prosessen», («More control over the proceeding»), the Norwegian daily, Aftenposten, 2 November 1993, p.15.
361. ESMV, «List of Events», No. 5 May 1994, p. 12.
362. But often under another name, for example, «tolerated stay» in A. Grahl-Madsen who believes that outside of Latin America, the states cannot accord diplomatic asylum, see «The Status of Refugees in International Law», Vol. II, 1972, p.46.

and Australian embassies. Other powerful images of the desperate resort to diplomatic asylum include images of the Vietnamese who tried to seek refuge at the US embassy in Saigon in 1975, and Chileans who sought refuge in different European embassies, following the coup d'Etat in 1973. Some persons have benefited from diplomatic protection over a period of several years, for example, the Hungarian Cardinal, Jozsef Mindszenty (1892-1975) who was granted refuge in the US Embassy in Budapest from 1956 to 1971.

Towards the end of the 1980s, the world witnessed a mass flight of East German nationals towards West German embassies in Warsaw, Budapest, and Prague. However in this instance, the embassies did not grant diplomatic asylum in the legal sense of the term, [363] as the persons concerned were already considered German citizens under West German law.

An example of «diplomatic asylum» which resulted eventually in «territorial asylum» took place in November 1994, when during the visit of President Clinton in Indonesia a group of militant students from East Timor, overrun by Indonesia in 1975, «occupied» the US Embassy in Djakarta. Portugal offered them asylum, which they accepted after ten days of occupation.

In spite of several instances of the practice of diplomatic asylum, as described above, there is still a certain international reluctance to accept the institution as established by international law.[364] No matter its legal status, it is a fact that diplomatic asylum contributes, under certain circumstances, to saving life and providing a form of protection. More often than not «diplomatic asylum» has satisfactory end results for the persons in need of protection. However, a successful outcome often depends on the willingness of the national authorities of the country of the person in need of protection, to provide guarantees which allow the person to leave the country safely.[365] Quiet diplomacy obviously has an impact in many of these cases creating solutions which allow for the least embarrassment to be caused to the host State.

---

363. E. Zoller, «Le droit d'asile», 1989, p.39.
364. A. Grahl-Madsen, «The Status of Refugees in International Law», Vol. II, 1972, p.46; E. Zoller, «Le droit d'asile», 1989, p.38; G. Goodwin-Gill, «The Refugee in International Law», 1983, p.102, and G. Fourlanos, «Sovereignty and the Ingress of Aliens», p.135.
365. See in this regard, the Caracas Convention on Diplomatic Asylum of 1954, article 5 which states that «Asylum may not be granted except in urgent cases and for the period of time strictly necessary for the asylee to depart from the country with the guarantees granted by the Government of the territorial State, to the end that his life, liberty, or personal integrity may not be endangered, or that the asylee's safety is ensured in some other way».

Asylum requests presented to embassies or international organizations

Asylum applications are sometimes presented at an embassy or to an international organization. The presentation of such a request by a person in need of protection is not motivated by a desire to stay at the premises of the embassy or the organization, but rather as a means of securing a grant of asylum in the home country of the embassy, or to be assisted by the organization, for example UNHCR through its quota system. It is evident that such practice eases the problem presented by large numbers of spontaneous asylum seekers who travel to asylum countries on their own without having been granted any right of entry.

However, there are several problems involved in seeking protection along these lines. First of all, refugees are often not able to approach embassies in their home country for fear of security police or others watching embassy premises. The same applies to international organizations. Secondly, a diplomatic mission, whether an embassy or an intergovernmental organization, always risks being accused of interference in the internal affairs of a host country whose citizens it assists in this way, and could be considered to be in violation of international law; although where violations of human rights are at stake, this could be viewed differently.

Nevertheless, a more practical alternative is, when the person in question has already fled, for example, to a neighbouring country and in that country deposits an asylum request in an embassy. For example, this was how the Danish «Visa Office» in Zagreb functioned during the conflict in former Yugoslavia. After the introduction of visa obligations for Bosnians in most European countries, Denmark established an office in Croatia where all citizens from Former-Yugoslavia could deposit asylum requests or applications for a residence permits for humanitarian reasons. However, once the borders between Croatia and Bosnia became almost hermetically sealed precisely in order to inhibit refugee flows, few refugees were actually able to take advantage of this offer of assistance and means to protection.

International protection does not always follow a strictly legal basis and procedure; rather, a recourse to diplomacy and politics is often necessary in order to uphold the international principles and obligations upon which the regime is based. There are cases in which persons in need of protection who enjoy a high profile outside their country in which they risk persecution, are granted or offered asylum, by another State, even without having to request protection. «Dethroned» Heads of State, diplomatic defectors, international celebrity adversaries to a regime, in particular writers and journalists and others have benefited from offers of protection in such circumstances. For example, the writer Taslima Nasreen, condemned to death by a «fatwa» declared by Muslim fundamentalists in her country, Bangladesh, was granted asylum in Sweden without request, during the summer of 1994. The objective of handling the asylum procedure in this way is, as it is in diplomatic asylum cases, to obtain guarantees which allow the person to leave the country safely. When such an «operation» succeeds, it is generally due to diplomatic negotiations on a bilateral level. The international pressure exerted in these situations may be such that the persecuting country prefers to rid itself of the problem and therefore allows the person to leave in order to avoid attracting further unwanted and critical attention from the international community. The role of diplomatic intervention is therefore more evident and more pertinent in such cases than a strictly legal basis for the granting of protection.

In certain cases, the attention of the international community or the media is the only possibility of saving persons in need of international protection. For example, in the 1980s, when Turkey refouled or threatened to refoul Iranian refugees to Iran by exchanging them with Turkish prisoners there, diplomatic pressure from various western embassies representing resettlement countries, helped in preventing refoulement. In cases in which refugee status had already been granted by UNHCR, according to the Statute of 1950[366] and the refugees had been accepted for resettlement by «third countries» which got involved, refugees were saved. However, for those who had not yet been given a UN refugee status, the risk of refoulement remained, even though they had been accepted by a resettlement country, and in spite of Turkey's international obligations under Article 3 of the European Convention on Human Rights and under regional customary law.[367]

Internationally protected areas

In order to try and prevent persons from leaving their country of origin, for example, for reasons of civil strife or other forms of generalized violence, the international community has created a way of offering «protection» by establishing so called «protected areas» within the borders of the home country.

---

366. Refugee determination was carried out by UNHCR on the basis of its mandate contained in the Statute of 1950 as Turkey had, and still has, maintained a geographical limitation to the 1951 Convention and thus excluding Iranians as refugees in Turkey. These had to be resettled as quota refugees in «third countries» upon presentation by UNHCR. Turkish authorities granted temporary «protection» on an «ad hoc» basis under the condition that they would all be received by «third countries». This meant great difficulties in Turkey for those who were not considered as refugees under the Statute of 1950, but who, nevertheless, could not or would not return to Iran.
367. See below, p. 151 and following.

For example, during the conflict between Kurdish groups and the authorities in Iraq in 1991, the UN created a security area[368] in Northern Iraq in order to protect the civilian population and to prevent an exodus of one million Kurdish refugees to Turkey. This international initiative came in the immediate aftermath of the Gulf war and was clearly motivated by the political interest on the part of Western powers in seeking to further curtail Saddam Hussein's power in the region. Nevertheless, the decision by the world community to defend the Kurdish population's basic right of survival was a new approach in the sense that Iraqi authorities had no way of refusing international «assistance». Until then, international humanitarian intervention has, as a rule, only taken place if the country in question has asked for it. This time it was the other way around. The world community asked to do it and the country could not refuse.

At the end of 1994, the conflict in the former Yugoslavia provided the background against which the UN again failed to effectively police and protect the «safe havens» of its own making. In this instance the UN peacekeeping force, UNPROFOR was unable to protect the civilian Bosnian population against Serb aggression in the UN protected areas, the most striking images of which emanated from the besieged enclave of Bihac. When the international community fails to such a degree that protected areas are no more than an illusion, it is fair to raise the question of whether such endeavours should ever be undertaken again unless sufficient human and economic resources are invested in the operation. The intervention of the international community for protection purposes, otherwise deteriorates into a gamble with human lives.

During the summer of 1994, French troops took a similar initiative in Rwanda for the protection of internally displaced persons and for repatriated refugees. In this instance, the principal political players in the region concerned, the Heads of state of Zaïre and Burundi, favoured and sought to create the conditions for the return of more than two million refugees to Rwanda and to this end proposed the creation of «protection areas» on Rwandan territory placed under UN control. In theory, this approach to dealing with the crisis appeared to be correct. However, in reality a very different scenario to the one envisaged unfolded, as refugee camps were attacked by Rwandan rebel groups with the support of the then opposition leader in Zaïre, Lawrence Kabila, who has since become the President of the now Democratic Republic of Congo. Allegations of war crimes committed by Kabila's soldiers are currently under UN investigation and the UN High Commissioner for Human Rights has not refrained from criticizing Kabila for lack of cooperation with

---

368. Resolution 688 of 5 April, 1991 of the Security Council.

these investigations.[369] When repatriation from the Democratic Republic of Congo to Rwanda began in November 1996, UNHCR and the High Commissioner for Human Rights initiated measures to ensure the safety of returning Rwandans by creating so-called «protection corridors» and stationing an international presence at points of entry to Rwanda. At the beginning of 1998, the number of refugees who remain hiding in the jungle in the Democratic Republic of Congo, is unknown.

UNHCR and the European Commission have criticized Kabila for not co-operating in the search for international solutions to the problems in the Great Lakes region which would enable Rwandan refugees to repatriate safely. In spite of such criticism, Kabila forcibly returned 800 Hutu refugees to Rwanda in September 1997, an act which according to UNHCR amounts to a violation of the non-refoulement principle and which therefore led the organization to suspend its operations in the country.[370] According to the High Commissioner, Ms. Ogata, the most basic conditions for protecting refugees in this instance had ceased to exist. According to the High Commissioner, UNHCR cannot protect refugees if the host governments do not abide by the principles and standards of law. Ms. Ogata received the support of the UN Security Council for her decision to suspend the activities of UNHCR in the region for the reason stated.[371]

The decision to suspend operations in the Great Lakes region was also endorsed by the Inter-Agency Standing Committee[372] chaired by the UN Emergency relief Coordinator, UN Department of Humanitarian Affairs (DHA). The Inter-Agency Committee expressed a grave concern over the erosion of respect for humanitarian principles and human rights which increasingly affects humanitarian operations in the Great Lakes region of Central Africa. While agreeing with the decision of UNHCR in the withdrawal of its assistance and protection activities in the Democratic Republic of Congo, the Inter-Agency Standing Committee nevertheless urged protection activities to be resumed, but only after having been given guarantees by Kabila's government that humanitarian principles would be respected and the security of staff ensured. Furthermore, the Inter-Agency Standing Committee, called

---

369. Newsweek, 6 October 1997, p. 12.
370. The High Commissioner for refugees informed the UN Security Council of this decision and its reasons on 9 September 1997.
371. NGO Coordination Unit, UNHCR, 19 September 1997.
372. The Committee comprises UN agency heads of the World Food Programme (WFP), UNHCR, UN Development Programme (UNDP), Food and Agriculture Organization (FAO), World Health Organization (WHO), and UN Children's Fund (UNICEF), as well as representatives of the International Organization for Migration, the Steering Committee for Humanitarian Response, InterAction, and the International Council of Voluntary Agencies (ICVA).

«…upon all parties in the region to ensure access to affected populations, the security of humanitarian workers and respect for human rights and international humanitarian law», in this statement on refugees, human rights, humanitarian law and principles in the Great Lakes region. As a prerequisite, it was also mentioned that UNHCR and other concerned humanitarian agencies and human rights observers must be permitted full access to repatriated refugees to ensure that their rights and safety are respected. [373]

Again, whether arranged on an «ad hoc» basis or whether institutionalized through UNHCR whilst carrying out its protection mandate, international protection in its varied forms has to be taken seriously by the world community at large, or else it does not work. Political will by each and every State actor is essential.

Protection must be based on principles of human rights and other principles of international law as well as on a shared sense of humanitarian responsibility. This having been said, it is also important to underline, that there are many reasons why international protection cannot depend solely on «ad hoc» solutions of various kinds, but must be firmly institutionalized both with an international agency, UNHCR, and in appropriate legal instruments by which States are legally bound on an equal basis. This is a founding philosophy of international public law. It may be wise also to acknowledge that beyond the nice and meaningful words of political statements, there is every reason to worry as «compassion fatigue» becomes synonomous with «protection fatigue».

5.2 Legal basis of the principle of non-refoulement
At the universal level

In international treaty law, the non refoulement principle has been incorporated into three different categories of conventions: Firstly, conventions for the protection of refugees,[374] secondly, extradition conventions,[375] and thirdly, conventions for the protection of human rights.[376]
Article 33 of the 1951 Convention stipulates that:

---

373. Inter-Agency Standing Committee, UN Department of Humanitarian Affairs, New York, 12 September 1997.
374. Article 33 of the 1951 Convention and Article II, paragraph 3 of the OAU Convention.
375. For example, Article 3 of the European Convention on Extradition of 1957.
376. For example, Article 3 of the Torture Convention of 1984 and Article 3 of the European Convention on Human Rights.

«No Contracting State shall expel or return ('refouler') a refugee in any manner whatsoever to the frontiers of territories where his life or freedom would be threatened on account of his race, religion, nationality, membership of a particular social group or political opinion».

According to the «travaux préparatoires» of the 1951 Convention, the difference in wording between Article 1A and Article 33 was not intended to introduce a stricter criterion. The reference in Atricle 33, «where his life or freedom would be threatened» was introduced to make it clear that the principle refers to not only the refugee's country of origin, but equally to any country where a person has reason to fear persecution.

Furthermore, at the universal level, the UN General Assembly[377] and the UNHCR Executive Committee have adopted numerous resolutions calling for respect for the non-refoulement principle and have repeatedly endorsed its fundamental character.[378] According to these resolutions, the non refoulement principle cannot be disregarded, either at the border or within the territory of a State, irrespective of whether the person concerned has been formally recognized as a convention refugee. For example, the Executive Committee Conclusion No. 22(XXXII) on protection of asylum seekers in situations of large-scale influx, states that «In all cases the fundamental principle of non-refoulement – including non-rejection at the frontier – must be scrupulously observed».[379]

Although «soft law» instruments such as these are not, as a starting point, considered mandatory, legally binding, they may nevertheless contribute to the creation of customary law.[380] Resolutions containing reference to the in-

---

377. For example, in Resolutions 44/137 of 1989, 45/140 of 1990, 47/105 of 1992, etc., all resolutions on the Office of the United Nations High Commissioner for Refugees.
378. See, first of all Executive Committee Conclusion No. 6 (XXVIII) on non-refoulement. Other examples of Executive Committee Conclusions in which the principle is referred to are: Conclusions No. 15 (XXX) on refugees without an asylum country adopted in 1979, Conclusions No. 19 (XXXI9 on temporary refuge in 1980, No. 22 (XXXII) on protection of asylum seekers in situations of large-scale influx in 1981, No. 58 (XL) on problem of refugees and asylum seekers who move in an irregular manner from a country in which they had already found protection in 1989, and further in i.a. the following General Conclusions No. 46 (XXXVIII) (1987), No. 50 (XXXIX) (1988), No. 55 (XL) (1989) and No. 65 (XLII) (1|991), No. 68 (XLIII) (1992).
379. Such is not always the case. Recent examples of refugees in mass-influx situations include Haitians being stopped by the US Coast Guard and Albanians being stopped by the Italian Coast Guard.
380. On the emergence of customary law from «soft law» instruments, see above, p. 38–42 and more specifically on non-refoulement as a customary rule of law, see below, p. 157–161.

violability of the non-refoulement principle are repetitious, a characteristic which proves that the international community has wished to reaffirm its importance time and again. The fact that the universal «soft law» instruments pertaining to the non-refoulement principle are imperative in their language further strengthens their authority. The universal «soft law» instruments are indeed an expression of international consensus on the inviolability of the principle. Furthermore, they provide guidelines for the interpretation of treaty law and its development. General adherence by States to the principle in practice, incorporation of the non-refoulement principle into national legislation and national case law also demonstrate the fundamental character of the principle and that States consider themselves legally bound by it.

A «soft law» instrument of particular importance in this regard and which is considered as having contributed to the evolution of asylum law,[381] is the UN Declaration on Territorial Asylum of 1967, which, according to its Article 3, prohibits both refoulement from a territory and non admission at a border by stating:

«No person referred to in Article 1, paragraph 1, shall be subjected to measures such as rejection at the frontier or, if he has already entered the territory in which he seeks asylum, expulsion or compulsory return to any State where he may be subjected to persecution».

International human rights law supplements the above mentioned instruments of refugee law. Article 3 of the Convention against Torture of 1984 stipulates that no State shall expel, return («refouler») or extradite a person to another State where there are substantial grounds for believing that he or she would be in danger of being subjected to torture. Article 7 of the International Covenant on civil and political rights has also been interpreted as prohibiting the return of persons to places where torture or persecution is feared.

As opposed to the universal refugee law instruments which foresee exceptions to the prohibition of refoulement,[382] the universal human rights instruments contain an absolute prohibition against refoulement. Regional human rights and refugee law instruments equally contain provisions which permit no derogation.

---

381. P. Weis, «The United Nations Declaration on Territorial Asylum», reprinted from «The Canadian Yearbook of International Law» 1969.
382. See below, p. 164–165.

At a regional level

Africa and Asia

At a regional level, the OAU Convention expresses the mandatory legal obligation of the non- refoulement principle. Its Article II(3) states:

«No person shall be subjected by a Member State to measures such as rejection at the frontier, return or expulsion, which would compel him to return to or remain in a territory where his life, physical integrity or liberty would be threatened for the reasons set out in Article I, paragraphs 1 and 2.»

The expanded refugee definition of the OAU Convention,[383] acknowledges that the beneficiaries of the non refoulement principle are both victims of persecution and victims of generalized violence. The principle is clear, but in Africa, as elsewhere, there are examples of violations of international refugee law. A recent example, as already mentioned, was the refoulement of Rwandan refugees from the Republic of Congo in September 1997 which caused UNHCR to suspend its activities there.[384]

Another reference to the non-refoulement principle is contained in the so called «Bangkok principles», adopted by the Asian-African Legal Consultative Committee in 1966 which state that:

«No one seeking asylum in accordance with these principles, should, except for overriding reasons of national security or safeguarding the populations, be subjected to measures such as rejection at the frontier, return or expulsion which would result in compelling him to return to or remain in a territory if there is a well-founded fear of persecution endangering his life, physical integrity or liberty in that territory».

It should be noted that Asian States have shown great reluctance in adhering to the 1951 Convention and no regional mandatory legal instrument for refugee protection exists. Refugee movements in Asia have caused protection problems where violation of the non-refoulement principle have occurred. This is, in other words, another region where initiatives should be taken for the development of a regional protection instrument modeled on the OAU Convention and the Cartagena Declaration.

The Americas

In Article 22(8) of the American Human Rights Convention of 1969, the non-refoulement principle is expressed in the following way:

«In no case may an alien be deported or returned to a country, regardless of whether or not it is his country of origin, if in that country his right to life or

---

383. See above, p. 103–107.
384. See above, p. 145.

personal freedom is in danger of being violated because of his race, nationality, religion, social status or political opinions.»

However, this provision did not prevent the U.S. practice of intercepting and forcibly repatriating Haitian refugees which dealt a severe blow to the respect of the non-refoulement principle. In June 1993, in the so called Haiti case»,[385] the U.S. Supreme Court, ruled by a majority of 8-1, that interception by the U.S. Coast Guard outside of U.S. territorial waters and the subsequent return of Haitian asylum seekers, including those who had good reason to fear persecution, was not a violation of the principle of non-refoulement and Article 33 of the 1951 Convention. The practice was regarded as taking place outside of U.S. territorial jurisdiction and therefore the non-refoulement principle was not seen to apply in this case; a viewpoint which does not have any bearing in international law. In March 1997, the Inter-American Commission on Human Rights pronounced disagreement with the U.S. Supreme Court's ruling and stated that U.S. practice had been in violation of the right to seek and receive security.[386] The practice was interpreted as contrary to the American Convention on Human Rights. The Supreme Court decision does not alter a State's international obligations and the principle of non-refoulement regulates State practice wherever it takes place.[387] This is equally in line with UNHCR's view.

In Latin America, the prohibition of refoulement is found in various instruments.[388] The Cartagena Declaration of 1984 is particularly explicit in emphasizing the importance of non-refoulement for the protection of refugees. Not only does it reaffirm the importance and the meaning of the non-refoulement principle, rejection at the frontier included, but it also describes it as the cornerstone of international protection of refugees. In the context of refugee protection, the Cartagena Declaration, recommends that the non-refoulement principle be acknowledged and observed as a rule of «jus cogens». Without attempting a discussion of the concept of «jus cogens» here, it should be noted that such a reference to an imperative norm adds great value to the general regional interpretation of the non-refoulement principle.

---

385. Acting Commissioner, Immigration and Naturalization Service, et al., petitioners versus Haitian Centers Council Inc., et al., to the United States Court of Appeals for the Second Circuit, 21 June 1993.
386. OAS Decision, The Haitian Center for Human Rights et al. V. U.S., Case 10-675, Report No. 51-96, Inter American Commission on Human Rights, OEA – SER.L– V – II. 95, Doc. 7 rev., p. 550, 1997.
387. G. Goodwin-Gill, «The Refugee in International Law», 1996, p. 143.
388. See for example the Treaty on International Penal Law of 23 January 1889 and the Convention on Diplomatic asylum of 28 March 1954.

Europe
The Council of Europe approach
To date, a mandatory European legal refugee instrument, containing the non-refoulement principle has not been adopted. However, the view of European States has been expressed on many occasions, in the countless resolutions and recommendations adopted by various organs of the Council of Europe, which have collectively affirmed a European commitment to the non-refoulement principle. Furthermore, the principle has been consolidated through the application of Article 3 of the European Convention on Human Rights.[389]

In 1961, the Consultative Assembly of the Council of Europe adopted Recommendation 293, on the right of asylum,[390] which recommended that the Committee of Ministers should take the initiative of including an article on the right of asylum in a second protocol to the European Convention on Human Rights. It also recommended the inclusion of an article on the non-refoulement principle in conformity with Article 33 of the 1951 Convention. The Recommendation was never carried out.

In 1965, the Consultative Assembly adopted Recommendation 434,[391] on the granting of the right of asylum to European refugees. It recommended that governments, while waiting for the elaboration of an international instrument designed to give full legal recognition to the practice of granting asylum, the Member States of the Council of Europe, should take immediate steps «…to guarantee refugees the right not to be returned to a country where they would be in danger of persecution (recognition of the principle of prohibition of return (non-refoulement))». The Assembly equally reminded governments that they should interpret the refugee concept «liberally» and referred to Recommendation E of the Conference of Plenipotentiaries to the 1951 Convention. Furthermore, the intention of the Consultative Assembly at that time, was to link the non-refoulement principle to Article 3 of the Convention on Human Rights.[392]

In 1967, the Committee of Ministers adopted Resolution (67)14, on asylum to persons in danger of persecution. The Resolution marked a significant

---

389. Other provisions of the European Human Rights Convention have equally been invoked in order to halt deportation cases such as Article 8 which includes the right to private and family life, Article 13 on the right to an «effective remedy before a national authority» in case of the violation of a person's fundamental rights and freedoms and very rarely, Article 4 on the prohibition of slavery, servitude and «forced or compulsory labour» and Article 5 on the right and liberty and security of person.
390. Adopted on 26 September 1961.
391. Adopted on 1 October 1965.
392. G. Stenberg, «Non-Expulsion and Non-Refoulement», p. 256.

breakthrough in European governmental thinking, because the representatives of the governments themselves, when referring to Article 3 of the Convention on Human Rights, urged member governments to do all that is possible to assure security and protection to persons in danger of persecution. In addition, it also recommended that governments should act in a «...particularly liberal and humanitarian spirit in relation to persons who seek asylum on their territory». Furthermore, and in the same spirit, they were called upon to»...ensure that no one shall be subjected to refusal of admission at the frontier, rejection, expulsion or any other measure which would have the result of compelling him to return to, or remain in, a territory where he would be in danger of persecution for reasons of race, religion, nationality, membership of a particular social group or political opinion». The principles of Resolution 67(14) were strengthened through the Declaration on Territorial Asylum, adopted by the Committee of Ministers in 1977, which made explicit reference to the provisions of this resolution. The principle of non-refoulement was further consolidated in Resolution No. R (84)1, adopted by the Committee of Ministers in 1984, which explicitly recognizes the non-refoulement principle as a general principle applicable to all persons. In other words, applicable regardless of whether or not a person is considered a Convention refugee.

In spite of numerous attempts by the Member States of the Council of Europe Parliamentary Assembly to promote the inclusion of the right to asylum in a protocol to the European Convention on Human Rights,[393] or to elaborate upon a separate European convention on territorial asylum,[394] little has so far been accomplished. However, the Assembly has continuously insisted on the prohibition of refoulement.[395]

The numerous recommendations by the Council of Europe Parliamentary Assembly which, as regards the non-refoulement principle, have been followed-up by the Committee of Ministers and confirmed by State practice, demonstrate that European States consider themselves as being under the obligation to respect the principle of non-refoulement. Moreover, the opinion and jurisprudence of the European Commission and of the European Court

---

393. For example in Recommendations 293 (1961), 1088 (1988) and 1236 (1994).
394. For example in Recommendations 842 (1978), 1016 (1985), 1088 (1988) and 1236 (1994).
395. For example in Recommendations 434 (1965) and 773 (1976). See also Recommendation 1237 (1994) on the situation of asylum seekers whose applications have been rejected in which the Parliamentary Assembly recommends to the Committee of Ministers to confer basic rights, as provided for in Conclusion No. 22 (XXXII) adopted by UNHCR's Executive Committee. (Conclusion No 22 refers to the non-refoulement principle as an absolute principle, applicable in all circumstances).

of Human Rights, have confirmed and further developed the fundamental character of the principle.

Article 3 of the European Convention on Human Rights
Article 3 of the European Convention on Human Rights states that: «No one shall be subjected to torture or inhuman or degrading treatment or punishment».

This is an imperative rule which, according to Article 15 of the European Convention on Human Rights, permits no derogation; not even in times of war or other public emergencies which threaten the life of a nation. Article 3 applies to any person, irrespective of the person's own citizenship, who finds himself within the jurisdiction of one of the Member States of the Council of Europe. It is therefore a rule which, in the refugee context, concerns not only 1951 Convention refugees, but equally «de facto» refugees and others who cannot return to an area where their life or security would be threatened.

In cases involving deportation, asylum seekers therefore invoke Article 3 and the European Commission of Human Rights has accepted the logic of its applicability on a number of occasions, as has the European Court of Human Rights.[396] The European Court of Human Rights has clearly proclaimed the relevance of Article 3 in relation to extradition or expulsion if the person being extradited, risks being submitted to torture, inhuman or

---

396. For a profound analysis, see M. Joao Madureira, «La jurisprudence des organes de la Convention européenne des Droits de l'Homme et la Charte sociale européenne concernant l'entrée et la sortie des étrangers du territoire d'un Etat», Colloquy «Droits de l'Homme sans Frontières», Strasbourg, 30 November – 1 December, 1989., H.D.M. Steenbergen, «The Relevance of the European Convention on Human Rights for Asylum Seekers», Studie-en informatiecentrum Mensenrechten, SIM Special, No. 11, 1991, p.45–68. For recent examples see: Petition No. 22408/93, H. versus Sweden which concerns an asylum applicant from the Middle-East who invoked the applicability of Article 3 in the case of expulsion; Petition No. 15658/89, Abdel-Qader Hussein Yassin Mansi versus Sweden which concerns a Jordanian asylum seeker (of Palestinian origin) expulsed in Jordan; Petitions No. 17550/90 and No. 17825/91, V. And P versus France which concerns an asylum applicant from Sri Lanka whose request had been refused (only the first case was declared admissible by the Commission). Petition No. 18560/91, S., N., and T. versus France concerning administrative detention in the international zone of an airport of three nationals of Sri Lanka, of Tamil origin, who deposited asylum requests and were later returned to Sri Lanka, even though the President of the European Commission declared it desirable to not return the applicants before the Commission had had the possibility of fully examining the request. Petition No. 21649/93, D. et al. versus Sweden concerning a family from Peru which was to be deported to the country of origin. This case was taken off the Commission's list when the family obtained a permanent residence permit.

degrading treatment in the country of destination. The Soering case of 7 July 1989[397] marks the beginning of such application of Article 3. In this case, the European Court of Human Rights found, that the extradition of a German citizen from Great Britain to the United States, where he risked the death penalty, constituted a violation of Article 3. It was not the death penalty in itself which would be contrary to Article 3, but the death row phenomenon was considered «inhuman punishment». The European Commission and Court of Human Rights require a certain level of gravity of «ill treatment» in order to consider a potential treatment as amounting to a risk of «torture», «inhuman», or «degrading treatment.[398] In fact, to date, only one Court decision, that of Aksoy versus Turkey in 1996, has explicitly found that there was an incidence of torture.[399] The assessment of a minimum level of «ill-treatment» under Article 3 depends on the circumstances of the case, the duration of treatment and its physical and mental effects.[400]

In 1991, the European Court of Human Rights ruled on the applicability of Article 3 in the Cruz Varas et al. case.[401] In this case, the Court confirmed that the ruling on extradition which derived from the Soering case, also should apply to expulsion decisions. However, in this particular case, it ruled that there was no violation of Article 3.[402]

---

397. The Soering case (i/1989/161/217), series A No. 161, of 7.VII.89, p. 35.
398. K. Hailbronner, «Non-refoulement and 'Humanitarian' Refugees: Customary International Law or Wishful Legal Thinking?», p.141. In this regard, see also G. Stenberg, «Non-Expulsion and Non-Refoulement», p. 206 and p. 219.
399. See the case of Aksoy versus Turkey of 18 December 1996. While the person concerned was kept in police custody, he was tortured in a way which, the Court ruled, must have caused severe pain at the time it was carried out and which had led to a lasting paralysis of both arms of the victim.
400. See, C. Ovey, «Prohibition of refoulement: The Meaning of Article 3 of the ECHR», ELENA, International Course on the European Human Rights Convention in Relation to Asylum», Strasbourg, 23–26 May 1997.
401. The Cruz Varas et al. case (46/1990/237/307), of 20 March 1991 concerns the members of a Chilean family who entered Sweden in 1987 as asylum seekers. They were refused asylum and expelled. Swedish authorities were asked to authorize a suspension before expelling the family. This was, however, not abided by.
402. In the Vilvarajah et al. case versus Great Britain in 1991, the Court no longer judged that it was a violation of Article 3 when the Sri Lankan applicants were expelled from Great Britain, case /457199072367302-306), 30 October, 1991.

It is worth noting, that in connection with this case, the Commission of Human Rights, in conformity with Rule 36 of the Rules of procedure of the European Commission of Human Rights, had, as in other cases, requested the expelling State (Sweden) to suspend the expulsion until the Commission had had an opportunity to examine the application.[403] The Swedish government did not comply with this request. The Court commented that if an expelling State decides not to comply with such a request by the Commission, it risks assuming the responsibility of violating Article 3 of the Human Rights Convention.

The non-compliance with a request by the Commission, to grant suspensive effect to a deportation order, until the Commission has had time to examine the case, provides the background for an interesting proposal made in 1997 by the Committee on Migration, Refugees and Demography of the Parliamentary Assembly of the Council of Europe. This Committee proposes that Rule 36 of the Rules of Procedure of the European Convention on Human Rights should be reformed to make it a mandatory obligation for signatory States.[404]

In the course of the 1990s, the European Court of Human Rights has made several rulings which have significantly contributed to the development of the interpretation of Article 3, with regard to the refoulement of asylum seekers and the absolute nature of Article 3. In the case of Ahmed versus Austria,[405] the European Court of human Rights found that the person concerned, if he were deported and returned to Somalia, which was in a state of civil war, would risk being subjected to treatment contrary to Article 3. With regard to the absolute nature of Article 3, this conclusion was upheld in spite of the fact that no State authority existed in Somalia at that time and that the fighting was a result of rival clans aiming at control of the country.

In the Chahal versus the United Kingdom case,[406] an Indian national was about to be deported to India because it was claimed that he had been involved in terrorist activities and therefore posed a risk to the national security of the United Kingdom. Although the Court expressed an understanding of the difficulties faced by States, with regard to terrorist activities on their territory, it nevertheless found that the prohibition against torture, inhuman or

---

403. The Cruz Vargas case, (46/1990/237/307), p.19, paragraph 53. Article 36 of the internal regulation is used in the only cases in which it is established that the application of the measure would result in irreparable damage. This may include the hypothesis of an imminent expulsion or extradition, if the person affirms that he would probably receive treatment contrary to Article 2 or 3 of the Convention in the State of destination.
404. Draft report, AS/PR (1997) 2 revised of 19 February 1997.
405. Judgement of 17 December 1996.
406. Judgement of 15 November 1996.

degrading treatment, is absolute, irrespective of a person's conduct. In the opinion of the Court, therefore, Chahal could not be returned.

According to the second paragraph of Article 33 of the 1951 Convention, a State would not necessarily be obliged to protect a refugee against refoulement, if he were seen as posing a threat to the security of the country. In other words, the protection offered by Article 3 of the Human Rights Convention is absolute and therefore goes further than the universal principle of non-refoulement contained in the 1951 Convention which permits derogation under certain circumstances.[407]

The practice which has been described offers reassurance as regards European interpretation of the non-refoulement principle. However, it should be kept in mind that very few cases are brought before the bodies of the Council of Europe pertaining to the European Convention of Human Rights compared to the total number of asylum seekers and refugees who are being deported, or who risk deportation, from European countries every day. In order to ensure effective European refugee protection, the need for a European refugee convention which, i.a. incorporates a supplementary refugee definition and a non-refoulement principle which covers all refugees according to this expanded definition, is required.

The European Union approach
In various instruments adopted or elaborated upon in the European Union context, Member States of the European Union refer to the non-refoulement principle as a mandatory principle. In this regard reference is made to Article 33 of the 1951 Convention, Article 3 of the European Convention of Human Rights and other human rights instruments, for example Article 3 of the Torture Convention of 1984.

One example of such an EU instrument is the Resolution on a Harmonized approach to questions concerning host third countries,[408] adopted in 1992 in relation to the Dublin Convention. Another example is the 1995 EU Resolution on Minimum Guarantees for Asylum Procedures.[409] In spite of the references to the non-refoulement principle, the question remains whether, while applying instruments like those mentioned, the EU Member States do actually take all necessary precautions. For example, while applying the «safe third country concept» according to the 1992 Resolution and the Dublin Convention, there is an inherent risk of violating the non-refoulement principle.[410] Therefore, before a refugee is returned to another State

---

407. On exceptions, see below, p. 164.
408. Adopted by the Ministers of the Member States of the European Communities responsible for Immigration, in London 30 November 1992.
409. Adopted by the European Council on 20 June 1995.

which is considered responsible for the examination of the asylum request, the sending State must ensure that the refugee does not risk a chain deportation and thereby in the worst scenario, refoulement.

It should be noted that in its 1997 proposal to the Council for a Joint Action based on Article K.3 2(b) of the Treaty on the European Union, concerning Temporary protection of Displaced Persons, the European Commission aims at introducing a protection regime for persons who are in need of international protection, owing to armed conflict, persistent violence, systematic or widespread human rights abuses. Even though the Council proposal does not specifically refer to the non-refoulment principle, it is evident that it is indeed this principle which underpins the endeavour to reach agreement among the fifteen Member States of the European Union regarding a protection regime for those who are not considered covered by the 1951 Convention. Equally, it is the non-refoulement principle that lies behind the safeguard mechanisms, proposed in order to evaluate the appropriate moment for lifting the temporary protection regime. According to the proposed Article 4, return of the persons concerned can only take place «...if the situation in the country of origin allows a safe return under humane conditions». The outcome in the Council of the Commission's initiative is impossible to predict.

In conclusion, EU Member States' harmonization of refugee and asylum policy and their explicit reference to the non-refoulement principle is in itself a good sign which shows, that as «law makers», these States are conscious of the importance of the principle as it is laid down in various instruments of refugee law and human rights law. However, the same consciousness is not always reflected in practice. As will be discussed under Chapter 7, for example, in the context of the «safe third country concept», there are still legal safeguards which need to be adopted in order to ensure full adherence to the non-refoulement principle when EU instruments are being applied.

5.3 Legal developments of the principle of non-refoulement

From treaty law to customary law

The question relating to an evolution of the non-refoulement principle as it is contained in treaty law into customary law, remains controversial as does the question regarding the scope of the principle. Legal theory on the subject reflects two schools of thought. Some commentators acknowledge only the

---

410. For more details on the application of the «safe third country» concept, see below, Chapter 7.

conventional character of the principle, of which the most puritan view is that it relates only to Article 33 of the 1951 Convention.[411] Strictly speaking, this would signify two things. Firstly, that only States which have ratified the 1951 Convention are obliged to respect the non-refoulement principle and, secondly, that only 1951 Convention refugees are protected against refoulement. Other commentators regard the principle of non-refoulement as a legal obligation deriving both from treaty law (refugee law and human rights law), as well as from State practice. According to this view, the principle of non-refoulement has evolved into a principle of customary law[412] which implies that all States have a legal obligation to respect the non-refoulement principle and that all refugees are its beneficiaries.

In order to assess the fundamental character and the scope of the non-refoulement principle, it should always be kept in mind that refugee law cannot be interpreted without reference to international human rights instruments. It must also be kept in mind, that where universal refugee law sets barriers, for example by application of the «exclusion clauses» of the 1951 Convention[413] or allows for exceptions to the non-refoulement principle,[414] the human rights instruments allow no derogation if returning a person signifies that his life or security would be threatened. In other words, in the absence of a refugee status, a person can still not be returned according to the non-refoulement principle as contained in the human rights instruments.

---

411. For example, K. Hailbronner, who contends that the lack of State practice and of significant «opinio juris» makes it unrealistic to suggest that the non-refoulement principle forms part of customary international law, K. Hailbronner, «Non-refoulement and «Humanitarian» Refugees: Customary International Law or Wishful Legal Thinking», p. 123-124. In 1972, A. Grahl-Madsen asserted, that in spite of repeated calls by the UN General Assembly, urging respect for the principle of non-refoulement, the principle was still not considered as having attained general acceptance, see A. Grahl-Madsen, «The Status of Refugees in International Law», Vol. II, 1972, p. 94 and onwards. Ten years later, however, he asserted that the scrupulous respect for the non-refoulement principle should clearly be considered as a rule engraved in international law, binding on all law-abiding States, see A. Grahl-Madsen, «Refugees and Refugee Law in a World of Transition» in «Transnational Legal Problems of Refugees», Michigan Yearbook of International Legal Studies, 1982, p.72.
412. See e.g. G. Stenberg, «Non-Expulsion and Non-Refoulement», p.288; K. Hailbronner, «Non-refoulement and Humanitarian Refugees: Customary International Law or Wishful Thinking», p.129; and G. Goodwin-Gill, The Refugee in International law», 1996, p. 123. See, E. Zoller, «Le droit d'asile», p. 32 and P. Weis, «The United Nations Declaration on Territorial Asylum», p. 143 and 144. However, both authors indicate that the non-refoulement principle does not apply as a customary norm in mass-influx situations.
413. See above, p. 89–94.
414. Article 33(2) of the 1951 Convention, see below, p. 164–165.

5.3 LEGAL DEVELOPMENTS OF THE PRINCIPLE OF NON-REFOULEMENT

In cases in which persons risk torture or other forms of inhuman or degrading treatment, if refouled, the fundamental quality of the non-refoulement principle is indisputable.[415] The prohibition of torture as a fundamental principle of international law, has been incorporated into numerous international instruments and was considered a universal customary rule of international law long before it was finally consolidated in a «lex specialis» instrument, the Torture Convention of 1984. It should also be noted that the Torture Convention offers the right of individual petition, to which individuals who risk being deported to a country where they fear being submitted to torture can refer, provided the sending country has accepted the responsibility of individual petition. The Convention therefore established a Committee against Torture, whose function is to determine whether there are substantial grounds for believing that a person would be in danger of being subjected to torture. If this is the case, the Committee has the right to pronounce that the State party has an obligation to refrain from forcibly returning the person in question.[416] In spite of the fact that there have been few cases and that not all signatory States have adhered to the right of individual petition, the Committee against Torture, nevertheless constitutes a supplementary international body whose aim is also to ensure the protection of refugees.

The customary status of the principle of non-refoulement remains controversial in international legal doctrine.[417] Some authors consider that the non-refoulement principle does not form part of universal customary law, but is a norm «in statu nascendi» and that it only constitutes customary regional law in Western Europe, the Americas and Africa.[418] It has been alleged that the fact that States do not return refugees to territories where they risk persecution, does not necessarily imply that they consider themselves to be legally obliged not to do so and therefore «opinio juris» is lacking.[419]

---

415. K. Hailbronner, «Nonrefoulement and 'Humanitarian' Refugees: Customary International Law or Wishful Legal Thinking», p. 124, cf. p. 140 and after. See equally, E. Zoller, «Le droit d'asile», p. 27.
416. See for example, Committee against Torture concerning Communication No. 41/1996 CAT/C/16/D/41/1996, Ms. Pauline Muzonzo Paku Risoki versus Sweden. The case concerned a Zairian citizen who had sought refugee status in Sweden claiming that her forced return to Zaïre would constitute a violation by Sweden of Article 3 of the Convention against Torture. Another similar example and in which the Committee against Torture drew the same conclusion, is that of Motumbo versus Switzerland, Communication No. 13/1993, CAT/C/12/D/13/1993.
417. G. Stenberg, «Non-Expulsion and Non-Refoulement», p. 288.
418. W. Kälin, «Das Prinzip des Non-refoulement», p. 353; K. Hailbronner, «Nonrefoulement and 'Humanitarian' Refugees: Customary International Law or Wishful Legal Thinking», p. 129; G. Stenberg, «Non-Expulsion and Non-Refoulement», p. 288.

Asian and Middle-Eastern States, and until recently all of the Eastern European States, have expressed that without certain qualifications, they do not consider themselves bound by the non-refoulement principle. For example, during the negotiations of the UN Declaration on Territorial Asylum in 1967, these same States declared that the non-refoulement principle should not be considered as having legal, but only moral consequences for them.[420]

This declaration should be considered in the context of today's interpretation, thirty years after its adoption. International endeavours in the field of refugee and human rights law and State practice since then cannot be disregarded. Even so, it must also be acknowledged that even today, there exists no consensus among States concerning their legal obligations with regard to the limits of the non-refoulement principle.

The majority of present day refugees are refugees who have fled their countries, often in situations of mass exodus, in order to escape from civil war, military occupation and human rights violations. According to K. Hailbronner, it is a mistake to assume that despite State practice and domestic legislation in Western countries, the non-refoulement principle should be considered as having been extended to apply to every «humanitarian refugee». Moreover, Hailbronner maintains that State practice should not be confused with the extended mandate of UNHCR and the development of «soft law».[421] It must be acknowledged that indivdual State practice, domestic legislation, UNHCR's extended mandate, etc., do not necessarily signify that an international customary norm has been established. However, when all these developments, both at the universal level and at a regional level, are assessed as a whole, the argument is no longer valid. The strength of the claim that the non-refoulement principle has developed into a customary norm lies precisely in the fact that so many legal developments have taken place and consistently so over a long period of time. This is reflected in State practice (legislative, administrative and judicial) and in international jurisprudence as well as in the adoption of numerous international «soft law» instruments on refugee protection together with the development of human rights law. The fact that most of today's refugees are «de facto» refugees strengthens rather than weakens the argument. In principle, the 1951 Convention offers adequate protection to those who are to be considered Convention refugees. It is in order to offer adequate protection to other refugees that a legal development has taken place. Adequate protection for «de facto» refugees cannot but encompass respect of the non-refoulement principle. Refugee law and refugee

---

419. See, W. Kälin, Ibid, p. 352 and K. Hailbronner, Ibid, p. 123 and 124.
420. W. Kälin, Ibid.
421. K. Hailbronner, «Non-refoulement and «Humanitarian» Refugees: Customary International Law or Wishful Legal Thinking», p, 123-124 and 130.

protection would be meaningless otherwise as would the fundamental belief that international law does develop.

Against this background, notwithstanding the controversy which still exists, it seems realistic to claim that the non-refoulement principle has developed into customary international law at the universal level in cases in which return of a refugee would put him at risk of torture or of violations of other fundamental human rights from which no derogation is permitted. As regards the regional level, as far as Europe, Africa and Latin-America are concerned, the customary norm of the non-refoulement principle must be interpreted in conjunction with the interpretation of «who is a refugee».[422] The proposed definition for a new European refugee convention, draft Article 1 provides the answer to who is in need of protection and therefore for whom refoulement must be prohibited.[423]

5.4 Particular aspects related to the non-refoulement principle

Non-rejection at the border

In practice, States usually allow refugees to enter when they present themselves at the border, but this is not without exception. Access to a territory as well as access to asylum procedures, at least access on a temporary basis, is a fundamental part of refugee protection. Asylum applicants at the border, be it on an individual or group basis should be considered in need of protection until the opposite can be proved.

If the non-refoulement principle is to have sense, it must therefore apply irrespective of whether persons have yet been formally recognized as refugees. Access to the territory is therefore a logical consequence of this. Access to the territory is also a logical follow-up to refugees' right to seek asylum in accordance with Article 14 of the Universal Declaration of Human Rights.[424] Indeed, in order for the 1951 Convention itself to make sense, refugees must have access to refugee determination procedures which implies that they must have had access to the territory of a State in the first place. According to this view, refusal of admittance at the border could be interpreted as a violation of the whole meaning of the 1951 Convention, notably, for States to offer protection to refugees.

Article 33 of the 1951 Convention was incorporated as a safeguard for the life and security of refugees. It does not, however, contain any explicit in-

---

422. See above, Chapter 3 and 4.
423. See below, Chapter 8.
424. See below, p. 172–173.

structions regarding an obligation not to refuse admission at the border. As Article 33 is meant to prevent the return of refugees to countries where they risk persecution, protection should not depend on the fact of whether or not they have succeeded in physically crossing the border.[425]

With the adoption of the Declaration on Territorial Asylum, in 1967, the international community took an explicit step forward in the interpretation of the non-refoulement principle to include the prohibition of rejection at the border in Article 3. However, in 1977, during the Conference for the establishment of a Convention on Territorial Asylum,[426] the opposite viewpoint was expressed as it was impossible to reach agreement concerning an automatic right to entry.[427]

Following this failure, UNHCR's Executive Committee adopted Conclusion No. 6 (XXVIII) on non-refoulement in 1977. This conclusion confirms the «...fundamental importance of the observance of the principle of non-refoulement – both at the border and within the territory of a State».[428] At a regional level, both the OAU Convention and the Cartagena Declaration specifically emphasize that refoulement, means that both rejection at the frontier and return or expulsion from the territory, is prohibited. A similar interpretation of the non-refoulement principle is found in the European context, for example in the Council of Europe's Resolution 14 (1967) on asylum to persons in danger of persecution.[429]

In general, the opinion of legal doctrine today accepts that non-refusal at the border is covered by the non-refoulement principle,[430] but it cannot be ignored that such an acceptance is not without dispute. [431]

States hesitate about obligations to allow the entry of persons on to their territory. This is especially so in view of developments in connection with the application of the «first country of asylum»/«safe third country» concept.[432]

---

425. P. Weis, «Territorial Asylum», 1966, p. 183.
426. See below, p. 176–179.
427. E. Zoller, «The Right of Asylum», p. 31
428. Adopted during the Committee's 28th session.
429. See also Recommandation 773 (1976) in which the Parliamentary Assembly of the Council of Europe explicitly invites governments not to refuse admission. In recommendation 953 (1982) the Assembly also recommends that in large-scale influx situations, asylum seekers should be admitted at least on a temporary bases. This equally implies non-refusal at the border.
430. See G. Stenberg, «Non-Expulsion and Non-Refoulement», p. 200–201; G. Goodwin-Gill, «The Refugee in International Law», p.87 and «Non-Refoulement and the New Asylum seekers» in «The New Asylum Seekers: Refugee Law in the 1980's», Martinus Nijhoff Publishers, 1988, p.105. See also O. Kimminich, «Völkerrechtlige und gründgesetzliche Grenzen der Asylrechtsreform», in Fortschritt im Bewusstsein der Grund-und Menschenrechte, Festschrift für Felix Ermacora, N.P. Engels Verlag, Kehl am Rhein, 1988, p.397.

Thus there is a need for legal clarification in this context. This and other aspects concerning non-refoulement must be incorporated into the proposal for a new regional protection instrument.[433]

Non-expulsion and non-extradition

Article 33 of the 1951 Convention includes an explicit reference to non-expulsion of a refugee and Article 32 emphasizes that States may not expel refugees except for reasons of national security.

Non-extradition, on the other hand, is not specifically mentioned. The essential difference between expulsion and extradition is that whereas expulsion concerns the execution of an order to leave the country, extradition signifies transfer from one jurisdiction to another. One could consider that non-extradition is a logical consequence of the non-refoulement principle, but the opinion of States is not unanimous in this respect.[434]

The right of extradition forms a fundamental part of the sovereignty of a State. Extradition is, nevertheless, widely regulated in extradition treaties and generally regarded in national penal law as an intergovernmental mutual assistance institution. At a universal level, no conventional law exists but at a regional level, the issue is more widely regulated.[435] For example, as recently

---

431. For example, in 1953, N. Robinson, in his commentary on the 1951 Convention, declared that no State is obliged to accept a refugee at the border, N. Robinson, «Convention Relating to the Status of Refugees», p. 163. Similarly, A. Grahl-Madsen and K. Hailbronner both assert that the non-refoulement principle concerns only those who are already present in the territory of a State. See, A. Grahl-Madsen, «The Status of refugees in International Law», Vol. II, p. 94; and K. Hailbronner, «Non-refoulement and «Humanitarian» Refugees: Customary International Law or Wishful Thinking?», p. 128,
432. See below, Chapter 7.
433. See below, Chapter 8 containing the proposed new European Convention, draft Article 4.
434. G. Goodwin-Gill, «The Refugee in International Law», 1983, p.81.
435. For example, in the Inter- American Convention on Extradition, Article 13, which states: «No provision of this Convention should be interpreted as a limitation on the right of asylum as long as it is applicable». In Recommandation R (80)9 of the Committee of Ministers of the Council of Europe on extradition to the non-party states of the European Convention on Human Rights of 1950, it was recommended to government to not permit extradition in the case in which there exists substantial reasons to believe that article 3 (2) of the European Convention on Extradition of 1957 is applicable. On the universal level, the non-extradition principle for political offenses is not part of the Geneva Convention, but the UNHCR Executive Committee declared itself on the matter, in Conclusion No. 17 (XXI) adopted in 1980 during the 31st session in 1980, which stipulates that a refugee should not be extradited to territories in which he fears persecution for reasons enumerated in the definition of the 1951 Convention.

as 1996, Member States of the European Union signed a Convention relating to extradition between Member States of the EU.[436]

With respect to extradition for political offenses, it could be argued that State practice has contributed to an expansion of the interpretation of the non-refoulement principle, to cover non-extradition of refugees.[437] There may be reason to be more cautious. In spite of the clear tendency by States to extend the non refoulement principle to include non-extradition there is still an absence of international unanimity.[438]

Exceptions to the principle of non-refoulement

The non-refoulement principle as contained in Article 33 of the 1951 Convention is not absolute in character. Article 33, second paragraph, permits derogation of the principle in circumstances in which there are serious grounds for regarding a refugee as «... a danger to the security of the country in which he is, or who, having been convicted by a final judgment of a particularly serious crime, constitutes a danger to the community of that country».

It is within the jurisdiction of the host country to decide if a refugee constitutes a danger. There is therefore a risk that a given country may invoke this paragraph in order to relieve itself of refugees who create difficulties for other reasons. A situation where this may be the case is, for example, when the acceptance of certain refugees has political ramifications for the diplomatic relations between the host country and the country of origin.

In order to prevent States from taking their own political interest into consideration when they consider using Article 33, second paragraph, a certain degree of proportionality in the application of the article is required. Such proportionality relates to, on the one hand, the risk a refugee would be exposed to in case of return and, on the other hand, the risk a country of asylum runs if it keeps him in its territory. If, upon return, a person risks becoming the victim of violations of non-derogable human rights principles, such as being subjected to torture or to slavery, the second paragraph of Article 33 must not be applied.

---

436. Signed by the Ministers of Justice and Home Affairs of the EU on 27 September 1996 in Dublin.
437. J. Swieconek considers that such is the case, see «Souveraineté territoriale et asile», p.16. See also P.J. van Krieken, «Torture or Asylum», Israel Yearbook on Human Rights, Vol. 16, 1986, p.144 in which he states that the non-refoulement principle prevails over any other obligation, including an extradition treaty.
438. See, G. Goodwin-Gill, «The Refugee in International Law», p. 78 and 79; and E. Zoller, «The Right of Asylum», 1989, p.37.

States have referred to «danger to the security of the country» in connection with mass influx situations. In 1991, for example, Turkey referred to national security when Iraqi Kurds crossed the border from Iraq and if the international community had not interfered, the border would have remained closed.

The 1951 Convention does not explicitly distinguish between situations involving individual arrival and those involving mass influx. The fact that the authors of the 1951 Convention were mainly concerned with individual persecution, should, however, not preclude the taking into account of contemporary situations involving mass influx. In this context, it should also be remembered that Recommendation E of the Final Act of the Conference of Plenipotentiaries, expressed the hope that the 1951 Convention could have «value as an example» and thus exceed the contractual scope of the Convention. This line of thought conforms with UNHCR's Executive Committee Conclusion No. 22 (XXXII), concerning protection of asylum seekers in situations of large-scale influx, which states that the principle of non-refoulement must be scrupulously observed in all cases.[439]

However, the UN Declaration on Territorial Asylum of 1967 states, in its Article 2, second paragraph, that «Exception may be made to…» the non-refoulement principle «…only for overriding reasons of national security or in order to safeguard the population, as in the case of a mass influx of persons». Some commentators refer to this Declaration while considering that States are not obliged to guarantee temporary refuge to refugees in a mass influx situation, and that if they do, then it is based on humanitarian considerations rather than legal obligations.[440]

It should be kept in mind that thirty years have passed since the adoption of the UN Declaration on Territorial Asylum of 1967. Indeed, the wording of the Declaration of 1967 and the second paragraph of Article 33 of the 1951 Convention should be regarded as being out of date because most contemporary refugee crises concern situations of mass exodus. It is also worth noting that at the regional level, the OAU Convention and the Cartagena Declaration permit no derogation of the non-refoulement principle. These instruments, as well as UNHCR's Executive Committee Conclusion No. 22 (XXXII), should be the model for a new European refugee convention.

---

439. Adopted during the 32nd session of the UNHCR's Executive Committee in 1981. This point of view is in conformity with the Report of the International Institute of Humanitarian Law, «Round Table» on the problems relative to large flows of asylum seekers, San Remo, June 1981, p.2.
440. E. Zoller, «Le droit d'asile», p. 27 and p. 32. See also P. Weis, «The United Nations Declaration on Territorial Asylum», p. 143 and 144.

5.5 Proposal in part for a new European convention on refugee protection

Against the background of the previous chapters, a new European instrument must contain specific clarification regarding the scope of the non-refoulement principle. The evaluation of the non-refoulement principle is of importance in many situations, for example, when refugees are being refused access to asylum procedures on «first country of asylum» grounds, [441] when repatriation after a period of temporary protection is being evaluated, when an asylum application is rejected and the asylumseeker is about to be returned to his country of origin, when a war breaks out and large numbers of the population approach the border of a neighbouring country, etc. The application of the non-refoulement principle is the fundamental safeguard of refugee protection and it is unacceptable that the scope of State responsibility remains unclear.

To this effect, a new European Convention would have to contain the following provisions relating to the non-refoulement principle:[442]

Draft Article 4 NON-REFOULEMENT

No person claiming to be a refugee shall be subjected to measures such as rejection at the frontier or, if he has already entered the territory, return, expulsion or extradition which would compel him to return to or remain in a territory where his life, physical integrity or safety would be threatened for the reasons set out in Article 1.[443]

As can be seen in the wording of this provision, the language is modeled on Article II (3) of the OAU Convention. The concept of «non-extradition» has, however, been added. Draft Article 4 should be read with draft Article 1 of the proposed European refugee convention, which contains the expanded refugee definition. With this link, the non-refoulement principle would apply to every person in need of international protection. It also applies regardless of whether the refugee is at the frontier or in the territory of a State.

Draft Article 4 is an absolute rule as suggested in UNHCR's Executive Committee Conclusion No. 22 (XXXII), no derogation is permissible, either for reasons of national security or for reasons of mass influx.

---

441. See below, p. 250–251.
442. See the full text of the proposed Convention below, Chapter 8.
443. On the proposed Article 1, see above p. 133–135.

Draft Article 5 REPATRIATION

(1) Repatriation may take place when circumstances in the country of origin allow for it to take place in safety and dignity. Due regard must be given to principles of international law – civil and political rights as well as economic, social and cultural rights. Before repatriation takes place, UNHCR should be consulted and the organization should play a coordinating role in cooperation with regional organizations.

(2) The provisions of the preceeding paragraph shall not be applied to any person who can invoke compelling reasons arising out of previous persecution or other circumstances. The personal circumstances of the person concerned must be taken into account.

Draft Article 5 of the proposed European Convention, also relates to the principle of non-refoulement, in the sense that when it refers to repatriation as a solution, it stipulates that repatriation cannot take place unless the situation in the country of origin is such that return can take place in safety and dignity. In order to ensure international cooperation and harmonization in matters of repatriation, UNHCR is given a clear consulting and coordination role. The reference to «regional organizations» is included to allow for an opening for the institutional knowledge which regional institutions have.[444]

The expression «in safety and dignity», implies two points. Firstly, it implies the existence of a safeguard, with respect to the physical well-being of the person, in other words the protection of his life and security and secondly, the existence of a safeguard, with respect to certain minimum socio-economic conditions, which must prevail in the country to which the person is being returned. This concept is difficult to incorporate in absolute terms, because it is dependent on certain conditions which need to be met, conditions which differ from one situation to another and from one culture to another. What is important, however, is that there are two sets of human rights, both civil and political rights as well as social, economic and cultural rights which are emphasised and taken into consideration. This explains the reference in draft Article 5.

The second paragraph of draft Article 5 is modeled largely on the cessation clause in the second paragraph of Article 1(C)(6) of the 1951 Convention.[445] In addition to past occurrences, such as previous persecution or treatment which would make it inhumane to request a person to return,

---

444. See further on this below under the discussion on temporary asylum, p. 191 and following.
445. See above, p. 87–89.

other personal reasons should also be taken into consideration before a person is compelled to leave. Such reasons could include, for example, family links, assimilation in a host society or prolonged stay. Sometimes such circumstances are impossible to foresee and it is therefore appropriate not to make an exhaustive list of examples but rather to leave this clause open for interpretation.

The non refoulement principle is of fundamental importance in connection with the application of the «first country of asylum»/«safe third country» concept which is dealt with in draft Article 8 of the proposed new refugee convention.[446]

---

446. This provision will be discussed under Chapter 7, see p. 273–280.

CHAPTER 6
Asylum

Due to fear of relinquishing part of their sovereignity, States have always reacted reluctantly when faced with efforts to develop international law concerning the admission of foreigners to their territory. One example of this is evident in the fact that the 1951 Convention does not contain any provision of substantive law on asylum.[447] This is a serious flaw of the 1951 Convention. Another example of State reluctance in this matter, was the failure of the 1977 UN Conference of Plenipotentiaries to establish an international instrument on territorial asylum. Such a state of affairs is evident in the fact that that nearly fifty years after the adoption of the 1951 Convention, there is still no universal rule concerning an obligation to grant asylum to refugees. The issue of the right to asylum was addressed in 1949 when the UN Commission of International Law included the issue on its agenda for discussion with a view to creating conventional law on the topic.[448] One proposal was to include the right to asylum in the International Covenant on Civil and Political Rights of 1966, but the initiative failed.

The legal lacuna on the right to asylum still exists, in spite of efforts to the contrary and in spite of the fact that States have recognized the right to grant asylum at their own discretion, and that many have accepted that they even have a duty to do so.[449] The lack of a right to asylum is a deficiency, which could be overcome through an initiative, whereby the right to asylum becomes an appropriate part of international law, preferably at the universal level. Such an initiative could occur as a logical progression of continuing re-

---

447. The Preamble of the 1951 Convention does, however, contain a reference to «asylum» when acknowledging that the institution may place unduly heavy burdens on some States which calls for international cooperation in the field of refugee protection. See also Recommendation D of the Final Act of the Conference of Plenipotentiaries on «International cooperation in the field of asylum and resettlement» in which the authors of the Convention recommend that «…Governments continue to receive refugees in their territories and that they act in concert in a true spirit of international cooperation in order that these refugees may find asylum and the possibility of resettlement».
448. In this regard, see also M. Garcia-Mora, «International Law and Asylum as a Human Right», Public Affairs Press, Washington D.C., 1956, p.3.
449. E.Zoller, «Le droit d'asile», Académie de droit international de La Haye, Martinus Nijhoff, 1990, p.16.

gional endeavours, such as the proposed new European refugee convention. When considering the right to asylum, two considerations have to be taken into account. Firstly, there needs to be a balance between the protection needs of refugees on the one hand, and the need for States to control who enters their territory, for which purpose and for how long, on the other. Secondly, the establishment of a right to asylum necessitates a discussion on its content, with regard to protection needs. This leads to an acknowledgment of the need for asylum on a permanent basis, in some cases, and asylum on a temporary basis in others.

In order to explore the concept of asylum and its requirements, an assessment of the present status of the institution of asylum needs to be made. The assessment must also include endeavours which have been made, but which have failed.

At the universal level, provisions relating to asylum are found in the Universal Declaration of Human Rights and in other instruments which are not mandatory in character, the most important of which is the UN Declaration on Territorial Asylum of 1967. The General Assembly has also repeatedly asked governments to respect the non-refoulement principle and to grant asylum.[450] At a regional level, Latin America has progressed further than other regions, in the development of asylum law. One particularity of this region which has had a certain influence elsewhere, is also the institution of diplomatic asylum.[451]

At the national level, the right to asylum and State duty to grant it, has been incorporated into constitutions and domestic legislation.[452] Convention refugee status is often a prerequisite for asylum.[453] However, this generosity in domestic law, as opposed to the lack of it in international law has not created a customary international norm with regard to State responsibility to

---

450. For example, in the following resolutions: 36/125 of 14 December 1981, 37/195 of 18 December 1982, 40/118 of 13 December 1985 and 45/140 of December 1990.
451. See above, p. 139–141.
452. France, for example, is among the States which have incorporated the right of asylum in their constitutions. The Preamble of the Constitution of the Fourth Republic states that any man persecuted on account of his action in favour of liberty, has the right to asylum in the territory of the Republic. See J.Y. Carlier, «L'état du droit international», p.45. In Norway, the alien's legislation contains a provision which stipulates that refugees in the sense of the 1951 Convention have the right to asylum. For a listing of different constitutions and national legislation in this respect see «Asile en Europe, Guide à l'intention des associations pour la protection des réfugiés», Editorial: ECRE and France Terre d'Asile, 1990, «Asylum in Europe-an Introduction», London, April 1993 and ECRE, «Review of Refugee and Asylum Procedures in Selected Countries», Vol. II, London, October 1994. See also R. Plender, «International Migration law», 1988, p.404–411.

grant asylum. It could be argued that States grant asylum as a principle of law in their domestic legislation and for humanitarian reasons, but that States do not consider themselves mutually bound by international obligations.[454] This is in line with G. Goodwin-Gill's assertion that despite the existence of humanitarian practice, a sense of obligation is missing.[455]

The following section will examine the institution of asylum in light of existing international instruments, conventional law and «soft law». Based on the need for international clarification and harmonization, the right to asylum must be seen as an important part of the proposal for a new European protection convention.

6.1 Asylum at the universal level

When UNHCR was established, the General Assembly of the UN called on governments to cooperate with the organization, by admitting refugees to their territories.[456] Asylum as such was not specifically mentioned, but implied.[457] According to the «travaux préparatoires» of the 1951 Convention, efforts had been made during the Conference of Plenipotentiaries to introduce a provision on entry into the territory of a State, but this attempt failed. However, the reference to asylum in the preamble of the 1951 Convention demonstrates the recognition of the institution of asylum as a consequence of refugee status, but otherwise the right to asylum is, as already indicated, left entirely to the discretion of each State.

Due to its protection role UNHCR advises States on their asylum practice. Examples of issues of major importance brought forward by UNHCR include the importance of the institution of asylum as a fundamental form of international protection, the necessity of respecting the right to seek asylum as it is enshrined in the Universal Declaration of Human Rights, access to territory and to refugee determination procedures and the obligation to respect the non-refoulement principle.

---

453. P. Weis, «Recent Developments in the Law of Territorial Asylum, Revue des Droits de l'Homme, Vol. I, No. 3, 1968, p.14 and E.W. Vierdag, « 'Asylum' and 'Refugee' in International Law», Netherlands International Law Review, Vol. XXIV, 1977, p.297.
454. A. Grahl-Madsen, «The Status of Refugees in International Law», Vol. II, p.130.
455. G. Goodwin-Gill, «The Refugee in International Law», p.107.
456. Resolution 428 (V) of the UN General Assembly of December 14, 1950, see paragraph 2.
457. Articles 31, 32 and 33 implicitly contain at least the safeguard of temporary asylum.

Article 14 of the Universal Declaration of Human Rights

In order for a person to be granted asylum, he must first have had the possibility of asking for protection. This was acknowledged by the international community in the Universal Declaration of Human Rights, adopted by the UN in 1948. Article 14 states that «Everyone has the right to seek and to enjoy in other countries asylum from persecution». With this inclusion in the Universal Declaration, a formal link was established between the protection of human rights and the protection of refugees.

There is no doubt, that a State has the right to admit a person into its territory.[458] Asylum is thus a privilege granted by States, as a function of their sovereign rights. States have difficulties in formally recognizing the right of the individual to attain asylum although in practice, States grant asylum to individuals all the time.[459] In other words, Article 14 ensures a person the right to «seek asylum», but no State is obliged to grant asylum unless it has undertaken specific obligations, for example, in regional conventions or according to national legislation.

During the negotiations on the Universal Declaration of Human Rights, the initial draft of Article 14 was, «everyone has the right to seek and be granted asylum from persecution in other countries». Several States protested at this wording, because they believed it carried the risk of being interpreted as implying an individual right to asylum. Another proposal, that of including a right for the UN to grant asylum also met with very clear opposition.

In spite of the limited scope of Article 14, its importance should not be underestimated. The question can be raised if it is not contrary to the intent of both Article 14 and to the purpose and aim of the 1951 Convention when States hinder flight from persecution. In order for refugees to be able to seek asylum and in order for the 1951 Convention to have any meaning, refugees must have the possibility of escape. When potential asylum States hinder flight, for example, through the imposition of restrictive measures such as

---

458. For more details, see, A. Grahl-Madsen, «The Status of Refugees in International Law», Vol. II, p.23 and P. Weis, «The Draft United Nations Convention on Territorial Asylum», reprinted by UNHCR from the British Yearbook of International Law, 1979, p.152.
459. For more details on asylum, see P. Leuprecht, «Le droit d'asile en Europe» in «Droit d'Asile», Ed. F.Rigaux, E. Story-Scientia, Brussels, 1988, p. 71 in which he claims that the subjective right to asylum does not exist in international law, that there is no human right to attain asylum, but only the right of a State to accord it or not. See also: A.Grahl Madsen, «The Status of Refugees in International Law», Vol. II, p.101, E. Zoller, «Le droit d'asile», p.20 and 21, G. Goodwin-Gill, «The Refugee in International Law», p.121, J.Y. Carlier, «L'état du droit international», p.44 and 49 and G. Fourlanos, «Sovereignty and the Ingress of Aliens», p.137 and 138.

visa requirements and carrier sanctions,[460] the refugee no longer has a genuine right to seek asylum. Governments need to be constantly reminded of this fundamental right to seek asylum and of the reasons for activating international responsibility for the protection of refugees. Both UNHCR and the NGO community have important functions in this regard.

The UN Declaration on Territorial Asylum of 1967

In 1957, the French member of the Human Rights Commission presented a draft declaration on the right of asylum to the Commission. In 1960 it was adopted and presented to the UN General Assembly.[461] After ten years of negotiations, the proposition had evolved into the UN Declaration on Territorial Asylum of 1967.[462]

Because of the lack of a mandatory legal instrument on territorial asylum, this declaration has an importance which goes beyond the majority of UN declarations.[463] It contains two principal elements regarding asylum, the non-refoulement principle and the principle of international solidarity; both principles to which the UN and other international organizations continue to refer in the search for international solutions.[464]

The UN Declaration on Territorial Asylum refers to Article 14 of the Universal Declaration of Human Rights. In Article 1 it states that «Asylum granted by a State, in the exercise of its sovereignty, to persons entitled to invoke article 14..., shall be respected by all States». It continues in the third paragraph by stating that the evaluation of the grounds for the granting of asylum, is the sole responsibility of the State which is granting asylum.

---

460. See below, p. 225–229.
461. For a thorough analysis on the steps taken regarding the adoption of the Declaration on Territorial Asylum of 1967, see P. Weis, «Human Rights and refugees», p.38 and after; and G. Goodwin-Gill, «The Refugee in International Law», p.105.
462. Adopted unanimously by the UN General Assembly on 14 December 1967 in Resolution 2312 (XXII).
463. This point of view is supported by A. Grahl-Madsen, «Territorial Asylum», p. 45.
464. The OAU was, for example inspired by the UN Declaration on Territorial Asylum of 1967 when, in 1969, it adopted the OAU Convention on governing specific aspects of refugee problems in Africa. Article II (3) of the OAU Convention states: «No person shall be subjected by a Member State to measures such as rejection at the frontier, return or expulsion, which would compel him to return to or remain in a territory in which his life, physical integrity, or liberty would be threatened. . .» Article II (4) consolidates the aspect of international solidarity.

The Declaration explicitly refers to the granting of asylum as an exercise in State sovereignty[465] and thus the Declaration can be viewed as constituting a conservative instrument.[466] The fact that it refers to Article 14 of the Universal Declaration of Human Rights and not to the 1951 Convention is of specific relevance. The enumeration of human rights in Article 2 of the Universal Declaration on Human Rights[467] to which Article 14 refers, defines a range of protection rights which are more expansive than those enumerated in the definition of the 1951 Convention and which are considered, at least by some, to be exhaustive.[468] The UN Declaration on Territorial Asylum could, therefore, be seen as covering refugees who are not strictly covered by the 1951 Convention, but who are nevertheless in need of international protection. In practice, however, at least in the European context, persons who are not considered as refugees under the terms of the 1951 Convention, are not usually granted asylum in the classical sense of the word, but are often granted alternative forms of protection, for example, residence permits for humanitarian reasons.[469]

Article 3 of the Universal Declaration on Territorial Asylum of 1967, reiterates the non-refoulement principle, which includes an obligation not to refuse admission of refugees at the border. The second paragraph of Article 3, however, allows for a derogation of the principle for «overriding reasons of national security or in order to safeguard the population, as in the case of a mass influx of persons».

As a concluding remark regarding the Declaration, it should be noted that it does not cite the term «right» and therefore it does not pertain to the individual's right to asylum.

---

465. See Article 1 which declares that asylum is granted by a State «... in the exercise of its sovereignty, to persons entitled to invoke article 14 of the Universal Declaration of Human Rights...».
466. A. Grahl-Madsen, «The Status of Refugees in International Law», Vol. II, p.102.
467. Article 2, first paragraph of the Universal Declaration of Human Rights reads: «Everyone is entitled to all the rights and freedoms set forth in this Declaration, without distinction of any kind, such as race, colour, sex, language, religion, political or other opinion, national or social origin, property, birth or other status».
468. See E. Lapenna, «Le Réfugié et l'Emigrant dans le Cadre des Droits et Libertés Fondamentaux», AWR, No. 1–2, 1984, p.52 and after. On the definition of the 1951 Convention, see above, p. 72 and following.
469. See above, p. 138–139.

Conclusions on Asylum adopted by UNHCR's Executive Committee

Although UN Member States did not wish for UNHCR to be given the right to grant asylum, the Conclusions of the Executive Committee have repeatedly stated the need for States to respect the principle of asylum. In 1977, In its initial Conclusion on Asylum, the Executive Committee simply requested governments «...to follow, or continue to follow, liberal practices in granting permanent or at least temporary asylum to refugees who have come directly to their territory...».[470]

Following this Conclusion, the Executive Committee has repeatedly declared its view on asylum. Conclusion No. 15 (XXX) of 1979,[471] explicitly states that «States should use their best endeavours to grant asylum to bona fide asylum seekers;...» and Conclusion No. 65 of 1991, emphasizes «...the primary importance of non-refoulement and asylum as cardinal principles of refugee protection...». In 1983, the Executive Committee, whilst recognizing the problems posed by asylum requests which are manifestly unfounded or abusive,[472] expressed its concerns on the restrictive tendencies of States, with regard to the institution of asylum and the determination of refugee status.[473]

In 1990, the Executive Committee acknowledged that «...the current size and characteristics of the refugee and asylum problem necessitate appropriate reassessment of international responses to the problem to date, with a view to developing comprehensive approaches to meet present realities».[474] With this objective the High Commissioner created an internal Working Group on protection, which was given the task of proposing a strategy for reinforcing international protection. The observations of this group were presented in 1992, in the Note on international protection.[475]

In 1992, the report of the Executive Committee's 43rd session, on the rein-

---

470. Adopted at its 28th session in 1977.
471. Adopted at its 30th Session in 1979.
472. See Conclusion 30 (XXXIV) adopted during its 34th session in 1983. On the same subject, see also the preceding Conclusions: Conclusion No. 8 (XXVIII) adopted during the 28th session in 1977, Conclusion No. 15 (XXX) adopted during the 30th session in 1979 and Conclusion No. 28 adopted during the 33rd session in 1982.
473. Conclusion No. 29 (XXXIV) adopted during the 34th session of the Executive Committee in 1983. See also, Conclusion No. 33 (XXV) adopted during the 35th session in 1984.
474. Conclusion No. 62 (XLI) adopted during the Executive Committee's 41st session.
475. UN Document, A7AC.96/799, 1992. On asylum, see p.6–8.

forcement of international protection, clearly recognized that despite the traditional need for attention to be given to refugee status, the size and complexity of population displacements had created serious tension concerning traditional refugee protection.[476] Furthermore, if stated that international solidarity has indeed been weakened and that the asylum principle has been put in jeopardy at a time when conflicts have reinforced the importance and urgent need for coherent, solid, and flexible structures, capable of preserving the fundamental principles of international protection.

The Working Group on refugee protection, reiterated that asylum is the fundamental principle underlying refugee protection and that UNHCR should continue to promote the right of all refugees to seek asylum and to benefit from it. Recognizing the impossibility of granting asylum in grand-scale operations, the Working Group accepted that asylum could be granted temporarily, by making reference to Conclusion No. 22 (XXXII) of the Executive Committee on the protection of asylum seekers in situations of large-scale influx,[477] which contains fundamental protection principles.[478] It also indicated other ways in which to address the problem of protection, for example, by focusing more on the responsibility of «refugee-producing» States, or by strengthening prevention measures. The Working Group did not, however, consider it timely to take an initiative for legal clarification on the concept of asylum nor to take the initiative for a new international asylum instrument.[479]

The failure of creating a Universal Convention on Territorial Asylum in 1977

In the beginning of the 1970s, following a request by the UN General Assembly, initiatives were taken to establish a Convention on Territorial Asylum.[480] In 1971, during the international Colloquy on Territorial Asylum and Refugee Protection held in Bellagio, Italy, three articles were adopted: an article on the granting of asylum, an article on non-refoulement and an article on international solidarity. Due to time restrictions, the rest of the text

---

476. UN Document, A/AC.96/804, 1992, p .32.
477. Adopted during the Executive Committee's 32nd session in 1981.
478. UN Document, A/AC.96/799, p.6 and 7.
479. UN Document, A/AC.96/799, p.7. See also, Note on International Protection by the UNHCR Executive Committte's 45th session in 1994, UN Doc. A/AC.96/830, p. 6.
480. For a thorough examination of the work on the Convention on Territorial Asylum, see P. Weis, «The Draft United Nations Convention on Territorial Asylum», p.151–171, A. Grahl-Madsen, «Territorial Asylum», p.61–68.

was left to a Working Group, which met in Geneva in January 1972 and which added articles on non-extradition, temporary stay during the examination of a request, voluntary repatriation, cooperation with the UN, the peaceful characteristic of asylum, the right of qualification, the regime of beneficiaries of asylum and «bona fide» refugees. In its entirety, this text was called «the Bellagio draft» and was revised by a Group of Experts, established by the UN and representing 27 different States, meeting between 28 April and 9 May 1975, in Geneva.[481]

Although some experts were in favour of adding a subjective right to asylum for the individual, the majority maintained the position that the granting of asylum forms part of State competence, derived from State sovereignty. Finally, the text did not include any obligation to grant asylum, but instead made only a limited proposal that States should make «all efforts» to do so.

In the final version of the draft, the text of Article 1, the key provision, stated that: «Each contracting State, acting in the exercise of its sovereign rights, shall make all efforts, in a humanitarian spirit, to grant asylum in its territory to all persons meeting the required conditions in order to benefit from the provisions of this Convention».

As far as personal applicability was concerned, Article 2 contained a description of the conditions that need to be met in order for a person to be considered a refugee in need of territorial asylum. The article was true to the formulation of the 1951 Convention definition and went on to add an implicit reference to political offenders. The second part of the article enumerated the reasons for which a person was not eligible under the draft convention, for example, by excluding persons who had committed a crime against peace, a war crime, or a crime against humanity within the terms of international instruments.[482]

The principle of non-refoulement in Article 3 of the draft convention was deemed applicable only to persons already on the territory of a State, because certain members of the Group of Experts considered that the principle did not apply to non-rejection at the border. A previous proposal to incorporate a provision on non-extradition, in harmony with the non-refoulement principle, was also taken out of the text by the Group of Experts.

With these amendments, the text was brought to the Conference of Plenipotentiaries,[483] which met in January and February of 1977. During their meeting, the final text was weakened, indeed, the second article was modified almost beyond recognition.[484]

---

481. See Resolution 3272 (XXIX) of the UN General Assembly of 1974.
482. See above on the «exclusion clauses» of the 1951 Convention, p. 89–94.
483. With the participation of 92 States.
484. P. Weis, «The Draft United Nations Convention on Territorial Asylum», p. 169.

Nevertheless, two positive aspects did emerge from the Conference of Plenipotentiaries. Firstly, the inclusion of an additional paragraph proposing that asylum should not be refused on the grounds that it could have been requested in another State and secondly, a declaration on the non-refoulement principle as a non-derogable principle.

Unfortunately, the Conference of Plenipotentiaries on Territorial Asylum was concluded without achieving its task of adopting a convention. On 4 February 1977, the Conference acknowledged that it had not been able to fulfill its mandate, but nevertheless considered that efforts should be pursued in view of drafting a convention on territorial asylum. This recommendation was adopted without opposition.[485] The failure of the Conference of Plenipotentiaries on Territorial Asylum was, in part, caused by the discussions which took place during the conference, but was also a result of the international events of the time, which had created a general fear of refugee flows. Furthermore, the prevailing view of governments at that time, was that it was not in their interest to commit themselves to taking on mandatory, legally binding international obligations.[486] The question of the possibility of a future adoption of binding rules on asylum, was left to the General Assembly.

Since the failure of the Conference of Plenipotentiaries on Territorial Asylum, the General Assembly has continuously advised governments to respect the non-refoulement principle and to grant asylum to refugees,[487] but it has not considered it timely to reopen discussions on the content of the notion of asylum, and through implication, on the goal of adopting a universal rule on the institution.

None of the instruments mentioned above have really contributed to providing a legal definition of the concept of asylum. With respect to the reinforcement of the institution of asylum, adopted texts, such as the UN Declaration on Territorial Asylum of 1967, the Conclusions of the UNHCR Executive Committee, and the resolutions emanating from the UN General Assembly, belong to the family of UN «soft law». The Common denominator of all these instruments is that they are, in principle, deprived of obligatory force in international law. Nevertheless, they have contributed to the devel-

---

485. E. Zoller, «Le droit d'asile», p.17, note 12. (Doc. A/CONF.78/12 of April 12, 1977, p.6).
486. See G. Goodwin-Gill, «The Refugee in International Law», p.111–112 where he cites the political events which resulted in refugee flows in different regions of the world, such as the division of Pakistan in 1971–1972, the colonial battles in Africa thoughout the 60s and the 70s and the flights provoked by the totalitarian regimes in Latin America, such as the coup in Chile in 1973.
487. See for example, Resolution 32/67 of December 8, 1977, Resolution 33/26 of November 29, 1978, Resolution 39/140 of December 14, 1984, Resolution 46/106 of December 16, 1991.

opment of humanitarian practice, which should not be underestimated. The legal evolution of «soft law» cannot be excluded.

6.2 Asylum at a regional level

At a regional level, Latin America and Africa have adopted legally binding instruments pertaining to asylum. Europe, on the other hand, has so far based its international endeavours in «soft law» instruments, such as the Council of Europe recommendations and resolutions, none of which recognize the right to asylum. In addition to this, European cooperation has inspired new initiatives for the harmonization of asylum policies at an inter-governmental level among Member States of the EU, but this has not led to a harmonization of a right to asylum. There remains an urgent need that the issue be debated in a pan-European context, in order to ensure asylum as a subjective right contained in international law, and as binding on all European States.

The OAU Convention was inspired by the UN Declaration on Territorial Asylum of 1967, which also explains why it contains two innovative aspects of international law, namely a broadened refugee definition and a conventional provision on asylum.

The first paragraph of Article II, stipulates that «Member States of the OAU shall use their best endeavours consistent with their respective legislations to receive refugees...», whereas the second paragraph contains a reference to the wording of the UN Declaration on Territorial Asylum, which regards asylum as a peaceful and humanitarian act. The non-refoulement principle is guaranteed, both at the border and within the territory. However, the OAU Convention does not ensure a right to asylum. The wording stipulates that States should «use their best endeavours» and this allows too much leeway for States not to offer asylum if they so choose.

The so called «Bangkok principles» of 1966, on the treatment of refugees,[488] are not legally binding. It should be noted, however, that Article III of these principles, emphasizes State sovereignty in referring to asylum as being dependent on the right of a State to grant or refuse asylum. The principles give no indication that a refugee should have a right to asylum. Nevertheless, according to the Bangkok principles, a refugee may be offered the protection of «temporary» asylum, so as to enable him, if in danger, to request asylum in another country.

In Latin America the institution of asylum has a long tradition, which is

---

488. Adopted by the Legal Committee on Africa-Asia during its 8th session, which was held in Bangkok 8–17 August 1966.

partly a result of the fact that the region has undergone many upheavals. Persons in power today risk being the refugees of tomorrow and vice-versa and it has therefore been in the interest of all, to regulate rights pertaining to protection. The principles of asylum were first adopted in the Treaty on International Penal Law, signed in Montevideo in 1889. Several other instruments, which refer specifically to the institution of asylum, have also been adopted.[489] The most significant of these is the Caracas Convention of 1954 on Territorial Asylum which reaffirms the sovereign right of States to grant asylum[490] and the duty of the other States to respect it.[491] This Convention further allows the State which granted asylum not to expel or permit the extradition of persons who are persecuted for political reasons or for political crimes.[492]

In its Recommendation No. 4, the Cartagena Declaration of 1984, emphasises the «...peaceful, non-political and exclusively humanitarian nature of the grant of asylum or recognition of the status of refugee...». However, the Declaration does not contain an additional right of asylum for the individual.

European approaches

When examining asylum policy in the European context, it is important to remember that although EU Member States have assumed the lead role in the region on these issues, it was in the context of the Council of Europe that refugee and asylum matters were initially discussed. The Parliamentary Assembly of the Council of Europe has continued to act on refugee and asylum matters, but its recommendations are not always followed up by the Committee of Ministers, which represents governments, and thus forms the decision making body of the organization.

The shift of governmental discussion to Brussels has not proved reassuring, because the purpose of EU cooperation is not the same as that of the Council of Europe. The EU is chiefly concerned with economic cooperation and the development of a single market, and EU member States, on the whole, deal with asylum issues in order to protect themselves against refugee

---

489. The Convention on asylum of 20 February 1928 (Havana), the Convention on Political Asylum of 26 December 1933 (Montevideo), the Convention on Diplomatic asylum of 28 March 1954 (Caracas), The Inter-American Convention on Extradition of 25 February 1981 (Caracas) and the Cartagena Declaration of 1984.
490. See Article I.
491. See Article II.
492. See Article III and IV.

influx. In contrast, one of the main purposes of the Council of Europe is to safeguard and develop human rights principles.[493] Moreover, the Council of Europe includes forty European Member States, whereas the European Union only includes fifteen, all of whom are also members of the Council of Europe. It would seem, therefore, that the Council of Europe is the more appropriate pan-European forum in which to conduct a continuous European debate on asylum and refugee issues.

The Council of Europe
The European Convention on Human Rights of 1950, has made a significant contribution as a legal international safeguard for the fundamental human rights of the individual. The Convention does not contain any explicit provisions on the rights of refugees or on the right of asylum. Its provisions do, nevertheless, apply to refugees and asylum seekers, since the Convention is applicable to all those who are within the jurisdiction of one of the signatory States. The European Court of Human Rights has, for example, highlighted the principle of the unity of the family, guaranteed by Article 8 of the Convention. Even more importantly, in the context of refugee protection, is the practice of both the Commission of Human Rights and the Court of Human Rights regarding the application of Article 3 in cases concerning the possible refoulement of refugees and asylum seekers.[494] According to the Commission and the Court «...expulsion by a Contracting State of an asylum seeker may give rise to an issue under Article 3, and hence, engage the responsibility of that State under the Convention, where substantial grounds have been shown for believing that the person concerned faces a real risk of being subjected to torture or to inhuman or degrading treatment or punishment in the country to which he is returned».[495] This shows, that although the European Convention on Human Rights does not contain provisions on asylum, it does ensure protection to refugees and asylum seekers, at least on a temporary basis.

Two other provisions in conventional European Human Rights instruments have implications for refugees. Firstly, Article 4 of the Additional Pro-

---

493. See also Christian Bruschi, «Le droit d'asile: l'Europe a l'heure des choix», Migrations Société, Revue de presse (Vaulx-en Velin), Vol. 2, No. 12, Nov.-Dec. 1990, p.52.
494. On the relation between Article 3 of the European Convention on Human Rights and the non-refoulement principle, see above, p. 153–156.
495. European Commission of Human Rights in the case of Sharif Hussein Ahmed versus Austria (Case No. 25964/94) of 5 July 1995. The Commission's viewpoints were upheld by the European Court in its judgment of 17 december 1996 on this case (71/1995/577/663).

tocol No. 4 to the European Convention for the protection of human rights and fundamental freedoms, which secures certain rights and freedoms other than those already included in the convention and in the first protocol;[496] and secondly, Article 1 of the Additional Protocol No. 7 to the European Convention for the protection of human rights and fundamental freedoms.[497] The first provision mentioned is interesting with respect to asylum, because it prohibits collective expulsions of persons, whereas the second indicates conditions which need to be met regarding the expulsion of foreigners.

In addition, instruments of «soft law», which give an indication of European political thinking in connection with asylum, have been adopted. For example, Recommendation 293, adopted by the Council of Europe's Consultative Assembly on 26 September 1961, recommended that the Committee of Experts of Human Rights should introduce an Article on asylum in a protocol to the European Convention of Human Rights of 1950. The Committee of Experts was, however, not in favour of an additional protocol which would guarantee an individual right of asylum.

On 29 June 1967, the Committee of Ministers adopted Resolution (67)14, on asylum to persons in danger of persecution,[498] which was influenced by Parliamentary Assembly Recommendation 293. According to resolution (67)14, governments are recommended to «...act in a particularly liberal and humanitarian spirit in relation to persons who seek asylum on their territory», and «...in the same spirit, ensure that no one shall be subjected to refusal of admission at the frontier, rejection, expulsion or any other measure which would have the result of compelling him to return to, or remain in, a territory where he would be in danger of persecution for reasons of race, religion, nationality, membership of a particular social group or political opinion;».

Resolution 817, on certain aspects of the right to asylum, adopted by the Parliamentary Assembly in 1977,[499] and the Declaration on Territorial Asylum of the Committee of Ministers, also adopted in 1977,[500] both reiterate the content of Resolution (67)14. The Declaration on Territorial Asylum was adopted by European States as a reaction to failure of the Conference of Plenipotentiaries to adopt a universal Convention on Territorial Asylum. The European Declaration on Territorial Asylum not only refers to the refugee con-

---

496. Signed on 16 September 1963 and entry into force on 2 May 1968.
497. Signed on 22 November 1984 and entry into force on 1 November 1988.
498. Adopted by the Delegates of Ministers on 29 June 1967.
499. Adopted during the 29th session of the Parliamentary Assembly in 1977.
500. Adopted during the 278th meeting of the Delegates of Ministers on 18 November 1977.

cept of the 1951 Convention and confirms the right to grant asylum to persons covered by this instrument, but also refers to «...any other person they (member States) consider worthy of receiving asylum for humanitarian reasons». This expansion is worth noting.

Both Recommendation 787 of 1976 on the harmonization of eligibility practice under the 1951 Geneva Convention on the Status of refugees and the 1967 Protocol[501] of the Parliamentary Assembly, and Recommendation No. R (81)16, adopted by the Committee of Ministers in 1981,[502] address the issue of harmonization as regards the interpretation of the 1951 Convention. However, they do not add any new elements to the concept of the right of asylum, except that they refer to Resolution (67)14 and the European Declaration on Territorial Asylum. Despite the fact that these texts contribute little to the clarification of the concept of asylum, they should be interpreted as expressions of good will on the part of European States.

It was not until 1988 that the Parliamentary Assembly finally adopted a Recommendation on the right to territorial asylum. In Recommendation 1088, on the right to territorial asylum,[503] the Parliamentary Assembly expresses its wish «...to preserve fully the rights to territorial asylum as one of the generous liberal traditions of democracy, and to pursue and to extend the work of the Council of Europe in this field», and «...to continue work on the harmonization of the legal rules in respect of territorial asylum in the Council of Europe member states...».

This recommendation is also of interest because it shows the Council of Europe responding to new trends of cooperation on asylum matters, among the Member States of the then European Community. One example of such cooperation involved a European agreement on responsibility for examining asylum applications. This issue was being discussed within the framework of intergovernmental negotiations of the EU States and led to the adoption of the Dublin Convention.[504] The Council of Europe has never finalized an agreement on the responsibility for examining an asylum request, although, its draft[505] is, according to the Parliamentary Assembly, superior to the Dublin Convention. The reason given by the Parliamentary Assembly for such an opinion, is that the European Council draft has been debated in the Council

---

501. Adopted during the 28th session of the Parliamentary Assembly, on 16 September 1976.
502. Adopted on 5 November 1981 during the 339th meeting of the Delegates of Ministers.
503. Adopted on 7 October 1988 during the 40th session of the Parliamentary Assembly.
504. More on the Dublin Convention, see below, Chapter 7.
505. See below, p. 232.

of Europe context and formulated against the background of all the other legal instruments of the Council of Europe.[506] Nevertheless, it is the Dublin Convention which has been adopted and ratified.

The efforts of the Parliamentary Assembly of the Council of Europe to balance the restrictive developments taking place in the context of the EU, with humanitarian commitments, by which European States are also bound, should be recognized and followed. Recommendation 1237, on the situation of asylum seekers whose applications have been rejected, adopted by the Parliamentary Assembly on 12 April 1994, is an important reminder to European States. It emphasises that the 1951 Convention, the European Convention on Human Rights and the relevant national instruments in the field of humanitarian law must «...provide the basis for harmonizing asylum policies and regulations in all the Council of Europe member states».

The Parliamentary Assembly's engagement in asylum matters reached a high point with the adoption, in April 1994, of Recommendation 1236, on the right of asylum.[507] This Recommendation referred to the changes which had taken place with regard to the right to territorial asylum, both in the Member States of the Council of Europe and otherwise at the international level, in the five years which had passed since the adoption of Recommendation 1088(1988) on the right to territorial asylum. The changes were seen as resulting from the fall of communist regimes in Eastern Europe, the civil war in Former Yugoslavia, economic disparity between industrialized countries and poorer countries, and on-going human rights abuse both in Europe and in the world at large. According to the Assembly, all these aspects combined, had created a situation whereby the number of refugees seeking asylum in the Member States of the Council of Europe had reached proportions not seen since the Second World War.

The Parliamentary Assembly therefore, suggested that «...since two of the aims of the Council of Europe are bringing its member states closer together and protecting human rights, now should be the time to take common action in the Council of Europe, to ensure fairness to all persons in need of protection, and to reduce friction over sharing asylum responsibilities between its member states by initiating collective European cooperation. The right of asylum is a pan-European problem that requires a pan-European solution».

Recommendation 1236 continued by recommending the Committee of Ministers to «...amend the Convention for the Protection of Human Rights

---

506. See Council of Europe, Parliamentary Assembly, Committee on Legal Affairs and Human Rights, Report on the right of asylum, Doc. 7052 of 23 March 1994, p.17.
507. Adopted by the Parliamentary Assembly on 12 April 1994.

and Fundamental Freedoms to include a right of asylum...». Failing such incorporation, it was recommended to «...draw up ...a separate agreement on the right of asylum, containing not only a clarification of the legal status of asylum seekers and displaced persons, but also laying out model (harmonized) procedures for determining refugee status in full compatibility with the 1951 Geneva Convention, the 1967 New York Protocol and other relevant principles of international law». Furthermore, Recommendation 1236 called on the Committee of Ministers to «...draw up a legal instrument for the protection of de facto refugees...».

Recommendation 1236 also contains a variety of other suggestions worthy of note. For example, the need to handle the root causes of current refugee problems, through such measures as the implementation of minority rights in Member States, improvement in human rights work outside Europe, the combat of racism, xenophobia, anti-Semitism and intolerance, etc. Furthermore, the Parliamentary Assembly urges particular care to be taken by all Member States of the Council of Europe, when harmonizing asylum procedures or when trying to establish a «fairer» distribution of responsibilities in such matters as applications classified as «manifestly unfounded», the application of the «safe third country» principle, etc.[508] Moreover, the recommendation not only refers to previous recommendations cited above, in order to improve, for example, the situation of asylum seekers whose applications have been rejected but also to UNHCR Executive Committee Conclusion No. 22 (XXXII), on the protection of asylum seekers in situations of large-scale influx.

There had been no governmental follow up to these proposals within the Council of Europe until the Norwegian government proposed that the Member States draw up a European convention on refugees and asylum seekers during the meeting of the Committee of Ministers in November 1997.

The Parliamentary Assembly had also adopted a recommendation to this effect, notably Recommendation No. 1324, adopted in April 1997, as a contribution to the Second Summit of Heads of State and Government of the Council of Europe. It recommends Member States to draw up a European convention on the protection and rights of refugees and asylum seekers, and in so doing, reiterates its call for new instruments, as stated in 1994, in Recommendation 1236.

The proposal for a new European refugee convention contained in this book is in harmony with Recommendations 1324 and 1236. The proposal would fill the various gaps in international refugee law by way of one single new European instrument, rather than several separate instruments. Such an

---

508. On these practices, see further below, Chapter 7.

instrument would include a supplementary refugee definition, the right to asylum and other forms of protection and finally, it would contain provisions on sharing of responsibility with regard to which country should be responsible for an asylum request.[509]

The European Union

Following the creation of an area of free movement in Europe, Member States of the European Union have, since 1986, taken initiatives to introduce «compensatory» measures, in order to avoid an increasing numbers of asylum seekers entering their territory. It would seem that strengthened control of external borders and efforts to hinder access to asylum procedures and asylum, are two seemingly indispensable aspects of present day European asylum policy. In order to succeed in this enterprise, EU Member States have, so far, refrained from introducing a common definition of the concept of asylum or from clarifying the individual right of asylum in a harmonized manner. Instead, they have negotiated rules governing the responsibility for examining an asylum request made in one of the Member States.[510]

In its Communication on asylum in October 1991,[511] the European Commission, in the light of the increasing influx of asylum seekers into the European Union,[512] insisted on the need for European cooperation and remarked on the particular importance of having a common asylum policy. The Commission elaborated on two essential reasons for a common approach: Firstly, the prevention of the abuse of the asylum institution and secondly, the need for harmonization, with regard to form and substance, of the right of asylum.[513] In order to achieve these aims, the Commission proposed to harmonize, among other things, the application of the 1951 Convention, the definition of «country of first asylum», the definition of «safe country», the definition of an «unfounded asylum request» and the treatment of «de facto» refugees. Furthermore, it proposed to establish procedures for the exchange of information concerning countries of origin. The problems which needed to be solved in 1991 are, with few exceptions, largely the same as those worrying European Union Member States today.

---

509. See below, Chapter 8.
510. On the Schengen and the Dublin Conventions, see below, Chapter 7.
511. Communication by the Commission to the Council and the European Parliament, SEC (91) 1857 Final, of 11 October 1991.
512. In 1981, approximately 71,000 asylum applicants arrived in the Member States of the European Community (excluding Luxembourg and Ireland) whereas in 1991, 420,000 asylum applicants arrived in these same countries, cf. Statistics given in St.meld . No. 17, 1994/95 (report to the Norwegian Parliament) on refugee policy, p.37.
513. See the Communication of 1991.

Based on the advice contained in the 1991 European Commission and on a report by the ministers responsible for immigration,[514] the European Council, in 1991, laid out four priorities in its so-called work programme concerning asylum. Firstly, the implementation of the Dublin Convention with particular emphasis on the need to adopt common interpretations of the concepts used in the convention and on the establishment of a practical manual. Secondly, the harmonization of rules of substance in relation to asylum issues, which is of importance, for example, in order to assess so-called «manifestly unfounded» asylum applications. Thirdly, the harmonization of expulsion policies, including a common evaluation of the situation in countries of origin and fourthly, the creation of a clearing house, the Centre for Information, Discussion and Exchange on Asylum (CIREA), whose main aim would be to exchange information on legislation, policies, jurisprudence, and statistics.[515] The creation of CIREA, following a decision by the ministers responsible for immigration, at their meeting in Lisbon in 1992, is, in fact, a forerunner of the Dublin Convention which, in its Article 14, seeks to enshrine mutual exchange between States on legislation and national practice in the area of asylum, statistics, information of a general character on new tendencies regarding asylum applications, country of origin, etc.

In December 1992, during their London-meeting, the European Community ministers responsible for immigration, adopted three resolutions of importance in connection with asylum; the first on manifestly unfounded applications for asylum, the second on a harmonized approach to questions concerning host third countries (the Resolution on «safe third countries»)[516] and the third on countries in which there is generally no serious risk of persecution.[517] The legal status of these resolutions has not been defined within the framework of community law, but they are applied in practice and are incorporated into national legislation. It remains uncertain, however, as to whether the European Court would consider their application as being within its jurisdiction.[518]

As regards the Resolution on manifestly unfounded asylum applications, the ministers insisted that cases involving manifestly unfounded asylum requests should be the object of an accelerated examination process, with a

---

514. Ad hoc Group on Immigration, SN 4038/91 (WG 930), Brussels, December 3, 1991.
515. W. Lobkowicz, «L'Union européene et le droit d'asile», p.16 and 17.
516. The Resolution on safe third countries addresses the issue of harmonization of the application of the concept of «first country of asylum»/«safe third country» and is a follow up to the Dublin Convention. See, below, p. 262–267.
517. All three resolutions were adopted on 30 November 1992.
518. See R. Plender, «Asylum Policy», p. 8.

«first instance decision» being taken within a month. The implementation of this policy is left to the discretion of each signatory State.[519] An application is to be considered manifestly unfounded if it is clear that, it does not concern persecution, or there is an attempt to abuse asylum procedures, or if the asylum applicant is considered covered by the resolution on safe third countries. Inclusion of the latter condition has been criticized by UNHCR[520] and by the NGO community [521] because of the danger of a violation of the non-refoulement principle.

The Resolution on countries where there is no risk of persecution, is less imperative in its language and concerns basic criteria for assessing the situation of countries to which asylum seekers may be returned: the so called «safe» countries. Unofficial lists of «safe» countries exist, but the wording of the Resolution leaves it to the discretion of each State to decide which countries are «safe».

The justification given for the 1992 Resolutions, was the need to distinguish between asylum seekers, who are «bona fide» refugees, and economic migrants. This argument, however, is not entirely convincing, as seen, for example, in the application of the concept of «first country of asylum». According to this practice, an asylum seeker may be sent to another country, which is considered responsible for the examination of his request. The deportation decision is often made by means of an accelerated procedure, which excludes a thorough examination of the merits of the case. Without an examination of the case, it is not possible to assess whether or not a person is a refugee, under the terms of the 1951 Convention, or an economic migrant not in need of protection.

The European Parliament has promoted a number of studies on migration and asylum policies and it has adopted several resolutions on the topic. In October 1992, the Committee of Civil Liberties and Internal Affairs presented a report on the harmonization of asylum law and policy in the European Community. Furthermore, on 18 November 1992, the European Parliament, in full session, adopted a Resolution on the harmonization of asylum law and policies within the European Community.[522] In this Resolu-

---

519. See the Communication to the European Council and the Parliament 1994, p. 29.
520. See as an example the letter from the High Commissioner, Ms. Ogata to the Minister of the interior of the United Kingdom of 27 November 1992 and UNHCR's Note on «Fair and Expeditious Asylum Procedures» of November 1994, p. 3 and 4.
521. See, for example, ECRE, «Una politica europea sull'asilo alla luce dei principi consolidati», April 1994, p. 5 and 6.
522. Resolution A3-0037/92, Official Journal of the European Communities, C 337, Vol. 35, 21 December 1992.

tion, the Parliament requested the Council and the Commission to put forward proposals for harmonizing visa requirements, laws on aliens and the right of asylum, and also called on them to draw up a Common European policy on refugees. It should be noted that the Council of Ministers had also acknowledged the urgency of implementing the Commission's recommendations for the post-Maastricht period.[523]

With the entry into force of the Treaty of Maastricht in November 1993, the role of the European Community institutions in the harmonization process were, for the first time, defined under Title VI of the Treaty. Up to that point, work had been carried out at an intergovernmental level. During its meeting in Brussels in October 1993, the European Council asked the Council of Ministers of Justice and Home Affairs to prepare a specific plan of action on a common approach to the right of asylum, visa policy, judicial cooperation, relations with third countries, and readmission agreements. This plan of action was approved by the European Council in December 1993. The plan considered two issues for priority attention in 1994, the harmonized application of the refugee definition of Article 1(A) of the 1951 Convention and the establishment of minimal norms for asylum procedures.[524] As a follow-up to these priorities, the Joint Position on the harmonized application of the definition of the term «refugee» in Article 1 of the Geneva Convention of 28 July 1951 relating to the status of refugees, was adopted on 4 March 1996.

In early March 1995, European Union Member States reached agreement on minimum guarantees in asylum procedures, which was formally adopted by the Ministers of Justice and Home Affairs in June 1995 in the Resolution on minimum guarantees for asylum procedures. This resolution contains principles which are supposed to guarantee effective and equitable procedures in conformity with the 1951 Convention. It includes guarantees on the examination of asylum applications, which means, for example, that all applications should be examined in an «individual, objective, and impartial» manner. The resolution also states that the asylum applicant should have the possibility of proving his case, and includes provisions on certain rights for an asylum seeker during the proceedings, for example, the use of an interpreter.

However, UNHCR has voiced concern that the adopted principles on minimum guarantees impede the possibility of appeal for an asylum seeker whose case has been rejected and that they threaten the right of an asylum

---

523. See, Communication of the Commission to the Council and the European Parliament, 1994, p.2.
524. Communication by the Commission to the European Council and Parliament, 1994, p.24.

seeker to remain in the asylum country until a final decision has been taken on his application. The Resolution also allows for exceptions, with respect to the suspensive effect of appeals, which is contrary to international refugee law.[525]

The concept of asylum, meaning the right to asylum as a principle of international law, has not been specifically elaborated upon, at either the intergovernmental level or within EU institutions, following the entry into force of the Treaty of Maastricht. The European Union Member States appear to suggest that, according to the European tradition, asylum should be granted to persons who are considered refugees within the terms of the 1951 Convention. This explains EU Member States' concern about harmonizing the interpretation of the conventional refugee concept, because granting refugee status provides an indirect definition of asylum. No need has been identified, therefore, for harmonizing the content of the asylum institution beyond existing practice.

The application of the Joint position on the interpretation of Article 1(A) of the 1951 Convention varies from one Member State to another and, therefore, the practice of granting or not granting protection varies. Equally, practice by Member States concerning «de facto» refugees differs from one Member State to another. These discrepancies bear witness to the fact that European Union Member States do not have a common asylum policy and a common policy on the content of the concept of asylum. This is a clear confirmation of the need for an international initiative in this regard and a pan-European approach to this problem would seem the most appropriate solution.[526]

In 1994, the European Commission wrote to both the European Council and the European Parliament, stating that «It is clear that much remains to be done, if the Union wishes to develop and implement a common policy on immigration and asylum. Achieving and implementing a common policy on immigration and asylum will not be possible without greater reliance on legally binding instruments, procedures to ensure uniform interpretation of those common rules and the development of common policies in relation to areas of both substantive and procedural law that have not yet been addressed».[527] Without wishing to appear naive, there is a lot of merit in this conclusion drawn up by the Commission which could develop into taking

---

525. See Johannes van der Klaauw, «Refugee Protection in Western Europe: A UNHCR Perspective», Kluwer Law International, 1997, p. 238.
526. See therefore below, Chapter 8 which proposes a new European Convention on refugee protection.
527. The 1994 Communication from the Commission to the Council and the European parliament, p. 10.

both the needs of States and of refugees into consideration. From this perspective, the words therefore remain equally applicable in 1998 and for the foreseeable future. The need to develop such policies, however, should not be limited to the fifteen West European States only, but to all European States. This is why a pan-European proposal is necessary. An internationally harmonized mandatory rule on the right to protection is of vital importance. A broadened refugee definition necessitates further debate. When establishing a European harmonized approach to the question of «who is a refugee», priority must also be given to defining what should be the legal content of State obligations towards refugees.

In March 1997, the European Commission made a proposal to the Council for a Joint Action concerning temporary protection, the outcome of which will certainly be of importance for the content of asylum and protection in Europe.[528]

6.3 Temporary protection

The need for international protection presupposes that it is impossible for the person concerned to return home to his country of origin. If circumstances change and the person concerned can return in safety and dignity then international protection is, in principle, no longer required and international responsibility therefore – whether legal or humanitarian – can cease to exist. The very same philosophy is reflected in the «cessation clauses» of the 1951 Convention.[529]

Throughout the era of the «Cold War», asylum granted in the Northern hemisphere has traditionally been of a permanent character. The institution of asylum has thus developed according to the historical and political context of the time. For example, refugees seeking asylum in Western Europe during the Cold War tended to be refugees fleeing violations of human rights taking place behind the «Iron Curtain», or from other totalitarian regimes. The permanency of these regimes therefore, more often than not, dictated that protection on a permanent basis was required. The granting of permanent asylum by a Western country to a refugee fleeing persecution under a Communist regime was also very much a political statement of moral superiority over governments which were founded on a political ideology to which the West was fundamentally opposed.

However, the granting of asylum on a permanent basis has not always been

---

528. See below, p. 201–205.
529. See above, p. 86–89.

the foundation of European refugee protection. Those who fled the Spanish civil war between 1936-39 were granted temporary refuge especially by France and the U.K. Likewise, when the U.S.S.R. invaded Hungary in 1956 and the Czech Republic in 1968, the refugees who joined the consequent mass exoduses, received temporary refuge, this time mainly in Austria. In the decades that followed the relative absence of mass exoduses towards Western Europe kept the issue of temporary protection off the European agenda. However, because of the events following the dissolution of the U.S.S.R. at the end of the 1980s and the war in Former Yugoslavia which forced millions into exile at the beginning of the 1990s, Western governments were forced to address the issue of temporary protection again.

In other parts of the world, protection needs, in addition to individual persecution, arise frequently from generalized violence such as war and internal strife. Countries neighbouring those thus affected usually deal with the mass exoduses which result, by offering protection on a temporary basis. For example, in the Democratic Republic of Congo and in Zambia, there are at present third generation Angolan refugees who were granted protection on a temporary basis, and are waiting to return to Angola. Repatriation is considered the evident solution to this refugee problem, not only by the countries of exile, but also by the international community as a whole. UNHCR and other international organizations are already in Angola waiting to implement the repatriation programmes. In the Middle-East, Africa, and Asia, where there is a long tradition of large refugee flows and temporary protection, (such as Palestinian refugees in Lebanon, Afghan refugees in Pakistan, and Cambodian refugees in Thailand), the fact that the stay is considered «temporary», although it may last for many years, is not an issue for discussion. At the end of the 1970s, UNHCR implored South-East Asian governments («first asylum countries») to admit Vietnamese refugees and grant temporary protection based on «prima facie» determination, before they were resettled elsewhere.[530] The «first asylum countries» agreed, in the main, to respect the non-refoulement principle and granted access to their territory on the notable condition of resettlement guarantees and economic assistance from «third countries». The fact is, that although forced repatriation has been carried out, there are still Vietnamese refugees left in camps in South East Asia, for example in Hong Kong. This is another example of temporary protection lasting longer than foreseen, although it must also be borne in mind that some of the inhabitants of the camps are newly arrived asylum seekers.

---

530. On the «boat people» and the history of international cooperation at the end of the 1970s and the beginning of the 1980s in view of finding solutions to the exodus of Vietnam, see Goodwin-Gill, «The Refugee in International Law», 1983, p.87–92.

The preliminary condition of granting protection to victims of generalized violence in these regions has always been that the refugees will repatriate when the situation in the country of origin allows for repatriation to take place. It is also worth noting that certain refugee groupings have, indeed, even a self-interest in maintaining that the protection granted to them is temporary in character. For example, Palestinian refugees who want to return to their homeland. The same would apply to Serb refugees at present in the Federal Republic of Yugoslavia wishing to return home to the Krajina-region.

Different situations obviously require different solutions and with the new trend of mass outflows of refugees in Europe as well, arrangements of a more temporary character have found their way into European practice and legislation. As a consequence of contemporary history, the European Commission has prepared a proposal to the European Council for a Joint Action concerning temporary protection which is being debated in the Council of Ministers.

In order to expand on international cooperation further in this field and as a consequence of the concrete proposal contained in this book on a supplementary refugee definition and other protection measures, it is necessary to further examine the concept of temporary asylum in the context of a form of protection which may be suitable under certain circumstances and given certain conditions.

The underlying principle of any moves to institutionalize and harmonize the practice of temporary protection must be, that temporary protection should, under no circumstances, be seen as a substitute for permanent asylum. It should be seen as a supplementary interim protection method, to be used whilst permanent solutions are being sought after. On an international level, in principle the usefulness of an institution of temporary protection is not disputed. However, disagreement does exist about whether it should be part of an internationally harmonized legal system, as suggested by the EU Commission, or if the utilization of temporary protection should be left to unilateral «ad hoc» policies or to «soft law» initiatives.

With this debate in mind it is necessary to analyse the present state of affairs and the lessons learned from the recent experience of temporary protection accorded to refugees from the Former Yugoslavia in various countries. From such an analysis, it will be possible to define who should be the beneficiaries of a temporary protection regime and which should be the benchmarks for the lifting of temporary protection. Furthermore, it is necessary to address the issue of the rights which should be accorded to persons enjoying protection, and the question of a time limit on the duration of such a regime which would indicate its essential character as an interim asylum institution to be succeeded by permanent asylum or by another adequate solution.

Legal developments of temporary protection
UNHCR

In 1979, an Australian proposal in UNHCR's Sub-Committee on the Whole on International Protection, replaced the term «permanent asylum» by the term «durable asylum» in order to give the illusion to governments, which already received large numbers of refugees, that the duration of stay was not meant to be permanent. The term «durable» contains an interim connotation whereas «permanent» connotes everlasting.[531]

The concept of a protection being limited in time was not unknown to the authors of the 1951 Convention. Both Articles 31 and 32 recognize that States must accord temporary protection even to refugees whose entry or presence is illegal in their territory. Even more importantly, through the «cessation clauses» contained in the 1951 Convention, the refugee definition itself recognizes and allows for the fact that under certain circumstances refugee status is no longer necessary and therefore ceases to exist.[532] This must be seen as an implicit acceptance in international refugee law, that protection can be of a temporary character.

Specific reference to temporary protection has also been made in several other international instruments. For example, Article II(5) of the OAU Convention declares that «Where a refugee has not received the right to reside in any country of asylum, he may be granted temporary residence in any country...»; while Article 3(3) of the UN Declaration on Territorial Asylum of 1967 refers to the necessity of granting «provisional asylum» in cases where a State decides to use the exception to the non-refoulement principle contained in the same article. However, the Cartagena Declaration does not address the issue as temporary protection as such, but in its Recommendation No. 5, the authority of the principle of non-refoulement is underlined and the prohibition of rejection at the frontier is specifically stated. From this it can be deduced that for the countries in Latin America which have incorporated the recommendations contained in the Cartagena Declaration, the granting of temporary protection is part of their refugee protection regime.

Notwithstanding the above examples, it is in the context of UNHCR's Executive Committee that the concept has developed further and been refined in relation to emergency situations and situations of mass influx. For example, in Conclusion No. 5 (XXVIII) of 1977 on «Asylum»,[533] governments are requested to grant «...at least temporary asylum...». In Conclusion No. 15

---

531. G.J.L. Coles, «Solutions to the Problem of Refugees and the Protection of Refugees», p.192.
532. See above, p. 86–89.
533. Adopted during the Executive Committee's 28th session.

(XXX) of 1979 on «Refugees without an asylum country»,[534] the Executive Committee points out that in cases of large-scale influx, persons seeking asylum should «...always receive at least temporary refuge». Conclusion No. 19 (XXXI) which dealt specifically with temporary refuge was adopted the following year.[535] This latter Conclusion, apart from referring to previously mentioned Conclusions on the subject of large-scale influx and burden-sharing among States, stresses the exceptional character of temporary refuge and «...the essential need for the humanitarian legal principle of non-refoulement to be scrupulously observed in all situations of large-scale influx». The non-refoulement principle can in fact be seen as having prompted the development of the concept of temporary protection. This also explains the link between the non-refoulement principle and temporary protection in other international instruments.[536]

Traditionally, in practice and in international documents, allusion has been made to temporary protection as a «crisis solution» of «exceptional character», such as situations of mass outflows of refugees. For example, Conclusion No. 19 (XXXI) on temporary refuge referred to above. The content of this Conclusion is a reflection of this line of thinking and has since been upheld by UNHCR by its reference to temporary protection as «a tool for dealing with situations of mass outflow».[537] This can be seen, for example, in General Conclusion No. 68(XLIII), adopted in 1992. The same opinion was reiterated in UNHCR's Note on International Protection in 1994.[538] ECRE has also expressed a similar opinion.[539]

Temporary protection as a crisis solution has equally been reflected in the international debate which followed the handling of the refugee crisis in Europe caused by the conflict in the Former Yugoslavia. Both the European Union and the Council of Europe are, in order to handle a future large scale influx of refugees, considering the creation of new and harmonized approaches

---

534. Adopted during the Executive Committee's 30th session.
535. Adopted during the Executive Committee's 31st session.
536. See, for example, the UN Declaration on Territorial Asylum of 1967, Article 3 (3), the OAU Convention article II (5), the Bangkok principles of 1966 Article III (4), Resolution (67)14 of the Council of Europe of 1967 Article 3. In the draft UN Convention on territorial asylum, its Article 3(3) equally contained this link. The proposal was adopted unanimously by the Conference on territorial asylum in 1977 which, as we know, did not materialize into a Convention after all.
537. UNHCR – Legal Information, Note by UNHCR: Temporary Protection of 16 July 1997.
538. See UN Doc. A/AC.96/830, 1994, p. 22.
539. ECRE, «Una politica europea sull'asilo alla luce dei principi consolidati», 1994, p. 3.

to temporary protection. Similarly on a national level the nature and pace of events in recent years is increasingly forcing a reassessment and revision of national legislation. Until the crisis in former Yugoslavia, persons in need of protection who were not considered to meet the criteria of Convention status refugees were nevertheless granted protection, for example, on humanitarian grounds or, as reflected in the practice of the Scandinavian countries, on a permanent basis. Following the experience of countries which received refugees from the former Yugoslavia, the inadequacy of existing legislation in such situations of mass influx has been recognized by the governments of Western Europe and thus the move towards adjusting national legislation to incorporate the principle of temporary protection in the event of mass influx situations.

In spite of the political dynamic which now seems to exist for concrete steps to be taken on this issue, the question still remains whether States are, according to international law, obliged to grant temporary protection in order to ensure respect for the non-refoulement principle. Current legal thinking seems to be developing along these lines, although some authors may be somewhat sceptical about the obligatory character of granting temporary protection. For example, K. Hailbronner, does not consider that the granting of temporary protection forms part of international customary law. In his opinion, States have not yet undertaken mandatory legal obligations towards «de facto» refugees by their humanitarian practice. This would imply that States can in fact refuse admission and the granting of temporary protection to every refugee who is not a 1951 Convention refugee.[540] Some authors share this view.[541] It is difficult to understand how these authors would suggest making a determination at the border, in case of mass influx, between those who are 1951 Convention refugees and those who are not. It is equally difficult to perceive how, in case the persons in question are admitted, States would not be obliged to grant temporary protection to those considered «de facto» refugees without violating the principle of «non-refoulement».

This leads to agreement with other authors who, on the contrary, consider that the granting of temporary protection is an obligation which prohibits forced repatriation of «de facto» refugees according to international customary law. For example, G. Goodwin-Gill, believes that temporary protection

---

540. K. Hailbronner, «Nonrefoulement and 'Humanitarian' Refugees: Customary International Law or Wishful Legal Thinking?», in «The New Asylum Seekers in the 1980's», Ed. D. Martin, 1988, p.132 and following.
541. For example, M.R. Garcia-Mora in «International Law and Asylum as a Human Right», Washington, 1956, p.151. G. Fourlanos, also has some difficulties in accepting that temporary protection should be obligatory, quoted in G. Fourlanos, «Sovereignty and the Ingress of Aliens», 1987, p.158.

is the logical and necessary corollary of the non-refoulement principle.[542] Perluss and Hartmann also consider that a combination of necessity and humanism has resulted in the emergence of such an essential norm in humanitarian law.[543] The Group of Experts on temporary refuge in situations of large-scale influx whose work was finalized by the adoption of the UNHCR Executive Committee of Conclusion No. 22 (XXXII) on protection of asylum seekers in situations of large-scale influx in 1981,[544] considered that States should grant at least temporary protection in cases when life is threatened.[545] Conclusion No. 22 (XXXII) reiterated the principles adopted by the Group of Experts on temporary refuge. It contains fundamental conditions pertaining to the use of temporary protection, including the condition of respect for the non-refoulement principle. It states: «In all cases the fundamental principle of non-refoulement – including non-rejection at the frontier – must be scrupulously observed». With respect to temporary protection it states: «In situations of large-scale influx, asylum seekers should be admitted to the State in which they first seek refuge and if that State is unable to admit them on a durable basis, it should always admit them at least on a temporary basis...».

In its Note on International Protection of 1994, UNHCR spoke of an international responsibility, generally accepted by States, for the provision of protection to refugees fleeing armed conflict and civil strife, whether or not such persons are deemed to fall within the terms of the 1951 Convention.[546] In the same year, the Executive Committee considered the content of international protection and ways in which to extend protection to all who require it. UNHCR was urged to further develop comprehensive and regional approaches in consistency with recognized principles of asylum and protection, as laid down by international refugee instruments and other human rights standards. This would mean extending protection to all persons who fall under UNHCR's protection mandate. Subsequently, in the Sub-Committee of the Whole on International Protection,[547] UNHCR emphasized the need for legal protection of refugees in the context of mass influx and also drew attention to the burden placed on particularly impoverished countries

---

542. G. Goodwin-Gill, «Entry and Exclusion of Refugees», Michigan Yearbook of International Legal Studies, 1982, p.306.
543. See D. Perluss & J.F. Hartmann, «Temporary Refuge: Emergence of a Customary Norm», Virginia Journal of International Law, 1986, p.554.
544. Adopted during the Executive Committee's 32nd session.
545. Report of the Meeting of the Group of Experts on Temporary Protection, Doc. EC/SCP/16 of 3 June 1981.
546. See Note on International Protection, UN. Doc. A/AC.96/830, p.19 and 20.
547. Doc. EC/1995/SCP/CRP.3.

hosting large refugee populations. In the 1995 Note on International Protection, UNHCR underlined the desirability of global efforts to address the important problem of refugees in large scale influx situations and stressed the need for liberal asylum policies which, as it is stated in the Note, «...need not presuppose permanent settlement...». [548] The emphasis put on a protection-based comprehensive approach of UNHCR's 1996 Note on protection, stresses that appropriate reference to the international refugee instruments be included. This means that the non-refoulement principle, including non-rejection at frontiers, must be respected under all circumstances. Furthermore, the need for displaced persons receiving admission to safety and the need for UNHCR to be given unrestricted access to persons of concern is underlined. There is, however, no indication of durable asylum being the most sought after solution. On the contrary, UNHCR sees its role as being one of prevention in trying to avert mass flows of refugees which implies addressing the «root causes» of refugee situations («preventive protection») and, if flight has occurred, that the organization should facilitate return and reintegration of refugees in safety and dignity in their home country («curative protection»).

Usually, temporary protection is granted on the basis of group determination which means each individual refugee does not have his claim assessed, at least not immediately and sometimes never. The reason behind this is twofold. Firstly, because of the need for speedy decisions and secondly, so as not to overburden refugee determination procedures. When the examination of an individual refugee claim is postponed, as was the case in many countries receiving refugees from the Former Yugoslavia, it must be kept in mind, that according to the 1951 Convention, asylum- seekers have an inherent right to have their application for asylum examined according to the Convention, and on the assumption that, until proved otherwise, they may qualify for Convention status. However, disagreement may and does arise about the point in time at which an individual examination of an application must take place. For example, as the 1951 Convention contains rights for refugees which normally extend beyond those that are conceived for refugees in an emergency situation, it is evident that there must be a limit to the duration of temporary protection and the premise of group determination on which it is based, so that the persons in question can make use of their rights.

In order to respect the principle of non-refoulement, the cessation of a temporary protection regime can only occur if, either the situation in the country of origin improves to the extent that the person can safely return, or the country in which the person is a beneficiary of temporary protection, or

---

548. Note on International Protection at the Executive Committee of the UNHCR's 46th session, 1995.

another country grants asylum or an equivalent form of permanent protection. The question which still remains is what interim period of time, during which a person is protected without being admitted to an individual asylum procedure and without the full rights pertaining to permanent refugee status, should be acceptable as an international standard. Apart from the analogy to temporary protection provided by the «cessation clauses» of the 1951 Convention, there is no universal mandatory binding agreement on temporary protection. Therefore, notwithstanding the guidance provided by UNHCR Executive Committee Conclusion No 22. (XXXII) on protection of asylum seekers in situations of large-scale influx (1981), the time limits as well as status, rights, and benefits of those under temporary protection vary greatly from one country to another. Therefore efforts are needed to harmonize these aspects at a regional level.[549]

The European Union
When the war in the Former Yugoslavia broke out in 1990, UNHCR referred to the principle of international protection in the regional context. In 1991 the High Commissioner initially called upon States to extend temporary protection to persons fleeing Croatia and in 1992, UNHCR officially requested governments to grant «temporary protection» to those in need of international protection on account of the conflict and human rights violations.[550] A number of international meetings were convened in order to debate assistance and protection to these refugees and the use of temporary protection began to emerge again in the European context in specific national legislation or in various combinations of existing laws and administrative decisions and practice,[551] be it called «temporary admission» as in France, «exceptional leave to remain» as in the U.K., or «collective protection» as in Norway.

In other words, even in the context of the crisis and international response provoked by the conflict in former Yugoslavia, UNHCR's initiative did not immediately result in international harmonization attempts. Nor within the EU, did the fact that asylum policy is defined as a matter «of common interest» according to the Maastricht Treaty, spur efforts at resolving on a European level a clearly pressing and urgent issue. During the crisis, in spite of the fact that nearly all Member States of the Union made special arrangements to

---

549. See below, Chapter 8.
550. See «Comprehensive Response to the Humanitarian Crisis in Former Yugoslavia», Geneva 21 January 1993.
551. See in this regard, «Survey on the Implementation of Temporary Protection», Humanitarian Issues Working Group of the International Conference on the Former Yugoslavia», 18 March 1994, p. 1–62.

make accelerated decisions on temporary admission to people escaping the conflict in the Former Yugoslavia, there was, at the time, no real cooperation between the Member States in the devising of a uniform system to deal with a common crisis. Thus, while no harmonized means of guaranteeing the rights of displaced persons from the former Yugoslavia emerged, the effect of the ad hoc measures which were put in place by individual States was to postpone access to the full eligibility procedures to refugee status normally guaranteed and underpinned by the 1951 Convention. According to UNHCR, however, such an approach to dealing with the refugees in this situation of mass influx was not contrary to the protection purpose of the 1951 Convention, but rather a flexible and practical form of according protection. [552]

In its 1994 Communication to the European Council and Parliament,[553] the European Commission stated that it should be possible to derive something from the experience of granting temporary protection to refugees from the Former Yugoslavia by way of harmonizing national legislation on temporary protection of the Member States. The aim would be to create a uniform European system of temporary protection which would ensure a minimal level of protection, in regard to which Member State were to offer their protection in the future. This was also considered a way of avoiding refugee flows to one particular State or States as a result of differences between national legislation and thereby ensuring a more equitable sharing of the burden among States.

In 1995, the Commission announced that it would take an initiative to draw up a general coordinated policy for admission on a temporary basis of persons in need of international protection. In September 1995, the Council adopted a Resolution on burden-sharing with regard to the admission and residence of displaced persons on a temporary basis.[554] This resolution was intended to regularize access to the territory and distribute displaced persons in future mass-influx situations in a balanced manner. The Resolution also listed the beneficiaries as those who have been held in prisoner-of-war or internment camps, those who are injured or seriously ill, those whose life is under direct threat and whose protection in their region cannot be secured, those who have been assaulted sexually, and those who come directly from combat zones. War criminals are explicitly excluded from entry as are those who have committed a serious non-political crime.[555] The capacity of a

---

552. See Note on International Protection of 1994, UN Doc. A/AC.96/830, p.15 and p.22 and following.
553. Communication from the Commission to the Council and the European Parliament, COM(94) 23 final of 23 February 1994, p. 25 and 26.
554. Official Journal of the European Communities No. C 262/1 of 7 October 1995.
555. Cf. above, on «exclusion clauses» p. 89–94.

Member State should, according to the Resolution, be taken into consideration from a political, social, and economic point of view, criteria which, according to J. Van der Klaauw, UNHCR's senior European Affairs Officer in Brussels, refer to the size of the population, the size of the territory and the gross domestic product of the host State.[556]

Following the Resolution, the Council adopted a Decision on an alert and emergency procedure for burden-sharing with regard to the admission and residence of displaced persons on a temporary basis in March 1996.[557] In order to implement the content of the 1995-Resolution and to assess whether an emergency situation exists, the Presidency, a Member State or the Commission can, according to the Decision, call for the convening of a Coordinating Committee. The Decision also refers to consultation with UNHCR.

The notion of burden-sharing contained in this Decision differs from the one envisaged by UNHCR in the past where burden sharing was not meant as a means of restricting or distributing the number of persons in need of protection, but «...as an underlying principle of international refugee law, inextricably linked to the concept of international solidarity».[558] It could perhaps be seen as an example of both: a repartitioning among the Member States of the number of refugees to be admitted by each State, on the one hand, and, on the other hand, an acknowledgement by the 15 EU Member States, (in the spirit of international solidarity) of an international responsibility of receiving displaced persons who are not necessarily covered by the 1951 Convention, but who are in need of international protection.

Finally, in March 1997, the EU Commission presented a proposal to the Council for a Joint Action based on Article K.3 2(b) of the Maastricht Treaty concerning Temporary Protection of Displaced persons. When the proposal was presented, the EU Commissioner Anita Gradin, responsible for Home and Justice Affairs, referred to the lack of cooperation in connection with the Bosnia crises and urged Member States to build on the experiences of the mass influx from Bosnia and «...make sure that a fair and dignified reception can be offered in all Member States» the next time the EU Member States are faced with such a situation.[559] Gradin also underlined that the proposal was intended as a complement to the 1951 Convention.

---

556. See Johannes van der Klaauw, «Refugee Protection in Western Europe: A UNHCR Perspective», p. 243–245.
557. Official Journal of the European Communities No. L 63/10 of 13 March 1996.
558. Johannes van der Klaauw, «Refugee Protection in Western Europe: A UNHCR Perspective», p. 244.
559. Press release on Commission proposal on Joint Action for temporary protection of Displaced Persons, Doc. IP/97/178 of 5 March 1997.

The draft is the Commission's first proposal for an EU instrument in the asylum area. It is of a binding nature and according to the Rapporteur of the Civil Liberties and Internal Affairs Committee of the European Parliament, Jan Kees Wiebenga, it should be treated as a form of legislation, even though the Parliament does not have a right of veto, the European Court of Justice has no power over its implementation, and the incorporation into Member States' national legislation will be unclear.[560] It is difficult to predict the Council's reaction and the time needed for its elaboration on the subject, especially since the adoption of the Proposal by the Council will require a unanimous decision.

The purpose of this proposed Joint Action is to create a framework for common decision making between the EU Member States regarding the access, prolongation or cessation of temporary protection regimes in cases of mass influx of displaced persons in need of international protection. This means that the Joint Action is not supposed to apply when there is not a mass influx. According to draft Article 1 of the proposal, «mass influx» means « ... a significant number of arrivals within the Union of persons who claim to be in need of international protection or a strong probability that such a situation may soon arise;».

As is implied in the Council Resolution Laying Down Priorities for Cooperation in the Field of Justice and Home Affairs for the Period 1 July 1996 to 30 June 1998,[561] the Council of Ministers recognize that a distinction should be made between temporary protection and burden sharing on the one hand, and other forms of protection accorded to «de facto» refugees, such as, for example, residence permits on humanitarian grounds. It has been argued that the distinction should be maintained and that temporary protection should only be applied in an emergency situation where individual refugee status determination cannot be carried out and where temporary protection will enhance admission to the territory.[562] There may be differing views on the upholding of the distinction as it could be seen as creating more difficulties than actually bridging the existing gap in international law between those in need of protection who fall within the 1951 Convention and the non-1951 Convention refugees. A distinction serves the purpose of main-

---

560. European Parliament, Working Document on the proposal for a Joint Action concerning temporary protection of displaced persons (COM(97)0093 final - 97/0081 (CNS)), Committee on Civil Liberties and Internal Affairs, Rapporteur Jan Kees Wiebenga, Doc EN`/DT/326/326311 of 2 June 1997.
561. Official Journal of the European Communities C 319/1 of 26 October 1996.
562. ECRE, «Comments from the European Council on Refuees and Exiles on the Proposal of the European Commission Concerning Temporary protection of Displaced Persons», 1997 and ECRE, «Position of the European Council on Refugees and Exiles on Temporary Protection in the context of the Need for a Supplementary refugee definition», March 1997.

taining the existing categorization of refugees: convention refugees, on the one hand, and «de facto» refugees on the other hand, who receive protection on humanitarian grounds. Upholding distinctions might result in adding a third category of refugees: «emergency refugees».

However, in the proposal for a new European refugee convention presented in this book, this distinction would cease to exist as the principles for refugee protection would derive from a combined refugee definition in draft Article 1 which includes 1951 Convention refugees, war refugees and other refugees in need of international protection. The only distinction to be made would be one based on what the protection need of the individual is.[563] Draft Article 1 would therefore include refugees who have escaped violations of human rights and risk being subjected to torture, inhuman or degrading treatment if returned to their country of origin, refugees sometimes referred to as «Article 3 refugees».[564] Some commentators would suggest that the «Article 3» refugees should not fall within the scope of the temporary protection institution. The fact remains, however, that all the refugees concerned may have differing protection needs – some refugees can never return and thus need protection on a permanent basis, whereas some are in need of urgent and sudden shelter, but only on a temporary basis. States should take the differing needs into consideration when harmonizing their protection obligations, thus allowing, notably, for a distinction to be made between refugees only on the basis of differing protection needs of the individual.

The EU Joint Action also aims to establish a minimum level as regards rights and benefits for persons who are beneficiaries of a temporary protection regime. These rights concern i.a. work, education, social welfare, housing, family reunification. The content of the Joint Action in this regard will at least ensure that the standard of reception and protection of refugees does not vary between countries to the extent that it does today. The rights proposed are minimum rights and it is therefore envisaged that national legislation could go further in the standard of rights granted, according to the Rapporteur of the Committee on Civil Liberties and Internal Affairs.[565] This would, however, create new differentials in standards of treatment in different countries. It would therefore seem more logical and consistent with the overall purpose of the harmonization behind the proposal to set the standards at a level above the minimum and thus ensure adequate rights throughout Europe.[566]

---

563. See below, Chapter 8, draft Article 1 and draft Article 2.
564. Article 3 of the European Convention on Human Rights, see above p. 153–156.
565. European Parliament, Working Document, Doc. EN/DT/326/326311 of 2 June 1997.
566. See, for example, the proposal for a new European refugee convention, below, Chapter 8, draft Article 3.

One of the more contentious points of the proposal for a Joint Action concerns the length of time during which the normal asylum procedure for beneficiaries of a temporary protection regime should be postponed. The proposal contains an article which states that the examination of an application for asylum under the 1951 Convention, introduced by a beneficiary of a temporary protection regime, may be postponed for as long as the Council has not adopted a decision on the phasing out of the temporary protection regime, but in any event, the period may not exceed five years from the beginning of the temporary protection regime. This article has prompted differing reactions from those concerned with the content of the Proposal. For example, ECRE, considers that «...access to full and fair asylum procedures should be granted as soon as practically possible...» but acknowledges that at least there is an absolute maximum after which postponement is not acceptable. [567] This viewpoint has a lot of merit. Neither for governments nor for the refugees concerned is there, in principle, a reason to postpone the refugee status determination procedure. Only for practical reasons in the case of mass influx, when meeting other immediate considerations is the priority, such as provision of protection and shelter, should individual determination be delayed. Such a delay should, however, never exceed a maximum of five years after which time an asylum seeker must be allowed entry to the normal asylum procedure. This recommendation is also contained in the proposal for a new European refugee convention.[568] Another view, which has been put forward concerning this element of the proposal for a Joint Action, is that of the Division on International Protection in UNHCR. While commenting on the present proposal for new legislation on temporary protection in Denmark, in which a time limit of five years equal to the EU Joint Action has been proposed,[569] the Division of International Protection has indicated that the time span should not exceed two to three years.

Provided that the crucial provision of a maximum time limit to temporary protection is adhered to by the European Council of Ministers, it must be acknowledged that the initiative taken by the European Commission on this topic is as a positive contribution for future international discussions. Nevertheless, an important concern remains, that a European temporary protection regime should not be limited to the fifteen Member States of the EU. Rather, to ensure a truly harmonized regional approach to the resolution of this issue, a pan-European approach is required. It is therefore necessary to uphold the suggestion of institutionalizing temporary protection in a broader

---

567. ECRE, «Comments on the Proposal of the European Commission Concerning Temporary protection of Displaced persons».
568. See below, Chapter 8, draft Article 2(3).
569. See Berlingske Tidende, (a Danish daily), 1 October 1997.

European context, notably in a new European Protection Convention which should be debated under the auspices of the Council of Europe.

The Council of Europe
In the context of the Council of Europe, the debate on temporary protection has taken place in the Committee on Migration, Refugees and Demography of the Parliamentary Assembly. In September 1996 the Committee produced a report on temporary protection of persons forced to flee their countries. [570] This report discusses the underlying principles of, and the reasons for, temporary protection, defining both the beneficiaries and the rights which should be accorded to non-1951 Convention refugees in need of international protection. It does not, however, suggest that a legally binding instrument on this topic should be debated in the Council of Europe. Instead the Committee concludes that regulation of temporary protection is best left to a «soft law» instrument.

In the same report, the Parliamentary Assembly Committee of the Council of Europe recognized that temporary protection may be defined as «…a flexible and pragmatic means of providing protection…» and identified three categories of potential beneficiaries: war refugees who are not covered by the 1951 Convention; refugees fleeing on a mass-scale which renders it impossible for national authorities to process asylum applications individually; refugees in need of protection for «humanitarian reasons» who would otherwise be refouled following rejection of their applications.[571] As explained by the Rapporteur for the Committee, Ms. Arnold, refugees from countries such as Rwanda, Afghanistan, Liberia, Somalia and Sudan fall into this latter category and therefore benefit from this protection in different European countries.[572] According to the Rapporteur, there is a need for «common guiding principles» in Europe on temporary protection, which should be drawn up by relevant bodies of the Council of Europe, particularly the CAHAR, and adopted by the Committee of Ministers in the form of a recommendation to the Member States.

The proposals for a new European refugee protection convention contained in this book start from a different point. Further development of a

---

570. See Preliminary draft report, AS/PR (1996) 21 of 18 September 1996, Rapporteur Ms. Arnold.
571. See also Recommendation 1237 (1994) on the situation of asylum seekers whose asylum applications have been rejected, adopted by the Parliamentary Assembly of the Council of Europe.
572. See further below, p. 220–221 on beneficiaries as defined by the Committee on Migration, refugees and Demography of the Parliamentary Assembly of the Council of Europe.

harmonized temporary protection regime is suggested as part of the institution of asylum to which all refugees must have the right. This right can only be guaranteed through the adoption of a legally binding instrument.

From the examples of State practice, recommendations by UNHCR and the present ongoing debate in European fora described above, it is possible to draw certain conclusions about how temporary protection is defined and applied at the current time. The first rule of temporary protection is that refugees are admitted to safety in an asylum country. The asylum country is obliged to respect the principle of non-refoulement and it is equally obliged to provide treatment according to standards which include the respect for basic human rights principles and which are in accordance with international humanitarian principles. Finally, the temporary protection that is granted should last only until conditions in the country of origin permit repatriation.[573]

In addition to these essential components of a temporary protection institution, any discussion about the revision of such an institution should take place within a framework which addresses the need for international harmonization of temporary protection. Accordingly the proposal contained in this book is based on this essential premise, as it seeks to bring the various elements of missing links in international refugee law into one protection convention. In addition to draft Article 1 of the proposed new European convention indicating who the beneficiaries of protection should be, any institutionalization of temporary protection should equally reflect a progressive improvement of the rights to be accorded to refugees who are protected under a temporary protection regime. The rights should be equivalent to those of 1951 Convention refugees. An explicit time limitation on the duration of temporary protection must also be included and internationally harmonized and permanent solutions must in the meantime be sought after. To guarantee the effective realization of all the above aspirations, an international mechanism whereby the principles of international solidarity and burden sharing are ensured must equally be conceived.

6.4 Proposal in part for a new European convention on refugee protection

International refugee protection is in a crisis. Responsibility for the grave situation can be attributed to all the actors involved for different reasons. States

---

573. These four elements are in conformity with UNHCR's view. See Note on International Protection, UN Doc. A/AC/96/830, of 7 September 1994, p. 23.

stand accused of pursuing the priority of protecting themselves against refugees arriving in their territory through the imposition of restrictions, rather than prioritizing the search for new ways of ensuring that those who are in need of protection are protected, through international consultation. The failure of States to develop a mechanism whereby international burden sharing does not simply remain at a theoretical level, but contributes to a fairer division of responsibility for the protection of refugees in both practical and fiscal terms, has also contributed to the reluctance of individual States to assume the protection responsibilities they are obliged to undertake as signatories to the 1951 Convention. Charges could also be laid at the door of those who are not in need of protection and misuse the asylum institution in order to gain access to the labour market of the Northern hemisphere.

The issue of solidarity among those who are forced to flee in order to protect their life and security is also an issue in this regard. When protection against a threat to a person's life or security is no longer needed, the space provided by the international community ought to be ceded to someone else who is in need of protection or who may need protection in the future. Voluntary repatriation, therefore, ought to be a solution adhered to more willingly by those who are no longer in need of international protection and who do not need to remain in exile for other pertinent reasons.

In order to reverse the negative spiral of misapprehension and misperception in the field of refugee protection, States and other international actors should be encouraged to evaluate the whole range of humanitarian and legal duties objectively and as a whole. Only then will they fully appreciate that refugee protection can not be disassociated from the general issue of human rights and fundamental freedoms which the international community, through the UN and other international bodies has engaged itself to promote and encourage. The issue at stake is to find the best way of ensuring that this is done in a manner which responds to and satisfies the needs of both refugees and States.

With this in mind, the proposal for a new European protection regime in this book primarily emphasizes the need for a refugee definition which covers both the 1951 Convention refugee and the «de facto» refugee before going on to highlight the standard of protection which is required by these refugees.

Until now the concept of asylum has not been internationally defined and an unprecedented opportunity therefore exists to take into consideration all the necessary elements which have been brought forward in this chapter. Among other important aspects the concept of «asylum» should not be assessed solely from the perspective of permanent duration of protection, but equally in view of the need to provide temporary protection.

Such an approach may contribute to a change in attitude towards the present negative trend of States protecting themselves against the arrival of refugees. By introducing a concept of asylum which acknowledges both the temporary and permanent character of protection, European States would be able to see that ensuring refugee protection in a reciprocally binding instrument would be an obligation undertaken according to need, sometimes of a short duration sometimes of a permanent duration. In this regard, the proposed convention would equally ensure a system of fairness in European responsibility sharing[574] and thereby benefit States.

The existing lack of international harmonization in the protection area leads to unequal practices not only as regards interpretation of the refugee concept and the protection accorded to refugees, but also as regards differentiation in the implementation of the whole range of rights pertaining to the treatment of refugees. The EU institutions have shown that they are aware of this. It has been acknowledged in relation to «Agenda 2000»,[575] in which the Commission expresses its opinion on the prospects of accession to the Union by the Associated countries in Central and Eastern Europe[576] and Cyprus, by the inclusion of criteria that need to be fulfilled by the acceding States. These criteria include the level of stability of institutions guaranteeing democracy, the rule of law, human rights, and respect for and protection of

---

574. See also in this regard J. Hathaway, «Toward the reformulation of International Refugee law», Research report 1992–1997, who emphasizes the need for a system of international burden sharing in order to find new mechanisms of the international system of refugee protection. He lists five key principles: Firstly, «Interest Convergence Groups» which reflect States' binding commitments, based on common interests, to a wide variety of regional and sub-global organizations; secondly, «Common but Differentiated Responsibility» whereby it is recognized that different States can best contribute to refugee protection in different ways; thirdly, «Solution-Oriented temporary protection» which acknowledges the basic rights of refugees and which prepares for return and thereby lays the best groundwork for solutions; fourthly, «Residual Solutions» which pertain to an allegation of significant numbers of refugees wanting to return and therefore the need to ensure viable repatriation if the international community consistently and effectively intervenes in response to human rights abuse; and finally, «Viable Repatriation» whereby refugee protection should be understood as a human rights remedy in which return home is a vital element. See also, Joanne Thorburn, «Transcending Boundaries: Temporary Protection and Burden-sharing in Europe», International Journal of Refugee Law, Vol. 7, No. 3, 1995.
575. Published by the EU Commission on 16 July 1997.
576. The Commission recommends that besides Cyprus, five out of the ten: Hungary, Poland, the Czech Republic, Slovenia and Estonia would be considered eligible for opening of accession negotiations in early 1998 on a basis of a comprehensive and objective evaluation of how the countries meet the criteria mentioned.

minorities.577 In a bilateral meeting with the Luxembourg Presidency of the Council in July 1997, the evaluation of the applicant States' ability to join the EU by monitoring the evolution of their asylum policies was placed as one of the Commission's priority areas.

Rather than passively monitor progress in this field, there is a more pertinent and more efficient way of ensuring that the countries of Central and Eastern Europe honour, in their national legislation, their commitment to upholding the human rights and refugee law standards of international law. This way would consist of proactively engaging these countries and others, in a debate in an arena in which forty European States gather, notably in the Council of Europe. Areas of concern in this context which would need to be included in the discussion and incorporated into a new European instrument are:

- the content of the concept of «asylum»; the duty of States and the right of the individual
- the duration of asylum, permanent asylum and temporary asylum, including maximum duration of temporary protection
- solutions if temporary asylum is lifted
- international solidarity and burden sharing
- the beneficiaries
- basic rights (treatment of refugees)

The right to asylum and its duration

To this effect, a new European refugee convention would have to contain the following provisions on asylum:578

Draft Article 2 ASYLUM

(1) Refugees entitled to invoke Article 1 of the present Convention have a right to seek asylum in other countries and to obtain protection.

(2) Refugees entitled to invoke Article 1 of the present Convention have a right to asylum. Asylum shall not be granted to any person who has committed a crime against peace, a war crime, or a crime against humanity or

---

577. See further on this matter in Johannes van der Klaauw, «The Provisions on Human Rights and Asylum in the revised Treaty on European Union», The Netherlands Human Rights Quarterly, October 1997.
578. See below, Chapter 8.

to any person guilty of acts contrary to the purposes and principles of the UN. The granting of asylum by a State to a person in need of international protection, is a peaceful and humanitarian act and cannot be regarded as unfriendly by any other State.

(3) Asylum may be granted on a permanent or on a temporary basis. Asylum on a temporary basis must not under any circumstances exceed five years from the moment a refugee first seeks protection, and contracting States will do everything in their power to facilitate examination of individual applications and to facilitate solutions as quickly as possible. If conditions in the country of origin or in the home country are such that repatriation would be in violation of Article 4 and/or Article 5 of the present Convention, the asylum country shall offer asylum on a permanent basis. In the search for solutions, due regard shall equally be given to the principle of international solidarity as contained in Article 6 of the present Convention.

As regards draft Article 2(1), there is generally no disagreement on a refugee's right to seek asylum as it is incorporated in the Universal Declaration on Human Rights. [579] More importantly for a new instrument, is the inclusion of a refugee's right to access to a country to seek protection. This is in addition to the extension of the non-refoulement principle to non-rejection at the frontier which is explicitly stated in draft Article 4. Furthermore, no derogation for reason of mass-influx situations is permitted.

In draft Article 2(2), the right to asylum is explicitly incorporated as an «answer» to the wording in draft Article 1 which says that international protection shall be accorded to persons who are to be considered refugees within the draft convention. Reference to reasons of excluding a person from the right to be granted asylum, is largely modeled on the 1951 Convention Article 1(F). States' competence, in the exercise of their sovereignty, of granting asylum is not questioned. The phrase defining asylum as a peaceful and humanitarian act to be respected by all other States is modeled i.a. on the UN Declaration on Territorial Asylum of 1967. [580]

---

579. See, above, p. 172.
580. Cf. the UN Declaration on Territorial Asylum of 1967, Article 1 (1). In the case of conflict, this respect is put to a harsh test, for example, when a country which has received refugees by according them asylum is occupied by the country of origin, or by a country which has activated ethnic cleansing. Such was the case during World War II, for example, when Jewish refugees were deported from their land of asylum by the German occupiers. Such was also the case when the agents of a country of origin delivered a refugee from his country of asylum to the occupiers. There are still allegations to this effect, but which are difficult to verify and for this reason there has been little said.

This new instrument would therefore carry an obligatory responsibility for States to accord asylum to refugees, which in turn would bring the right to asylum to the level of mandatory legally binding refugee law.

As regards draft Article 2(3), it will be noted that it contains a reference to both permanent protection and temporary protection as simply «asylum». In national and international usage, different terms have been used to describe temporary protection such as «to grant refuge temporarily», «to grant temporary protection», etc. The concept of asylum is often reserved to describe a permanent solution. It seems that different terms are used to express the same concept, namely «protection». The proposal therefore seeks to simplify the usage by using one term: «asylum». This clarification would also contribute to the elimination of different «classes» or categories of refugees inadvertently created at present. These categories can be described as being 1951 Convention refugees who are considered «first class» refugees and who acquire asylum, «de facto» refugees or those with «B status» or equivalent who are considered «second class» refugees, and who receive residence permits on humanitarian grounds or on a temporary basis, and the category which is now developing of «war refugees» and other refugees in mass flight situations who are considered «third class» refugees and who are given temporary protection or «protection on a collective basis», etc. To counter such classification which may have direct and detrimental consequences for the level of protection awarded to those in need, the proposal for a new European refugee convention focuses on two clear terms: «refugee» and «asylum». This presupposes an understanding of asylum as something which is granted according to the protection needs of the individual refugee.

The proposed institutionalization of temporary asylum has advantages for refugees as well as for governments. Temporary asylum permits simplified asylum procedures in situations such as mass influx which demand quick action and access to safety. It also allows for protection to be granted to more people. Temporary protection can also ease the burden on receiving States and thereby inspire a greater generosity in granting refugee protection which would be manifested by the elimination or reduction of restrictions. Such action on the part of governments would of course also depend on the establishment of an international mechanism for the purpose of burden sharing. Institutionalization of temporary asylum could also, to some extent, prevent irregular movements and diminish abusive asylum applications. Economic migrants would perhaps be less inclined to misuse the asylum procedure if there were less chance of obtaining a right to long-term stay. The implementation of correct, but adequate border control and return to the country of origin of those who are not in need of international protection are other prerequisites for States' willingness to engage themselves further in developing a refugee protection regime along the lines described.

Nevertheless, proposals to institutionalize temporary protection have been criticized in view of the risk of weakening the institution of permanent asylum. In this respect, it is necessary to distinguish between practice and theory. In practice, permanent asylum is accorded to only a small percentage of asylum seekers in Europe. From a realistic point of view, finding new ways of safeguarding the institution of asylum and international protection now seems to be the only option. Continued reference to how things should be does not necessarily change the restrictive attitude of States. Furthermore, asylum is granted only to 1951 Convention refugees and most refugees in need of protection are «de facto» refugees. The reality of the situation being acknowledged, those who are concerned with safeguarding the 1951 Convention status should also recognize the urgent need to find a solution to the problems created by the increasingly restrictive application of its terms.

In theory, the concept of asylum is «sacred». It is, however, necessary to recognize that asylum has not been codified internationally in a manner which guarantees refugees' right to asylum. Creating an asylum institution is therefore a challenge that European States should meet and undertake and one which presents the opportunity to address the dual issues of permanent and temporary asylum, as suggested in draft Article 2 of the proposed new convention. It can be presumed that the public at large in the European countries would show support for a proposal which takes both refugees' needs and the needs of the host countries into consideration by introducing an institutionalization of asylum, whereby the duration of protection is based on the actual need as a principal rule. It implies that international protection lasts as long as it is necessary, but no longer. This could contribute to turning the negative trends of present day public opinion and instead enhance people's basic feelings of justice and tolerance towards refugees.

It is evident that the institutionalization of temporary protection would have disadvantages, mainly for those who, until now, would have the advantage of permanent asylum or permanent residence permits on humanitarian grounds. Temporary protection implies repatriation. This means even forced return to the country of origin in the event that the person in question does not depart voluntarily. The condition is that circumstances allow for return, as described in draft Article 5 on repatriation.[581] Draft Article 2 should therefore, as regards temporary protection, be read in conjunction with draft Article 5. There may be many valid reasons, other than those relating to protection, which cause unwillingness to return. For example, reasons of a more personal character such as not having anyone or anything left at home to which to return. However, in a world with limited resources for offering as-

---

581. For a detailed examination of draft Article 5, see above, p. 167–168.

sistance and protection to refugees, the space granted for protection, must be connected to the need for protection of a person's life and security, and not to other reasons. Therefore, when such specific protection is no longer needed, the principal rule must be that the space which one refugee occupied is ceded to someone else who is in need of protection.

«Forced repatriation» as opposed to «voluntary repatriation» is indeed a fairly new approach which has met with criticism in various quarters. For example, UNHCR has been criticised for its repatriation programmes of Vietnamese asylum seekers in transit in Hong Kong, in spite of the use of individual screening of refugee claims whereby the repatriated are those who are not deemed to be in need of international protection. When the host country is no longer willing to host refugees, the home country is obliged by international law to receive its citizens back, [582] and if a person, following an individual refugee determination procedure is found not to be in need of protection, then it can be argued that forced repatriation is the only solution and an acceptable one. This is quite different in the case when a host country deports refugees against the advice of UNHCR because the circumstances in the country of origin are not such that return is safe either in general, or for specific reasons relating to the particular situation of the person concerned. Forced repatriation under such circumstances amounts to a violation of the non-refoulement principle. This is taken into consideration in draft Article 5 of the proposal for a new European refugee convention contained in this book.

Furthermore, the importance of UNHCR's involvement in connection with repatriation is also emphasized in draft Article 5. Firstly, UNHCR should play a coordinating role, in cooperation with a regional organization, to ensure just international treatment for all, because often more than one asylum country at the same time is considering repatriation of refugees. Secondly, in countries which have not adhered to the 1951 Convention, UNHCR must make an individual assessment of refugee claims in order to know who can be repatriated and who cannot. Thirdly, UNHCR could and should play an important consultancy role for countries in general when they are debating the issue of repatriation and whether circumstances in the country of origin really do allow for repatriation.

The insecurity of a temporary protection regime could be compensated in the following way. Firstly, by ensuring that the treatment and rights accorded to persons granted temporary asylum are in harmony with international humanitarian standards,[583] and to the extent possible, equivalent to those ac-

---

582. Article 13 of the Universal Declaration of Human Rights.
583. Draft Article 3 contains the provision on treatment. See below, p. 221.

corded to the 1951 Convention refugee. Secondly, by establishing that temporary asylum can not exceed the maximum duration period of five years, as indicated in draft Article 2(3). Refugee protection is first and foremost about protecting people's life and security. However, it must also be recognized that at a certain point, the person concerned must, together with his family, be able to settle on a more permanent basis (also for reasons of more personal convenience), and a time limit of five years would therefore seem to be reasonable. These considerations also clearly indicate that the counting of the five years must start from the moment a refugee crosses a border in search of protection and registers with the authorities in the asylum country. This is an important qualifying argument for example, in situations in which refugees spend a long time in transit camps. This is also reflected in the proposed Article 2(3).

At the same time it should be kept in mind that refugees are victims in need of protection and every effort should be made for individual eligibility procedures to take place as soon after arrival as possible. There are, for example, persons who cannot be expected to return to their country of origin even if circumstances change. This explains why States, in draft Article 2(3), are urged to do their best to shorten the waiting period for individual screening as much as possible.

Solutions if temporary asylum is lifted

Draft Article 2(3) indicates that in order to lift temporary asylum three solutions can be envisaged and the contracting States are to do everything in their power to facilitate those solutions. The first solution envisaged is repatriation to the country of origin. «Facilitation» in this regard includes both preparing the refugees for return while in exile, and the active promotion of peace and stability in the country of origin by States through international cooperation. Follow-up activity in democracy building and rebuilding of a civil society including monitoring of the respect for human rights once a peace accord has been established, are also important elements in the promotion of voluntary repatriation. Only if conditions are such will peace be sustainable and only then will refugees see repatriation as a solution they have confidence in and will risk undertaking. [584] Repatriation cannot take place if return would be in violation of draft Article 4 which contains the non-refoulement principle: the fundamental rule for assessing whether or not a refugee can repatriate.[585]

---

584. See more on viable repatriation in J. Hathaway, «Toward the reformulation of International Refugee law», Research report, 1992–1997.
585. On the non-refoulement principle of draft Article 4, see above, p. 166.

Furthermore, repatriation, according to draft Article 5, can only take place, provided the «…conditions in the country of origin allow it».[586]

The second solution envisaged in draft Article 2(3) is that which refers to draft Article 6 on international solidarity and burden sharing.[587] This provision pertains to the case where refugees are in continued need of international protection at whatever stage their case is examined and at the latest, after five years. Rather than remain the sole responsibility of the country having granted protection on a temporary basis, it could, according to this provision, become the responsibility of a third country through a resettlement programme facilitated by an established burden sharing mechanism which should be coordinated by UNHCR in cooperation with a regional organization, for example the Organization for Security and Cooperation in Europe (OSCE).

The third solution envisaged, pertains to a continued need for protection, according to the criteria set out in draft Article 1, at the time when the individual refugee case is examined (at the latest after a maximum of five years). If the other two solutions are not possible, permanent asylum should then be offered in the same country which had granted temporary asylum.

If the reasons for allowing the persons concerned to stay are of a personal nature and not because of protection needs, then the asylum institution should not be used. This would be evaluated through an individual eligibility procedure. It would, however, be an advantage to both the refugee and the government concerned, if eligibility procedures were carried out as soon as possible after the refugee's entry. In a mass influx situation, it may take longer, whereas for other refugees, an individual screening process should take place promtly. This is reflected in draft Article 2(3).

Two sets of criteria need to be taken into account when repatriation or transforming temporary asylum into permanent asylum, are being considered by the receiving State. The first set pertains to objective elements which concern the circumstances in the country of origin. Return cannot take place unless conditions are such that the person concerned can return in safety and dignity.[588] The second set of criteria is related to subjective elements pertaining to the refugee in question, such as experiences he may have been subjugated to in his country of origin which would make involuntary return an inhumane act, his family situation and integration in the new country, etc.

It is interesting to note that Denmark, which initially had granted temporary protection to refugees from Bosnia, granted protection on a permanent

---

586. See the discussion on draft Article 5, above, p. 167–168.
587. See below, p. 216–219 on the discussion on draft Article 6.
588. See draft Articles 4 and 5 below, Chapter 8.

basis after only two years. This country is now in the process of changing its domestic legislation in order to introduce a maximum duration of five years. In Norway, where protection on a «collective basis» was lifted before the foreseen duration of temporary protection was exhausted, the experience has been that very few refugees have taken the opportunity to apply for 1951 Convention refugee status and few refugees have returned. Many are still apparently waiting for more assurances that it is safe to return. In order for refugees in such situations to be able to evaluate conditions in the country of origin and to feel secure enough to return, access to many sources of information must be ensured and a harmonized policy on repatriation must be directed by the appropriate bodies, if necessary at a supranational level. In this context , the unilateral endeavours undertaken by Germany and Switzerland as regards the lifting of temporary protection and repatriation to Bosnia was a wholly damaging blow to international cooperation in the field of refugee protection. For such repatriation to take place UNHCR should and would be the appropriate international coordinator.[589]

International solidarity and burden sharing

A proposal for a European refugee convention should, apart from taking into consideration the protection needs of the refugees, also assess the problems that States are faced with. The concrete proposition for a provision on international solidarity of a new European convention as regards the need for international burden sharing in relation to asylum, is therefore contained in the first paragraph of draft Article 6. [590]

Draft Article 6 INTERNATIONAL SOLIDARITY

(1)When a Signatory State to the present Convention finds difficulty in granting or continuing to grant asylum to refugees, such a State may appeal directly to other Signatory States, and these States shall, in the spirit of international solidarity and international cooperation, individually or jointly, and through the intermediary of UNHCR and/or regional organizations, take appropriate measures to lighten the burden of the Signatory State granting asylum. Such measures may include, among other things, fiscal contributions for the protection of refugees in the State granting asylum or willingness to resettle refugees from the State granting asylum to other States.

---

589. The EU Commission's proposal to the Council for a Joint Action on temporary protection also includes UNHCR's role in this regard.
590. The rest of draft Article 6 will be presented and discussed, below, p. 280–282.

The responsibility sharing among States need not only be one of offering resettlement places, but can also be one of economic assistance. Refugee problems are international in character and the establishment of a harmonized orchestration for the benefit of both refugees and States is therefore both logical and useful. However, international solidarity, although consistently referred to as part of the institution of asylum in existing instruments, in practice usually turns out to be void of all content and application. The preamble of the 1951 Convention, for example, appeals to international solidarity while it affirms «...that the grant of asylum may place unduly heavy burdens on certain countries...» Article 2(2) of the UN Declaration on Territorial Asylum of 1967, also appeals to «...a spirit of international solidarity» in order to ease the burden on a State which has difficulties in granting or continuing to grant asylum. UNHCR's Executive Committee Conclusion No.22 (XXXII) on protection of asylum seekers in situations of large-scale influx, Part IV, concerns international solidarity, burden-sharing and duties of States and recognizes the need for international cooperation and the setting up of mechanisms facilitating voluntary repatriation, local settlement or resettlement in a third country. It also calls for finding solutions within the regional context and cooperation with UNHCR. At a regional level, Article II, paragraph 4 of the OAU Convention, in recognition of the difficulties an asylum State may be faced with, refers to «the spirit of African solidarity» while calling on other Member States to take appropriate measure.

Based on these theoretical precedents, draft Article 6(1) of the proposal is modeled on the wording of the OAU Convention and on the spirit of UNHCR's Executive Committee Conclusion No. 22 (XXXII). The reason for the inclusion of this Article is that experience has proved that nothing happens automatically as far as international solidarity is concerned. It must be initiated. It is evident that UNHCR, as the global organization charged with the responsibility of assisting and protecting refugees, must play a role as intermediary in a solidarity assessment. Reference to a regional organization was added in order to strengthen the regional responsibility and because a regional organization, such as a the Council of Europe or the OSCE would have particular institutional knowledge for making such an evaluation. However, first and foremost, it is necessary that States themselves acknowledge that they would benefit from a coordinated system. Moreover, States must show willingness to extend their horizon to a global perspective of refugee protection and not seek only short term solutions from a national interest or regional interest perspective.

There are examples of international cooperation which have proved to be generally in the interests of refugees and States. Austria allowed Hungarian refugees to transit in Austria on their way to resettlement countries in the aftermath of the Hungarian crisis in 1956. From 1975 onwards, approximately one and a half million people fled Vietnam, Laos, and Cambodia. After a number of refugees had drowned in outer seas after having been towed away from land by the Coast Guard, for example, off the coast of Malaysia, the «countries of first asylum» eventually allowed access to their borders on condition that the refugees would be resettled elsewhere. Despite UNHCR's and «third countries'» resettlement efforts, many refugees remained in the «countries of first asylum» and this called for a need to find new solutions. In 1989, a UNHCR Conference was held in Geneva on South-East Asia and a comprehensive Plan of Action to provide solutions – including refugee status determination and repatriation for Vietnamese and Laotian refugees – was adopted and carried out. These examples serve to illustrate that the principle of international solidarity can and does have meaning when put into practice. However, a major difficulty in this regard is always that it takes time after a crisis has occurred for the international community to act together to find solutions. For example, the Comprehensive Plan of Action in South-East Asia is considered successful, but it was drawn up late in the day, and after this, repatriation could no longer be considered as entirely based on the will of the person concerned.

However, in 1988, an attempted concrete burden sharing scheme was proposed by the Parliamentary Assembly of the Council of Europe when it asked Member States of the Council of Europe, for humanitarian reasons, to assist Turkey which had received more than 50,000 Iraqis on its territory. The proposal concerned resettlement in other European countries, sharing of financial costs, or both.[591] This initiative did not result in much, but it pointed to a need which did not end in 1988. In the 1990s, Europe has been faced with the greatest refugee flow since the Second World War and there is every reason to state that the coordination between the receiving countries could have been handled better had a mechanism for that very purpose been established. The receiving burden in the various countries was totally out of proportion, and the protection issue remained in the hands of each and every State. The EU Resolution on certain guidelines as regards the admission of particularly vulnerable persons from the former Yugoslavia was one exception.[592] The resolution provided a framework for the concept of temporary protection, but emphasis was given to what is termed «the approach of UNHCR», that protection should be provided in the region of origin. EU Member States committed themselves to the aim of creating safe

---

591. Recommendation 1088 (1988) on the right of asylum.
592. Adopted by the Ministers of the member States of the European Communities responsible for immigration in the member States of the European Communities, meeting in Copenhagen on 1 and 2 June 1993.

conditions for Bosnian refugees and sufficient funds for them to be able to remain in these areas. Member States, however, did not honour their commitment as shown by their lack of action in July 1995, when the UN declared areas of «safe havens» for Bosnian Muslims, Screbrenica and Zepa, fell.[593]

The EU Commission's proposal for a Joint Action concerning temporary protection of displaced persons of March 1997, is an improvement in European thinking which is a step in the right direction. It is, however, limited to the fifteen Member States of the EU even though the issue of temporary protection is one with which all of Europe is faced. As with the other elements of refugee law and policy discussed which can only be resolved through a harmonized approach, the appropriate forum for discussion of this issue is the Council of Europe.

Beneficiaries of asylum

In its Note on International Protection of 1994, UNHCR raised the issue of how to extend international protection to all those in need: 1951 Convention refugees and «de facto» refugees.[594] The draft convention, as already indicated, attempts to bring forward further suggestions in this regard as the draft Article 1 merges the 1951 Convention refugee and the «de facto» refugee into one broadened refugee definition. A refugee is thus a person in need of international protection for reasons specified as persecution and for reasons of other threats to life or security. Furthermore, according to draft Article 2, refugees have a right to asylum and States have an obligation to grant asylum.

In connection with the ongoing international debate on temporary protection, beneficiaries of temporary protection include both persons who clearly qualify as 1951 Convention refugees and others who may not qualify. The need to provide international protection to persons fleeing armed conflict and civil strife, whether or not they come within the terms of the 1951 Convention definition, but whose eligibility examination for 1951 Convention refugee status is postponed, has been generally accepted in practice by States as a humanitarian responsibility in Europe. Elsewhere responsibility is also derived from treaty obligations. Furthermore, at a national level several countries have adopted or are considering adopting legislation specifically author-

---

593. Elspeth Guild, «The Developing Immigration and Asylum Policies of the European Union», Kluwer Law International, 1996, p. 297–309.
594. Note on International Protection, UN Doc. A/AC.96/830, of September 7, 1994, p.21.

izing protection on behalf of persons in need of international protection other than those covered by the 1951 Convention.

In this context and with respect to refugees fleeing the conflict and human rights abuses in the Former Yugoslavia, temporary protection was recommended for:[595]

- persons who had fled from areas affected by conflict or violence;
- persons who had been or would be exposed to human rights abuses, including those belonging to groups compelled to leave their homes by campaigns of ethnic or religious persecution; and
- persons who for other reasons specific to their personal situation are presumed to be in need of protection.

The latter category was added in order to take into consideration those persons for whom the need of protection was based on other circumstances, such as deserters, conscientious objectors, and persons of mixed ethnic origin or mixed couples. The EU Commission's proposal for a Joint Action on Temporary Protection of Displaced Persons, inspired by the categories of persons in need of international protection listed in UNHCR's Note on International Protection of 1994, are the same as the recommendations concerning the Former Yugoslavia.[596] In addition to adhering to the same categories, the Committee on Migration, Refugees and Demography of the Parliamentary Assembly of the Council of Europe, suggests including other categories to the definition, such as people fleeing from natural or ecological disasters.[597]

This latter category is a suggestion which can be understood in the context of the Council of Europe's idea of creating guidelines for persons having to flee in emergency situations. On the other hand, the discussion concerns «international protection» of refugees, and when discussing protection granted to refugees, according to whether their flight is caused by persecution or man made disasters of a more generalized character, the international protection in question is of a different kind. More often than not, it concerns protection

---

595. Humanitarian Issues Working Group of the International Conference on the Former Yugoslavia, Annex to the Survey on the Implementation of temporary Protection of 8 March 1995. See also UNHCR's Note on International Protection, UN Doc. A/AC.96/830.
596. Ibid.
597. The Committee on Migration, Refugees and Demography of the Parliamentary Assembly of the Council of Europe, Preliminary draft report on temporary protection of persons forced to flee their countries (Doc. AS/PR (1996) 21 of 18 September 1996.

of civil and political human rights principles whereas needs pertaining to shelter and other humanitarian assistance in an emergency situation caused by natural disasters concern other international responsibilities. Refugee law has always upheld the distinction between humanitarian assistance needs of victims of natural disasters on the one hand and, on the other hand, humanitarian and human rights needs of victims of man made violence. It is important that this distinction remains clear. This view is, therefore, reflected in the proposal for a new European Refugee convention which concerns refugees and refugees' needs only.[598]

The proposal for a new European convention contained in this book seeks otherwise to eliminate the existing distinctions between different categories of refugees, and to concentrate on refugees' protection needs. Discussions taking place in the different European organizations and countries are important contributions in providing protection frameworks for refugees other than the 1951 Convention refugees, but none of them go as far as to merge the refugee concepts into one. Already most European States agree that «de facto» refugees exist as well as 1951 Convention refugees, and that all should be beneficiaries of protection. It should therefore not be impossible to combine the two as proposed in draft Article 1 of the new European convention.

Treatment of refugees

The concrete text which is proposed concerning provision on the treatment of refugees in a new European refugee convention is:

Draft Article 3 TREATMENT

Asylum countries shall abide by all international principles of refugee law, human rights and humanitarian law. The treatment of refugees shall be governed by the rights pertaining to refugees contained in the Convention relating to the Status of Refugees of 28 July 1951. In the case of a mass influx situation, refugees must, as a minimum, be treated in accordance with the humanitarian standards contained in UNHCR's Executive Committee Conclusion No. 22 (XXXII). Contracting States undertake, in particular, to adopt similar rules pertaining to rights, such as education, employment and family unity.

---

598. Cf. draft Article 1 of the proposed convention, see above, p. 133–134.

The reference in draft Article 3 relates to all international human rights principles, civil and political rights as well as economic, social and cultural rights as contained in i.a. the Universal Declaration on Human Rights, The International Covenants of 1966, the Torture Convention of 1984 and the European Convention on Human Rights of 1950. Reference to humanitarian law principles relate to protection rights pertaining to civilian populations in situations of conflict as set forward in the 1949 Geneva Conventions and the 1977 Protocols.

Reference is made to the 1951 Convention in draft Article 3 as this instrument accords specific rights to those who are recognized as 1951 Convention refugees: for example, that refugees' personal status shall be governed by the law of the country of domicile, that refugees' rights acquired previously shall be respected, particularly rights pertaining to marriage, that refugees shall be treated as favourably as possible as regards the acquisition of movable and immovable property, that refugees shall have the right to participate in non-political and non-profit-making associations and trade unions, have free access to courts, have the rights to engage in wage-earning employment, etc. Furthermore, the 1951 Convention contains regulations as to a refugees' right to education, housing, freedom of movement, identification and travel documents, etc.

The rights of «de facto» refugees protected under other protection schemes such as the granting of residence permits on humanitarian grounds, vary enormously in different European States as do rights provided under temporary protection schemes.[599] However, there does seem to be general acceptance of the principle which sets a progressive standard according to the length of stay, that is, the longer the stay of the refugee the more extensive the rights granted to him. As far as refugees from the Former Yugoslavia are concerned, this «upgrading» has already occurred in most of the receiving States.

It is important that, in situations of mass influx, refugees are, as a minimum, treated according to UNHCR's Executive Committee Conclusion No. 22 (XXXII) on protection of asylum seekers in situations of large-scale influx. A specific reference to the Conclusion has therefore been made in draft Article 3 which would also ensure that this important «soft law» instrument would become a mandatory, legal basis in Europe on minimum treatment to be accorded in mass influx situations. The principle elements are: respect for the non-refoulement principle, respect for family unity and enjoyment of civil rights as set out in the Universal Declaration on Human Rights. Furthermore, refugees in a mass influx situation should, according to Conclu-

---

599. Humanitarian Issues Working group of the International Conference on the Former Yugoslavia of 8 March 1995.

sion No. 22, also be given all necessary assistance, food, shelter, etc. and voluntary repatriation or other durable solutions should be facilitated and sought after.

Rights to welfare, education, employment, and family reunification are of such fundamental importance to the refugees concerned and equally to the asylum countries, that they should indeed be harmonized at a regional level. This explains the urgent call, in draft Article 3 of the proposed convention, for States' future harmonization efforts to specifically focus on rights pertaining to these issues.

A new European regime must not in any way prejudice the 1951 Convention. Therefore, if rights accorded to refugees in a large scale influx situation are less favourable than the rights contained in the 1951 Convention, then it is of the utmost importance that refugees, who have not had their case individually examined by the time temporary protection ends after a maximum five years,[600] are guaranteed access to an individual examination of their application. If the person in question is still in need of international protection and asylum on a permanent basis is granted, the rights granted to him should be modeled on those contained in the 1951 Convention and may not, under any circumstances, be inferior to the rights contained therein.

---

600. Cf. draft Article 2(3) of the proposed convention, see above, p. 210.

CHAPTER 7
State responsibility for asylum requests

Modern transportation allows refugees to travel far in search of protection. In the 1980s, European governments became increasingly alarmed at the rise in the number of asylum seekers arriving in the countries of Western Europe. Two characteristics were identified in the upward trend of arrivals: firstly, that the majority of the new asylum seekers came from the South[601] and secondly, that with the fall of the Berlin wall and the democratic revolutions of Eastern and Central European countries, these were becoming transit countries opening up new and accessible travel routes for persons from the Middle East, Africa, and Asia. The conflicts in the Former Yugoslavia and the Caucasus in the 1990s, produced the largest refugee movements in Europe and its neighbouring regions since the Second World War, and further induced fear among the Western countries which were required to receive and host large numbers of refugees on their territory.

Such events form the background to the adoption by many Western European countries of restricive deterrent measures intended to prevent or limit the access for asylum seekers to their territories and to their asylum procedures. These measures are unilateral in the form of national legislation and bilateral in the form of readmission agreements. Since the beginning of the 1990s, the measures have, however, been increasingly regional as the Member States of the European Union have developed policies of cooperation and harmonization. The measures include the introduction of visa regulations, carrier sanctions which involve i.a. penalizing airline companies which transport asylum seekers without identity papers, the implementation of accelerated asylum procedures in order to prove asylum applications unfounded, detention of asylum seekers, restrictive interpretation of the 1951 Convention, and the application of the concept of «first

---

601. See in this respect, L. Gordenker, «Global trends in Refugee Movements», In Defense of the Alien, Vol. V. 1982, p.4 where he indicates the three principal factors causing flight from the Southern countries as being violence, the nationalist syndrome, and structural changes of societies.

country of asylum»/«safe third country concept».602 The application of the latter concept has been assisted by the establishment of so called «international zones» at airports as a means of preventing asylum seekers from gaining access to the territory and to asylum procedures. Detaining asylum seekers in these international zones, until they can be deported to the home country or to the «first country of asylum», enables States to evade their protection responsibilities under international law. The burden is shifted to another country, which is designated as responsible for examining the asylum seeker's application.

Restrictive practice and legislation gives rise to many concerns with regard to States' respect for and commitment to the upholding of obligations under international refugee law. For example, according to the practice of carrier sanctions, airlines risk being sanctioned if they allow asylum seekers on board without valid documents. Refugees are often not in possession of valid passports and visas. Therefore airline personnel, charged with the responsibility of controlling travel documents at the point of departure, end up deciding who should be allowed international protection.

Hindering flight and thus preventing access to protection for those who are in need of it, is contrary to the very purpose of the 1951 Convention which was created and adhered to by States precisely to extend protection to refugees. It is also contrary to the right to seek asylum as enshrined in Article 14 of the Universal Declaration of Human Rights. Both these instruments presuppose, as already indicated, that refugees have the possibility of flight, access to a territory, and access to asylum procedures.

The question has also been raised as to whether restrictions which hinder flight in fact constitute a violation of the non-refoulement principle. It could be argued that it would be stretching the principle too far to assume that non-refoulement envisages a prohibition against hindering asylum requests while the refugee in question is in his home country or in another coun-

---

602. The concept of «first country of asylum» indicates that the country of final destination in which the asylum seeker asks for asylum considers another country responsible for the examination of the asylum request. Traditionally it was the «first country» into which the asylum seeker entered in which he would ask for asylum and thus the terminology «first country». In spite of flight to distant lands having developed, the term «first country» has been kept. In this context, the term is a misnomer as, more often than not, the country of final destination returns the asylum seeker to the immediately preceeding country rather than the very first he had entered. In the context of cooperation among the EU countries, the concept of «first country» signifies the EU country into which an asylum seeker first enters whereas a new expression has been invented as regards countries considered responsible which are outside of the EU cooperation: hence the term «safe third country».

try.[603] The non-refoulement principle, in its strictest sense, only has territorial application and concerns return from the territory and admission at the border.[604] However, the consequences of hindering flight in this way should not be ignored.

In practice, when applying the concept of «first country of asylum»/«safe third country concept», States do not normally distinguish between asylum seekers who are refugees in need of international protection and those who are not. Other than creating difficulties for refugees to obtain access to procedures eventually leading to protection, this practice of «first country of asylum» therefore entails a real risk of violation of the non-refoulement principle.[605]

Genuine concern has been prompted among UNHCR [606], NGOs[607] and

---

603. G. Stenberg, «non-Expulsion and Non-Refoulement», 1989, p.292. K. Hailbronner also believes that the non-refoulement principle only concerns the refugees who have fled or who have asked for protection at the border, as the motive of the non-refoulement principle has never been to facilitate access to a country of refuge, «The Right to Asylum and the Future of Asylum Procedures in the European Community», International Journal of Refugee Law, Vol. 2, No.3, 1990, p.354.
604. See above Chapter 5 on «non-refoulement»
605. See below, p. 250–251.
606. UNHCR and the NGO community have been following the restrictive developments in Europe closely and they have commented on various issues. See for example the concern expressed by UNHCR and ECRE regarding the resolution on minimum guarantees for asylum procedures approved on 9 March 1995 by the Council of Ministers of Justice and Home Affairs of the Member States of the European Union, ESMV, List of Events, No. 4, April 1995, p.2. See also in this regard, UNHCR, «Up date», UNHCR concerned by EU agreement on Asylum Procedures» of 10 March 1995. For more general commentaries, see UNHCR, «Current Asylum Issues», March 1992, «Briefing on UNHCR's Position regarding Resolutions on manifestly unfounded applications for asylum and on a harmonized approach to questions concerning host third countries» of 3 December 1992, «Readmission Agreements, 'Protection Elsewhere', and Asylum Policy», of August 1994, «Fair and Expeditious Asylum Procedures» of November 1994 and «Asylum applications and the entry into force of the Schengen Implementation Agreement: Some observations of UNHCR» of March 1995. See equally, the High Commissioner, Sadako Ogata in «Refugees and asylum seekers: A Challenge to European Immigration Policy», in Towards a European Immigration Policy, 1993.

other international organizations concerned with safeguarding democratic rights, such as the Council of Europe and its bodies,[608] regarding the imposition of restrictions in Europe (and elsewhere) in the course of the last decade.

---

607. See for example, Amnesty International, «Europe: Harmonization of Asylum Policy», 1992, ECRE: «The Schengen Convention in pursuance of the Schengen Agreement of 14 June 1985 in relation to the gradual abolition of internal borders», a commentary of November 1990, «The Convention determining the State responsible for examining applications for asylum lodged in one of the Member States of the European Communities», a commentary of November 1990, «Una politica europea sull'asilo alla luce dei principi consolidati» of April 1994 and «Position on the Implementation of the Dublin Convention» of 1 December 1997. See also The Danish Refugee Council and the Danish Center for Human Rights, «The Effects of Carrier Sanctions on the Asylum System», M. Kjærum, (Ed.), The Norwegian Organization for Asylum Seekers (NOAS), «Virkninger av EF's indre marked i forhold til asylsøkere og flyktninger i Norge», («The effect of the Internal Market of the European Communities for Asylum Seekers in Norway») November 1990, NOAS, «En mur rundt Europa – Konsekvenser for Norge», («A wall around Europe – Consequences for Norway»), 1992 and the Standing Committee of Experts on International Immigration, Refugee and Criminal Law, «Schengen», November 1991.

608. See Recommendation 1149 (1991) on Europe of 1992 and refugee policies in which the Parliamentary Assembly of the Council of Europe declares that «...the coordination of European refugee policies cannot just be based on common restrictive measures and limited to twelve Member States of the European Community». According to the Parliamentary Assembly, the 1951 Convention and the European Convention on Human Rights should be taken as a basis for the harmonization of policies and rules on asylum in all the Council of Europe Member States. It also invites Member States to «...intensify their cooperation policies that will contribute to a better protection of human rights and greater social and economic development in the asylum seekers' countries of origin so as to slow down the population flows towards Europe». See also Report on the arrival of asylum applicants in the European airports (Rapporteur Lord Mackie of Benshie), Council of Europe, Doc. 6490, of September 2, 1991; the Rreport on Europe of 1992 and refugee policies (Rapporteur Sir John Hunt), Council of Europe, Doc. 6413, April 12, 1991 and Recommendation No. R (94)5, adopted by the Committee of Ministers of the Council of Europe on 21 June 1994 concerning practice vis-à-vis asylum seekers in European airports and Ch. Giakoumopoulos, «L'étranger en 'zone internationale' et les garanties de la Convention des Droits de l'Homme», CAHAR (92) 3 of 19 June 1992. In January 1997, the Committee on Civil Liverties and Internal Affairs of the European Parliament (Rapporteur: Ms. Anne Van Lancker) added its voice and critical comments in a Report on the Functioning and Future of Schengen (Doc. A4-0014/97) based on Anne Van Lancker's Working Document «The operation of Schengen: an evaluation» of 15 October 1996 (Doc. EN7DT7305/305700).

This concern has been expressed in policy documents and in legal literature.[609]

The various international actors in the field of refugee protection, have a crucial role to play in actual refoulement situations. UNHCR, for example, has the duty to speak up each time it is aware of the risk of refoulement of refugees in all parts of the world – in mass exodus situations in Africa or Asia and on behalf of the individual asylum seeker at a European airport. UNHCR's presence and protection priorities are therefore essential. NGOs can also act on behalf of individuals and have successfully undertaken monitoring and reporting work as for example through an NGO network monitoring the consequences of the application of the «safe third country concept» in different countries.

If it is necessary to admit that States are, at present, neither obliged to grant asylum nor to facilitate access to their territory, the value of a European refugee protection regime must be called into question. This is surely contrary to the «European humanitarian tradition» which European countries so

---

609. See M. Moussalli in «Mémoire du HCR sur les questions d'actualié relatives à l'asile», Documentation-Réfugiés, no. 182, 1 May 1992, p.12. See also E. Mignon, who believes that the use of carrier sanctions, by preventing access to territory is a twist of the non-refoulement principle, «Réfugiés et compagnies aériennes», Revue du droit des étrangers, No. 56, 1989, p.295 and E. Feller, «Carrier Sanctions and International Law», International Journal of Refugee Law, Vol. 1, No.1, 1989, p.58, Danish Refugee Council, M. Kjærum, (Ed.), «The Role of Airline Companies in the Asylum Procedure», July 1988, p. 8 and 9 and the Permanent Commission of Experts on International Penal Law, Foreigners, and Refugees, «Carrier Sanctions», 1992, p.1; K. Hailbronner, «The Right to Asylum and the Future of Asylum Procedures in the European Community», International Journal of Refugee Law, Vol. 2, No. 3, 1990, p.353-354, G. Stenberg, «Non-Refoulement and Non-Extradition», p.289 and after; J.Y.Carlier, «Droit d'asile et démocratie», L'Express, 26 April 1995, p.22. G. Melander, «'Country of First Asylum', Issues: A European Perspective», p.101-107; N. Gamrasni-Ahlen, «Recent European Developments Regarding Refugees: The Dublin Convention and the French Perspective» in Asylum Law & Practice in Europe and North America, 1992, p.109-123; G. Goodwin-Gill, «Safe Country? Says Who?», Refugees, May 1992, p.37 and 38, P. Rudge, «Refugee Policy to 1992 and Beyond», Speech given during the commemoration of the 40th anniversary of the 1951 Convention, June 1991 and D. Martin, (Ed.) «The New Asylum Seekers: Refugee Law in the 1980's», 1988, Johannes van der Klaauw, «Refugee protection in Western Europe: A UNHCR Perspective, 1997, p. 227-248, Johannes van der Klaauw, «The Provisions on Human Rights and Asylum in the Revised Treaty on European Union», Netherlands Quarterly on Human Rights, 15/2, p. 365-369; and the U.S. Committee for Refugees, Fortress Europe's Moat: The «Safe Third Country Concept», July 1997.

readily refer to when criticizing incidents of violations of refugee law in other parts of the world. In 1988, the Parliamentary Assembly of the Council of Europe recommended Member States «... to make arrangements so that those who are still in the country where they are persecuted may be able to exercise their right to asylum with regard to Council of Europe Member States».[610] This recommendation should serve as a reminder to Member States of their obligations when States apply the «first country of asylum»/ «safe third country» concept. The question that States must address is whether it is justifiable to use the concept as a legal barrier against refugees obtaining access to asylum procedures, because the fundamental point remains, that if the 1951 Convention is to make any sense, asylum seekers must be guaranteed access to an asylum procedure.

Designating which country should be responsible for the examination of asylum requests therefore demands procedural rules to be drawn up between States of which defining international burden sharing principles would have to be an essential element. The application of the «first country of asylum» / «safe third country» concept also has substantial consequences for refugee determination procedures and therefore needs to be considered as part of a whole which works at the same time towards a harmonized approach to the refugee concept and to the right of asylum. Harmonization of legal safeguards for the protection of asylum seekers through the process of application of the «first country of asylum»/«safe third country» concept is also required. All these issues, if resolved as matters of material and procedural law, would serve to fill gaps in the existing internatioal refugee protection regime at a European regional level.

The issue of designating a responsible State, needs to be addressed in an appropriate international setting. It would seem logical that such a discussion also takes place within the framework of the Council of Europe in the context of negotiations for a new European refugee Convention as proposed in this book.

7.1 «First country of asylum»/«safe third country» concept

The «first country of asylum» concept is, as already indicated, known in the European context also as «safe third country concept», or as «principle of first receiving country» or «country responsible for examining an asylum request». Sometimes the term «protection elsewhere» is used to describe the same phe-

---

610. Recommendation 1088 of 7 October 1988.

nomenon, that protection has been sought or could have been sought in another country which is therefore, according to varying criteria, regarded as the country responsible for the asylum request.

The use of the term «first country of asylum» in this context, is an inadequate and misleading description of what the «first country of asylum»concept means in current practice. It implies wrongly that «asylum», is granted in the first country in which the asylum seeker arrives. In reality, the term is merely an indication of which country is meant to grant access to refugee status determination procedures, the result of which may or may not be acceptance and asylum, or rejection and deportation.

More often than not, asylum seekers travel through many countries before they reach the country in which the asylum request is presented. According to practice, it is therefore normally not the first country the asylum seeker entered to which he is returned, but the country immediately preceeding the deporting country. Sometimes one deportation leads to another giving rise to the phenomenen of so called chain deportations. These are a manifestation of the refusal, of all the countries through which the asylum seeker has passed, to give access to the asylum procedure. In this way countries are able to evade responsibility under international law to protect those in need and no one is held accountable for the fate of the individual refugee. As described by the US Committee for refugees, «...lip service to the non-refoulement principle and «general conditions of safety» given by officials in the deporting state will do little to help those who are being mistreated in a country farther down the chain because few mechanisms or safeguards now exist to provide accountability for those violations. The whole concept risks leading those responsible for upholding principles of protection into the trap of behaving according to the classic adage 'out of sight and out of mind'».[611]

The term «safe third country» provides a more accurate description of the reality of its application. The term is used by EU Member States in relation to countries which do not participate in their regional framework of cooperation in the field of refugee and asylum issues, but to which refugees and asylum seekers are deported on the presumption that such countries are «safe». In the London resolution on «safe third countries», safe is defined according to reference to various human rights instruments.[612] In relation to the EU framework otherwise, a «safe» country is, first of all, all other Member States. The concept is otherwise defined according to national law and practice.

---

611. U.S. Committee for Refugees (USCR), «European «Safe Country» System Creates a New Berlin Wall, 1997, p.10.
612. See below, p. 264.

Refugees have the right to seek asylum, but they do not, according to the way in which the concept of «first country of asylum» is currently applied and being codified regionally, have the right to choose the country in which refugee status will be determined and asylum possibly granted.[613] For example, if an asylum seeker from Congo travels through Cairo, Istanbul and Rome before he reaches Copenhagen, he risks being refused access to Danish refugee status determination procedures in reference to the «first country of asylum»/«safe third country» concept. The Danish authorities may in such a case consider Italy responsible for the asylum request since the asylum seeker had travelled through this country immediately before coming to Denmark and perhaps even spent a few days there. Deporting the asylum seeker to Italy would be an application of the concept of «first country of asylum». If, on the other hand, the Danish authorities were to discover that in spite of having travelled to Denmark directly from Italy, the asylum seeker had, on the way to Italy, travelled via Istanbul, they may decide to pass over Italy and return the person directly to Turkey. In this scenario the expression «safe third country» would be the appropriate term as Turkey is a country outside the cooperation of the EU Member States and therefore a «third country».

If the asylum seeker were to be sent from Copenhagen to Rome and on to Istanbul without the case being examined anywhere, he would become a victim of chain deportation and could be characterized as a refugee «in orbit». This is a situation which EU Member States supposedly wish to combat through their endeavours to harmonize their practice as regards the designation of the country which is responsible for an asylum request.[614] In the worst cases, chain deportations lead to a person actually being returned to the country from which he fled in order to avoid persecution or other threats to his life or freedom. If the asylum seeker's fear was well-founded, this deportation would constitute a violation of the non-refoulement principle, which A. Grahl-Madsen called the «principle of civilization».[615] According to the non-refoulement principle therefore, an asylum seeker may only be deported to another country if it is a «safe» country and thus the expression «safe third country concept».

The «first country of asylum»/«safe third country» concept is not an established principle of international law. Rather it is found in national legislation and bilateral instruments (refoulement accords or readmission accords)[616]

---

613. On asylum seekers' right to choose their own asylum country, see below, p. 260.
614. See below, p. 257 and following.
615. A. Grahl-Madsen, «International Refugee Law Today and Tomorrow», Archiv des Völkerrechts, 20, Band, 1982, p. 439.
616. For example between Germany and its neighbouring countries. Further on re-admission accords, see below, p. 270–273.

and in regional instruments.[617] The origin of the concept can appearently be traced to the Scandinavian countries.[618] At a regional level, from 1978-1988, the Council of Europe tried without success to establish a European agreement on the designation of responsibility for the examination of asylum requests. The Committee of experts CAHAR, which undertook the work, presented its final report in January 1989.[619] The report includes the draft project for a regulation on the determination of the country responsible for examining an asylum request, but which until recently had not been followed up on by the Committee of Ministers. In November 1997, the Committee of Ministers adopted a Recommendation which contains guidelines on the application of the «safe third country» concept.[620] The failure of the Council of Europe to arrive at a draft upon which all the Member States could find consensus arises from the conflict of interests which exists between those countries which have traditionally been «first» countries of asylum and those which have traditionally been «second» countries of asylum.[621] Moreover, as a result of the slowness and diversity of opinion within the Council of Europe context, however, intergovernmental negotiations among EU Member States took over the dynamic and the leading role for providing European standards in refugee and asylum law since the mid 1980s.

Issues relating to the «first country of asylum»/«safe third country» concept have since been addressed in various international instruments. The Convention Determining the State Responsible for Examining Applications for Asylum Lodged in One of the Member States of the European Communities (the Dublin Convention),[622] which entered into force on 1 September 1997 in twelve of the EU Member States, has incorporated the concept as one of

---

617. For example, the Benelux Treaty of 1960 between Belgium, Luxembourg, and Holland which is an agreement facilitating border control between these three countries. Other examples are the Treaty of Aix-la-Chapelle of 1969 between Germany, Belgium, and Holland; the Treaty between Germany and Luxemburg of 1977 and the Treaty between Germany and France of 1978. Other existing treaties which also concern countries not participating in the Schengen cooperation, are, for example, the Treaty between Germany, France, and Switzerland and Germany and the Nordic countries of 1954.
618. G. Melander, «Country of First Asylum» issues : A European Perspective» in «Asylum Law & Practice», Ed. J.Bhabac & G. Cole, Europe & North America, 1992, p.102.
619. CAHAR (88) Final of 25 January 1988. See also below, p. 249–250, on the recent developments on the «safe third country» concept in CAHAR,
620. Reccommendation No. R(97)22 of 25 November 1997.
621. See the commentaries on the CAHAR debates in the Report of the seminar «Responsibility for Examining an Asylum Request», Raoul Wallenberg Institute, Lund, 24–26 April 1985, published in 1986, M.O. Wiederkehr, p.17–21 and G. Melander, p. 9–16.

its criteria for determining which country should be responsible for an asylum request. As regards the remaining three State parties, the Convention entered into force in Austria and Sweden on 1 October 1997 whereas Finland is not expected to become party until sometime in 1998. The «first country of asylum»/«safe third country» concept can also be deduced from the Convention applying the Schengen Agreement of 14 June 1985 between the Governments of the States of the Benelux Economic Union, the Federal Republic of Germany, and the French Republic, on the Gradual Abolition of Checks at their Common Borders (the Schengen Convention). Since the original five States adopted the Schengen Agreement as a Convention on 19 June 1990, all EU countries, with the exception of the UK and Ireland, have joined, or stated their intention to join the Convention.[623] The Schengen Convention has been in force since 26 March 1995 in France, Germany, Portugal, Spain and the Benelux-countries.

During its London meeting in November/December 1992, the Ministers of Immigration of the European Communities, adopted three resolutions of relevance to the application of the «safe third country» concept, the «London Resolutions».[624] Firstly, the Resolution on a harmonized approach to questions concerning host third countries (the «safe third country» Resolution), which moves refugee determination procedures out of the Union. Secondly, the Resolution on manifestly unfounded applications for asylum, which seeks to harmonize law and practice on accelerated procedures by which asylum seekers may be rejected. An example would be rejection on the grounds that the application falls within the provisions of the «safe third country» Resolution. In spite of the fact that these resolutions are «soft law» instruments, they have proved to be directive in character and their content has, as was expected, been incorporated into national legislation and practice of the EU Member States. The third London Resolution, the Conclusion on countries in which there is generally no serious risk of persecution, concerns the establishment of a concept which serves to harmonize the approach to appli-

---

622. The Dublin Convention was signed on 15 June 1990 by eleven member States of the then European Community. Denmark reserved itself. Ireland and the Netherlands depositing their final instruments of ratification on 13 June 1997
623. Italy signed the Schengen Convention in November 1990. Spain and Portugal signed in June 1991. Greece signed in November 1992 and Austria in April 1995. Denmark, Finland and Sweden signed in December 1996, and Norway and Iceland, not member States to the EU, signed association agreements for membership in December 1996. The agreements with Norway and Iceland need, however, to be renegotiated because of ICG's decision to incorporate the work undertaken in the Schengen coopertion context (the «Schengen acquis») into the Third Pillar of the EU cooperation.
624. On the introduction of the London Resolutions, see below p. 262–267.

cations from countries which give rise to a high proportion of clearly unfounded applications and thereby to reduce the pressure on asylum determination procedures.[625] This resolution is, as already noted, however, less imperative. The Dublin and Schengen Conventions and the London Resolutions form what will hereafter be referred to as the «Dublin/Schengen regime».

Harmonization efforts among EU Member States in particular have led to legislations being adopted accordingly at the national level. EU cooperation in this domain has also influenced other countries which, at the time of negotiations of the Schengen and Dublin Conventions, were outside the framework of cooperation. For example, Austria adopted a new Asylum Law in 1991 which includes the «first country of asylum» concept. In Norway, the concept has been used in practice for a long time and in 1988 it was incorporated into the Alien's Act. The adoption of the new German law in 1993 marked a turning point in the European context. As a consequence of a generous asylum policy and this country's particular geographical situation, the reception of asylum seekers in Germany reached its peak in 1992 with 438,191 arrivals. After the entry into force of the new legislation, there was a marked decrease of 70 % in the number of asylum seekers arriving in Germany. Asylum seekers have not, of course, simply disappeared, but have been shifted elsewhere by the application of the «first country of asylum»/«safe third country» concept. Consequently, the countries of Central and Eastern Europe which have found themselves at the receiving end of the change in German policy, are now contemplating or in the process of adopting «safe third country» laws to counteract the increase in numbers of asylum seekers they are experiencing as a result of West European restrictive measures.[626]

The application of the concept of «first country of asylum» is, above all, a European practice, but it is not restricted to this one continent. The consequences of its application are global. For example, in 1995 when refusing to receive Rwandan refugees who had stayed temporarily in Zaïre, the authorities in Tanzania referred to the concept of «first country of asylum» as it is applied in European asylum practice. Situations also arise in which countries considered to be «first countries of asylum» by others refuse to receive refugees back, as did Pakistan at the end of the 1980s, when the Pakistani author-

---

625. See, Elspeth Guild, «The Developing Immigration and Asylum Policies of the European Union», p. 177-189.
626. In 1995, 842 asylum seekers requested asylum in Poland while the 1996 figure was 3,205 asylum seekers. Similarly, in the Czech Republic, while there were 1,406 asylum applications in 1995, the figure had risen to 2,156 in 1996. See, USCR, «European «Safe Third Country» System Creates a New Berlin Wall».

ities refused to readmit the Iranian refugees who had spontaneously travelled to other countries in search of asylum. Those who were readmitted to Pakistan were held in custody for a long time. This was, no doubt, to demonstrate to other potential «queue jumping» asylum seekers, that leaving the «first country» and then hoping to return, once the next country had refused admittance to an asylum procedure, should not be taken for granted. The Pakistani policy of hindering readmission and detaining those who were allowed back into Pakistani territory also served as a signal to the sending countries, intended to discourage future application of the concept of «first country of asylum».[627] These examples indicate that the application and the consequences of the use of the «first country of asylum» concept are international and the policy should not, and indeed can not, be applied on merely a unilateral or regional level. The lack of internationally accepted common criteria governing a practice which is already universally known and applied is therefore a lacuna in international law which has negative effects on refugees and their protection.

In this context pan-European efforts of legal harmonization in this area, are urgently needed. There are several advantages to undertaking these under the auspices of the Council of Europe. First of all, as regards ensuring access to refugee determination procedures as a basic human right, the harmonization could tend towards the incorporation of legal safeguards, which prohibit the use of the «first country of asylum»/«safe third country» concept unless the «first country» explicitly agrees to receive them and to give access to asylum procedures there.[628] As a second point, broadening the scope of application of the concept to forty member countries instead of to the limited number of countries participating in the «Dublin/Schengen regime» and bilateral agreements, would contribute to an acknowledgement of the interests of not only the sending States, but also those of receiving States. The premise of burden sharing which would thus be introduced into the application of the concept, could then equally be upheld in relation to «third countries» outside Europe. There is no reason why such measures, based on the principle of international solidarity, should not form part of a regional instrument.

«Third countries» do not necessarily regard themselves as responsible for examining asylum requests of those returned to them, particularly, as is often the case, when asylum seekers are returned following a brief stay in transit at the airport. This should be kept in mind while assessing the provisions introduced by the «Dublin/Schengen regime» which state that one State, and only

---

627. M. Petersen, «Le pays d'asile», Séminaire européen d'avocats sur la notion de «pays de premier accueil», ECRE, April 1987, p.20.
628. See below, p. 273 and following on the proposals for a new European refugee Convention.

one State, should be responsible for the examination of an asylum request. As a starting point, this represents a step forward in that those States belonging to the regime thereby acknowledge responsibility directly – a fact which could constitute a fundamental guarantee for the asylum applicant that his case will be examined.[629] However, the rule does not apply outside of the Dublin/Schengen area. Therefore, in order to ensure that asylum seekers gain access to asylum procedures, when the «safe third country» concept is applied, agreements with those countries outside the area need to be adopted. These should contain a clause in which the receiving country undertakes the obligation of examining the asylum request. The introduction of a new European refugee convention containing a provision prohibiting return unless the «third country» is willing to examine the case would be an even better safeguard.

7.2 Determination of responsibility

In general, the «first country of asylum»/«safe third country» concept is interpreted unilaterally. State practice, and the conclusion of bilateral and regional agreements have, however, contributed to the development of some supplementary criteria for identifying the country responsible for examining an asylum request. Nevertheless there is no harmonized application of the concept – a lack of European cooperation which, just as with the restrictive versus generous interpretation of the refugee concept, has resulted in differentiation of procedural application. These varied applications have direct bearing on the travel route and the country of final destination chosen by an asylum seeker. As trafficking of people continues to increase, the better the chances of having an asylum application examined in one country, the higher the price is for those who are prepared to risk anything to escape threats to their life and security. While the different approaches to the application of the «first country of asylum»/«safe third country» concept in different countries are an additional boost to the trafficking business, the pressure on the more «generous» countries in terms of the number of asylum seekers choosing them as destination countries, also increases. Instead of sharing of responsibilities, the result is an evasion by some and an overburdening on a few.

In order to resolve the problem of refugees arriving in an irregular manner, international cooperation in the area of defining criteria for the designation

---

629. P. Stefanini and F. Doublet, «Le droit d'asile en Europe: La Convention relative à la détermination de l'Etat responsable de l'examen d'une demande d'asile présentée auprès d'un Etat membre des Communautés européennes», Revue du Marché Commun et de l'Union Européenne, No. 347, May 1991, p.391.

of the State responsible for asylum requests began at the end of the 1970s as the application of the «first country of asylum» concept was established in State practice.

These new developments prompted UNHCR to become engaged in the intergovernmental cooperation at an early stage, realizing, as they did, the repercussions which the application of the «first country of asylum» concept would have on the security of refugees. In 1979, UNHCR's Executive Committee adopted Conclusion No. 15 (XXX) on refugees without an asylum country in which advice was given on the adoption of common criteria for resolving the problem of identifying the country responsible for an asylum request. No results were seen on the creation of common criteria of a mandatory nature until recently at the European regional level, with the entry into force of the «Dublin/Schengen regime». In the meantime, due to the increase of asylum seekers arriving in an irregular manner in the 1980s, the Executive Committee had adopted Conclusion No. 58 (XL) on problems of refugees and asylum seekers who move in an irregular manner from a country in which they had already found protection.[630] While recognizing the problems which States face when asylum seekers move in an irregular manner, this Conclusion also reiterates the important legal and humanitarian safegurads necessary for an adequate refugee protection regime.

As described earlier, the Member States of the Council of Europe took it upon themselves to follow UNHCR's advice and started regional negotiations to find a common platform for designating which country should be responsible for an asylum request through CAHAR. In the «travaux préparatoires», CAHAR described the «first country of asylum» concept as a series of criteria excluding competence in connection with an asylum request.[631] The common denominator of such criteria was that they are based on the assumption that the asylum seeker could have requested asylum or should have requested asylum in another country. An asylum seeker should not, in other words, have the right to choose the country to which he will present his request and which, depending on the outcome of his application, may become his country of asylum.

The impossibility of reaching a consensus on a harmonized application of the «first country of asylum» concept in the CAHAR, was then, and is now, due to the many variations which exist in national practice. It is evident that for countries geographically closer to refugee producing areas, the risk of refugee influxes is ever present. This is why several countries consider that this

---

630. See below, p. 239–241.
631. Council of Europe, «First Country of Asylum. Refugees in Orbit. Responsibility for examining asylum request», CAHAR (86), of March 17, 1986, p.3.

geographic disadvantage must be taken into consideration when the «en route» concept [632] is being assessed in connection with discussions on international harmonization. «En route» implies that a mere transit country should not be considered the country responsible for examining the asylum request, as long as it can be proved that the asylum seeker only travelled through the transit country on his way to the country of final destination. Some countries, particularly those which are geographically located on the fringes of the main refugee flows, on the other hand, interpret «en route» restrictively and apply the «first country of asylum» concept liberally. This explains why some countries claim that having passed through passport control in another country is enough to consider that the asylum seeker was no longer «en route», whereas other countries consider that a time span of between three and six months would still be acceptable for the asylum seeker to be considered as being «en route».

Some national asylum laws require that in order for an asylum request to be examined, the person in question would have had to come directly from the territory where he was persecuted. This implies that a refugee must request asylum in the first country he enters after leaving his country of origin. Traditionally, and in most cases, this involves a neighboring country. In an age of ever greater mobility, such an approach would seem to be out of touch with reality, and contradictory to both the refugees' right to seek asylum which holds no geographical limitation and to the principle of international solidarity. While seeking refuge in neighbouring countries is the most used and the most immediate way for a refugee fleeing persecution to find protection, it cannot be seen as a rule.

The assumption that a condition of direct flight is based on Article 31 of the 1951 Convention also seems far fetched. Article 31 concerns the obligation of States not to impose a penalty on refugees who have entered illegally or reside in the asylum country illegally if they have come directly from the territory where their life or freedom was threatened. Some authors, however, believe that the link which is identified between the «first country of asylum» concept and Article 31 can be explained by the phrase incorporated in Article 31 which reads: «… coming directly from a territory where their life or freedom was threatened».[633] The assumption implied by this phrase is that States have an obligation only to refugees who have arrived without having stayed

---

632. «En route» signifies that an asylum seeker traverses more than one country on his way towards the country of his final destination. See further on the «en route» concept, below, p. 244–245.
633. See, as an example, E. Kjærgaard, «The Concept of Third 'Safe Country' in Contemporary European Refugee Law» ECRE, 6th international course of ELENA, Oxford, December 16–19, 1993, p.2

in an intermediary country. However, Article 31 does not have any purpose other than to lay down penal sanctions for illegal entry and stay. The Article does not concern the granting or withdrawal of refugee status, according to the route by which a refugee enters the country in which he seeks protection.[634]

The acceptance by UNHCR of the concept of «first country of asylum», is qualified by the great importance attached to the identification of appropriate applicable criteria.[635] The one fundamental prerequisite, is that the country to which an asylum seeker is returned must be «safe», in other words, that refugees' life or security would not be in danger upon return to a «first country». According to UNHCR, the strict procedural implementation of such a guarantee, by the identification of the country responsible and the respect of appropriate safeguards is essential in order to avoid situations of refugees «in orbit», to reduce the risk of refoulement, to eliminate multiple asylum requests, and in order to ease the effect on States of «irregular movements» of refugees and asylum seekers.[636]

In 1984, G. Jaeger was asked to undertake a study on the subject of «irregular movements» so that the international community could, depending on the conclusions of this study, agree on guidelines for the application of the «first country of asylum» concept.[637] The Executive Committee Conclusion which resulted from the study was only adopted in 1989: Conclusion No. 58 (XL), concerns the problem of refugees and asylum applicants who iregularly leave a country in which protection has already been accorded to them.[638]

Due to the fact that all asylum applicants are bound to travel in an irregular manner during flight, G. Jaeger believes that a very cautious approach must be taken in defining the concept of «irregular movements».[639] This need for prudence is also confirmed by D. Anker who states that if asylum is denied to all those arriving in a country with «irregular documents» or who travel further than the first transit country, asylum would become an ever

---

634. This viewpoint is shared by CAHAR, see CAHAR (86)1, p.4
635. See above, p. 237, on Executive Conclusions No. 15 (XXX) and No. 58 (XL).
636. UNHCR, working document, «Current Asylum Issues», of March 1992, p.5.
637. G. Jaeger, «Etude des déplacements Irréguliers des demandeurs d'asile et des réfugiés», UN Doc. WG/M/3, 1 August 1985. This study was presented during the 36th session of UNHCR's Executive Committee in 1985, see Note on International Protection, Doc. A/AC.96/680, of 15 July 1986, p. 8 and 9.
638. Adopted during the 40thth session of UNHCR's Executive Committee in 1989.
639. G. Jaeger, «Irregular Movements: The Concept and Possible Solutions», in «The New Asylum Seekers: Refugee Law in the 1980's», Martinus Nijhoff Publishers, 1988, p.23.

more narrow concept.[640] These warnings were sounded a decade ago and the trend which can be identified today is certainly not in contradiction with what was predicted then: it is becoming more and more difficult to gain access to asylum procedures and it is becoming more and more difficult to gain asylum, not least because of the restrictive practice of the «first country of asylum» concept.

In his study Jaeger divided refugee displacement into two categories: that which is spontaneous, unforeseeable displacement and that which can be called authorized displacement.[641] The latter which concerns displacement authorized by the receiving State in question, obviously has never been considered as irregular movement. Spontaneous displacements on the other hand, depending on the circumstances, could be either «regular» or «irregular». Spontaneous displacement was divided into two categories: firstly, direct arrival from the country in which the refugee fears being persecuted and secondly, arrival after having stayed for a certain amount of time in one or several other countries.

As a starting point, a displacement cannot be considered «irregular» if the asylum seeker has arrived directly from the country of persecution, except if the asylum request is abusive or unfounded. This kind of «irregular movement» is covered by UNHCR's Executive Committee Conclusion No. 30 (XXXIV) on the problem of manifestly unfounded or abusive applications for refugee status or asylum[642] which concerns asylum seekers who do not have any valid reason to be considered refugees. Another example of «irregular movement» concerns those who request asylum in a «second» or «third» country by so called «queue jumping». At the end of the 1980s, for example, Iranian refugees found themselves temporarily in Turkey while waiting to be resettled in a third country. Many tried to «queue jump» by leaving Turkey in order to reach third countries without waiting for an answer from UNHCR and potential resettlement countries. Some of these «queue jumpers» were returned to Turkey. However, because of the danger of refoulement from Turkey to Iran, most «queue jumpers» did in fact profit from their «irregular movements». This was a lesson to be learnt by the international community in the context of working to speed up existing but slow resettlement procedures. International solidarity when dealing with refugees is otherwise difficult to achieve and maintain. In this particular instance, as a result of the

---

640. D.E. Anker, «Irregular movement of refugees, discretion and US Asylum Law» in a speech on «Europe and North America Consultation», September 1986, p.8.
641. G. Jaeger, «Etude des déplacements irréguliers des demandeurs d'asile et des réfugiés», p.9 and 10.
642. Adopted during the 34th session of UNHCR's Executive Committee in 1983.

slow operation of resettlement programmes, not only was the security of the refugees in a transit country threatened, but protection responsibility was shifted in an irregular manner, away from designated resettlement countries to those to which the asylum seekers moved irregularly.

Conclusion No. 58 (XL), therefore, points at the difficulties created when refugees leave the country in which protection has already been accorded to them in an irregular manner, in search of asylum or resettlement elsewhere. The concern expressed in the Conclusion arises from the destabilizing effect which irregular displacement has on organized international efforts for offering durable solutions to refugees. According to the Conclusion, asylum seekers who leave a country in which they have already found protection in an irregular manner may be returned to that country. However, the same does not apply to asylum seekers who have not done more than travel through a country, «en route» towards the country of final destination. As a conclusion to the study, Jaeger considered that as far as «indirect arrival» is concerned, displacement is to be considered «irregular» only if the asylum seeker has left a country in which he has obtained adequate protection and not a country which is shown to be merely a transit country.[643] Following from this conclusion clarification is needed on two issues. First of all, what does the concept of adequate protection or «protection elsewhere» [644] constitute and secondly, what does the concept of «transit» [645] constitute?

Criteria

In spite of the international efforts which have been made to recommend and harmonize criteria which serve to identify the country responsible for the examination of an asylum request, the application of such criteria still varies considerably in different countries. In several countries, the «technical» elements such as the delay of stay in a third country, the concept of «en route» or direct travel are decisive factors in the consideration of which is the first country of asylum. In some countries the mere fact that the asylum seeker has travelled through a third country suffices for designating that country as the one responsible for examining the asylum application, whereas in others,

---

643. See G. Jaeger, «Irregular movements: The concept and possible solutions», 1988, p. 25 and the commentaries of D.A. Martin (Ed.), «The New Asylum Seekers: Refugee Law in the 1980s», Introduction, p. Viii.
644. «Protection elsewhere» gives an indication not only of a country which has already granted asylum or equivalent protection, but it is also used to describe a country in which the asylum seeker could have sought protection. More on the concept, see below, p. 246–250.
645. See below, p. 244–245.

it is the nature of the stay upon which an assesment of whether the concept of «protection elsewhere» can be applied correctly, is based. The practice of not examining asylum requests of persons who had the option of requesting asylum elsewhere but did not do so, has been called the «pure criteria» of the «first country of asylum» concept.[646] According to this practice, even if the asylum seeker had perfectly valid reasons for not requesting asylum in the transit country, he risks being returned there all the same. In practice, States take a combination of different criteria into consideration, and often make a decision without specifying the exact reasons for their assessment. In order for a fair and realistic evaluation to be made, all elements of relevance to the case should be examined, including for example, the special links a person may have to a country in which he seeks asylum, for example, because of friends or family members already residing there.

Right to choose an asylum country
According to current policy and practice in the upholding of States' protection obligations towards refugees, asylum seekers do not have the right to choose their country of asylum, notwithstanding the fact that their future, according to such a choice, may well be at stake. The application of the «first country of asylum» concept is accordingly more often the rule than the exception.[647] In this regard neither European practice nor the new developments in European refugee law are in conformity with UNHCR's Executive Committee's Conclusion No. 15 (XXX)[648] which requests that States, to the extent possible, take the asylum seekers' own wishes into consideration.

As K. Hailbronner has recommended, it would seem important in the context of the limited resources of receiving States, and in order to limit the waste created by multiple or parallel requests, that in a framework of regional European cooperation, it is guaranteed that each request will be examined once. The idea of multiple requests and free choice for the asylum seekers should, however, according to Hailbronner, be abandoned if each asylum seeker has the possibility of having his request examined by at least one of the European countries.[649] To hinder free choice may appear unfair, not vis-à-vis the person who has already obtained «protection elsewhere», but rather vis-à-vis the person who was «en route» and who had not yet made an asylum request. It is not necessarily evident to the asylum seeker that any transit coun-

---

646. CAHAR (86)1, p.5.
647. See also, G. Melander, «'Country of first asylum' issues: A European Perspective», p.103.
648. Adopted during the 30th session of the Executive Committee in 1979.
649. CAHAR (91), Strasbourg, 4 September, 1991, Report by K. Hailbronner, «The concept of 'safe country' and expedient asylum procedures», p.25 and 26.

try is an appropriate asylum country even if objective criteria for safety are fulfilled. Subjective elements also matter to the individual and can reasonably be considered to influence the final destination. However, according to current European practice it is the travel route, and not the identification of a final safe destination which can turn out to be the decisive factor for the asylum seeker. Although free choice for the asylum applicant may not be the most important element of refugee protection, States should nevertheless be requested to show a certain degree of flexibility in line with UNHCR's Executive Committee Conclusion No. 15 (XXX).

The «first country of asylum» concept has developed to the advantage of the States involved in the decision-making as a way of coordinating the designation of the State responsible for the examination of an asylum request. Mechanisms of international cooperation should enable States to arrive at a better system of coordination among themselves, to an extent where due regard can also be given to asylum seekers' wishes to seek asylum in a particular country. These wishes may well be linked to considerations in addition to, or other than, the guarantee of safety, such as the wish to be in a particular country where family members and friends already reside. The fact that such considerations exist should be acknowledged by States involved in regional cooperation for the designation of a responsible asylum State in the generous spirit they are directed to by UNHCR Conclusion No. 15.

Links to a particular State
If an asylum seeker has already been granted asylum or other adequate protection by another State, a «second country» of asylum does not normally examine his new asylum request. The same applies if an asylum request by the same person is made in a country other than the one which is in the process of examining it. Hindering such so called multiple asylum requests by the same person was one of the motives behind the European cooperation which resulted in the «Dublin/Schengen regime». The system is meant to guarantee that each request is examined only once and is thereby intended to eliminate the problem of «asylum shopping», which contributes to the overloading of States' asylum systems. The most appropriate and adequate State to be responsible for examining the asylum request would in many instances be the State to which the asylum seeker has special links. UNHCR's Executive Committee Conclusion 15 (XXX) on refugees without an asylum country contains guidelines enhancing such links.

According to this Conclusion, pertinent links may be of an economic, social, or cultural character. For the individual asylum seeker it may sometimes be difficult to justify his motives and this is why G. Melander, rather than rely on personal criteria, believes that the principal rule for the evaluation of «first country of asylum» should be based on formal criteria such as concepts of «en route» and «protection elsewhere».[650] While there is a lot of merit in Melander's viewpoint on objective criteria, if possible and particularly if the asylum seeker expresses them, the more personal elements should not be disregarded.

Transit and «en route»

In practice, and during debates regarding the concept of «first country of asylum» in the CAHAR in the 1980s, a certain amount of time is allowed between the point of embarkation and debarkation in defining the country which is considered to be «en route» and therefore not responsible for the asylum claim. Such a criteria is intended to apply in the case of the asylum seeker not having any special links with the transit State.[651] The same line of thinking is reflected at the universal level in UNHCR's Executive Committee Conclusion No. 15 (XXX) which declares that «...asylum should not be refused solely on the ground that it could be sought from another State». In other words, the fact alone that an asylum seeker could have sought asylum while «en route», does not oblige the transit State to undertake responsibility for the examination of the case.

Two issues must be considered in the evaluatuon of whether a transit country is to be considered an «en route» country, or not. Firstly, the question concerning the nature of the stay, must be evaluated according to an assessment of whether it could be considered «regular» or «irregular». For a «second country», evaluating if the asylum seeker was «en route», the stay in transit must not, according to practice, necessarily have been of a regular nature in order for it to apply the «first country of asylum» concept. Secondly, the question concerning the duration of the stay needs to be evaluated. Policy in this regard also varies. Being «en route» can be a question of five minutes or six months, but the longer the stay the greater the assumption of presuming a link between the person requesting asylum and the «first country». The problem lies in determining an internationally acceptable duration of the stay to support this presumption.

Setting a criterion on which tends towards specifing a lengthy duration of stay is evidently in the interest of countries located geographically close to refugee producing areas. Although these countries may regard themselves as «transit countries», through which refugees are required to pass in order to seek protection elsewhere, other countries are more likely to consider them as «first countries of asylum» and therefore responsible for asylum requests. By

---

650. G. Melander, «'Refugees in Orbit', African Refugees and the Law», p.36.
651. CAHAR (86)1, p.27

contrast, the countries which find themselves farthest from conflicts, the «second countries», tend towards the view that the length of time required to define a country as a «transit country» should be limited. The different interests also explain why the signatory countries to the Dublin and Schengen Conventions have avoided the incorporation of the concept of transit and its effects into these instruments. Such an ommission is also an indication of the fact that West European countries no longer regard the concept of «en route» as being very important – an attitude which allows greater leeway and flexibility in the consideration of other countries outside their framework of co-operation as responsible for asylum requests.

Such a disregard for the concept of «en route» is also to be found outside the EU context. According to Norwegian practice the «first country of asylum» concept eliminates the concept of «en route» from the moment an asylum seeker crosses the border. Passing through passport control is considered to be enough for a country to be considered the responsible State. The reasoning behind this practice is that from this moment on, the asylum seeker is considered as having entered another country in which he could deposit an asylum request.[652] German practice is even stricter. Mere transit at an airport may be enough to consider an asylum seeker as having entered another country and therefore as having had the opportunity of requesting asylum there.

The «ping pong effect», where «second countries» apply the «first country of asylum» concept in a strict manner and where «first countries» refer to the concept «en route» in order to deny receiving asylum seekers back, has as a consequence, that refugees are deported from country to country. Chain deportations may very well and sometimes do end up in a vicious circle. While situations of refugees «in orbit» are created, the risk of refoulement to countries of persecution or other threats to the person's life or security is also heightened.

---

652. See E. Fisknes, «Utlendingsloven» («The Alien's Act»), Universitetsforlaget, 1994, p.191. The most outstanding example of Norwegian practice, was that of an asylum seeker from Africa who, «en route» towards Norway, was in transit at Brussels airport. He noticed that the brand of cigarettes he wished to buy were not found in the tax free transit area, so he passed through passport control with his identity papers in order to purchase cigarettes outside before continuing his flight to Oslo. Norwegian authorities considered that by leaving the transit area, the asylum applicant had entered Belgium, and applying the concept of «first country of asylum», he was returned to Belgium.

«Protection elsewhere» and «safe country» concept

In order to identify the concept of «protection elsewhere», the starting point must be an assumption that adequate protection had been offered and that it will be given if an asylum seeker is returned there. It is therefore not possible to reach agreement on the meaning of «irregular movements» before the interpretation of the notion of «protection» is universally harmonized.[653] The evaluation of the possibility of «protection elsewhere» clearly constitutes the cornerstone of the concept of «first country of asylum». The asylum seeker is refused access to procedures for the determination of his refugee status on the basis that he has already obtained protection in another country or the presumption that he could have requested asylum in this other country. In other words, the application of the «first country of asylum» concept depends on the assessment of «protection elsewhere». It is the nature and the quality of rights and possibilities for the refugee which need to be evaluated.

Simply being in transit has normally not been considered as sufficient to apply the concept of «protection elsewhere».[654] Even in Norway, a country with a limited understanding of the concept «en route», a person would at least have had to enter the country considered as «first country» – albeit very briefly. Through the application of the «first country of asylum»/«safe third country» concept, a notion of «protection elsewhere» has deveolped which includes transit countries as countries in which the asylum seeker could have asked for protection implying that transit is no longer considered as being «en route». UNHCR's Executive Committee Conclusion No. 58 (XL) addresses the issue of irregular movements of refugees and supports the position that asylum seekers who have obtained «protection elsewhere» may be refused protection by the «second country». The Conclusion does not, however, suggest that asylum seekers may be removed to countries where they have not already explicitly been granted protection.

The crucial element of protection is knowing whether the country assumed responsible for the examination of an asylum request can be considered a «safe country». The concept of «safe country» means, in simple terms, that the protection accorded or which could be accorded, corresponds to international obligations and standards of refugee and human rights law. The guarantee of life and security of the person must be real.[655]

Conclusion No. 58 (XL) provides guidelines on conditions which need to be met in order for a refugee or an asylum seeker to be returned to a «first country of asylum»: that asylum seekers are protected against refoulement and are authorized to remain in the «first country of asylum» and treated in

---

653. Ibid, p.31.
654. G. Jaeger, «Irregular movement: Concept and possible solutions», p.30.

conformity with recognized humanitarian norms until a durable solution can be offered. Furthermore, the «second country» must be sure that the asylum seeker does not risk persecution in case of return and that his physical security and liberty would not be threatened.

The fundamental element of the concept of «safe country» is obviously respect for the non-refoulement principle. Another element which should be assessed in relation with «safe country», is that an asylum seeker should not be returned to a country from where he risks being sent on and thus eventually become a refugee «in orbit». Legal literature contains diverging views on the concept of «safe country» in this regard. M. den Hond, for example, esteems that exposing refugees to «in orbit» situations is not contrary to international law.[656] K. Hailbronner, on the other hand, considers that the risk of violating the non-refoulement principle is very present in «in orbit» situations. According to him, refugee «in orbit» situations should therefore be avoided.[657] Refugee «in orbit» situations could be avoided if the «second country», before applying the «first country of asylum» concept, assured itself that the receiving State would give access to its territory and to its asylum procedures. This ought always to be a prerequisite for the application of the «first country of asylum»/«safe third country» concept and is incorporated into the proposal for a new European refugee convention.[658]

In practice, reference to «safe country» often implies a country which adheres to the 1951 Convention;[659] and obligations imposed by the 1951

---

655. The term «safe country» may, in refugee law, mean either a non- refugee producing state (country of origin) or a country of asylum in which the refugees live in safety (country of asylum). With respect to the «safe countries of origin», the Member States of the European Union adopted Conclusions on countries in which there is generally no serious risk of persecution, of 30 November, 1992, according to which a policy is envisioned in which asylum requests of nationals of certain countries considered to be «safe» may be excluded «ex officio» from eligibility procedures. See K. Hailbronner, «The concept of 'safe country' and expedient asylum procedures». See in particular p. 8-16 in which he cites state examples of the application of «safe country». Thus, it is a sort of «collective ineligibility», as G. Loesscher has called it, «The European Community and Refugees», p. 624. Regarding the application of first country of asylum, the term «safe country» evidently refers to «country of asylum».
656. M. den Hond, «Jet-Age Refugees: In Search of Balance and Cooperation» in «The New Asylum Seekers: Refugee Law in the 1980s», Marinus Nijhoff Publisheres, 1988, p.53.
657. K. Hailbronner, «The Concept of 'safe country' and expedient asylum procedures», p. 25.
658. See below, on the proposed new refugee convention, Chapter 8, draft Article 8.
659. See G. Jaeger, «Etude des déplacements irréguliers des demandeurs d'asile et des réfugiés», p.23 and 24.

Convention should, in principle, guarantee that refugees are treated according to its purpose and spirit. However, formal adherance is never sufficient; it is practice which counts and which must be assessed before the concept of «first country of asylum»/«safe third country concept» is applied. In this context it is of great concern that the interpretation of the 1951 Convention now is generally restrictive and that «de facto» refugees are not considered covered by the 1951 Convention. Also in this regard therefore, a new European refugee convention which broadens the definition of «refugee», would imply a broadened State responsibility when the assessment of safety is made.

Application of the «first country of asylum» concept implies that an asylum request is not examined in substance by the «second country». This responsibility is left to the «first country» of asylum. When applying the «first country of asylum» concept, the majority of countries therefore do not distinguish between 1951 conventional refugees, other persons in need of protection, or persons abusing the institutionalization of asylum procedures by presenting unfounded asylum requests or doing «asylum shopping». If it were invariably the case that the «first country of asylum» concept was not applied unless the receiving «first State» agreed to grant the asylum seeker access to procedures, this would constitute less of a problem. However as practice is now, there is simply no guarantee that distinction will be made between «bona fide» refugees (in the broad sense of the term) and those not in need of protection at any stage before deportation to another country with all the potential for refoulement which this entails, takes place. While waiting for a European harmonized development to this effect, countries should at the least take measures to ensure that an asylum seeker is not deported without supplying him with a document stating that he has not had his asylum request examined and that the «first country» is therefore requested to do so.

When it comes to the definition of what constitutes a «safe country», G. Jaeger is in favour of rather expansive criteria in order for it to be considered that protection is adequate in the «first country».[660] M. den Hond maintains the opposite point of view. According to him, the concept of «protection elsewhere» does not constitue anything more than minimum protection.[661] K. Hailbronner is also in accordance with M. den Hond's opinion, stating that «reasonably safe» is sufficient.[662] Hence, on the one hand, there are those who believe that a «safe country» is one which respects human rights (civil and political, as well as social, economic, and cultural) and, on the other

---

660. G. Jaeger, «Irregular movements: The concept and possible solution», p.31.
661. M. den Hond, «Jet-Age Refugees: In Search of Balance and Cooperation», p.49 and after.
662. See K. Hailbronner, «The Concept of 'safe country' and expedient asylum procedures.», p.32.

hand, there are those who esteem that in order to consider a «first country» as «safe», only a minimum is required, notably, respect for the non-refoulement principle. In this context, the interrelationship between refugee law and human rights law must be considered. While respect for the non-refoulement principle is an absolute minimum safeguard, this does not mean that other human rights can be disregarded in the assessment of criteria which need to be met in order to consider a country as «safe».

While evaluating the application of the «first country of asylum»/«safe third country concept», States should follow the guidelines of UNHCR's Executive Committee and make sure that the following conditions in the «first country» are met: ratification and respect for the principles contained in the 1951 Convention, the non-refoulement principle in particular, ratification and respect for principles contained in the international human rights instruments, readmission of refugees and asylum seekers while the examination of their requests and permanent solutions can be found, and adherance to fundamental humanitarian norms for the treatment of asylum seekers and refugees.[663]

A further and recent reference which States would be wise to observe is Recommendation No. R(1997)22, adopted by the Committee of Ministers of the Council of Europe on guidelines on the application of the «safe third country» concept. This Recommendation lays down conditions under which a country may be considered «safe» in order to provide appropriate and effective protection for asylum seekers and refugees. The Council of Europe recommends that a «third» State must meet all the criteria listed in order to be considered «safe» in each individual case. The criteria are: observance of international human rights standards, including compliance with the principles laid down in Article 3 of the European Convention on Human Rights; observance of the international principles of the 1951 Convention and its 1967 Protocol, including observance of the principle of non-refoulement and willingness by the «third country» to provide protection against refoulement and the possibility to seek asylum. This criterion is linked to the preamble which recommends that asylum seekers are given an opportunity to have their claims examined by one State. The guidelines also refer to the hypothetical case in which the asylum seeker has already received «protection elsewhere». This is deemed to include instances where he could have asked for protec-

---

663. UNHCR, «Current Asylum Issues», March 1992, p.6. These same principles are to be found in Conclusion No. 58 (XL), adopted during the 40th session of the UNHCR Executive Committee in 1989. On the concept of «safe country», see also the ECRE proposal in «Una politica europea sull'asilo alla luce dei principi consolidati», p.7. In addition to referring to the same principles as UNHCR, ECRE also emphasizes the need for guaranteeing access to eligibility procedures for refugee status in the «first country of asylum».

tion, but did not do it. This is in line with current practice, but is nevertheless not a criterion European States ought to apply.[664]

7.3 Consequences of application of the «first country of asylum»/«safe third country» concept

Refugees «in orbit»/danger of refoulement

A phenomenon of non responsibility leading to situations of refugees «in orbit» has developed as a result of the fact that States are not legally obliged to grant asylum. This has been compounded by the move towards the imposition of restictive policies by those States which have traditionally received refugees – policies which have as a basic premise the aim to prevent asylum seekers from gaining access to refugee status determination in the first place. In the absence of harmonization at an international level, the application of the «first country of asylum» concept[665] is not only restrictive but also counter productive.

Application of the «first country of asylum» concept creates refugee «in orbit» situations in three instances. Firstly, the situation results when asylum seekers who are not granted access to refugee status determination procedures because they are returned to a country where they were in transit, are returned from the transit country to the preceding country.[666] The second instance would apply when asylum seekers who are not readmitted by the «first country», for lack of agreement on readmission conditions, are consequently returned to the «second country of asylum». Finally, the situation arises when asylum applicants whose requests are deemed unfounded on account of a lack of identity papers or false papers, are refused access at the point of entry and returned to the country of transit.[667]

A refugee in an «in orbit» situation is not necessarily endangered when refused refugee status. He is not necessarily deported or returned. It may simply be that the person continues to reside without a residence permit because he has not dared to formalize his situation out of fear of deportation of refoulement.[668] However, in situations where the concept of «first country of asylum»/«safe third country» is applied, the asylum applicant is often in danger of

---

664. See further below, p. 277–278.
665. Exception made for the efforts of certain European countries as well as more limited bilateral or regional accords.
666. This is the «domino effect» addressed by S. Teloken in «The Domino Effect», Refugees, December 1993, p.38.
667. See, G. Melander, «Country of First Asylum» Issues: A European Perspective», p.102 and after.

being refused access to eligibility procedures in one country after another[669] and there are examples of violations of the non-refoulement principle where the country to which the person is returned sends the person back to the country he fled due to fear of persecution. This danger exists not least because of the differentiation which exists in the legislation and practice of different States on several aspects pertaining to the refugee determination procedure. The lack of international harmonization on basic tenets of refugee law, such as the interpretation of the 1951 Convention refugee definition or the «de facto» refugee concept, the criteria for the assessment of adequate protection, the definition of «safe country», means that refugees and asylum seekers can not be returned in safety unless all legal guarantees are provided in order to avoid the phenomenon of refugees «in orbit» and thereby eliminate the risk of refoulement.[670]

It is worth noting that as in Conclusion No. 15 (XXX) of UNHCR's Executive Committee on refugees without an asylum country, the Conference of Plenipotentiaries which negotiated the failed Convention on Territorial Asylum in 1977, had also proposed that asylum should not be refused for the sole reason that it could have been requested in another state. In 1977 there was consensus on the matter. As we know, the convention was never adopted, however, and the good will which States demonstrated at this time does not appear to count for much twenty years later. Nevertheless, it would be timely to remember the consensus of 1977 and to respect the guidelines adopted in Conclusion No. 15 (XXX) while proposing a new European regime. The only means of combating the phenomenon of refugees «in orbit» would be to create a mandatory instrument of international law which not only contains provisions identifying the State responsible for examining an asylum request, but which also designates guarantees which should accompany the application of the concept.[671]

Lack of international solidarity

As a consequence of the application of the «first country of asylum» concept, an asylum seeker is returned to the State designated responsible without due consideration to the capacity of the first country to readmit and grant an asylum seeker access to asylum procedures and adequate protection. The appli-

---

668. See Jean-Pierre Alaux, on persons who cannot provide identity papers, etc., «Plus d'asile pour ceux qui fuient guerres et misères», Le Monde Diplomatique-August 1992, p.23.
669. See G. Melander, «Responsibility for Examining an Asylum Request», International Migration Review, Summer 1986, Vol. XX, No. 2, 1986.
670. See M. Moussalli, «Mémoire du HCR sur les questions d'actualité relatives à l'asile», Refugees, No. 182, 1992, p.14.
671. See below, Chapter 8, draft Article 7 and 8 of the proposal for a new convention.

cation of the «first country of asylum» concept is derived from protectionism rather than a commitment to the protection of refugees as supposedly provided for in international refugee law. Complete ignorance or disregard by rich West European countries towards Central and East European and Southern countries' economic problems and of their lack of capacity and infrastructure to handle refugee flows, is not in harmony with the international philosophy of international solidarity and burden sharing to which they are otherwise ready to refer. Readmission agreements which give due regard to the principle of international solidarity and an assessment of receiving States' capacity to receive and absorb refugees, should serve as minimum standards. An international mechanism to evaluate and give advice on this issue should be established.[672] Between the lack of an international obligation to grant asylum and the obligation to respect the non-refoulement principle, the international community has the responsibility for protecting refugees and resolving their problems.[673] In order to succeed, a new approach in which international solidarity has its place, is not only necessary, but crucial.

In 1994, the European Commission proposed that the European Council of Ministers and the European Parliament should consider the development of «… a monitoring system for absorption capacities and creation of a mechanism which would make it possible to support Member States who are willing to assist other Member States faced with mass influx situations; similarly to support projects of Member States or third transit countries faced suddenly with new pressures».[674] This philosophy should be applied not only in the context of the limited number of European Union Member States, but should equally be developed at a broader regional and eventually, universal level. Countries which find themselves defined as «first countries» should have a voice in deciding upon the way in which responsibility for the world refugee problems is divided and shared. Only when this becomes reality can «international solidarity», beyond the lip service of political manifestos, be hoped for.

In the meantime, institutionalization of a system of burden sharing by means of a mediator or the convening of bilateral or international consultations should be contemplated.[675]

---

672. See below, p. 280–282 on draft Article 6 of the proposal for a new European refugee regime.
673. G. Melander, «Responsibility for Examining an Asylum Request», p.225.
674. Communcation of the Commission to the Council and the European Parliament on Immigration and Asylum Policies, 1994, p.42.
675. See A. Grahl-Madsen, «Refugees in Orbit – Some Constructive Proposals», Round Table on Refugees «In Orbit», International Institute of Humanitarian Law, 1979, p.16. See also below, Chapter 8 on the proposal for a new European protection regime.

7.4 Harmonization experience in the European context

The «Dublin/Schengen regime»

Harmonization so far on the level of the EU has arisen from a perceived need to tackle a growing problem of increasing numbers of arrivals.[676] Furthermore, cooperation on a common approach to asylum issues among the Member States has been spurred by concern over asylum requests considered to be abusive, in the context of the need to conciliate the opening of borders[677] with the national legislation and practices of the right of asylum. The increase of asylum applications through the 1980s was accompanied by three different phenomenons: firstly, important internal displacements within the Community which led to serious inbalance between the States; secondly, the phenomenen of the same asylum seeker presenting an asylum application in several different countries within the Community, «asylum shopping»; and thirdly, the impossibility encountered by some asylum seekers in finding a

---

676. The increase in the number of asylum seekers was unequally experienced by different States in the European Community. In the German Federal Republic, it was significant (37,000 requests in 1982, 99,700 in 1986), in the Netherlands (1,800 requests in 1982, 5,900 in 1986), in Belgium (2,900 requests in 1982, 7,700 in 1986) and in France (22,500 requests in 1982, 26,290 in 1986). In 1989, 15,000 asylum requests were registered in Great Britain as opposed to 6,000 the year before, 8,100 in Belgium, 9,000 in the Netherlands, 130,000 in the German Federal Republic, and 61,000 in France. These statistics were provided in a non-published paper by the French Ministry of the Interior and Public Security, «Le droit d'asile en Europe: La Convention relative à la détermination de l'Etat responsable de l'examen d'une demande d'asile présentée auprès d'un Etat membre des Communautés européennes», p. 4. The restrictions imposed in order to diminish the number of asylum seekers were effective in several countries. In Belgium, for example, approximately 27,000 asylum requests were deposited in 1993, whereas in 1994, the figure fell to 14,000, see «List of Events», ESMV, No. 2, February 1995, p.1. In Germany, the percentage of asylum applicant diminished by 60%, from 322, 599 asylum requests in 1993 to 127,210 asylum requests in 1994, see «List of Events», No.1, January 1995, p.2.
677. The Single European Act of 1987 created an objective within the European Communities of an area without internal frontiers for the movement of persons because with an internal market without frontiers, not only Community citizens, but also third country nationals, would be able to cross freely. This is why the so called «compensatory measures» – restrictions so as to facilitate control of foreigners, refugees and asylum seekers included, were introduced. An opening up of borders would otherwise have allowed asylum seekers to present their request in twelve different countries at the same time. See further on this in Elspeth Guild, «The Developing Immigration and Asylum Policies of the European Union» p. 113 and following.

country willing to examine their request, and thereby creating the situation of refugees «in orbit».

Designating which State should be responsible for an asylum request formed part of the cooperation which in 1990 led to common criteria being adopted at a governmental level for the application of the «first country of asylum» concept in the Dublin and Schengen Conventions which were complemented by the London Resolutions in 1992.[678] In the development of this framework of cooperation not only did it seem necessary to identify the State responsible for examining an asylum request, but it was equally important to designate that this State would be the only responsible State.

The Dublin Convention and Chapter 7 of the Schengen Convention deal with similar and duplicate asylum matters.[679] The pertinence of asylum provisions in the Schengen Convention, given that this instrument mostly deals with security problems, has been questioned also in light of the fact that refugee and asylum matters had not been specifically mentioned in the Schengen Accord.[680] The Schengen Convention includes rules on external border control, visas, police cooperation, narcotics, armed weapons, and the creation of the Schengen Information System (SIS).[681] As a result of the Intergovernmental Conference, the Schengen cooperation has now been incorporated into the third pillar issues of the EU.[682] As regards Chapter 7 of the Schengen Convention, the Executive

---

678. The entry into force of the Dublin Convention constituted «the entry into force» of the London Resolutions as well. As already indicated their legal status is, however, uncertain. It should be noted that the Commission of the European Communities expressed the opinion that, the need to procure legal security in this domain for the asylum seekers as well as member States, could justify that the content of the resolutions should be transformed into treaty law, Communication by the Commission to the European Council and Parliament, COM (94) final, paragraph 86, p.25. Proposals to this effect have later been reiterated by the EU Commissioner on asylum matters Anita Gradin, but no proposal merging all EU «soft law» instruments has yet emerged.
679. For a comparative analysis, see, C. Bruschi, «Le droit d'asile: L'Europe à l'heure des choix», Center for Information and studies on International Migration, Press Review, Vol. 2, No. 12, Nov.-Dec. 1990. P.47-72.
680. R. Dedecker, «Le droit d'asile dans Schengen», Université Libre de Bruxelles, August 1991, p.30 and J.J. Bolten, «From Schengen to Dublin», Nederlands Juristenblad, Vol. No. 5, 1991, p. 168.
681. SIS is a data base system for police cooperation in the Schengen countries in which information is gathered on undesirable persons, a classification under which arms smugglers, drug traffickers and asylum seekers are grouped together. This has caused repeated critique by refugee organizations and scholars, not least in the Nordic countries while these assessed joining in the Schengen cooperation.
682. H. Blanc, «Schengen: Le chemin de la libre circulation en Europe», Revue du Marché Commun et de l'Union européenne, No.351, October 1991, p.723.

Committee of Schengen, meeting in Bonn in April 1994, had already decided that the provisions on asylum of the Schengen Convention should be replaced by the Dublin Convention when this Convention entered into force.[683]

When the Schengen Convention entered into force in March 1995, this became the most comprehensive instrument regulating State responsibility for examining asylum requests and the «first country of asylum»/«safe third country» concept became institutionalized at a broader international level. Signatory States of the «Dublin/Schengen regime» and other European countries had already prior to its entry into force, begun to introduce domestic legislative measures to restrict access to the territory and to facilitate the return of asylum seekers.[684] The «Dublin/Schengen regime» can also be de-

---

683. Final Communication of the Meeting of the Schengen Executive Committee, held in Bonn on 26 April, 1994.
684. K. Hailbronner, «The Right to Asylum and the Future of Asylum Procedures in the European Community», p. 344 and 345 mentioned that Switzerland installed accelerated procedures for unfounded procedures in 1988. In July 1989, Sweden also adopted a new legislation which authorizes restrictive measures vis-à-vis asylum seekers such as detention and immediate return of those presenting manifestly unfounded asylum requests. The Belgian law of 1988 also allows refusal of access to the territory when requests are unfounded. On 24 August 1993, France adopted a new legislation on immigration and on 19 November 1993, Parliament approved an amendment of the Constitution with respect to asylum. The aim was to reduce the number of asylum seekers in France and to bring the Constitution into conformity with the Schengen Convention. A sentence was added which permits, but does not obligate, the rejection of an asylum seeker whose request has already been rejected in another member State of the Schengan cooperation. (ESMV, «List of Events», No. 9, September 1993, p.1). Spain adopted new legislation on asylum in the summer of 1994, which distinguishes between refugees within the terms of the 1951 Convention, and «asilados», i.e. «de facto» refugees and other humanitarian cases. Since this law was implemented, only 1951 Convention refugees are accorded asylum in Spain. The most important change is that which permits «non-access to procedures» for unfounded asylum requests or when another State is considered responsible for examining the request or when there is a «safe third country» (ESMV, «List of Events», No. 6/, June/July 1994, p. 3 and 4). The Dutch law on migration and asylum was modified in 1993 in order to be adapted to the «Schengen regime». According to the new legislation, an asylum request will not be examined if it has already been rejected by another State and if the asylum applicant has traversed another country in which he could have requested asylum before arriving in the Netherlands. If it is possible to show that the asylum applicant has the nationality of a State where he could be protected or where he has deliberately produced false identity or other documents, the decision not to examine his request may be taken after an accelerated procedure. The right of appeal for a rejected asylum request was also abolished in the new legislation. (ESMV, List of Events, No. 9, September 1993, p.4).

scribed as a formalization of already existing systems of multilateral treaties on border control and police cooperation.

In order to designate the responsible State, various criteria have been incorporated into the «Dublin/Schengen regime», of which the «first country of asylum»/«safe third country» concept is but one. These criteria include consideration of whether the State in question has issued a visa, and whether the asylum applicant has family links with the State in which he is lodging his asylum claim. Application of the «first country of asylum» is the last resort to be applied only if none of the other criteria are found to be applicable. With respect to countries outside of the cooperation, it is the «safe third country» concept which pertains as the principal rule by which the decision is taken as to whether or not to deport the asylum seeker. In order to put this concept into practice, Article 3(5) of the Dublin Convention was complemented by the London Resolution on «safe third countries» of 1992. Article 29(2) of the Schengen Convention also allows for the application of the concept without indicating that it must always be applied. If a «third country» cannot be selected as responsible for the examination of the asylum request, for example, because it cannot be considered «safe», the criteria on internal cooperation among the Member States are applied.

State autonomy as regards application of the «Dublin/Schengen regime» on access to the territory and asylum procedures has not been changed by these instruments.[685] A harmonization of rules on asylum was not sought,[686] although during the drafting of the Dublin Convention, the question was asked if it were not necessary to bring the harmonization efforts further than originally intended, for example, by harmonizing asylum criteria in relation to the interpretation of refugee status. The reasoning which was offered in support of this suggestion was that the determination of refugee status, according to objective criteria, can only be wholly acceptable as part of an international cooperation if all States apply equal procedural and substantial rules as regards the granting of refugee status and asylum. This way equality in treatment would also have been ensured irrespective of in which country the application would be examined. However, States did not consider it necessary to go this far. [687]

The instruments of the «Dublin/Schengen regime» were not adopted as legal instruments of the European Community. The way in which the intergovernmental negotiations were handled has in fact been criticized because of the lack of transparency and the lack of democratic control which accompa-

---

685. See Article 3(3) of the Dublin Convention and Article 32 cf. Article 135 of the Schengen Convention.
686. J.J. Bolten, «From Schengen to Dublin: The New Frontiers of refugee Law», p. 167.

nied the adoption of the instruments, and which would have been provided had the negotiations been conducted on the Community level, by consultation of the European Parliament before adoption.[688] However, a certain element of democratic control can be pointed to in the final stages of the process as being instruments of public international law, the Schengen and Dublin Conventions had to be ratified by national parliaments in order to enter into force. This is not to say that a parliamentary «yes or no» is enough to consider that the need for democratic control has been met. As far as judicial control is concerned, no international tribunal which would be competent in the matter has yet been instituted, which was one of the reasons why final ratification took so long. The Netherlands, for example, initially required the introduction of the competence of the European Court in Luxemburg as a prerequisite for ratification. Since it was a «pre-Maastricht-instrument», this condition did not find accord with the other Member States. The Dublin Convention did, however, introduce an administrative resolution mechanism.

Examination by at least one State
According to the preamble of the Dublin Convention, Member States undertake to «…provide all applicants for asylum with a guarantee that their applications will be examined by one of the Member States …and to ensure that applicants for asylum are not referred successively from one Member State to another without any of these States acknowledging itself to be competent to examine the application for asylum». Article 3 states that «Member States undertake to examine the application of any alien who applies at the border or in their territory to any one of them for asylum». In theory, these provisions guarantee that situations whereby refugees remain «in orbit», should no longer be created. Article 29(1) of the Schengen Convention also seeks to ensure that the contracting States undertake to process any application for asylum lodged by an alien within the territory of any one of them.

Against this background, the adoption of common rules which designate

---

687. See, the French Ministry of the Interior and Public Security, «Le droit d'asile en Europe», Office français de protection des réfugiés et apatrides (O.F.P.R.A)., 1992, p. 9. The Ministry also declared that a middle way had been explored by the European Commission in an informal proposal. Without asserting total harmonization, the proposal sought to assure a certain balance between national practices on according refugee status by instituting a European Consultative Committee in charge of issuing opinions on the definitive negative decisions on refugee status, an opinion which could then be imposed on Member States.
688. See W. De Lobkowicz, «La Convention de Dublin: Un utile complément au droit humanitaire international», Objectif Europe, New series No. 10, 1990, p. 10.

the State responsible for examining an asylum request, may be regarded as a fundamental innovation in refugee law. Until the adoption of the «Dublin/Schengen regime», there was no legally binding international instrument explicitly obliging States to examine asylum requests, although the 1951 Convention would not make sense unless States are obliged to undertake a refugee determination procedure. However, such an obligation to examine asylum requests, cannot be interpreted as equally signifying a recognition of refugee status,[689] nor can it be viewed as concerning only the country in which the asylum request was initially introduced. The underlying philosophy is that an asylum request is considered to be a request for protection and, to the extent that protection could have been requested elsewhere, the asylum request will not be examined by the country of final destination.[690]

The «Dublin/Schengen regime» has, while referring to the provisions of the 1951 Convention, preserved the right of all contracting States to return an asylum seeker to a third country. Article 3(5) of the Dublin Convention states that «Any Member State shall retain the right, pursuant to its national laws, to send an applicant for asylum to a third State, in compliance with the provisions of the Geneva Convention, as amended by the New York Protocol». This principle allowing for the «safe third country concept» to be applied has been supplemented by the 1992 Resolution on host third countries.[691] Article 29(2), paragraph 2, of the Schengen Convention equally declares, that in spite of the signatory States' undertaking the obligation to process asylum applications, they «…retain the right to refuse entry or to expel any applicant for asylum to a «third country» on the basis of its national provisions and in accordance with its international commitments». Reference to human rights instruments, such as the European Convention of Human Rights of 1950 and the Torture Convention of 1984, could have been incorporated, although they are no less valid for not having been mentioned specifically.

According to Article 8 of the Dublin Convention, in cases where there is

---

689. French Ministry of the Interior and Public Security, «Le droit d'asile en Europe», p.8. See also, P. Stefanini and F. Doublet, «Le droit d'asile en Europe: La convention relative à la détermination de l'Etat résponsable de l'examen d'une demande d'asile presentée auprès d'un Etat membre des Communautés européennes», p. 395.
690. See, J.J. Bolten, «From Schengen to Dublin», 1991, p.172 in which she refers to the European doctrine of asylum by A. Grahl-Madsen, according to whom the grant of asylum means that the individual has the right to stay in the territory of the asylum State, not for ever, but as long a time as the person retains refugee status or until the moment in which he acquires a residence permit in another country, «Territorial Asylum», p. 52.
691. See below, p. 262–267.

no country to which an asylum seeker can be returned, one of the Member States must give access to its refugee determination procedure. Responsibility to examine such an application then rests with the Member State in which the asylum application was first lodged. This is the case, for example, in situations where it is difficult to prove which country or countries an asylum seeker has traversed, or, in situations where the «first country of asylum» can be identified, but may not be considered «safe» or may even refuse to readmit the asylum seeker. What is new for asylum seekers in Europe, therefore, is that they acquire a guarantee that if there is no «third State» to which they can be returned, one of the signatory States will examine their request.[692]

In situations where the responsibility for examining an asylum request belongs to a Member State, its obligation is firstly, to allow the asylum seeker access onto its territory and to readmit an asylum seeker who finds himself, in an irregular manner, in another Member State and secondly, to proceed to the examination of the asylum request according to conditions set forth by its national legislation and in accordance with the 1951 Convention.

However, with the exception of cases where there is no «third country» to which an asylum seeker could be returned, it would not be safe to assume that there is indeed a guarantee that at least one signatory State will assume responsibility for examining an asylum request and thereby solve the phenomena of refugees «in orbit». In practice, States have clearly demonstarted that they first and foremost apply the «safe third country concept», often without obtaining the prior consent of the country considered responsible.[693] This practice has developed in spite of the explicit aim of the drafters of the Dublin Convention, as outlined in the Preamble of the Convention, to prevent asylum seekers from being referred successively from one State to another without any single State acknowledging responsibility for the examination of the asylum request. Indeed, if the declared aim of the Preamble had been followed, not only among Member States of the Dublin Convention, but in general, then cases involving «in orbit» refugees would cease. It is precisely because of the lack of adequate cooperation between Member States of the Dublin Convention and the rest of the world's approximately 170 States, that the problem of «in orbit» refugees continues to persist.

---

692. See in this respect, W. De Lobkowicz, «La Communauté européenne et le droit d'asile», Flüchtlingsproblem eine Zeitbombe?, Schweizerisches Institut fur Auslandsforschung, Verlag Rüegger, 1991, p.53. See also the rules of implementation of the Dublin Convention in Article 3 of the Resolution on «safe third countries» and Article 30(3) of the Schengen Convention.
693. See, in this regard, the examples of refugees «in orbit» in «Safe Third Countries», Myths and Realities, ECRE, 1995.

Criteria according to the «Dublin/Schengen regime»

The preamble of the Dublin Convention guarantees common adhesion to the 1951 Convention and its Article 2 reaffirms the obligations of Member States within the terms of the 1951 Convention, as well as their commitment to cooperate with the UNHCR. Article 28 of the Schengen Convention reiterates this aim, as do the London Resolutions of 1992.

These references to the 1951 Convention should be interpreted in good faith and should form a sufficient guarantee to ensure that the application of the concept of «first country of asylum»/«safe third country» concept should not be used contrary to the letter or the spirit of the 1951 Convention. The risk remains, however, that the reference to this fundamental instrument for refugee protection, to which all the contracting States have adhered, will remain symbolic. Firstly, because implementation and practice of receiving States is seemingly more important than the formality of having adhered to the instruments themselves, a fact which is not always taken into consideration in practice. Secondly, because the 1951 Convention is now, more often than not, interpreted in a restrictive manner. Thirdly, because «de facto» refugees are not covered. Fourthly, because the application of the «safe third country» concept, and in particular the definition of what constitutes «safe», varies from one country to another and consequently so does the interpretation of what constitutes «refoulement», according to the 1951 Convention and finally, because the application of the «first country of asylum»/«safe third country» concept, triggers chain deportations, which creates problems of non-accountability.

When determining which country should be responsible for an sylum request, neither the Dublin Convention nor the Schengen Convention, aim at taking the intentions of the asylum seeker into consideration, though the personal situation of the asylum seeker may be taken into account. This has been repeatedly criticized[694] and it is in contradiction with UNHCR's Executive Committe guidelines outlined in Conclusion No. 15 (XXX) of 1979.

Article 4 of the Dublin Convention, concerning the principle of «family unity», is the first of the criteria which is taken into accout when determining which of the contracting parties is responsible for an asylum request. Articles 5 and 7 concern the issuance of residence permits and visas. The underlying principle of the Dublin Convention is, that the responsibility for handling an asylum request should belong to the Member State which has played the most significant role in causing the arrival of the asylum seeker into the territory covered by the Convention. However, Article 8 states that in the event

---

694. See, for example, E. Kjærgaard, «The Concept of 'Safe Third Country' in Contemporary European Refugee Law», p.6.

that none of the above mentioned criteria are applicable, responsibility for the examination of an asylum request should fall on the Member State in which the asylum request was first presented. In other words, the «first country of asylum»-concept applies only in cases where none of the other criteria are applicable, including cases involving the «safe third country» concept.

According to Article 1(d) of the Resolution on «safe third countries», the provisions of the Dublin Convention are applicable only if the asylum applicant is not returned to a «safe third country». Thus it is up to the «second country», which in this instance would be a Dublin Convention contracting party, to define which should be a «first country» and, therefore, the responsible country. Article 3(b) of the Resolution on «safe third countries» states that if the country responsible for the asylum request is one of the contracting parties, the latter cannot decline the responsibility for examining an asylum request by invoking that the petitioning Member State should have sent the applicant to a «safe third country». However, due to Article 3(c) of the same Resolution, the Member State considered responsible maintains the right to send an asylum seeker to a third country. Article 30 of the Schengen Convention includes similar principles. It could thus be assumed, that among the Member States of the «Dublin/Schengen regime» there is an understanding of not burdening each other unless it is necessary. An equivalent attitude vis-à-vis «third countries» is more difficult to establish.

It is important to note, however, that neither Article 3(4) of the Dublin Convention nor Article 29(4) of the Schengen Convention obligate States to apply the «first country of asylum»/«safe third country» concept. In addition, Article 1(e) of the Resolution on «safe third countries» states that «Any Member State retains the right, for humanitarian reasons, not to remove the asylum applicant to a host third country» and, in accordance with the preamble of the Resolution on manifestly unfounded asylum requests, States are, in exceptional cases and in conformity with their national legislation, allowed to grant «…exceptional stay of aliens for other compelling reasons outside the terms of the Geneva Convention». In each instance the decision to use these «opt out» clauses rests with the «second State». However, in order for Article 3(4) of the Dublin Convention to be applied, the asylum seeker must have given his consensus. This does not, however, allow for an asylum seeker to request the use of the clause, a right which would have been of significance, for example, in order to make the deciding State aware of the personal interests of the person involved, and whose future is at stake.

The London Resolutions

In its Report of 3 December 1991, the «Ad hoc Group on Immigration»[695] (Ministers of Immigration of the Member States of the European Community) listed three options for the application of a «first country of asylum» concept. Firstly, in harmony with the practice of several countries, that the return of refugees to «first countries of asylum» should only take place after the asylum procedure has begun, and refugee status has been declared well-founded. Secondly, that the concept be applied to every asylum seeker, without prejudice to his refugee status, which would imply that no examination of an asylum request would be carried out if a «first country of asylum» existed. Thirdly, a mixture of the two former options was envisaged, with the use of the first option for asylum seekers already on the territory of a contracting party and the second option for those at the border.[696]

West European governments retained the second option for their harmonization project as Article 3(5) of the Dublin Convention was complemented by the London Resolutions of 1992 which include criteria for implementing the «first country of asylum» concept, vis-à-vis «third countries». According to Article 1(a) of the Resolution on «safe third countries», the formal identification of a host third country precedes the substantive examination of the application for asylum and its justification, which has resulted in the creation of a «filter system».[697] As long as there is a «third country», the examination of the request for refugee status may be refused and the asylum seeker may be returned there (Article 1(c)).

The Schengen countries did not adopt instruments similar to the London Resolutions. However, the signatory States of the Schengen Convention are, to a large extent, the same as those which adopted the Dublin Convention and the London resolutions, indicating that the priority given to the application of the concept of «first country of asylum» is the same as has been confirmed by practice, since the entry into force of the Schengen Convention. In spite of the uncertain legal weight of the London Resolutions, the contracting States also agreed to incorporate the principles contained in the resolutions into national legislation and existing State practice

The aim of the Resolution on «safe third countries» was to harmonize Member States' practice with regard to the return of asylum seekers to countries outside the EU and thereby, in a unilateral[698] manner, to consider these

---

695. Document SN 4038/91 (WG 930), Brussels, December 3, 1991, p.41 and 42.
696. See in this regard, R. Fernhout and H. Meijers, «Asylum» in «A New Immigration Law for Europe», Nederlands Centrum Buitenlanders, Utrecht, 1993, p.16.
697. If the asylum seeker cannot, in practice, be returned to a «safe third country», the provisions of the Dublin Convention are applicable, (Article 1(d)).

«third countries» responsible for the asylum request. The Resolution expresses its concern with « ... the problem of refugees and asylum seekers unlawfully leaving countries where they have already been granted protection or have had a genuine opportunity to seek such protection ... » and the conviction that a concerted response should be made.[699] The first part of the Resolution deals with those persons who have already found protection elsewhere and refers to UNHCR's Executive Committee Conclusion No. 58 (XL), concerning the problem of refugees and asylum seekers who move in an irregular manner from a country in which they have already found protection. The second part of the Resolution, however, which regards refugees and asylum seekers who have not found protection, but who are nevertheless considered as having had an opportunity to seek it whilst travelling towards a country of final destination, is based on the established practice, whereby contracting States use every opportunity to rid themselves of responsibility. UNHCR did not participate in the making of this Resolution, indeed, it should be noted that the current High Commissioner for Refugees has expressed that the «first country of asylum»/«safe third country» concept should not be applied to an asylum seeker, if he has only transited through a country, to which he has no links and in which he had no contact with the authorities.[700]

Article 1 of the Resolution on host third countries contains certain procedural principles, such as the «safe third country» concept, which are applied to all applicants, irrespective of whether they are refugees or not, and in individual cases, certain criteria to be taken into account before the «safe third country» concept is applied. This means that not even a superficial consideration of an asylum claim is necessary before the applicant is removed to a third country.

Article 2, clauses a, b, c and d, set out the criteria which must be assessed before an asylum seeker is returned to a country considered a «safe third country»:

(a) In those third countries, the life or freedom of the asylum applicant must not be threatened, within the meaning of Article 33 of the Geneva Convention.

---

698. «Unilateral» in the sense that EU Member States in unison have adopted an instrument which allows for the return asylum seekers to the territory of other States without these «third countries's» consent.
699. See the Preamble of the Resolution on «Safe Third Countries».
700. See, letter by Ms. Ogata to the British Minister of the Interior, of 27 November 1992, p.4. See also Elspeth Guild, «The Developing Immigration and Asylum Policies of the European Union», p. 169–171.

(b) The asylum applicant must not be exposed to torture or inhuman or degrading treatment in the third country.
(c) It must either be the case that the asylum applicant has already been granted protection in the third country or has had an opportunity, at the border or within the territory of the third country, to make contact with that country's authorities in order to seek their protection, before approaching the Member State in which he is applying for asylum, or that there is clear evidence of his admissibility to a third country.
(d) The asylum applicant must be afforded effective protection in the host third country against refoulement, within the meaning of the Geneva Convention.

Article 2 is meant to form a comprehensive set of safeguards which assess whether or not a country may be considered «safe» and thus a country to which an asylum seeker may be returned. However, Article 2 is limited in several respects: Firstly, the non-refoulement principle to which the Resolution is referring in clauses (a) and (d), is limited to the definition of non-refoulement as contained in the 1951 Convention. This actively excludes persons who are not recognized as refugees within the definition of the 1951 Convention, but who are nevertheless equally in need of international protection and for whom the principle of non-refoulement applies as a principle of international law, irrespective of their refugee status. Furthermore, it does not address the issues which are still controversial as regards the scope of the non-refoulement principle.[701]

Limiting the clauses to reference to the 1951 Convention is therefore a weakness in terms of the provision of legal safeguards. Secondly, there is no reference to the Torture Convention of 1984, the European Convention on Human Rights or other human rights instruments, by which the contracting parties are bound, although their absence does not free States from their existing obligations under such human rights instruments. Thirdly, with regard to the harmonized approach underlying Article 2, countries through which an asylum seeker has merely transited, are responsible for examining the asylum request, a practice with which UNHCR does not agree and which does not, in its entirety seem fair. Fourthly, the definition of «safe» covered by Article 2 is unreliable, because as long as there is no mutual understanding of the concept of «safe», there will always be differing interpretations and thus differing national practice with regard to which countries are to be considered «safe third countries». Furthermore, a country that may have been considered «safe» at one point, may not necessarily continue to be so in the fu-

---

701. See above, Chapter 5 on the principle of non-refoulement.

ture. It is therefore crucial to make not only a careful ongoing assessment of the situation in the «third country» itself, but also an assessment of its political views, with respect to which countries it considers «safe», in case of further deportation.

The Resolution on «safe third countries» and the Resolution on manifestly unfounded asylum requests are intrinsically connected. The Resolution on manifestly unfounded asylum requests seeks to harmonize law and practice, relating to the rapid rejection of certain asylum applications in the Member States. Article 1 of the Resolution on manifestly unfounded asylum requests, considers an asylum request to be manifestly unfounded «…if it is clear that it meets none of the substantive criteria under the Geneva Convention…». In other words, there is clearly no substance concerning the fear of being persecuted or the request is based on a deliberate deception or is an abuse of asylum procedures.

An asylum request is also considered «manifestly unfounded» if it falls within the provisions of the Resolution on «safe third countries» (Article 1(b). Hence, asylum requests presented by persons having crossed a «third country» are considered as belonging to the same category as fraudulent and abusive asylum requests. This is, at best, worth questioning.

Decisions regarding the application of the «safe third country concept» may be examined in the light of the accelerated procedures foreseen by Article 2 of the Resolution on manifestly unfounded asylum requests. Procedural guarantees with respect to an accelerated procedure are limited and imply, for example, that a complete examination at each stage of the processing is not necessary.

The procedural safeguards set out in the Resolution on manifestly unfounded asylum requests, could offer legal security to asylum seekers in several ways. The preamble of the Resolution not only refers to the «common humanitarian tradition» of the contracting parties, but also guarantees that Member States will conform to the 1951 Convention. Article 3 sets a time limit for reaching initial decisions on asylum applications which should be made no later than one month after an asylum request is first presented. Appeals or procedural reviews should be completed as soon as possible. The aim of these provisions is to speed up the decision making process and thereby reduce the unnecessary suffering caused by long waiting periods, during which the fate of an asylum seeker remains uncertain. The provisions are also relevant in the context of the application of the «safe third country concept», because too long a delay would create problems for the countries considered to be responsible for examining the request as would claims against transport carriers. Article 3 also foresees an appeals procedure, albeit a more simplified one than those generally available in the case of other rejected asylum applications. According to Article 4, the decision to reject an asylum request must be taken by a competent authority fully qualified in asylum or refugee matters. This article also serves as a guarantee to such procedures, so that an asylum applicant has an opportunity to present his case to a competent authority before a final decision is taken in his case.

However, in June 1995, the Council of Ministers of Justice and Internal Affairs adopted the text of a new Resolution on minimum guarantees for asylum procedures.[702] According to this resolution, asylum requests that are considered manifestly unfounded shall, with certain exceptions, be treated in the manner envisioned by the Resolution on manifestly unfounded asylum requests, but a special procedure is envisioned concerning asylum requests presented at the border. Asylum applicants who have crossed a «third country», to which the «safe third country concept» is applicable, are generally at the border when they present their request. As a consequence, following the new rules of the 1995 Resolution, such asylum applicants will not only be denied access to the territory but will also be denied access to refugee status determination procedures and the consequent in depth examination of the merits of the case. Furthermore, they will be submitted to an accelerated procedure, which denies the possibility of appeal. Procedural guarantees are becoming increasingly restrictive and the return of asylum seekers is facilitated with minimal effort. UNHCR and others have expressed concern for such exceptions, which exclude the right of appeal and suspensive effect to asylum applications presented at the border.[703]

Two elements are of paramount importance in this context. The first element to consider, is that each asylum seeker is a potential refugee within the terms of the 1951 Convention, to which all the States in question have adhered. This adhesion implies certain responsibilities with respect to the persons the Convention seeks to protect, mainly against refoulement. Such protection is not guaranteed in all cases where the «safe third country» concept is applied, for example, if a chain deportation leads to a refugee «in orbit» situation and eventually to refoulement. The danger of error in a decision to return an asylum seeker increases proportionately according to how much a procedure is accelerated.

The second element to consider is that the non-refoulement principle, for European countries, is a principle of customary international law, which not only covers refugees under the 1951 Convention, but also other persons in need of international protection.[704] Thus the States concerned have a man-

---

702. Adopted on 20 June 1995.
703. UNHCR, «Update», 10 March 1995. ECRE has equally expressed its fears in this regard, ESMV, «List of Events», April 1995, p.1
704. See above, p. 160–161.

datory legal obligation to guarantee that the principle of non-refoulement is not violated with respect to refugees, be they 1951 Convention refugees or «de facto» refugees. The issue at stake is whether this obligation, with respect to the procedural provisions on the application of the «safe third country» concept as envisaged by the «EU» provisions, is respected in all cases. The right to appeal and suspensive effect are rights to which exception should not be allowed.[705] The principles contained in UNHCR's Executive Committee Conclusion No. 30 (XXXV), concerning the problem of manifestly unfounded or abusive applications for refugee status or asylum of 1983,[706] should be respected. These Conclusions, whilst accepting that States may ultimately apply special provisions to treat manifestly unfounded requets more speedily, since they do not merit an in depth examination, warns of the serious consequences of an erroneous decision and the necessity to follow up the decision taken with appropriate procedural guarantees, such as, examinations made by qualified authorities, the safeguard of the right of appeal, etc.

Present day practice
As a consequence of the «Dublin/Schengen regime», Member States of the EU have to a large extent disclaimed responsibility for asylum requests, through the application of the «first country of asylum»/«safe third country» concept and through the adoption of readmission agreements.

One country which has clearly demonstrated these practices is Germany. Germany has, for both historical and geographical reasons, played a defining role with regard to European asylum policies and, as such, is a country whose practice is worth examining in detail.

Since Germany introduced comprehensive asylum reforms in 1993 which, among other things, allowed for the use of the «safe third country» concept thousands of asylum seekers attempting to find protection in Germany, have been returned to «safe third countries». On 14 May 1996, two rulings by the German Federal Constitutional Court on the law concerning asylum seekers arriving from «safe third countries», upheld this practice as constitutional.[707]

The first case concerned an Iraqi woman, who had fled from Northern Iraq to Germany via Turkey and Greece and is an illustration of the difficulties involved when countries apply the «safe third country» concept unlilaterally. Upon arrival in Germany, the border police refused the woman in question access to refugee status determination procedures on the grounds that she should have sought asylum in Greece, a country considered «safe», de-

---

705. This same point of view was expressed by the UNHCR in its commentary «Fair and Expeditious Asylum Procedures», Brussels, November, 1994., p.3
706. Adopted at the 34the session of the Executive Committee.
707. Bundesverfassungsgericht, 2 BvR 1938/93, 2 BvR 2315/93 of 14 may 1996.

spite the fact that she had only spent a few hours there, before flying to Frankfurt. After a hearing by a German Administrative Court, the Federal Office for the recognition of Refugees reviewed the case, but upheld that she could have sought asylum in Greece and that her asylum claim in Germany was therefore invalid. In other words, the woman should have sought asylum in the first country possible. In an analysis of the case, conducted by the U.S. Committee for Refugees, attention was drawn to the problem that each of the countries through which the woman had passed, had a different answer concerning which country should be regarded as responsible for examining the asylum request. In this case, Germany considered that Greece was responsible for the asylum request. Greece, on the other hand, does not accept asylum applications from persons who do not come directly from the country of persecution and her travel via Turkey therefore disqualified her from access to asylum procedures in Greece. With regard to Turkey, the geographical limitation of the 1951 Convention still applies, and an Iraqi woman is therefore, by definition, not eligible for refugee status according to Turkish law. This leaves the woman with no options.[708] Germany would return the woman in question to Greece. Greece, in turn, would return the woman to Turkey, clearly placing the woman in an «in orbit» situation, and Turkish practice would put the non-refoulement principle at risk.

The second case concerned an Iranian man, who travelled to Germany via Hungary and Austria. When requesting asylum in Germany, his case was dismissed, on the grounds that he could have sought asylum in Austria, to where he was subsequently deported. The asylum seeker then applied for asylum in Austria which, in turn, denied him access to asylum procedures, on the grounds that he could have sought protection in Hungary. In addition, Austrian State practice also rejects asylum seekers who have been previously rejected by Germany. This case clearly demonstrates that access to refugee determination procedures is not only denied by Germany itself, through the application of the «safe third country» concept, but also in a country which Germany regards as responsible for the asylum request. This is the classical «in orbit» situation, a situation the «Dublin/Schengen regime» was meant to abolish.

In July 1996, a Syrian citizen of Kurdish origin arrived in Norway, where his brother had obtained refugee status, and applied for asylum, after having been in transit in Germany and Greece. Norway regarded Germany as the responsible «first country of asylum» and consequently the asylum seeker was deported to Germany. Germany, however, regarded Greece as the «first coun-

---

708. See U.S. Committee for Refugees, «European 'Safe Third Country' System Creates a New Berlin Wall», p. 9.

try of asylum» and the asylum seeker was deported to Greece. A Norwegian lawyer, acting on behalf of the asylum seeker, claimed that asylum procedures in Greece were questionable, because of documented cases involving the refoulement of Syrians, in need of protection, to Syria, via Bulgaria and Turkey. Through a joint cooperation initiative between Norwegian and Greek NGOs, the asylum seeker was finally brought back to Norway, in order to have his asylum request heard there. Despite the fact that the Norwegian authorities should not have applied the concept of «first country of asylum» with regard to Greece, because it was common knowledge that Greece was not a «safe» country with respect to all asylum seekers, it was at least logical that the case should be examined in Norway, where the asylum seeker had close family links.

In other instances the final fate of asylum seekers remains unknown. For example, in September 1995, two Rwandan asylum seekers arrived at Moscow airport on a direct flight from Nairbi, Kenya, and tried to request asylum. Their claims were refused by the Federal Migration Service, presumably on the grounds that Kenya was the «first country of asylum», and they were subsequently deported to an unknown destination, without their asylum requests being considered.

Another example of an «in orbit» situation and the risk of refoulement can be seen in the case of a woman from Sri Lanka, who arrived in Copenhagen in July 1996 and applied for asylum. On her way to Copenhagen the woman in question had travelled through Rome and Hong Kong airports. In Denmark, the asylum seeker was denied access to asylum procedures on «safe third country» grounds and was returned to Rome. The Italian authorities, on the other hand, agreed not to deport her to Hong Kong, where the risk of refoulement to Sri Lanka was imminent, only if the Danish authorities would agree to readmit her, which they subsequently did. It is worth noting, that according to the Italian authorities, «mere transit» through Rome airport would not constitute a basis for considering Italy responsible for examining an asylum request.

It is often difficult to monitor the application of the «first country of asylum»/«safe third country» concept because representatives of UNHCR and the NGO-community are not necessarily present at points of entry, where asylum seekers are refused access to asylum procedures. More often than not, organizations come to learn of deportations to countries which are not «safe», through family members and friends of the asylum seekers who are at risk, and who are often aware that somebody is travelling. In February 1995, ECRE issued a report on European practice in a study[709] containing sixteen

---

709. ECRE, «Safe Third Countries», Myths and Realities, 1995.

case histories, which illustrate the consequences of chain deprtations, refugee «in orbit» situations, and violations of the non-refoulement principle. The Danish Refugee Council has followed up this monitoring project and published a report in November 1997 on the practice of the «safe country concept» in various European countries and strategies for their improvement. It is also worth to noting, that as a follow-up to the evidently crucial monitoring of «safe third country» practices, the British Refugee Legal Centre has taken an initiative to continue collecting information, through the establishment of a formal network of NGOs and Immigration practitioners throughout Western Europe.

As the examples illustrate, there are safeguards in existence which, in theory, should be taken into consideration but which are not necessarily complied with in practice. Refugees in need of protection are sometimes at risk when the «first country of asylum»/«safe third country» concept is applied. It is of great concern that mistakes are sometimes only found out and corrected at random and such a state of affairs leads to an inevitable questioning as to the extent of undiscovered mistakes. States do have a responsibility not to violate international law in their national practice. States are also responsible, from a moral point of view, for endeavouring to fill existing legal gaps in refugee protection.

Readmission agreements
Due to the application of the «first country of asylum»/«safe third country» concept, several States have used readmission agreements in order to facilitate return of asylum seekers to countries deemed responsible for the examination of asylum requests. These constitute a kind of fore-runner to the «Dublin/Schengen regime». Readmission agreements have been adopted at both a bilateral level, as well as a multilateral level. As early as 1991, in the Communication of the EU Commission to the EU Council and Parliament,[710] the usefulness of readmission accords with «third countries» was mentioned as a vehicle for solving problems in connection with countries of origin and of transit. At a multilateral level, for example, the Schengen Member States adopted a multilateral readmission accord with Poland in 1991. At a bilateral level, Germany has, due to its geographical situation, concluded readmission accords with all its neighboring countries.

In conformity with the 1992 bilateral readmission accord, concluded between Germany and Romania, 72,000 asylum seekers who presented themselves in Germany after having passed through Romania during the first ten

---

710. Communication of the Commission to the European Council and Parliament, 1994, paragraph 114, p.32.

months of 1993, had to be readmitted by Romania.[711] It is interesting to note that this bilateral readmission accord has repercussions on another country: Denmark. Romanians do not always present their asylum requests in Germany, as they risk being returned on account of the bilateral accord, and therefore they continue their journey to Denmark. Other asylum seekers also cross the border between Germany and Denmark in order to seek asylum for the same reasons, for example, Albanians, Armenians, Pakistanis, Lebanese, and Russians. They are all returned from Denmark to Germany as «first country of asylum».[712]

When asylum reform measures were being discussed in Germany, refugee and human rights advocates criticized the application of the «safe third country» approach towards Poland and the Czech republic, because the asylum procedures in these countries were already overwhelmed and mass deportations would ultimately result in refoulement. In light of this, the German government agreed to limit the number of deportations to Poland to 10,000 for 1993. It also extended an aid package of DM 120 million to Poland, in order to help set up structures to receive and to accommodate asylum seekers and refugees.[713] In February 1994, German authorities complained that the bilateral readmission accord with Poland, which was signed in 1993, was not being respected by the Polish authorities. Poland had readmitted fewer asylum seekers than had been agreed to in the accord, because the passports of the asylum seekers had not been stamped by the Polish border control authorities, which made it impossible for German authorities to prove that the asylum seekers in question had traversed Poland before arriving in Germany.

In September 1994, the German Government and the Bulgarian Government signed a readmission accord, allowing for the rapid repatriation of rejected Bulgarian asylum seekers, as well as other illegal immigrants.

As early as March 1994, in anticipation of the entry into force of the Schengen Convention, the Netherlands began returning all asylum seekers arriving from Belgium and Germany. Initially, Belgium refused to cooperate, fearing a flow of asylum seekers, but eventually an interim accord, concerning the return of asylum seekers according to the «first country of asylum» concept, was concluded between the Netherlands, Belgium and Germany. In January 1995, the Netherlands adopted a new law on «safe countries» which was designed to ensure that all asylum seekers, having crossed a safe country before arriving in its territory (German model), could be returned to the pre-

---

711. ESMV, «List of Events», No. 11, November 1993, p.2.
712. The Danish daily «Berlingske Tidende», 10 February 1995, p. 3
713. See, U.S. Committee for refugees, «European 'Safe Third Country' System Creates a New Berlin Wall», p. 6.

ceding country. Belgium protested, fearing that this would inevitably mean the return to Belgium of all asylum seekers, who traversed Belgium before arriving in the Netherlands, which would be the classic situation of the application of the concept of «first country of asylum».

In November 1993, during the first meeting of the Council of Ministers of Justice and Internal Affairs in Brussels, under the Third Pillar of the Treaty of Maastricht, the Council decided that certain guidelines needed to be incorporated into readmission accords between the Member States of the EU and «third countries», with a view to furthering improved immigration controls in the area as a whole. In November 1994, the Member States adopted a Recommendation concerning a specimen bilateral readmission agreement between a Member State of the European Union and a third country.[714]

The application of the «first country of asylum» concept covered by the readmission accords may have important consequences for «third countries» as well as for the asylum seekers who are returned. The transit countries, who are obliged to readmit returned asylum seekers, have and will continue to be confronted with considerable financial and technical tasks. Indeed, in a 1994 Communication to the Council and the European Parliament, the EU Commission, urged Member States of the European Union to show a particular understanding towards this issue.[715]

States which have to readmit thousands of asylum seekers attempting to enter Western Europe, consider that they are themselves forced to introduce restrictions in order to hinder entrance onto their territory. Such has been the effect, for example, of the readmission agreement between the Czech Republic and Germany, which explains why the Czech Republic introduced obligatory visas for nationals from Yugoslavia, Azerbaidjan, Georgia, and Tadjikistan. In addition, the readmission accords have had the effect of increasingly limiting access to the countries in which asylum applicants could deposit their applications. The pressure caused by asylum applications in Europe has steadily been pushed further East and South.

Another fear with respect to readmission agreements, is that the asylum seekers are returned to countries which do not have sufficient means to handle their cases and accord adequate protection. This is why UNHCR advised the Member States of the European Union to incorporate clauses in their readmission agreements to ensure, first of all, that the receiving country guarantees responsibility for examining the asylum request and secondly, that the sending country makes it clear on what grounds it has decided not to exam-

---

714. Adopted on 30 November 1994.
715. Communication of the Commission to the Council and the European Parliament, 1994, paragraph 116, p.32.

ine the merits of the case, rather than simply return the asylum seeker to the «first country of asylum».[716]

If asylum seekers are returned to «third countries» with whom there are no readmission agreements, or if the question of re-entry of asylum seekers has not been regulated in another form, it cannot be assured that the generosity of these «third countries», will encompass an agreement to receive the asylum seekers back and give them access to their refugee status determination procedures. In this context, the fundamental guarantee on which the Dublin Convention was based, that each asylum request will be examined by at least one State, again risks remaining merely a theoretical commitment, without being worth much in practice.

Thus, the unscrupulous application of the «first country of asylum»/«safe third country» concept engenders fear. If the adoption of harmonized rules on the application of the concept were really motivated by the concern to guarantee that each asylum request be examined in order to avoid the creation of situations of refugees «in orbit», then supplementary guarantees must be incorporated into the EU cooperation in this area and better still, supplementary guarantees should be incoporated into a pan-European refugee convention.[717] In the meantime, no country should, as a minimum guarantee, apply the concept of «first country of asylum»/«safe third country» concept, unless the receiving country guarantees an asylum seeker access to its territory and to its asylum procedures. This would ensure that asylum seekers do not become refugees «in orbit» and it would constitute a safeguard against the risk of refoulement.

7.5 Proposal in part for a new European convention on refugee protection

The application of the «first country of asylum»/«safe third country» concept, is generally considered so favourably by States, that no proposal would eliminate its usage. The only alternative is to propose the improvement of legal and humanitarian safeguards and their incorporation into European legislation and practice at a pan-European level. As the examination of present rules and national practice has shown, there is no reason why West European States should

---

716. «UNHCR concerned with a document adopted by the EU Justice and Home Affairs Council on 30 November 1994 which could enable the transfer of asylum seekers to third countries», 1 December 1994, p. 1. See, «UNHCR Position on Standard Bilateral Readmission Agreements Between a Member State and a Third Country», December 1994.
717. See below, Chapter 8 on the proposed new European refugee convention.

consider their work on this subject completed. Harmonization efforts among the EU States have repercussions which go far beyond the area of the European Union and the region of Europe as a whole. It would therefore seem an appropriate moment for States to review the existing gaps in international refugee law and re-evaluate the dangers pertaining to the use of the «first country of asylum»/«safe third country» concept, with a view to developing new proposals.

Two elements should be given particular attention: firstly, repercussions concerning asylum seekers and the need to avoid the situation of refugees «in orbit», and the consequent risk of violation of the non-refoulement principle and secondly, repercussions concerning the countries considered responsible for examining asylum claims, with particular attention to the need to address the issue of international burden sharing and international solidarity. It is a fact that reciprocal agreements on the matter are, after all, limited and a unilateral practice does not foresee any mutual advantage, only the advantage of the sending State. As regards the Member States of the EU, the readmission agreements, first and foremost, are of advantage to these countries and do not benefit the «third countries». Adoption of readmission agreements should, however, reflect the interests of both sending and receiving States. A more equitable way of ensuring a fair division of responsibility would be to strive for a broader harmonization where the principles laid down are mutually beneficial to all parties involved. A pan-European initiative, to begin with, would at least ensure a fairer distribution of responsibility in the European context.

Safety of the asylum seeker

The very first prerequisite for the safety of an asylum seeker is that his case be examined according to the refugee determination procedures deriving from the 1951 Convention. In order to achieve this, he must first obtain access to the territory of a potential asylum State. States have the prerogative to decide to whom they are willing to give access, but these same States are also bound by their international obligations under the 1951 Convention and human rights and humanitarian law instruments as well as customary law. Despite the fact that the 1951 Convention does not oblige States to grant asylum, it must nevertheless be interpreted as obliging States to examine asylum requests when refugees, according to their right to seek protection in other States, ask for it. Since it has already been decided, through national and international practice, that it is not the refugee himself who decides which country should be responsible for his asylum request, it goes without saying, that if the State to which he addressess himself refuses responsibility, it must at least see to it that his case is examined by another State. Refugee protection would otherwise be hollow and completely void of meaning.

Ensuring refugees access to a territory and access to asylum procedures is therefore the most basic duty of States. Furthermore, admission to procedures should not depend on whether the asylum request is made at the point of entry or in the territory itself.[718] As far as European harmonization efforts are concerned, they have to a certain degree ensured access to their territory. More efforts remain to be taken in order to arrive at a fairer division of responsibility and European States should be expected to continue their international endeavours in order to ensure access to the «third countries» to which they are referring responsibility for asylum requets. The EU «internal» approach is not good enough because it does not provide a sufficient guarantee of protection for the asylum seeker by means of access to an asylum procedure.

Thus draft Article 7 of the proposed European convention on refugee protection, covers both access to the territory and to eligibility procedures and, more specifically, refers to draft Article 8,[719] with regard to the application of the «first country of asylum»/«safe third country»-concept. In addition to the legal safeguards, aimed at ensuring access to the territory and to procedures for the asylum seeker, draft Articles 7 and 8 also aim at taking the interest of States into consideration: The interests of the «second State» are taken into account by allowing for accelerated procedures and by allowing for the «first country of asylum»/«safe third country» concept to be applied, whilst the interests of the State considered to be the «first country of asylum» are accounted for through the incorporation of certain benchmarks which need to be met in order for the concept to be applied, a mechanism of international burden sharing and international solidarity included. [720]

Draft Article 7, which proposes the inclusion of a provision in the proposed new European refugee convention, on access to the territory of an asylum State and access to the refugee status determination procedures is as follows[721]:

Draft Article 7 ACCESS TO THE TERRITORY AND PROCEDURES

(1) Asylum seekers shall be guaranteed access to the territory of a State to ensure that persons covered by Article 1 of the present Convention, are given access to refugee status determination procedures which enables them to benefit from international protection.

---

718. See, UNHCR, in «Fair and Expeditious Asylum Procedures», p.2 and 3.
719. See below, p. 282–283, on draft Article 8.
720. See below, p. 278–282, on draft Article 6.
721. See the full text on the proposal for a new convention, below, Chapter 8.

(2) Fundamental procedural and substantive guarantees in virtue of international law, in particular as described in UNHCR's Executive Committee Conclusions No. 15(XXX) on refugees without an asylum country, No. 30(XXXIV) on the problem of manifestly unfounded or abusive applications for refugee status or asylum, and No. 58(XL) on the problem of refugees and asylum seekers who move in an irregular manner from a country in which they had already found protection, shall be fully respected. The right of access to counselling, tribunals, the right of appeal and the right of suspensive effect on a decision while an appeal is examined, shall be meticulously respected.

(3) A decision relating to the «first country of asylum»/«safe third country» concept may be taken in virtue of an accelerated procedure which does not entail an in depth examination, but only in compliance with safeguards as described in the preceeding paragraph.

«Protection elsewhere»
The concept of «protection elsewhere» and «safe» is another aspect which needs to be harmonized before it is possible to speak of a harmonized European asylum policy. [722] As of present the new guidelines on the «safe third country» concept adopted by the Committee of Ministers of the Council of Europe in November 1997, provides the most encouraging international agreement in this regard. Reference to the obligations of States under international refugee law, humanitarian law, and human rights, be they of a civil, political, economic, social or cultural nature, is essential as is the reference to the opportunity of seeking asylum.[723]

In addition, the following factors should be taken into consideration in the evaluation of a «third country»: ratification and implementation of the 1951 Convention, ratification and implementation of instruments for the protection of human rights, treatment of «de facto» refugees, the willingness of the «third country» to readmit asylum applicants and refugees, the willingness of the «third country» to authorize a lawful stay while the asylum request is being examined or while a durable solution is being sought, and finally, the respect by the «third country» for fundamental humanitarian norms in the treatment of asylum seekers and refugees.[724] All these factors should be incorporated into a new European instrument for refugee protection.

---

722. See above, p. 262–267, on the examination of Article 2 of the Resolution on «safe third countries».
723. See above, p. 249–250.
724. See, «Current asylum Issues», «Harmonization in Europe», March 1992, p.6. See also the examination of the concept of «protection elsewhere», above, p. 246–250.

Transit [725]

Another issue which remains to be discussed is the fairness of referring to the concept of «protection elsewhere», with respect to countries where protection has not been effectively granted, but where the asylum seeker could have requested asylum because he has transited the country at some stage. To presume the transit country's responsibility is simply not logical and therefore to consider an asylum request «unfounded» on these grounds is unfair.[726] An asylum applicant who has simply traversed a country, should not be compared to abusive asylum seekers who have already found protection elsewhere. Similarly, it is hardly fair towards the country of transit to apportion responsibility, merely because persons traversed its territory.

This should also be taken into consideration in a new European refugee convention. The difficulty lies in making a fair assessment between a case where there is no link between the asylum seeker and the State he traversed «en route», and a case where the person stayed for a period long enough to consider that the country should be responsible for an asylum request and to decide how to interpret whether or not protection could have been sought in a transit country.[727] Either the Scandinavian model, which allows only for a rigid «en route» criteria should be adopted or a system which favours a longer and more flexible interpretation of the definition of «transit». Finding an international agreement on the topic of «transit», is as imperative today as it was in the 1980s, when debate was taking place under the auspices of the Council of Europe. This problem should not be disregarded by reference to the concept of «protection elsewhere». However, as practice in this regard is far from coherent, the issue seemingly remains open for debate among States, within or outside of the EU-context, but without international agreement on this issue, the problem of refugees «in orbit» cannot be solved.

In order for the concept of «transit country» to retain a meaning, it is necessary to reach an agreement on the interpretation of «protection elsewhere» as was the intention of UNHCR's Executive Committee Conclusion No. 58 (XL) of 1989.[728] The interpretation must allow for an indication that an asylum seeker has received protection elsewhere, but must exclude from the concept, the possibility that he «could have asked» for protection elsewhere. Transit in an airport, where the asylum seeker does not so much as move

---

725. See below, p. 281–282, on the proposal for a new European convention on refugee protection, draft Article 6(3).
726. Cf. Article 1(2) of the Resolution on manifestly unfounded asylum applications.
727. Cf. Article 2(c) of the Resolution on «safe third countries».
728. On the contents of Conclusion No. 58 (XL), see above, p. 236 and following.

from the transit area, should never be considered as entry and should therefore not provide grounds for return, according to the «first country of asylum»/«safe third country» concept. In contrast to this view, the new guidelines adopted by the Council of Europe[729] seem to accept current European practice by which the fact that an asylum seeker has had «the opportunity» (at the border of within the territory) to seek protection, could be enough to consider that the «safe third country» concept may apply. In other words, the Recommendation does not contain any reference to the duration and nature of stay, or transit in a «third country». This is unfortunate.

Burden sharing and international solidarity

In current practice, allowing the application of the «first country of asylum»/«safe third country» concept without distinction between whether asylum seekers are moving in an irregular manner or whether they are traversing a country «en route» to a country of final destination, has profound consequences for both the border countries and transit countries. Eastern and Central Europe have become the main areas of transit. The transit phenomenon not only concerns nationals from neighboring countries, but also asylum seekers coming from Asia, Africa, and the Near-East, «en route» towards Western Europe,[730] who often arrive as part of the business of trafficking in human beings.[731]

Western European governments anticipated the flow of immigrants and refugees from Central and Eastern Europe, resulting from the fall of the Berlin Wall and the dissolution of the Soviet Empire, but these movements did not create significant problems for the Western European countries themselves, because the displacements mainly took place in the neighbouring

---

729. Recommendation No. R(97)22 of 25 November 1977.
730. Traditionally, Eastern Germany was the intermediary country for the German Federation. Czechoslovakia was the point of entry to the German Federation. Austria, France, and Poland were the transit countries necessary for reaching Scandinavia. See M. Arnould, «Asylum in Europe: Shift to the East», Forum by the Council of Europe, No. 3, September 1994, p.20.
731. It has, for example, been reported that many asylum seekers coming from Iraq, Iran, and Somalia crossed the border between Russia and Norway in an irregular manner. The Baltic States are also transit bases for asylum seekers coming from Asia and the Near-East who try to enter Finland, Sweden, Denmark and Norway. The trafficking of human beings has grown in these States. They are the new «boat people» because they often embark on small boats in order to reach the Swedish and Danish coasts. In Southern Europe, nationals from North Africa pass through the island of Lampedusa into Italy and on to other West European States.

countries.732 The management of the problem of persons in need of protection is thus more serious in Eastern Europe than in Western Europe. These countries have fewer means and less developed mechanisms for taking care of asylum seekers and refugees. For example, it is not without just cause that procedural and substantive status for asylum seekers in Poland, has been described as being in a «legal limbo».733

Countries in the Asian and African continents represent the «first countries of asylum» which receive and lodge the greatest numbers of refugees in the world. One may wonder how it is possible that European States, apply the concept of «first country of asylum» vis-à-vis these countries. For example, how could Somali asylum seekers be returned to Kenya which in 1992 experienced a flow of some 3,000 asylum seekers per day from Somalia?734 Similarly, how can the return of Afghan asylum seekers to Pakistan, which had already received 1.5 million refugees, be explained or the return of asylum seekers to Zaïre in 1995, which had already received 1.4 million refugees from Rwanda be justified?735

The practice of the «first country of asylum» concept is imposed by a region which receives approximately only 5 % of the total number of refugees in the world. This is why, A. Grahl-Madsen called the application of the concept «an embarrassing humanitarian problem».736 If the explanation of the application of the concept, is that it constitutes a sharing of international responsibility, perhaps it would be necessary to recognize that the current «key

---

732. Since 1988, 150 conflicts have escalated in the former U.S.S.R. As a consequence, in the beginning of 1994, there were two million displaced persons, mainly Russians, arriving in Russia. These flows presented numerous problems to the Russian government, see G. Loescher, «Les mouvements de réfugiés dans l'après-guerre froide», in Politique étrangère, No. 3, 1994, p.712. In addition, there were already approximately 40,000 asylum seekers in Russia in 1994. Objectively this may seem a modest number, but for a country which has no tradition for determining refugee status and receiving asylum seekers, this number constitutes a serious problem, see M. Arnould, «Asylum in Europe: shift to the East», in Forum by the Council of Europe, No. 3, 1994, p.20. According to the ESMV «List of Events», May 1995, p. 9, a total of approximately 4 million persons were displaced as a consequence of the dissolution of the U.S.S.R. In Poland, the greatest number of refugees in the country, with the exception of Bosnians, have been Armenians, M. Arnould, Ibid, p.21. One should not ignore the fact that the conflict between Azerbaidjan and Armenia in the High-Karabakh provoked the displacement of approximately 500,000 persons, G. Loescher, Ibid, p.708.
733. M. Arnould, Ibid.
734. «Les réfugiés dans le monde», 1993, p. 83 and 95.
735. «The Christian Science Monitor», March 1, 1995, p.10-11.
736. A. Grahl-Madsen, «Territorial Asylum», 1980, p.101.

of division» is not equitable. Furthermore, this practice is for the most part unilateral, a fact that does not seem in keeping with international cooperation. Normally, a country cannot unilaterally impose responsibility on another country. As a consequence, countries without prior readmission agreements, tend to make the entry of returned asylum seekers more difficult and the refugees concerned, continue to be refused access to asylum procedures and the protection which they need.

It is time a real meaning were given to the concept of «international solidarity». One could, for example, imagine a division of responsibility which does not designate application of the concept of «first country of asylum» when the asylum applicants have not done anything more than traverse a country. In addition, the signatory States to the «Dublin/Schengen regime» should be encouraged to use the «opt out» clauses[737] of the Conventions, instead of applying the «safe third country» concept in cases where the receiving country would have difficulties in receiving, either because the burden in that country is already overwhelming, or because the country's social, political or economic infrastructure and overall response possibilities are otherwise limited.

Whilst giving due consideration to the problems of finding a more equitable «key» to the division of labour between State actors, draft Article 6 is designed not only to incorporate the aspects relating to international solidarity,[738] but also to give the necessary indications with regard to the use of the concept of «transit», «en route» and other factors, such as «protection elsewhere».

Draft Article 6, which proposes the inclusion of a provision on international solidarity and critera for the assessment of the use of the «first country of asylum»/«safe third country concept» in the proposed new European refugee convention,[739] is as follows:

Draft Article 6 INTERNATIONAL SOLIDARITY

(1) When a Signatory State to the present Convention finds difficulty in granting or continuing to grant asylum to refugees, such a State may appeal directly to other Signatory States, and these States shall, in the spirit of inter-

---

737. Article 3(4) of the Dublin Convention and Article 29(4) of the Schengen Convention.
738. On international solidarity from this perspective. Draft Article 6 (1) concerns an appeal for international solidarity in the case where a receiving country has difficulties in according international protection to refugees, for example, because of a mass-influx situation. See above, p. 216–219.
739. See the full text of the proposed new Convention, below, Chapter 8.

national solidarity and international cooperation, individually or jointly, and through the intermediary of UNHCR and/or regional organizations, take appropriate measures to lighten the burden of the Signatory State granting asylum. Such measures may include, among other things, fiscal contributions for the protection of refugees in the State granting asylum or willingness to resettle refugees from the State granting asylum to other States.

(2) In order to ensure equitable burden sharing among States regarding the responsibility to examine asylum requests, States agree to cooperate according to the same principles as set forth in the preceeding paragraph while assessing the application of the «first country of asylum»/«safe third country» concept. Asylum seekers should not be returned if the «first country» is already overburdened. Fiscal contributions should be considered. UNHCR shall have the right to initiate and call for consultations among States in this regard. These considerations should be met irrespective of whether or not the State concerned is a contracting party to the present Convention.

(3) In the assessment of State responsibility for the examination of an asylum request, transit is not to be considered as if protection has already been granted by another State. The examination of an asylum request shall therefore not be refused because asylum could have been requested in another State if the asylum seeker only transited through this State in an airport or was similarly «en route» to the country of his final destination.

(4) The examination of an asylum request may be refused and, according to principles set forth in Article 8 of the present Convention, responsibility may be tranferred to another contracting State, on the grounds that the asylum seeker had close links with that other State, family links, or otherwise. The same applies if protection has already been granted according to Article 2 of the present Convention or an equivalent level of protection.

In order to guarantee a fair practice, UNHCR, the organization most apt to have a global perspective of the pressures and movements of refugees, should be asked to play a supervisory and intermediary role. This explains the repetition of its duties in draft Article 6(2).[740] Through international consultation and UNHCR involvement, it should be possible to find a mechansim of di-

---

740. See the Executive Committee Conclusion No. 58 (XL) which envisages a consultative role for UNHCR and Conclusion No. 15 (XXX9 which also indicates that States should take appropriate measures to ensure an equitable burden sharing in the case of large-scale influx of asylum seekers, either on an individual basis or through UNHCR .

vision which proves equitable, so that States which are already overburdened are not used as «first countries of asylum» by European States, whether amongst themselves or vis-à-vis «Southern» countries. The call for international solidarity is meant to manifest itself both with regard to the non application of the «first country of asylum»/«safe third country» concept, because the country in question is already burdened and with regard to fiscal contributions in the event that the concept is applied.

From the perspective of international burden sharing, the concept of «transit» and the meaning of «en route» have been incorporated into draft Article 6(3). Draft Article 6(3) does not, however, give a clear indication of the amount of time a person can be «en route» before the «first country» could be seen as responsible. This leaves some flexibility, while the one condition, that the asylum seeker has not in fact asked for asylum while «en route» is added in draft Article 6(4). This paragraph also includes the concept of «protection elsewhere» and other criteria which indicate which country should be responsible for an asylum request. It is specified, that in cases where an asylum seeker has already been granted protection, according to the criteria laid out in draft Article 2 on asylum, an examination of the case is not necessary. This takes care of the phenomenon of «asylum shopping» and the whole range of problems with which UNHCR's Executive Committee Conclusion No. 58 (XL) is concerned.

As far as «links» to an asylum country are concerned, the reference is left flexible, with the exception of specifically indicating family links. The term «otherwise» is designed to cover cases of the «first country» having issued a visa or a residence permit, elements which are based on the «Dublin/Schengen regime», but which in the draft article are less specific. Indeed, there are some occasions where «links» can be explained only by the asylum seeker himself and this paragraph therefore leaves a State with room to manoeuvre, in order to take the asylum seeker's subjective wishes into consideration.

Draft Article 6 must be seen in conjunction with draft Article 8 which outlines the more specific conditions pertaining to the application of the «first country of asylum»/«safe third country» concept.

Draft Article 8 is as follows:[741]

Draft Article 8 «FIRST COUNTRY OF ASYLUM»/«SAFE THIRD COUNTRY» CONCEPT

No asylum seeker may be returned to a preceeding State before the State in question has been informed of the reason for return and has given its con-

---

741. See the full text on the proposed convention, below, Chapter 8.

sent to grant access to the territory and to refugee status determination procedures. In addition the following conditions must be met:

(i) That the person shall be treated in conformity with international law and basic humanitarian standards as laid down in Article 3 of the present Convention.

(ii) That the receiving State must have adopted and implemented all relevant instruments of international law relating to refugees, human rights and humanitarian law. Accordingly, the record of a receiving State concerning the implementation of the human rights principles laid down in such instruments, must be evaluated.

(iii) That every measure be taken to ensure that the asylum seeker is protected against refoulement within the meaning of Article 4 of the present Convention.

Draft Article 8 is designed to give the necessary guarantees, that before any asylum seeker is returned to a «first country», the sending country has assured itself that access will be given to the territory and to refugee status determination procedures. This presupposes an explicit assurance on the part of the receiving State of its willingness to undertake responsibility for the examination. Refugee «in orbit» situations, chain deportations and refoulement would no longer occur. It is unfortunate that the new guidelines on the «safe third country» concept adopted by the Committee of Ministers of the Council of Europe in November 1997, do not contain any specification, as a prerequisite for application of the concept, about the consent of the «third country» concerned. Certain additional conditions are equally incorporated in the draft. Reference to international legal instruments and assurances on their implementation is essential. After this, the question of return must be assessed according to, for example, the human rights record of the receiving country. This is in line with the above mentioned guidelines of the Council of Europe. In other words, draft Article 8 describes conditions which need to be met in order to consider a country «safe».

An international refugee tribunal

Finally, in order to solve problems raised in connection with the interpretation of the proposal for a new European refugee protection regime, a judicial organ needs to be established for the benefit of both refugees and States. In addition to the safeguarding of legal and democratic principles of the international community, a refugee tribunal would ensure an efficient and unitary approach in refugee and asylum matters – a fundamental precondition in order to achieve successful legal harmonization in this area. One of the difficulties relating to refugee law is the notable lack of judicial advice on its implementation. At present, only in some instances, are cases relating to refugees and asylum seekers brought before an international judiciary, for example, practice pertaining to the interpretation of Article 3 of the European Convention on Human Rights with regard to refoulement of persons in need of international protection.[742] Although fundamental, this represents but a fraction of all the questions which concern refugee and asylum matters. If, for example, agreement regarding the application of the «first country of asylum»/«safe third country» concept, together with an intervention by UNHCR, fail to solve the dispute, then the case could be brought before a European judiciary specialized in these matters for the benefit of the States concerned, but, even more importantly, for the benefit of the persons the protection convention is meant to serve – the refugees.

Draft Article 9, on the establishment of an international refugee judiciary is as follows:

Draft Article 9 JUDICIARY

The Signatory States to the present Convention undertake to establish an international judicial body for the interpretation of the present Convention. Its competence shall be modelled on the supervisory bodies of the European Convention on Human Rights.

---

742. On Article 3 of the European Convention on Human Rights, See above, p. 153–156

CHAPTER 8
Proposal for a new European convention on refugee protection

There is no reason to believe that changes proposed in this book would be easily achieved. Recent discussions have already shown that there is widespread scepticism in the different camps. To a certain extent this is a good sign. Caution is necessary as the danger is always there that in striving for an improvement, the opposite could come about. On the other hand, if scepticism stands in the way of further discussion, refugee protection will not progress beyond the current status quo.

The various actors are sceptical for different reasons. States hesitate to undertake further legal obligations. Other actors, both NGOs and UNHCR seem, at present, to be afraid to act in the present political climate, in spite of their own repeated calls for regional improvement.

Whilst due regard must evidently be paid to legitimate concerns, States need to be reminded of their already existing obligations in the field of human rights and refugee protection and the principle of international solidarity. The other actors need to be urged to seize the opportunity which has been presented by the adoption of Recommendation 1324, by the Parliamentary Assembly of the Council of Europe in April 1997 which recommends that the Member States draw up a Convention on the protection and rights of refugees and asylum seekers. Furthermore, the fact that in November 1997 one government formulated a proposal in the Committee of Ministers for a European refugee convention makes it imperative that UNHCR and NGOs respond constructively with substantive proposals. Needless to say, such opportunities are rare.

The following is but one proposal for a European convention on refugee protection and could be a basis for discussion. The proposal strives at maintaining a balanced approach in which consideration is shown to the needs of both refugees and States. It also aims at not disregarding already existing legal and policy texts on refugee protection, but offers a supplementary scheme in order to fill gaps in areas where defined legal obligations are missing or unclear and to merge these various aspects of refugee law and policy recommendations into one comprehensive legal instrument.

A successful outcome depends on the political will of European States to act in unity now, not only to their benefit but to the benefit of those who are in need of international protection.

The draft text is as follows:

European Convention on Refugee Protection

The Governments signatory hereto, being Members of the Council of Europe, Considering the importance of the Universal Convention relating to the Status of Refugees of 28 July 1951 as it has been expanded by the Protocol relating to the Status of Refugees of 31 January 1967 and the need for the said Convention to be interpreted in accordance with its spirit and content;

Acknowledging that the present European convention must in no way prejudice the importance and the meaning of the 1951 Universal Convention relating to the Status of refugees;

Recognizing the need for a suppematary regional convention on refugee protection to further enhance refugee protection the Europe;

Affirming their profound belief in and obligation to the principles of refugee law, human rights law and humanitarian law;

Affirming that the present Convention will be interpreted in good faith and in accordance with the principles laid down in international instruments pertaining to the protection of refugees as contained in instruments of refugee law, human rights law and humanitarian law, i.a. the Universal Declaration of Human Rights of 1948; the United Nations Declaration on Territorial Asylum of 1967; the International Covenant on Civil and Political Rights of 1966 and Protocol thereto; the International Covenant on Economic, Social and Cultural Rights of 1966; the Convention against Torture and Other Cruel, Inhuman or Degrading Treatment or Punishment of 1984; the Geneva Conventions relative to the Protection of Civilian Persons in Time of War of 1949 and Additional Protocols; the European Convention for the Protection of Human Rights and Fundamental Freedoms of 1950 and Protocols thereto as well as other instruments adopted by the Council of Europe, i.a. Resolution 14(1967) on asylum to persons in danger of persecution, Declaration on Territorial Asylum of 1977; and Recommendation 1236 (1994) on the right of territorial asylum. Due regard shall be given to the Conclusions adopted by the Executive Committee of the UN High Commissioner for refugees.

Have agreed as follows:

Article 1
Refugee definition
Within the terms of the present Convention, a refugee, to whom international protection shall be accorded, is a displaced person (or a group of persons) who has fled his country or who cannot or will not return there, due to well-founded fear of persecution within the terms of the Convention relating to the Status of Refugees of 28 July 1951 and the Protocol relating to the Status of Refugees of 31 January 1967, or a displaced person (or a group of persons) who cannot or will not return for analogous reasons.

Analogous reasons could include: when life, liberty and security are threatened by violations of fundamental human rights principles or principles of humanitarian law, or by generalized violence, foreign aggression, internal conflict or other circumstances seriously disturbing public order.

Article 2
Asylum
(1) Refugees entitled to invoke Article 1 of the present Convention have a right to seek asylum in other countries and to obtain protection.

(2) Refugees entitled to invoke Article 1 of the present Convention have a right to asylum. Asylum shall not be granted to any person who has committed a crime against peace, a war crime, or a crime against humanity or to any person guilty of acts contrary to the purposes and principles of the UN. The granting of asylum by a State to a person in need of international protection, is a peaceful and humanitarian act and cannot be regarded as unfriendly by any other State.

(3) Asylum may be granted on a permanent or on a temporary basis. Asylum on a temporary basis must not under any circumstances exceed five years from the moment a refugee first seeks protection, and contracting States will do everything in their power to facilitate examination of individual applications and to facilitate solutions as quickly as possible. If conditions in the country of origin or in the home country are such that repatriation would be in violation of Article 4 and/or Article 5 of the present Convention, the asylum country shall offer asylum on a permanent basis. In the search for solutions, due regard shall equally be given to the principle of international solidarity as contained in Article 6 of the present Convention.

Article 3
Treatment

Asylum countries shall abide by all international principles of refugee law, human rights and humanitarian law. The treatment of refugees shall be governed by the rights pertaining to refugees contained in the Convention relating to the Status of Refugees of 28 July 1951. In the case of a mass influx situation, refugees must, as a minimum, be treated in accordance with the humanitarian standards contained in UNHCR's Executive Committee Conclusion No. 22 (XXXII). Contracting States undertake, in particular, to adopt similar rules pertaining to rights, such as education, employment and family unity.

Article 4
Non-refoulement

No person claiming to be a refugee shall be subjected to measures such as rejection at the frontier or, if he has already entered the territory, return, expulsion or extradition which would compel him to return to or remain in a territory where his life, physical integrity or safety would be threatened for the reasons set out in Article 1.

Article 5
Repatriation

(1) Repatriation may take place when circumstances in the country of origin allow for it to take place in safety and dignity. Due regard must be given to principles of international law – civil and political rights as well as economic, social and cultural rights. Before repatriation takes place, UNHCR should be consulted and the organization should play a coordinating role in cooperation with regional organizations.

(2) The provisions of the preceeding paragraph shall not be applied to any person who can invoke compelling reasons arising out of previous persecution or other circumstances. The personal circumstances of the person concerned must be taken into account.

Article 6
International solidarity
(1) When a Signatory State to the present Convention finds difficulty in granting or continuing to grant asylum to refugees, such a State may appeal directly to other Signatory States, and these States shall, in the spirit of international solidarity and international cooperation, individually or jointly, and through the intermediary of UNHCR and/or regional organizations, take appropriate measures to lighten the burden of the Signatory State granting asylum. Such measures may include, among other things, fiscal contributions for the protection of refugees in the State granting asylum or willingness to resettle refugees from the State granting asylum to other States.

(2) In order to ensure equitable burden sharing among States regarding the responsibility to examine asylum requests, States agree to cooperate according to the same principles as set forth in the preceeding paragraph while assessing the application of the «first country of asylum»/«safe third country» concept. Asylum seekers should not be returned if the «first country» is already overburdened. Fiscal contributions should be considered. UNHCR shall have the right to initiate and call for consultations among States in this regard. These considerations should be met irrespective of whether or not the State concerned is a contracting party to the present Convention.

(3) In the assessment of State responsibility for the examination of an asylum request, transit is not to be considered as if protection has already been granted by another State. The examination of an asylum request shall therefore not be refused because asylum could have been requested in another State if the asylum seeker only transited through this State in an airport or was similarly «en route» to the country of his final destination.

(4) The examination of an asylum request may be refused and, according to principles set forth in Article 8 of the present Convention, responsibility may be transferred to another contracting State, on the grounds that the asylum seeker had close links with that other State, family links, or otherwise. The same applies if protection has already been granted according to Article 2 of the present Convention or an equivalent level of protection.

Article 7
Access to the territory and procedures
(1) Asylum seekers shall be guaranteed access to the territory of a State to ensure that persons covered by Article 1 of the present Convention, are given

access to refugee status determination procedures which enables them to benefit from international protection.

(2) Fundamental procedural and substantive guarantees in virtue of international law, in particular as described in UNHCR's Executive Committee Conclusions No. 15 (XXX) on refugees without an asylum country; No. 30 (XXXIV) on the problem of manifestly unfounded or abusive applications for refugee status or asylum, and No. 58 (XL) on the problem of refugees and asylum seekers who move in an irregular manner from a country in which they had already found protection, shall be fully respected. The right of access to counselling, tribunals, the right of appeal and the right of suspensive effect on a decision while an appeal is examined, shall be meticulously respected.

(3) A decision relating to the «first country of asylum»/«safe third country» concept, may be taken in virtue of an accelerated procedure which does not entail an in depth examination, but only in compliance with safeguards as described in the preceeding paragraph.

Article 8

«First country of asylum»/«safe third country» concept
No asylum seeker may be returned to a preceeding State before the State in question has been informed of the reason for return and has given its consent to grant access to the territory and to refugee status determination procedures. In addition the following conditions must be met:

(i) That the person shall be treated in conformity with international law and basic humanitarian standards as laid down in Article 3 of the present Convention.

(ii) That the receiving State must have adopted and implemented all relevant instruments of international law relating to refugees, human rights and humanitarian law. Accordingly, the record of a receiving State concerning the implementation of the human rights principles laid down in such instruments, must be evaluated.

(iii) That every measure be taken to ensure that the asylum seeker is protected against refoulement within the meaning of Article 4 of the present Convention.

Article 9
Judiciary

The Signatory States to the present Convention undertake to establish an international judicial body for the interpretation of the present Convention. Its competence shall be modelled on the supervisory bodies of the European Convention on Human Rights.

APPENDIX I

Convention relating to the Status of Refugees of 28 July 1951

United Nations Conference of Plenipotentiaries on the Status of Refugees and Stateless Persons, Geneva, 2–25 July 1951
22 April 1954

Preamble
The High Contracting Parties
Considering that the Charter of the United Nations and the Universal Declaration of Human Rights approved on 10 December 1948 by the General Assembly have affirmed the principle that human beings shall enjoy fundamental rights and freedoms without discrimination,

Considering that the United Nations has, on various occasions, manifested its profound concern for refugees and endeavoured to assure refugees the widest possible exercise of these fundamental rights and freedoms,

Considering that it is desirable to revise and consolidate previous international agreements relating to the status of refugees and to extend the scope of and protection accorded by such instruments by means of a new agreement,

Considering that the grant of asylum may place unduly heavy burdens on certain countries, and that a satisfactory solution of a problem of which the United Nations has recognized the international scope and nature cannot therefore be achieved without international cooperation,

Expressing the wish that all States, recognizing the social and humanitarian nature of the problem of refugees will do everything within their power to prevent this problem from becoming a cause of tension between States,

Noting that the United Nations High Commissioner for Refugees is charged with the task of supervising international conventions providing for the protection of refugees, and recognizing that the effective co-ordination of measures taken to deal with this problem will depend upon the cooperation of States with the High Commissioner,

Have agreed as follows:

Chapter I, General Provisions

Article 1
Definition of the term «Refugee»

A. For the purposes of the present Convention, the term «refugee» shall apply to any person who:

(1) Has been considered a refugee under the Arrangements of 12 May 1926 and 30 June 1928 or under the Conventions of 28 October 1933 and 10 February 1938, the Protocol of 14 September 1939 or the Constitution of the International Refugee Organization; Decisions of non-eligibility taken by the International Refugee Organization during the period of its activities shall not prevent the status of refugee being accorded to persons who fulfil the conditions of paragraph 2 of this section;

(2) As a result of events occurring before 1 January 1951 and owing to a well-founded fear of being persecuted for reasons of race, religion, nationality, membership of a particular social group or political opinion, is outside the country of his nationality and is unable or, owing to such fear, is unwilling to avail himself of the protection of that country; or who, not having a nationality and being outside the country of his former habitual residence as a result of such events, is unable or, owing to such fear, is unwilling to return to it.

In the case of a person who has more than one nationality, the term «the country of his nationality» shall mean each of the countries of which he is a national, and a person shall not be deemed to be lacking the protection of the country of his nationality if, without any valid reason based on well-founded fear, he has not availed himself of the protection of one of the countries of which he is a national.

B. (1) For the purposes of this Convention, the words «events occurring before 1 January 1951» in Article 1, Section A, shall be understood to mean either

(2) Any Contracting State which has adopted alternative (a) may at any time extend its obligations by adopting alternative (b) by means of a notification addressed to the Secretary-General of the United Nations.

C. This Convention shall cease to apply to any person falling under the terms of Section A if:

(1) He has voluntarily re-availed himself of the protection of the country of his nationality; or

(2) Having lost his nationality, he has voluntarily re-acquired it, or

(3) He has acquired a new nationality, and enjoys the protection of the country of his new nationality; or

(4) He has voluntarily re-established himself in the country which he left or outside which he remained owing to fear of persecution; or

(5) He can no longer, because the circumstances in connection with which he has been recognized as a refugee have ceased to exist, continue to refuse to avail himself of the protection of the country of his nationality;

Provided that this paragraph shall not apply to a refugee falling under Section A(1) of this Article who is able to invoke compelling reasons arising out of previous persecution for refusing to avail himself of the protection of the country of nationality;

(6) Being a person who has no nationality he is, because of the circumstances in connection with which he has been recognized as a refugee have ceased to exist, able to return to the country of his former habitual residence;

Provided that this paragraph shall not apply to a refugee falling under section A(1) of this Article who is able toinvoke compelling reasons arising out of previous persecution for refusing to return to the country of his former habitual residence.

D. This Convention shall not apply to persons who are at present receiving from organs or agencies of the United Nations other than the United Nations High Commissioner for Refugees protection or assistance.

When such protection or assistance has ceased for any reason, without the position of such persons being definitively settled in accordance with the relevant resolutions adopted by the General Assembly of the United Nations, these persons shall ipso facto be entitled to the benefits of this Convention.

E. This Convention shall not apply to a person who is recognized by the competent authorities of the country in which he has taken residence as having the rights and obligations which are attached to the possession of the nationality of that country.

F. The provisions of this Convention shall not apply to any person with respect to whom there are serious reasons for considering that:

(b) he has committed a serious non-political crime outside the country of refuge prior to his admission to that country as a refugee;

(c) he has been guilty of acts contrary to the purposes and principles of the United Nations.

Article 2
General obligations
Every refugee has duties to the country in which he finds himself, which require in particular that he conform to its laws and regulations as well as to measures taken for the maintenance of public order.

Article 3
Non-discrimination
The Contracting States shall apply the provisions of this Convention to refugees without discrimination as to race, religion or country of origin.

Article 4
Religion
The Contracting States shall accord to refugees within their territories treatment at least as favourable as that accorded to their nationals with respect to freedom to practise their religion and freedom as regards the religious education of their children.

Article 5
Rights granted apart from this Convention
Nothing in this Convention shall be deemed to impair any rights and benefits granted by a Contracting State to refugees apart from this Convention.

Article 6
The term «in the same circumstances»
For the purposes of this Convention, the term «in the same circumstances» implies that any requirements (including requirements as to length and conditions of sojourn or residence) which the particular individual would have to fulfil for the enjoyment of the right in question, if he were not a refugee, must be fulfilled by him, with the exception of requirements which by their nature a refugee is incapable of fulfilling.

Article 7
Exemption from reciprocity
1. Except where this Convention contains more favourable provisions, a Contracting State shall accord to refugees the same treatment as is accorded to aliens generally.

2. After a period of three years' residence, all refugees shall enjoy exemption from legislative reciprocity in the territory of the Contracting States.

3. Each Contracting State shall continue to accord to refugees the rights and benefits to which they were already entitled, in the absence of reciprocity, at the date of entry into force of this Convention for that State.

4. The Contracting States shall consider favourably the possibility of according to refugees, in the absence of reciprocity, rights and benefits beyond those to which they are entitled according to paragraphs 2 and 3, and to extending exemption from reciprocity to refugees who do not fulfil the conditions provided for in paragraphs 2 and 3.

5. The provisions of paragraphs 2 and 3 apply both to the rights and benefits referred to in Articles 13, 18, 19, 21 and 22 of this Convention and to rights and benefits for which this Convention does not provide.

Article 8
Exemption from exceptional measures
With regard to exceptional measures which may be taken against the person, property or interests of nationals of a foreign State, the Contracting States shall not apply such measures to a refugee who is formally a national of the said State solely on account of such nationality. Contracting States which, under their legislation, are prevented from applying the general principle expressed in this Article, shall, in appropriate cases, grant exemptions in favour of such refugees.

Article 9
Provisional measures
Nothing in this Convention shall prevent a Contracting State, in time of war or other grave and exceptional circumstances, from taking provisionally measures which it considers to be essential to the national security in the case of a particular person, pending a determination by the Contracting State that that person is in fact a refugee and that the continuance of such measures is necessary in his case in the interests of national security.

Article 10
Continuity of residence
1. Where a refugee has been forcibly displaced during the Second World War and removed to the territory of a Contracting State, and is resident there, the period of such enforced sojourn shall be considered to have been lawful residence within that territory.

2. Where a refugee has been forcibly displaced during the Second World War from the territory of a Contracting State and has, prior to the date of entry into force of this Convention, returned there for the purpose of taking up residence, the period of residence before and after such enforced displacement shall be regarded as one uninterrupted period for any purposes for which uninterrupted residence is required.

Article 11
Refugee Seamen
In the case of refugees regularly serving as crew members on board a ship flying the flag of a Contracting State, that State shall give sympathetic consideration to their establishment on its territory and the issue of travel documents to them or their temporary admission to its territory particularly with a view to facilitating their establishment in another country.

Chapter II, Juridical Status
Article 12
Personal status
1. The personal status of a refugee shall be governed by the law of the country of his domicile or, if he has no domicile, by the law of the country of his residence.

2. Rights previously acquired by a refugee and dependent on personal status, more particularly rights attaching to marriage, shall be respected by a Con-

tracting State, subject to compliance, if this be necessary, with the formalities required by the law of that State, provided that the right in question is one which would have been recognized by the law of that State had he not become a refugee.

Article 13
Movable and immovable property
The Contracting States shall accord to a refugee treatment as favourable as possible and, in any event, not less favourable than that accorded to aliens generally in the same circumstances, as regards the acquisition of movable and immovable property and other rights pertaining thereto, and to leases and other contracts relating to relating to movable and immovable property.

Article 14
Artistic rights and industrial property
In respect of the protection of industrial property, such as inventions, designs or models, trade marks, trade names, and of rights in literary, artistic, and scientific works, a refugee shall be accorded in the country in which he has his habitual residence the same protection as is accorded to nationals of that country. In the territory of any other Contracting State, he shall be accorded the same protection as is accorded in that territory to nationals of the country in which he has his habitual residence.

Article 15
Right of association
As regards non-political and non-profit making associations and trade unions the Contracting States shall accord to refugees lawfully staying in their territory the most favourable treatment accorded to nationals of a foreign country, in the same circumstances.

Article 16
Access to courts
1. A refugee shall have free access to the courts of law on the territory of all Contracting States.

2. A refugee shall enjoy in the Contracting State in which he has his habitual residence the same treatment as a national in matters pertaining to access to the Courts, including legal assistance and exemption from cautio judicatem solvi.

3. A refugee shall be accorded in the matters referred to in paragraph 2 in

countries other than that in which he has his habitual residence the treatment granted to a national of the country of his habitual residence.

Chapter III, Gainful Employment

Article 17
Wage-earning employment

1. The Contracting State shall accord to refugees lawfully staying in their territory the most favourable treatment accorded to nationals of a foreign country in the same circumstances, as regards the right to engage in wage-earning employment.

2. In any case, restrictive measures imposed on aliens or the employment of aliens for the protection of the national labour market shall not be applied to a refugee who was already exempt from them at the date of entry into force of this Convention for the Contracting State concerned, or who fulfils one of the following conditions: (a) He has completed three years' residence in the country, (b) He has a spouse possessing the nationality of the country of residence. A refugee may not invoke the benefits of this provision if he has abandoned his spouse, (c) He has one or more children possessing the nationality of the country of residence.

3. The Contracting States shall give sympathetic consideration to assimilating the rights of all refugees with regard to wage-earning employment to those of nationals, and in particular of those refugees who have entered their territory pursuant to programmes of labour recruitment or under immigration schemes.

Article 18
Self-employment

The Contracting States shall accord to a refugee lawfully in their territory treatment as favourable as possible and, in any event, not less favourable that that accorded to aliens generally in the same circumstances, as regards the right to engage on his own account in agriculture, industry, handicrafts and commerce and to establish commercial and industrial companies.

Article 19
Liberal professions

1. Each Contracting State shall accord to refugees lawfully staying in their territory who hold diplomas recognized by the competent authorities of that State, and who are desirous of practising a liberal profession, treatment as fa-

vourable as possible and, in any event, not less favourable than that accorded to aliens generally in the same circumstances.

2. The Contracting States shall use their best endeavours consistently with their laws and constitutions to secure the settlement of such refugees in the territories, other than the metropolitan territory, for whose international relations they are responsible.

Chapter IV, Welfare

Article 20
Rationing
Where a rationing system exists, which applies to the population at large and regulates the general distribution of products in short supply, refugees shall be accorded the same treatment as nationals.

Article 21
Housing.
As regards housing, the Contracting States, in so far as the matter is regulated by laws or regulations or is subject to the control of public authorities, shall accord to refugees lawfully staying in their territory treatment as favourable as possible and, in any event, not less favourable than that accorded to aliens generally in the same circumstances.

Article 22
Public education.
(1) The Contracting States shall accord to refugees the same treatment as is accorded to nationals with respect to elementary education.

(2) The Contracting States shall accord to refugees treatment as favourable as possible, and, in any event, not less favourable than that accorded to aliens generally in the same circumstances, with respect to education other than elementary education and, in particular, as regards access to studies, the recognition of foreign school certificates, diplomas and degrees, the remission of fees and charges and the award of scholarships.

Article 23
Public relief.
The Contracting States shall accord to refugees lawfully staying in their territory the same treatment with respect to public relief and assistance as is accorded to their nationals.

Article 24
Labour legislation and social security.
(1) The Contracting States shall accord to refugees lawfully staying in their territory the same treatment as is accorded to nationals in respect of the following matters:

(2) The right to compensation for the death of a refugee resulting from employment injury or from occupational disease shall not be affected by the fact that the residence of the beneficiary is outside the territory of the Contracting State.

(3) The Contracting States shall extend to refugees the benefits of agreements concluded between them, or which may be concluded between them in the future, concerning the maintenance of acquired rights and rights in the process of acquisition in regard to social security, subject only to the conditions which apply to nationals of the States signatory to the agreements in question.

(4) The Contracting States will give sympathetic consideration to extending to refugees so far as possible the benefits of similar agreements which may at any time be in force between such Contracting States and non-contracting States.

Chapter V, Administrative measures
Article 25
Administrative assistance.
(1) When the exercise of a right by a refugee would normally require the assistance of authorities of a foreign country to whom he cannot have recourse, the Contracting States in whose territory he is residing shall arrange that such assistance be afforded to him by their own authorities or by an international authority.

(2) The authority or authorities mentioned in paragraph 1 shall deliver or cause to be delivered under their supervision to refugees such documents or certifications as would normally be delivered to aliens by or through their national authorities.

(3) Documents or certifications so delivered shall stand in the stead of the official instruments delivered to aliens by or through their national authorities, and shall be given credence in the absence of proof to the contrary.

(4) Subject to such exceptional treatment as may be granted to indigent persons, fees may be charged for the services mentioned herein, but such fees shall be moderate and commensurate with those charged to nationals for similar services.

(5) The provisions of this Article shall be without prejudice to Articles 27 and 28.

Article 26
Freedom of movement.
Each Contracting State shall accord to refugees lawfully in its territory the right to choose their place of residence to move freely within its territory, subject to any regulations applicable to aliens generally in the same circumstances.

Article 27
Identity papers.
The Contracting States shall issue identity papers to any refugee in their territory who does not possess a valid travel document.

Article 28
Travel documents.
(1) The Contracting States shall issue to refugees lawfully staying in their territory travel documents for the purpose of travel outside their territory unless compelling reasons of national security or public order otherwise require, and the provisions of the Schedule to this Convention shall apply with respect to such documents. The Contracting States may issue such a travel document to any other refugee in their territory; they shall in particular give sympathetic consideration to the issue of such a travel document to refugees in their territory who are unable to obtain a travel document from the country of their lawful residence.

(2) Travel documents issued to refugees under previous international agreements by parties thereto shall be recognized and treated by the Contracting States in the same way as if they had been issued pursuant to this article.

Article 29
Fiscal charges.
(1) The Contracting States shall not impose upon refugee duties, charges or taxes, of any description whatsoever, other or higher than those which are or may be levied on their nationals in similar situations.

(2) Nothing in the above paragraph shall prevent the application to refugees of the laws and regulations concerning charges in respect of the issue to aliens of administrative documents including identity papers.

Article 30
Transfer of assets.
(1) A Contracting State shall, in conformity with its laws and regulations, permit refugees to transfer assets which they have brought into its territory, to another country where they have been admitted for the purposes of resettlement.

(2) A Contracting State shall give sympathetic consideration to the application of refugees for permission to transfer assets wherever they may be and which are necessary for their resettlement in another country to which they have been admitted.

Article 31
Refugees unlawfully in the country of refuge.
(1) The Contracting States shall not impose penalties, on account of their illegal entry or presence, on refugees who, coming directly from a territory where their life or freedom was threatened in the sense of Article 1, enter or are present in their territory without authorization, provided they present themselves without delay to the authorities and show good cause for their illegal entry or presence.

(2) The Contracting States shall not apply to the movements of such refugees restrictions other than those which are necessary and such restrictions shall only be applied until their status in the country is regularized or they obtain admission into another country. The Contracting States shall allow such refugees a reasonable period and all the necessary facilities to obtain admission into another country.

Article 32
Expulsion.
(1) The Contracting States shall not expel a refugee lawfully in their territory save on grounds of national security or public order.

(2) The expulsion of such a refugee shall be only in pursuance of a decision reached in accordance with due process of law. Except where compelling reasons of national security otherwise require, the refugee shall be allowed to submit evidence to clear himself, and to appeal to and be represented for the

purpose before competent authority or a person or persons specially designated by the competent authority.

(3) The Contracting States shall allow such a refugee a reasonable period within which to seek legal admission into another country. The Contracting States reserve the right to apply during that period such internal measures as they may deem necessary.

Article 33
Prohibition of expulsion or return («refoulement»)
(1) No Contracting State shall expel or return («refouler») a refugee in any manner whatsoever to the frontiers of territories where his life or freedom would be threatened on account of his race, religion, nationality, membership of a particular social group or political opinion.

(2) The benefit of the present provision may not, however, be claimed by a refugee whom there are reasonable grounds for regarding as a danger to the security of the country in which he is, or who, having been convicted by a final judgment of a particularly serious crime, constitutes a danger to the community of that country.

Article 34
Naturalization.
The Contracting States shall as far as possible facilitate the assimilation and naturalization of refugees. They shall in particular make every effort to expedite naturalization proceedings and to reduce as far as possible the charges and costs of such proceedings.

Chapter VI, Executory and transitory provisions
Article 35
Cooperation of the national authorities with the United Nations.
(1) The Contracting States undertake to co-operate with the Office of the United Nations High Commissioner for Refugees, or any other agency of the United Nations which may succeed it, in the exercise of its functions, and shall in particular facilitate its duty of supervising the application of the provisions of this Convention.

(2) In order to enable the Office of the High Commissioner or any other agency of the United Nations which may succeed it, to make reports to the competent organs of the United Nations, the Contracting States undertake

to provide them in the appropriate form with information and statistical data requested concerning:

Article 36
Information on national legislation.
The Contracting States shall communicate to the Secretary-General of the United Nations the laws and regulations which they may adopt to ensure the application of this Convention.

Article 37
Relation to previous Conventions.
Without prejudice to Article 28, paragraph 2, of this Convention, this Convention replaces, as between parties to it, the Arrangements of 5 July 1922, 31 May 1924, 12 May 1926, 30 June 1928 and 30 July 1935, the Conventions of 28 October 1933 and 10 February 1938, the Protocol of 14 September 1939 and the Agreement of 15 October 1946.

Chapter VII, Final clauses

Article 38
Settlement of disputes.
Any dispute between parties to this Convention relating to its interpretation or application, which cannot be settled by other means, shall be referred to the International Court of Justice at the request of any one of the parties to the dispute.

Article 39
Signature, ratification and accession.
(1) This Convention shall be opened for signature at Geneva on 28 July 1951 and shall hereafter be deposited with the Secretary-General of the United Nations. It shall be open for signature at the European Office of the United Nations from 28 July to 31 August 1951 and shall be re-opened for signature at the Headquarters of the United Nations from 17 September 1951 to 31 December 1952.

(2) This Convention shall be open for signature on behalf of all States Members of the United Nations, and also on behalf of any other State invited to attend the Conference of Plenipotentiaries on the Status of Refugees and Stateless Persons or to which an invitation to sign will have been addressed by the General Assembly. It shall be ratified and the instruments of ratification shall be deposited with the Secretary-General of the United Nations.

(3) This Convention shall be open from 28 July 1951 for accession by the States referred to in paragraph 2 of this Article. Accession shall be effected by the deposit of an instrument of accession with the Secretary-General of the United Nations.

Article 40
Territorial application clause.
(1) Any state may, at the time of signature, ratification or accession, declare that this Convention shall extend to all or any of the territories for the international relations of which it is responsible. Such a declaration shall take effect when the Convention enters into force for the State concerned.

(2) At any time thereafter any such extension shall be made by notification addressed to the Secretary-General of the United Nations and shall take effect as from the ninetieth day after the day of receipt by the Secretary-General of the United Nations of this notification, or as from the date of entry into force of the Convention for the State concerned, whichever is the later.

(3) With respect to those territories to which this Convention is not extended at the time of signature, ratification or accession, each State concerned shall consider the possibility of taking the necessary steps in order to extend the application of this Convention to such territories, subject, where necessary for constitutional reasons, to the consent of the governments of such territories.

Article 41
Federal clause.
In the case of a Federal or non-unitary State, the following provisions shall apply:

1. With respect to those Articles of this Convention that come within the legislative jurisdiction of constituent States, provinces or cantons which are not, under the constitutional system of the federation, bound to take legislative action, the Federal Government shall bring such Articles with a favourable recommendation to the notice of the appropriate authorities of States, provinces or cantons at the earliest possible moment.
2. A Federal State Party to this Convention shall, at the request of any other Contracting State transmitted through the Secretary-General of the United Nations, supply a statement of the law and practice of the Federation and its constituent units in regard to any particular provision of the Convention showing the extent to which effect has been given to that provision by legislative or other action.

Article 42
Reservations.
(1) At the time of signature, ratification or accession, any State may make reservations to articles of the Convention other than to Articles 1, 3, 4, 16(1), 33, 36-46 inclusive.

(2) Any State making a reservation in accordance with paragraph 1 of this article may at any time withdraw the reservation by acommunication to that effect addressed to the Secretary-General of the United Nations.

Article 43
Entry into force.
(1) This Convention shall come into force on the ninetieth day following the day of deposit of the sixth instrument of ratification or accession.

(2) For each State ratifying or acceding to the Convention after the deposit of the sixth instrument of ratification or accession, the Convention shall enter into force on the ninetieth day following the date of deposit by such State of its instrument or ratification or accession.

Article 44
Denunciation.
(1) Any Contracting State may denounce this Convention at any time by a notification addressed to the Secretary-General of the United Nations.

(2) Such denunciation shall take effect for the Contracting State concerned one year from the date upon which it is received by the Secretary-General of the United Niations.

(3) Any State which has made a declaration or notification under Article 40 may, at any time thereafter, by a notification to the Secretary-General of the United Nations, declare that the Convention shall cease to extent to such territory one year after the date of receipt of the notification by the Secretary-General.

Article 45
Revision.
(1) Any Contracting State may request revision of this Convention at any time by a notification addressed to the Secretary-General of the United Nations.

(2) The General Assembly of the United Nations shall recommend the steps, if any, to be taken in respect of such request.

Article 46
Notifications by the Secretary-General of the United Nations.
The Secretary-General of the United Nations shall inform all Members of the United Nations and non-member States referred to in Article 39:

IN FAITH WHEREOF the undersigned, duly authorized, have signed this Convention on behalf of their respective Governments,

DONE at GENEVA, this twenty-eighth day of July, one thousand nine hundred and fifty-one, in a single copy, of which the English and French texts are equally authentic and which shall remain deposited in the archives of the United Nations, and certified true copies of which shall be delivered to all Members of the United Nations and to the non-member States referred to in Article 39.

Appendix II
Protocol relating to the Status of Refugees of 31 January 1967

United Nations General Assembly, 16 December 1966
4 October 1967

Preamble
The States Parties to the present Protocol, Considering that the Convention realting to the Status of Refugees done at Geneva on 28 July 1951 (hereinafter referred to as the Convention) covers only those persons who have become refugees as a result of events occurring before 1 January, 1951.

Considering that new refugee situations have arisen since the Convention was adopted and that the refugees concerned may therefore not fall within the scope of the Convention.

Considering that it is desirable that equal status should be enjoyed by all refugees covered by the definition in the Convention irrespective of the dateline 1 January 1951,

Have agreed as follows:

Article 1
General provision 1. The State Parties to the present Protocol undertake to apply Articles 2 to 34 inclusive of the Convention to refugees as hereinafter redifined.

2. For the purpose of the present Protocol, the term «refugee» shall, except as regards the application of paragraph 3 on this Article, mean any person within the definition of Article 1 of the Convention as if the words «As a result of events occuring before 1 January 1951 and… «and the words»… a result of such events», in Article 1A(2) were omitted.

3. The present Protocol shall be applied by the States Parties hetero without any geographic limitation, save that existing declarations made by States already Parties to the Convention in accordance with Article 1B(1)(a) of the

Convention, shall, unless extended under Article 1B(2) thereof, apply also under the present Protocol.

Article 2
Cooperation of the national authorities with the United Nations 1. The State Parties to the present Protocol undertake to co-operate with the Office of the United Nations High Commissioner for Refugees, or any other agency of the United Nations which may succeed it, in the exercise of its functions, and shall in particular facilitate its duty of supervising the application of the provisions of the present Protocol.

2. In order to enable the Office of the High Commissioner, or any other agency of the United Nations which may succeed it, to make reports to the competent organs of the United Nations, the State Parties to the present Protocol undertake to provide them with the information and statistical data requested, in the appropriate form, concerning: (a) The condition of refugees; (b) The implementation of the present Protocol; (c) Laws, regulations and decrees which are, or may hereafter be, in force relating to refugees.

Article 3
Information on national legislation The State Parties to the present Protocol shall communicate to the Secretary-General of the United Nations the laws and regulations which they may adopt to ensure the application of the present protocol.

Article 4
Settlement of disputes Any dispute between State Parties to the present Protocol which relates to its interpretation or application and which cannot be settled by other means shall be referred to the International Court of Justice at the request of any one of the parties to the dispute.

Article 5
Accession The present Protocol shall be open for accession on behalf of all State Parties to the Convention and of any other State Member of the United Nations or member of any of the specialized agencies or to which an invitation to accede may have been adressed by the General Assembly of the United Nations.

Article 6
Federal clause In the case of a Federal or non-unitary State, the following provisions shall apply:

(a) With respect to those articles of the Convention to be applied in accordance with Article I, paragraph 1, of the present Protocol that come within the legislative jurisdiction of the federal legislative authority, the obligations of the Federal Government shall to this extent be the same as those of State Parties which are not Federal States;

(b) With respect to those articles of the Convention to be applied in accordance with Article I, paragraph 1, of the present Protocol that come within the legislative jurisdiction of constituent States, provinces or cantons which are not, under the constitutional system of the federation, bound to take legislative action, the Federal Government shall bring such articles with a favourable recommendation to the notice of the appropriate authorities of States, provinces or cantons at the earliest possible moment;

(c) A federal State Party to the present Protocol shall, at the request of any other State Party hetero transmitted through the Secretary-General of the United Nations, supply a statement of the law and practice of the Federation and its constituent units in regard to any particular provision of the Convention to be applied in accordance with Article I, paragraph 1, of the present Protocol, showing the extent to which effect has been given to that provision by legislative or other action.

Article 7
Reservations and declarations
1. At the time of accession, any State may make reservations in respect of Article IV of the present Protocol and in respect of the application in accordance with Article I of the present Protocol of any provisions of the Convention other than those contained in Articles 1, 3, 4, 16(1) and 33 thereof, provided that in the case of a State Party to the Convention reservations made under this Article shall not extend to refugees in respect of whom the Convention applies.

2. Reservations made by State Parties to the Convention in accordance with Article 42 thereof shall, unless withdrawn, be applicable in relation to their obligations under the present Protocol.

3. Any State making a reservation in accordance with paragraph 1 of this Article may at any time withdraw such reservation by a communication to that effect adressed to the Secretary-General of the United Nations.

4. Declerations made under Article 40, paragraphs 1 and 1, of the Convention by a State Party thereto which accedes to the present Protocol shall be deemed to apply in respect of the present Protocol, unless upon accession a notification to the contrary is adressed by the State Party concerned to the Secretary-General of the United Nations. The provisions of Article 40, paragraphs 2 and 3, and of Article 44, paragraph 3, of the Convention shall be deemed to apply mutatis mutandis to the present Protocol.

Article 8
Entry into force
1. The present Protocol shall come into force on the day of deposit of the sixth instrument of accession.

2. For each State acceding to the Protocol after the deposit of the sixth instrument of accession, the Protocol shall come into force on the date of deposit by such State of its instrument of accession.

Article 9
Denunciation
1. Any State Party hetero may denounce this Protocol at any time by a notification adressed to the Secretary-General of the United Nations.

2. Such denunciation shall take effect for the State Party concerned one year from the date on which it is received by the Secretary-General of the United Nations.

Article 10
Notifications by the Secretary-General of the United Nations The Secretary-General of the United Nations shall inform the States referred to in Article V above of the date of entry into force, accessions, reservations and withdrawals of reservations to and denunciations of the present Protocol, and of declarations and notifications relating hereto.

Article 11
Deposit in the archives of the Secretariat of the United Nations A copy of the present Protocol, of which the Chinese, English, French Russian and Spanish texts are equally authentic, signed by the President of the General Assembly and by the Secretary-General of the United Nations, shall be deposited in the archives of the Secretariat of the United Nations. The Secretary-General will transmit certified copies thereof to all State Members of the United nations and to the other States referred to in Article V above.

Bibliography

Books

BATIFFOL Henri and LAGARDE Paul, *Droit international privé*, 7th edition, Paris: Librairie Générale de Droit et de Jurisprudence, Vol. I, 1981, 448 p.

BERNHARD John and LEHMANN Tyge, *Den europæiske menneskerettighedskonvention belyst gennem menneskerettighedskommissionens og -domstolens praksis* (The European Convention on Human Rights Illustrated through the Practice of the Commission and the Court of Human Rights), Copenhagen: G.E.C. GAD, 1985, 190 p.

BODART Serge, *Les autres réfugiés: le statut des réfugiés «de facto» en Europe*, Louvain-La-Neuve: Academia, 1990, 88 p.

BUERGENTHAL Thomas and KISS Alexandre, *La protection internationale des droits de l'homme: Précis*, Kehl am Rhein; Strasbourg; Arlington, VA: Editions N.P. Engel, 1991, 261 p.

Council of Europe, *Le droit d'asile et des réfugiés: Tendances actuelles et perspectives d'avenir*, proceedings of the Sixteenth Colloquy on European Law, Lund, 15–17 September 1986, Strasbourg:Council of Europe, 1987, 169 p.

CRAWLEY Heaven, *Women as asylum seekers. A Legal Handbook*, Immigration Law Practitioners` Association and Refugee Action, London, 1997, 228 p.

ECRE, *Asylum in Europe. An introduction*, Vol. 1, London, April 1993, 105 p.

ECRE, ed., *Review of refugee and asylum procedures in selected countries*, Vol. II, London, October 1994.

ECRE and France Terre d'Asile, ed., *Asile en Europe. Guide à l'intention des associations pour la protection des réfugiés*, 1990.

EINARSEN, Terje, «Flyktningers rettsstilling i Norge», («The legal position of refugees in Norway»), Nordiske komparative studier om mottak av flyktninger, (Nordic comparative studies on the reception of refugees»), Fagbokforlaget Vigmostad & Bjørke AS, 1997, 144 p.

FISKNES Eli, *Utlendingsloven. Kommentarutgave* (The Aliens Act. A Commentary), Oslo: Universitetsforlaget, 1994, 466 p.

FLEISCHER Carl August, *Folkerett*, (International Public Law), 6th edition, Oslo: Universitetsforlaget, 1994, 284 p.

FOURLANOS Gerassimos, *Sovereignty and the Ingress of Aliens*, Stockholm: Almqvist & Wiksell International, 1986, 186 p.

GARCIA-MORA Manuel R., *International Law and Asylum as a Human Right*, Washington: Public Affairs Press, 1956, 171 p.

GOODWIN-GILL Guy S., *The Refugee in International Law*, Oxford: Clarendon Press, First Edition 1983, 318 p, Second Edition 1996, 584 p.

GRAHL-MADSEN Atle, *Makter og Mennesker: Studier i folkerett og fremmedrett* (Powers and People: Studies in International Law and Aliens Law), Oslo: Universitetsforlaget, 1991, 396 p.

GRAHL-MADSEN Atle, *The Status of Refugees in International Law*, Leyden: A.W. Sijthoff, Vol. I, 1966, 499 p. and Vol. II (Asylum, Entry and Sojourn), 1972, 482 p.

GRAHL-MADSEN Atle, *Territorial Asylum*, Stockholm: Almqvist & Wiksell International, 1980, 231 p.

GUILD Elspeth, *The Developing Immigration and Asylum Policies of the European Union*, The Hague: Kluwer Law International,1996, 528 p.

HATHAWAY James C., *The Law of Refugee Status*, Toronto: Butterworths Canada Ltd., 1991, 252 p.

HATHAWAY James C., ed. *Reconceiving International Refugee Law*, The Hague: Kluwer Law International, 1997, 208 p.

JOLY Danièle et. al., *Refugees. Asylum in Europe?*, London: Minority Rights Publications, 1992, 166 p.

KÄLIN Walter, *Das Prinzip des Non-Refoulment*, Bern-Frankfurt/M: Verlag Peter Lang, Europäische Hochschulschriften, Reihe II, Rechtswissenschaft, Vol. 298, 1982, 365 p.

LAMBERT, Helen, *Seeking Asylum. Comparative Law and Practice in Selected European Countries*, Dordrecht: Martinus Nijhoff Publishers, 1995, 220 p.

MARTIN David A., ed., *The New Asylum Seekers: Refugee Law in the 1980s*, Dordrecht: Martinus Nijhoff Publishers, 1988, 217 p.

MARTIN Susan Forbes, ed., *Refugee Women*, London: Zed Books, 1992, 140 p.

MELANDER Göran and NOBEL Peter, ed., *African Refugees and the Law*, Uppsala: Scandinavian Institute of African Studies, 1978, 98 p.

MERON Theodor, *Human Rights and Humanitarian Norms as Customary Law*, Oxford University Press, Clarendon Paperbacks, 1991, 263 p.

PLENDER Richard, *International Migration Law*, Dordrecht: Martinus Nijhoff Publishers, 1988, 587 p.

PLENDER Richard, *The Right of Asylum*, The present state of research carried out by the English-speaking section of the Centre for studies and research of the Hague Academy of International Law, 1989, Dordrecht: Martinus Nijhoff Publishers, 1990, p. 63–109.

PRAKASH SINHA S., *Asylum and International Law*, The Hague: Martinus Nijhoff, 1971, 366 p.

ROBINSON Nehemiah, *Convention Relating to the Status of Refugees. Its History, Contents and Interpretation*, New York: The Institute of Jewish Affairs, 1953, 238 p.

STENBERG Gunnel, *Non-Expulsion and Non-Refoulement*, Uppsala: Iustus Förlag, 1989, 309 p.

TERLOUW A. et. al., ed. *A new immigration law for Europe? The 1992 London and 1993 Copenhagen Rules on Immigration*, Utrecht: Netherland Centre for Immigrants, 1993, 96 p.

THIERRY Hubert et.al., *Droit international public*, 4th edition, Paris: Éditions Montchrestien, 1984, 799 p.

TIBERGHIEN Frédéric, *La protection des réfugiés en France*, 2nd edition, Presses Universitaires d'Aix-Marseille, Collection Droit Public Positif, 1988, 592 p.

UNHCR, *Les réfugiés dans le monde – L'enjeu de la protection*, Paris: Éditions La Découverte, 1993, 192 p.

UNHCR, *Handbook on Procedures and Criteria for Determining Refugee Status*, Geneva: January 1992, 107 p.

UNHCR Branch Office in Italy, ed., *For Forty Years, UNHCR Alongside Refugees*, Rome: Presidenza del Consiglio dei Ministri, Quaderni, 1991, 285 p.

Articles, Reports And Papers

Advisory Committee on Human Rights and Foreign Policy, *Harmonization of Asylum Law in Western Europe*, The Hague, 7 November 1990, 106 p.

AGA KAHN Sadruddin, «Refugees and Displaced Persons», Academy of International Law, The Hague, Vol. 149, Leyden: A.W. Sijthoff, 1977, p. 289–352.

AGA KAHN Sadruddin, «Mass Exodus», *In Defense of the Alien*, Vol. 5, 1982, p. 10–18.

AGA KAHN Sadruddin, «Asylum – Article 14 of the Universal Declaration of Human Rights», *Journal of the International Commission of Jurists*, Vol. VIII, N° 2, December 1967, p. 2–8.

ALAUX Jean-Pierre, «Plus d'asile pour ceux qui fuient guerres et misères», *Le Monde Diplomatique*, August 1992, 23 p.

Amnesty International, *Rapport 1994*, St. Pieters-Leeuw, Belgium: French edition, 1994, 381 p.

Amnesty International, «Europe: Harmonization of Asylum Policy», 1992, 21 p.

Amnesty International, «Europe: Human Rights and the Need for a Fair Asylum Policy», London: November 1991, 27 p.

ARBOLEDA Eduardo, «The Cartagena Declaration of 1984 and its Similarities to the 1969 OAU Convention – A Comparative Perspective», *Journal of Refugee Law*, Special Issue, July 1995, p. 87–101.

ARBOLEDA Eduardo, «Refugee Definition in Africa and Latin America: The Lessons of Pragmatism», *International Journal of Refugee Law*, Vol. 3, N° 2, 1991, p. 185–207.

ARNIM Ruprecht von, «Une Harmonization Européenne du Droit d'Asile», statement to the Seminar on Refugee Policy to 1992 and Beyond, organized by UNHCR, Brussels 20–21 June 1991, 7 p.

ARNOULD Michel, «Asylum in Europe: Shift to the East», *Forum, Refugees*, Council of Europe, N° 3, 1994, p. 20–21.

Asian–African Legal Consultative Committee, «Notes and Comments on the Proposed Convention on Territorial Asylum», 30th session of the UN General Assembly, New Dehli, 1975, 32 p.

BASHIR Layli Miller, «Female Genital Mutilation in the United States: An Examination of Criminal and Asylum Law», *American University Journal of Gender & the Law*, Spring 1996

BAUWENS Martin, «La définition du réfugié à la lumière de la jurisprudence du Commissariat General aux Réfugiés et aux Apatrides», *Revue du droit des étrangers*, Brussels: ADDE, N° 67, January – February 1992, p. 3–12.

BETTATI Mario, «Le statut juridique du réfugié en droit international», *The Refugee Problem on Universal, Regional and National Level*, Thessaloniki: Institute of International Public Law and Interntional Relations, 1987, p. 89–125.

BETTATI Mario, «L'asile politique en question», *Perspectives Internationales*, Paris: Presses Universitaires de France, 1985, 205 p.

BJÄLLERSTEDT Jöran, «Avvisning och principen om första asylland» («Rejection and the Principle of First Country of Asylum), *Asyl i Norden* (Asylum in the Nordic countries), Copenhagen: Danish Refugee Council, 1990, p. 52–71.

BLAKE Nicholas, «European Immigration and Asylum Policy and Respect for Human Rights», paper to the World Human Rights Conference from ILPA (Immigration Law Practitioners' Association), Vienna, 13 June 1993, 4 p.

BLANC Hubert, «Schengen: le chemin de la libre circulation en Europe», *Revue du Marché Commun et de l'Union Européenne*, N° 351, October 1991.

BLUM Carolyn Patty, «Refugee Status Based on Membership in a Particular Social Group: A North American Perspective», in Jacqueline Bhabha and Geoffrey Coll, ed., *Asylum Law & Practice in Europe and North America: A Comparative Analysis*, Washington, DC: Federal Publications Inc., 1992, p. 81–99.

BLUMENTHAL Ulrich von, «Dublin, Schengen and the Harmonization of Asylum in Europe», presentation submitted to the First European Lawyers Conference, Brussels, 14–15 February 1991, 12 p.

BOLTEN José J., «From Schengen to Dublin: The New Frontiers of Refugee Law», *Nederlands Juristenblad*, Vol. 5, 31 January 1991, p. 165–178.

BOLTEN José J., «The Right to Seek Asylum in Europe», *Netherlands Quarterly of Human Rights*, Vol. 7, N° 4, 1989, p. 381–412.

BRINGUIER Pierre, «Réfugiés et personnes déplacées: quelques problèmes de définition», *Les réfugiés en Afrique: situation et problèmes actuels*, Bordeaux: Institut Français de Droit Humanitaire et des Droits de l'Homme, Les Cahiers du Droit Public, 1986, p. 33–50.

BRUSCHI Christian, «Le droit d'asile: l'Europe à l'heure des choix», *Migrations Société*, Vol. 2, N° 12, 1990, p. 47–72.

BYRNE Rosemary and SHACKNOVE Andrew, «The Safe Country Notion in European Asylum Law», *Harvard Human Rights Journal*, Spring, 1996.

CARLIER Jean-Yves, «L'état du droit international», in F. Rigaux, ed., *Droit d'Asile*, Brussels: E. Story-Scientia, 1988, p. 29–64.

CARLIER Jean-Yves, «Harmonization of Refugee Policies in Europe: Practical Consequences and Compatibility with International Law and Standards: Access to the Territory», statement at ELENA seminar, Luxembourg, 7–10 May 1992, 8 p.

CELS Johan, «Responses of European States to 'de facto' Refugees», in Gil Loescher and Laila Monahan, ed., *Refugees and International Relations*, Oxford University Press, 1989, p. 187–215.

CHAUDRI Mohammed Ahsen, «The Problem of Refugees and International Humanitarian Law», in *Refugees and Displaced Persons*, Karachi: Pakistan Institute of International Affairs, 1985, p. 31–45.

CHEMILLE-GENDREAU Monique, «Le concept de réfugié en droit international et ses limites», *Pluriel*, N° 28, 1981, p. 3–11.

CHINKIN C.M., «The Challenge of Soft Law: Development and Change in International Law», *International and Comparative Law Quarterly*, Vol. 38, part 4, 1989, p. 850–866.

CISSE Bernadette Passade, «International Law Sources Applicable to Female Genital Mutilation: A Guide to Adjudicators of Refugee Claims Based on a Fear of Female Genital Mutilation», *Columbia Journal of Transnational Law*, 1997, p. 12–34.

COHEN-JONATHAN Gérard, «De l'effet juridique des 'mesures provisoires' dans certaines circonstances et de l'efficacité du droit de recours individuel: à propos de l'arrêt Cruz Varas de la Cour Européenne des Droits de l'Homme», *Revue Universelle des Droits de l'Homme*, Vol. 3, N° 6, 6 August 1991, p. 205–209.

COLELLA Alberto, «Les réserves à la Convention de Genève (28 juillet 1951) et au Protocole de New York (31 janvier 1967) sur le statut des réfugiés», *French Yearbook of International Law*, Paris: CNRS, XXXV, 1989, p. 446–475.

COLES G.J.L., «The Basis and Function of Refugee Law», in *The Refugee Problem on Universal, Regional and National Level*, Thessaloniki: Institute of International Public Law and International Relations, 1987, p. 655–667.

COLES G.J.L., «Solutions to the Problem of Refugees and the Protection of Refugees», a background study prepared for a Round Table organised by UNCHR and The International Institute of Humanitarian Law, San Remo, 1989, 326 p.

COLES G.J.L., «International Protection of Refugees and Displaced Persons», report prepared by Asian Working Group, 1980, 193 p.

COLES G.J.L., «The Human Rights Approach to the Solution of the Refugee Problem: A Theoretical and Practical Enquiry», in Alan E. Nash, ed., *Human Rights and the Protection of Refugees under International Law*, report from a conference in Montreal 29 November – 2 December 1987, Canadian Human Rights Foundation, 1988, p. 195–222.

COLES G.J.L., «Flyktningspørsmålet og menneskerettigheter – nye perspektiver» («The Refugee Question and Human Rights – New Perspectives»), *Mennesker & Rettigheter*, Oslo, N° 1, 1991, p. 3–13.

Comité Consultatif Asie–Afrique, «Note and Comments on the Proposed Convention on Territorial Asylum», 1975, 32 p.

Council of Europe, «The law of asylum and refugees: present tendencies and future perspectives», Proceedings of the Sixteenth Colloquy on European Law, Lund, 15th –17th September 1986, Strasbourg: Council of Europe, 1987, 169 p.

CRABB John, «The definition of refugees as belonging to international humanitarian law», *AWR Bulletin*, N° 1, 1983, p. 36–39.

CRUZ Antonio, «Carrier Sanctions in Five Community States: Incompatibilities between International Civil Aviation and Human Rights Obligations», *CCME Briefing Paper*, N° 4, 1991,

CUELLAR R. et. al., «Refugee and Related Developments in Latin America», *International Journal of Refugee Law*, Vol. 3, N° 3, 1991, p. 482–498.

CUÉNOD Jacques, «Assistance and Protection of Internally Displaced Persons», statement to the seminar on Refugee Policy to 1992 and Beyond, Brussels, 20–21 June 1992, 6 p.

DEDEKER Renée, «Le droit d'asile dans Schengen. Quelques réflexions à propos de l'avis du Conseil d'Etat néerlandais sur l'Accord de Schengen», Université Libre de Bruxelles, August 1991, 3 p.

DEDEKER Renée, «The Right of Asylum in Europe. Some Proposals on Accelerated

Procedures for the Twelve Member States», Université Libre de Bruxelles, January 1992, 86 p.

DENG Francis M., Introduction and Conclusion from a study presented at a Round Table on United Nations Human Rights Protection for Internally Displaced Persons, 5–6 February 1993, 11 p.

DIENG A., «Les politiques nationales et régionales dans le domaine des réfugiés: le tiers-monde», in Vera Gowlland and Klaus Samson, ed., *Problems and Prospects of Refugee Law*, Geneva: The Graduate Institute of International Studies, 1992, p. 133–145.

DUNBAR N.C.H., «The Myth of Customary International Law», *Australian Year Book of International Law*, Vol. 8, 1983, p. 1–19.

Dutch Refugee Council, «Refugees in Western Europe: Schengen Affects the Entire Refugee Law», Amsterdam, September 1989, 6 p.

Dutch Refugee Council, «Considerations, Conclusions and Recommendations of the International Conference Refugees in the World: The European Community's Response», The Hague, 7–8 December 1989, 63 p.

Dutch Refugee Council, «A Survey of Treatment of Asylum Seekers at International Airports in Western Europe», memorandum prepared for the colloquy «Human Rights Without Frontiers», Strasbourg, 30 November – 1 December 1989, 17 p.

ECRE, «Position of ECRE on Temporary Protection in the context of the Need for a Supplementary Refugee Definition», March 1997, 9 p. (Summary of Conclusions)

ECRE, «Analysis of the Treaty of Amsterdam in so far as it relates to asylum policy», 1997, 14 p.

ECRE, «Position on the implementation of the Dublin Convention in the light of lessons learned from the implementation of the Schengen Convention», 1997.

ECRE, «Position on asylum seeking and refugee women», 1997.

ECRE, «Convention Determining the State Responsible for Examining Applications for Asylum Lodged in one of the Member States of the European Communities», November 1990, 4 p.

ECRE, «Safe Third Countries – Myths and Realities», 1995, 20 p.

ECRE, «The Need for a Supplementary Refugee Definition», April 1993, 8 p.

ECRE, «Schengen Convention in Pursuance of the Schengen Agreement of 14 June 1985 in Relation to the Gradual Abolition of Internal Borders», November 1990, 3 p.

ECRE, «Una politica europea sull'asilo alla luce dei principi consolidati», April 1994, 22 p.

ECRE, «Observations on 'manifestly unfounded' applications for asylum and the notion of 'third host countries'», 20. November 1992, 5 p.

ECRE, «Airport Procedures in Europe», February 1993, 7 p.

ECRE, «Fair and Efficient Procedures for Determining Refugee Status», October 1990, 4 p.

ECRE/ZDWF, «Séminaire européen d'avocats sur la notion de 'pays de premier accueil'», 10–12 January 1986, edited by France Terre d'Asile, April 1987, 79 p.

EDMINSTER Steven, «European 'Safe Third Country' System Creates a New Belrin Wall», US Committee for Refugees, 1997, 40 p.

EGAN Suzanne and STOREY Andy, «European Asylum Policy: A Fortress Under Construction», in *Trócaire Development Review*, Dublin, 1992, p. 49–65.

EINARSEN Terje, «Mass Flight: The Case for International Asylum», *International Journal of Refugee Law*, Vol. 7, No. 4, 1995, p. 551–578

EINARSEN Terje, «The European Convention on Human Rights and the Notion of an Implied Right to 'de facto' Asylum», *International Journal of Refugee Law*, Vol. 2, N° 3, July 1990, p. 361–389.

ERGEC Rusen, «Le Conseil de l'Europe et les réfugiés», from *La reconaissance de la qualité de réfugié et l'octroi de l'asile*, Bruxelles: Editions Bruylant, Collection de droit internationale, 1990, p. 121–132.

FELLER Erika, «Carrier Sanctions and International Law», *International Journal of Refugee Law*, Vol. 1, N° 1, 1989, p. 48–66.

FERNHOUT R. et MEIJERS H., «Asylum», in A. Terlouw et. al., ed., *A New Immigration Law for Europe?: The 1992 London and 1993 Copenhagen Rules on Immigration*, Utrecht: Netherland Immigration Centre, 1993, p. 8–24.

FITZPATRICK Joan, «Revitalizing the 1951 Refugee Convention», *Harvard Human Rights Journal*, Spring 1996, p. 165–200.

FONTAINE Pierre-Michel, «Refugee Law and Protection of Human Life and Dignity», 11th seminar for international humanitarian law, Protection of Human Life and Dignity, Seoul: The Republic of Korea National Red Cross, 25 October 1990, p. 41–64.

FONTEYNE, Jean-Pierre L., «Burden Sharing: An Analysis of the Nature and Function of International Solidarity in Case of Mass Influx of Refugees», seminar on the problems related to international protection of refugees, Kensington, Australia, 2–3 August 1980, *The Australian Year Book of International Law*, Vol. 8, 1983, p. 162–188.

FOX Kristin M., «Note and Comment: Gender Persecution: Canadian Guidelines Offer a Model for Refugee Determination in the United States», *Arizona Journal of International and Comparative Law*, Spring 1994.

FULLERTON Maryellen, «A Comparative Look at Refugee Status Based on Persecution Due to Membership in a Particular Social Group», *Cornell International Law Journal*, 1993, p. 467–536.

GAMMELTOFT-HANSEN Hans, «Første asylland» («First Country of Asylum»), *Nordisk Tidsskrift for Internasjonal Rett* (Acta scandinavica juris gentium), Vol. 48, 1979, p. 173–185.

GAMRASNI-AHLEN Nina, «Recent European Developments Regarding Refugees: The Dublin Convention and the French Perspective», in Jacqueline Bhabha and Geoffrey Coll, ed., *Asylum Law & Practice in Europe and North America: A Comparative Analysis*, Washington, DC: Federal Publications Inc., 1992, p. 109–123.

GARIBALDI Oscar M., «The Legal Status of General Assembly Resolutions: Some Conceptual Observations», *American Society of International Law*, Proceedings from the 73rd Annual Conference, Washington DC, 26–28 April 1979, p. 324–333.

GARVEY Jack I., «Toward a Reformulation of International Refugee Law», *Harvard International Law Journal*, Vol. 26, N° 2, 1985, p. 483–500.

GERETY Tom, «Sanctuary: A Comment on the Ironic Relation Between Law and Morality», in David A. Martin, ed., *The New Asylum Seekers: Refugee Law in the 1980s*, Dordrecht: Martinus Nijhoff Publishers, 1988, p. 159–180

GIAKOUMOPOULOS Ch., «L'étranger en 'zone internationale' et les garanties de la Convention des Droits de l'Homme», Strasbourg: Council of Europe (CA-HAR), 10 June 1992, 17 p.

GOODWIN-GILL Guy S, «Refugee Identity and the Fading Prospect of International Protection», Conference on Refugee Rights and Realities, Human Rights Law Centre, University of Nottingham, 30 November 1996.

GOODWIN-GILL Guy S., «Nonrefoulement and the New Asylum Seekers», in David A. Martin, ed., *The New Asylum Seekers: Refugee Law in the 1980s*, Dordrecht: Martinus Nijhoff Publishers, 1988, p. 103–121.

GOODWIN-GILL Guy S., «Refugees: The Functions and Limits of the Existing Protection System», in Alan E. Nash, ed., *Human Rights and the Protection of Refugees under International Law*, Halifax: Canadian Human Rights Foundation, 1988, p. 149–182.

GOODWIN-GILL Guy S., «Safe Country? Says Who?», *Refugees*, May 1992, p. 37–38.

GOODWIN-GILL Guy S., «The Principle of Refuge: An Outline», at the ELENA seminar on The Legal Status of de facto Refugees and Rejected Asylum Seekers, 12–14 February 1988, 15 p.

GOODWIN-GILL Guy S., «Who is a Refugee?», paper prepared for the Conference on Refugees in the World – The European Community's Response, organised by the Dutch Refugee Council and the Netherlands Institute of Human Rights, The Hague, 7–8 December 1989, 32 p

GOODWIN-GILL Guy S., «Refugees: Definition and Admission», revised text of a paper presented to a Seminar on Problems in International Protection of Refugees, Kensington, Australia, 2–3 August 1980, 19 p.

GORDON Paul, *Fortress Europe? The meaning of 1992*, London: The Runnymede Trust, 1989, 40 p.

GORNIG Gilbert, «Das 'non-refoulement'-Prinzip, ein Menschenrecht 'in statu nascendi'», *Europäische Grundrechte*, Vol. 18, 1986, p. 521–529.

GRAHL-MADSEN Atle, «Refugees and Refugee Law in a World in Transition», in «Transnational Legal Problems of Refugees», *Michigan Yearbook of International Legal Studies*, 1982, p. 65–88.

GRAHL-MADSEN Atle, «International Refugee Law Today and Tomorrow», *Archiv des Völkerrechts*, Vol. 20, 1982, p. 411–467.

GRAHL-MADSEN Atle, «Refugees and Displaced Persons: Meeting the Challenge», *Nordisk Tidsskrift for International Ret*, Acta scandinavica juris gentium, Vol. 54, 1985, p. 3–10.

GRAHL-MADSEN Atle, «Refugees in Orbit – Some Constructive Proposals», proceedings from a Round Table on refugees in orbit, organised by the Institute of International Humanitarian Law, Florence, 4–6 June 1979, p. 13–18.

GRAHL-MADSEN Atle, «The Emergent International Law Relating to Refugees: Past-Present-Future», in *The Refugee Problem on the Universal, Regional and National Level*, Thessaloniki: Institute of Interntional Public Law and International Relations 1987, p. 58–62.

GRAHL-MADSEN Atle, «Fridtjof Nansen: den første høykommissær for flyktninger» («Fridtjof Nansen: The First High Commissioner for Refugees», in *Flyktning*, Oslo, N° 2, 1987, p. 18–21.

GROS ESPIELL Héctor, «American International Law on Territorial Asylum and Extradition as it Relates to the 1951 Convention and the 1967 Protocol Relating to the Status of Refugees», UNHCR, 1981, 46 p.

GUNNING Isabelle R., «Modernizing Customary International Law: The Challenge of Human Rights», *Virginia Journal of International Law*, Vol. 31, N° 2, 1991, p. 211–247.

GUNNING Isabelle R., «Expanding the International Definition of Refugee: A Multicultural View», *Fordham International Law Journal*, Vol. 13, N° 1, 1989–1990, p. 35–85.

HAILBRONNER Kay, «Nonrefoulment and 'Humanitarian Refugees*: Customary International Law or Wishful Legal Thinking?» in David A. Martin, ed., *The New Asylum Seekers: Refugee Law in the 1980s*, Dordrecht: Martinus Nijhoff Publishers, 1988, p. 123–158.

HAILBRONNER Kay, «The Concept of 'Safe Country' and Expedient Asylum Procedures», Strasbourg: Council of Europe (CAHAR), 4 September 1991, 35 p.

HAILBRONNER Kay, «The Right to Asylum and the Future of Asylum Procedures in the European Community», *International Journal of Refugee Law*, Vol. 2, N° 3, 1990, p. 341–360.

HANNUM Hurst, «The Status and Future of the Customary International Law of Human Rights: The Status of the Universal Declaration of Human Rights in National and International Law», *Georgia Journal of International and Comparative Law*, Fall 1995 / Winter 1996.

HARTLING Poul, «Concept and Definition of 'Refugee' – Legal and Humanitarian Aspects», statement at the Second Nordic Seminar on the Rights of Refugees, University of Copenhagen, 23 April 1979, 21 p.

HARTMAN Joan Fitzpatrick, «The Principle and Practice of Temporary Refuge: A Customary Norm Protecting Civilians Fleeing Internal Armed Conflict», in David A. Martin, ed., *The New Asylum Seekers: Refugee Law in the 1980s*, Dordrecht: Martinus Nijhoff Publishers, 1988, p. 87–101.

HATHAWAY James C., «Toward the Reformulation of International Refugee Law», Research Report, 1992–1997, 18 p.

HATHAWAY James C., «Reconceiving Refugee Law as Human Rights Protection», *Journal of Refugee Studies*, Vol. 4, N° 2, 1991, p. 113–131.

HATHAWAY James C., «A Reconsideration of the Underlying Premise of Refugee Law», *Harvard International Law Journal*, Vol. 31, N° 1, 1990, p. 129–183.

HOND Michiel den, «'Jet-Age Refugees': In Search of Balance and Cooperation», in David A. Martin, ed., *The New Asylum Seekers: Refugee Law in the 1980s*, Dordrecht: Martinus Nijhoff Publishers, 1988, p. 49–56.

HULL David, «Displaced Persons: 'The New Refugees'», *Georgia Journal of International and Comparative Law*, Vol. 13, N° 3, 1983, p. 755–792.

IOGNA-PRAT Michel, «The Notion of 'Membership of a Particular Social Group': A European Perspective», in Jacqueline Bhabha et Geoffrey Coll, ed., *Asylum Law & Practice in Europe and North America: A Comparative Analysis*, Washington, DC: Federal Publications Inc., 1992, p. 71–79.

IOGNA-PRAT Michel, «L'évolution du concept réfugié: Pratiques contemporaines en France», *Pluriel*, N° 28, 1981, p. 13–22.

JACKSON Ivor C., «The 1951 Convention relating to the Status of Refugees: A Universal Basis for Protection», *International Journal of Refugee Law*, Vol. 3, N° 3, 1991, p. 403–413.

JACKSON SMITH Alice, «Temporary Safe Haven for De Facto Refugees from War, Violence and Disasters», *Virginia Journal of International Law*, Vol. 28, N° 2, 1988, p. 509–560.

JAEGER Gilbert, «A succinct evaluation of the 1951 Convention and the 1967 Protocol relating to the Status of Refugees», Symposion des Diakonischen Werkes der Evangelischen Kirche in Deutschland, Stuttgart, 25–27 November 1980, 22 p.

JAEGER Gilbert, «Irregular Movements: The Concept and Possible Solutions», in David A. Martin, ed., *The New Asylum Seekers: Refugee Law in the 1980s*, Dordrecht: Martinus Nijhoff Publishers, 1988, p. 23–48.

JAEGER Gilbert, «The Definition of 'Refugee': Restrictive versus Expanding Trends», *World Refugee Survey*, 1983, p. 5–10.

JAEGER Gilbert, «Etude des déplacements irréguliers des demandeurs d'asile et des réfugiés», UN Document WG/M/3, Geneva 1985, 134 p.

JESSEN-PETERSEN Søren, «UNHCR i Norden» («UNHCR in the Nordic Countries»), *Asyl i Norden* (Asylum in the Nordic Countries), Copenhagen: Danish Refugee Council, 1990, p. 21–29.

JULIEN-LAFERRIERE François, «Treatment of Refugees and Asylum Seekers at Points of Entry», paper at the colloquy Human Rights without Frontiers, Strasbourg, 30 November–1 December 1989, 13 p.

KÄLIN Walter, «Well-Founded Fear of Persecution: A European Perspective», in Jacqueline Bhabha and Geoffrey Coll, ed., *Asylum Law & Practice in Europe and North America: A Comparative Analysis*, Washington, DC: Federal Publications Inc., 1992, p. 21–35.

KÄLIN Walter, «Protection from Forcible Return for de facto Refugees: Approaches and Principles in International Law», paper at an ELENA conference, 12–14 February 1988, p. 114–134.

KEBA M'BAYE M., «Les mouvements de population et les organes des droits de l'homme», *Yearbook of the International Institute of Humanitarian Law*, 1984, p. 21–40.

KIMMINICH Otto, «Völkerrechtlige und Grundgesetzliche Grenzen der Asylrechtsreform», in Manfred Nowak et al., ed., *Fortschritt im Bewusstsein der Grund- und Menschenrechte*, Festschrift für Felix Ermacora, Kehl am Rhein: N.P. Engels Verlag, 1988, p. 385–400.

KJÆRGAARD E., «The Concept of 'Safe Third Country' in Contemporary European Refugee Law», ECRE, 6th International ELENA Course, Oxford, 16–19 December 1993, 10 p.

KJÆRUM Morten, ed., *The Role of Airline Companies in the Asylum Procedure*, Copenhagen: Danish Refugee Council, 1988, 23 p.

KJÆRUM Morten, ed., *The Effects of Carrier Sanctions on the Asylum System*, Copenhagen: Danish Refugee Council, 1991, 34 p.

KJÆRUM Morten, «Visumpolitik og luftfartsselskaber» («Visa Policy and Airline Companies»), *Asyl i Norden* (Asylum in the Nordic Countries), Copenhagen:

Danish Refugee Council, 1990, p. 30–44.

KLAAUW Johannes van der, «The provisions on human rights and asylum in the revised Treaty on European Union», *Netherlands Quarterly on Human Rights,* Vol. 15, No. 3 (1997), p. 365–369.

KLAAUW Johannes van der, «The Dublin Convention, the Schengen asylum chapter and the treatment of asylum applications», in *Het Akkoord van Schengen en vreemdelingen»,* Utrecht: Netherland Immigration Centre, 1997, p. 37–47.

KLAAUW Johannes van der, «Refugee protection in Western Europe: a UNHCR perspective», in J.-Y. Carlier and D. Vanheule, ed., *Europe and Refugees: A Challenge?,* The Hague: Kluwer Law International, p. 227–248.

KOOIJMANS Peter H., «Trends and Developments in Asylum and Admission of Refugees», *Yearbook of the International Institute of Humanitarian Law,* 1986–87, p. 153–160.

KOOIJMANS Peter H., «Ambiguities in Refugee Law – Some Remarks on the Concept of the Country of First Asylum», in Manfred Nowak et al., ed., *Progress in the Spirit of Human Rights,* Festschrift für Felix Ermacora, Kehl am Rhein: N.P. Engel Verlag, 1988, p. 401–414.

LANDGREN Karin, «Gender Related Persecution», remarks at Symposium on Women and Asylum, Copenhagen, 3 March 1997.

LAPENNA Enrico, «Le Réfugié et l'Emigrant dans le Cadre des Droits et Libertés Fondamentaux», *AWR Bulletin,* N° 1–2, 1984, p. 50–58.

LAPENNA Enrico, «Les réfugiés de facto – un nouveau problème pour l'Europe», *AWR Bulletin,* N° 2–3, 1981, p. 61–68.

LAUTERPACHT Hersch, «The Universal Declaration of Human Rights», *British Yearbook of International Law,* 1948, p 354–381.

Lawyers Committee for Human Rights, «The Human Rights of Refugees and Displaced Persons: Protections Afforded Refugees, Asylum Seekers and Displaced Persons under International Human Rights, Humanitarian and Refugee Law», New York, May 1991, 28 p.

LEUPRECHT Peter, «Le droit d'asile en Europe», in F. Rigaux, ed., *Droit d'Asile,* Brussels: E. Story-Scientia, 1988, p. 69–77.

LEUPRECHT Peter, «La forteresse et les droits de l'homme», *L'événement européen, Dossier l'Europe et ses immigrés,* Vol. 11, 1990, p. 51–60.

LOBKOWICZ Wenceslas de, «La cooperation intergouvernementale dans le domaine des migrations de l'Acte unique à Maastricht», report presented to the European College, Bruges, 9 September 1993, 25 p.

LOBKOWICZ Wenceslas de, «La Communauté européenne et le droit d'asile», Schweizerisches Institut für Auslandsforschung, Verlag Rüegger, 1991, p. 39–59.

LOBKOWICZ Wenceslas de, «L'Union européenne et le droit d'asile», report presented to the colloquy Evolutions récentes du droit des réfugiés en Europe, Toulouse, 25 March 1993, 48 p.

LOBKOWICZ Wenceslas de, «La Convention de Dublin: un utile complément au droit humanitaire international», *Objectif Europe,* Nouvelle série, N° 10, 1990, p. 7–12.

LOESCHER Gil, «Les mouvements de réfugiés dans l'après-guerre froide», *Politique Étrangère,* N° 3, 1994, p. 707–717.

LOESCHER Gil, «The European Community and Refugees», *International Affairs*, Vol. 65, N° 4, 1989, p. 617–636.

MACKIE of BENSHIE Lord, «Rapport sur l'arrivée de demandeurs d'asile dans les aéroports européens», Council of Europe, Parliamentary Assembly, 2 September 1991, Doc. 6490, 15 p.

MADUREIRA M. Joao, «La jurisprudence des organes de la Convention européenne des Droits de l'Homme et de la Charte sociale européenne concernant l'entrée et la sortie des étrangers du territoire d'un Etat», the colloquy Human Rights without Frontiers, Strasbourg, 30 November –1 December 1989, 54 p.

MAHIGA Augustine Philip, «The Development Dimension of the Refugee Problem in Africa», in Vera Gowlland and Klaus Samson, ed., *Problems and Prospects of Refugee Law*, Geneva: Institute of International Studies, 1992, p. 73–77.

MARTIN David A, «Strategies for a Resistant World: Human Rights Initiatives and the Need for Alternatives to Refugee Interdiction», *Cornell International Law Journal*, 1993.

MARTIN David A., «New Developments in Refugee Law and Current Problems: Asylum Concept; Solidarity; and the Concept of Burden-Sharing», Proceedings from the Symposium on the Promotion, Dissemination and Teaching of Fundamental Human Rights of Refugees, Tokyo, 7–11 December 1981, Geneva: UNHCR, 1982, p. 61–71.

McDOWELL Roy, «Co-ordination of Refugee Policy in Europe», in Gil Loescher and Laila Nonahan, ed., *Refugees and International Relations*, Oxford University Press, 1989, p. 179–186.

McNAMARA Dennis, «Determinaton of the Status of Refugees-Evolution of the Definition», Proceedings from the Symposium on Promotion, Dissemination and Teaching of Fundamental Human Rights of Refugees, Tokyo, 7–11 December 1981, Geneva: UNHCR, February 1982, p. 76–78.

MEIJERS H., «Refugees in Western Europe. 'Schengen' Affects the Entire Refugee Law», *International Journal of Refugee Law*, Vol. 2, N° 3, 1990, p. 428–441.

MEIJERS H., «Foreword», in A. Terlouw et al., ed., *A New Immigration Law for Europe?: The 1992 London and 1993 Copenhagen Rules on Immigration*, Utrecht: Netherland Immigration Centre, 1993, p. 5–7.

MELANDER Göran, «Good Offices Refugees», *AWR Bulletin*, Vol. 4, 1972, p. 195–199.

MELANDER Göran, «Responsibility for Examining an Asylum Request», Lund: Raoul Wallenberg Institute, Report No. 1 1986, p. 9–16.

MELANDER Göran, «Refugees in Orbit», in Göran Melander and Peter Nobel, ed., *African Refugees and the Law*, Uppsala: Scandinavian Institute of African Studies, 1978, p. 27–40.

MELANDER Göran, «The Two Refugee Definitions», Lund: Raoul Wallenberg Institute, Report N° 4, 1987, p. 9–22.

MELANDER Göran, «'Country of First Asylum' Issues: A European Perspective», in Jacqueline Bhabha and Geoffrey Coll, ed., *Asylum Law & Practice in Europe and North America: A Comparative Analysis*, Washington, DC: Federal Publications Inc., 1992, p. 101–107.

MELANDER Göran, «Further Development of International Refugee Law», in *The*

Refugee Problem on Universal, Regional and National Level, Thessaloniki: Institute of International Law and International Relations, 1987, p 469–512.

MELANDER Göran, «Responsibility for the Examination of an Asylum Request, Asylum Seekers vs Quota Refugees», in the report from a seminar on restrictive asylum policy in Europe, Zeist, Holland, 16–18 January 1985, London: ECRE, March 1985, p 18–21.

MELANDER Göran, «Refugees in Orbit: Notions and Definitions», San Remo: International Institute of Humanitarian Law, 1979, p 6–12.

MIGNON Eric, «Réfugiés et compagnies aériennes», *Revue du droit des étrangers*, N° 56, 1989, p 287–296.

MINTER Shannon, «Sodomy and Public Morality Offenses Under US Immigration Law: Penalizing Lesbian and Gay Identity», *Cornell International Law Journal*, 1993, p. 561–609.

MIRANDA Carlos Ortiz, «Toward a Broader Definition of Refugee: 20th Century Development Trends», *California Western International Law Journal*, Vol. 20, N° 2, 1989–1990, p 315–327.

MOUSSALLI Michel, «Mémoire du HCR sur les questions d'actualité relatives à l'asile», *Documentation-Réfugiés*, N° 182, 1992, p 12–16.

MOUSSALLI Michel, «Human Rights and Refugees», *Yearbook of the International Institute of Humanitarian Law*, 1984, p. 13–20.

MUNTARBHORN Vitit, «Determination of the Status of Refugees: Definition in Context», Proceedings from the Symposium on the Promotion, Dissemination and Teaching of Fundamental Human Rights of Refugees, Tokyo, 7–11 December 1981, Geneva: UNHCR, February 1982, p. 83–90.

NANDA Ved P., «The Movement of Persons Across Borders – Part III: Refugees and Displaced Persons», *American Society of International Law*, 1991, 55 p.

NOAS (Norwegian Organization for Asylum Seekers), «Virkninger av EFs indre marked i forhold til asylsøkere og flyktninger i Norge» (The Effect of the Internal Market of the European Community for Asylum seekers and Refugees in Norway), November 1990, 43 p.

NOAS, «En mur rundt Europa – Konsekvenser for Norge» (A Wall Around Europe – Consequences for Norway), 1992, 15 p.

NOBEL Peter, «Protection of Refugees in Europe as Seen in 1987», Lund: Raoul Wallenberg Institute, Report N° 4, 1987, p. 23–41.

NOBEL Peter, «De facto-flyktningbegreppet i Norden» (The Concept of De Facto Refugees in the Nordic Countries), *Asyl i Norden* (Asylum in the Nordic Countries), Copenhagen: Danish Refugee Council, 1990, p. 102–118.

O'CONNOR Terry, «Gender and the Convention Refugee Definition», dissertation, London: Immigration Law Practitioners' Association (ILPA), April 1993, 20 p.

OLOKA-ONYANGO Joe, «Human Rights, the OAU Convention and the Refugee Crisis in Africa: 40 Years after Geneva», *International Journal of Refugee Law*, Vol. 3, N° 3, 1991, p. 453–460.

OVEY Clare, «Prohibition of Refoulement: The Meaning of Article 3 of the European Convention on Human Rights and Fundamental Freedoms», The International Course on the European Human Rights Convention in Relation to Asylum, ELENA, Strasbourg, 23–26 May 1997.

PASTORE C., «Refugees in Orbit (The Problem of Refugees without a Country of Asylum)», New Haven, Ct., Yale Law School, Lowenstein Human Rights Law Project, June 1986, 42 p.

PERLUSS D. and HARTMAN J.F., «Temporary Refuge: Emergence of a Customary Norm», *Virginia Journal of International Law*, Vol. 26, 1986, p. 551–626.

PETERSEN Michael, «Le pays d'asile», statement at a seminar of Europan lawyers on the concept of 'the first country of asylum', 10–12 January 1986, ECRE/ZDWF, April 1987, p. 19–23.

PLENDER Richard, «Asylum Policy», statement at the seminar «Joint research project on the third pillar of the European Union Treaty. Recent developments and problems», European College, Centre for European Law, Bruges, 19–20 September 1994, 29 p.

RAMCHARAN B.G., «The Good Offices of the United Nations Secretary-General in the Field of Human Rights», *The American Journal of International Law*, Vol. 76, 1982, p. 130–141.

REGENSBURGER O., «Le régime des visas pour les ressortissants yougoslaves», *Revue de politique internationale*, N° 941, 1989, p. 10–12.

ROGGE John R., «Some Comments on Definitions and Typologies of Africa's Refugees», *Zambian Geographical Journal*, N° 33–34, 1978–79, p. 49–60.

RUDGE Philip, «The Asylum Crisis: The Challenge for Lawyers: A European View», in Jacqueline Bhabha and Geoffrey Coll, ed., *Asylum Law & Practice in Europe and North America: A Comparative Analysis*, Washington, DC: Federal Publications Inc, 1992, p. 15–19.

RUDGE Philip, «Refugee Policy to 1992 and Beyond», intervention at the commemoration of the 40th anniversary of the Geneva Convention, Brussels, June 1991.

SAKSON A., «Hintergründe der polnishen Massenemigration – die De-Facto-Flüchtlinge aus Polen», *AWR Bulletin*, N° 3, 1990.

SCHWEBEL Stephen M., «The Effect of Resolutions of the UN General Assembly on Customary International Law», American Society of International Law, Proceedings from the 73 annual Conference, Washington DC, 26–28 April 1979, p. 300–309.

SEPULVEDA César, «Methods and Procedures for the Creation of Legal Norms in the International System of States: An Inquiry into the Progressive Development of International Law in the Present Era», *Georgetown Yearbook of International Law*, Vol. 33, 1990, p 432–459.

SIEMENS Maria, «Asylum and Protection in Latin America: The Cartagena Declaration of 1984», *Refugees*, October 1987, p 32–33.

SLOAN Blain, «General Assembly Resolutions Revisited (Forty Years Later)», *British Yearbook of International Law*, 1987, p. 39–150.

SOULIER Gérard, «Le respect du droit d'asile, preuve et garant du droit démocratique», in F. Rigaux, ed., *Droit d'asile*, Brussels: Story-Scientia, 1988, p. 101–107.

STAINSBY R.A., «Opinion – Asylum Seekers in Poland: Catalyst for a New Refugee and Asylum Policy in Europe», *International Journal of Refugee Law*, Vol. 2, N° 4, 1990, p. 636–641.

Standing committee on international migration, refugee and criminal law, «A New

Immigration Law for Europe? The 1992 London and 1993 Copenhagen Rules on Immigration», Netherland Immigration Centre, 1993, 96 p.

Standing committee on international migration, refugee and criminal law, «Carrier Sanctions», 1992, 6 p.

Standing committee on international migration, refugee and criminal law, «Schengen», November 1991, 22 p.

STEENBERGEN Hanneke D.M., «The Relevance of the European Convention on Human Rights for Asylum Seekers», in The New Refugee Hosting Countries: Call for Experience – Space for Innovation, *SIM Special* N° 11, 1991, p. 45–68.

STEFANINI Patrick and DOUBLET Frédérique, «Le droit d'asile en Europe: La Convention relative à la détermination de l'Etat responsable de l'examen d'une demande d'asile présentée auprès d'un Etat membre des Communautés européennes», *Revue du Marché Commun et de l'Union européenne*, N° 347, 1991, p. 391–399.

THORBURN Joanne, «Transcending Boundaries: Temporary Protection and Burden-sharing in Europe», *International Journal of Refugee Law*, Vol. 7, No. 3, 1995, p. 459–480.

TURPIN D., «Aspects Politico-Juridiques Internes de la Situation des Réfugiés en Afrique», in *Les réfugiés en Afrique – situation et problèmes actuels*, Bordeaux: Institut français de droit humanitaire et des droits de l'homme, Les cahiers du droit public, 1986, 101 p.

UNHCR, «UNHCR strategy towards 2000», PO1/02/97, 20 p.

UNHCR, «Note on Temporary Protection in a Broader Context», 1997.

UNHCR, «Survey on the Implementation of Temporary Protection», Humanitarian Issues Working Group of the International Conference on the Former Yugoslavia, 8 March 1995, 90 p.

UNHCR, «Populations of Concern to UNHCR. A Statistical Overview. 1993», May 1994, 34 p.

UNHCR, «Fair and Expeditious Asylum Procedures», November 1994, 5 p.

UNHCR, «Briefing on UNHCRs Position with Regard to the Resolutions which Relate to Procedures for Manifestly Unfounded Applications for Asylum, Host Third Countries and Countries in which there is in General no Serious Risk of Persecution, as Approved on 30 November 1992 by the Ministers of the Member States of the European Communities Responsible for Immigration», 3 December 1992, 2 p.

UNHCR, «UNHCRs Position on Standard Bilateral Readmission Agreements Between a Member State and a Third Country», December 1994, 2 p.

UNHCR, «Asylum applications and the entry into force of the Schengen Implementation Agreement: Some observations of UNHCR», March 1995, 3 p.

UNHCR, «Readmission Agreements, 'Protection Elsewhere' and Asylum Policy», August 1994, 4 p.

UNHCR, «Information note on article 1 of the 1951 Convention», March 1995, 5 p.

UNHCR, «Current Asylum Issues Harmonization in Europe», March 1992, 8 p.

UNHCR, «UNHCR Concerned by EU Agreement on Asylum Procedures», in *UNHCR up date*, 10 March 1995, 2 p.

VEEN Job van der, «Does Persecution by Fellow-Citizens in Certain Regions of a

State Fall within the Definition of 'Persecution' in the Convention Relating to the Status of Refugees of 1951? Some Comments Based on Dutch Judicial Decisions», *Netherlands Yearbook of International Law*, Dordrecht: Martinus Nijhoff, Vol 11, 1980, p. 167–174.

VEUTHEY Michel, «Réfugiés, droits de l'homme, droit humanitaire, paix et sécurité», in Vera Gowlland and Klaus Samson, ed., *Problems and Prospects of Refugee Law*, Geneva: The Graduate Institute of International Studies, 1992, p. 49–58.

VIERDAG E.W., «The Country of 'First Asylum': Some European Aspects», in David A. Martin, ed., *The New Asylum Seekers: Refugee Law in the 1980s*, Dordrecht: Martinus Nijhoff Publishers, 1988, p. 73–84.

VIERDAG E.W., «'Asylum' and 'Refugee' in International Law», *Netherlands International Law Review*, Vol. 24, special edition 1/2, 1977, p. 287–303.

VILLALPANDO Waldo, «L'asile dans l'histoire», *Quaderni*, 1991, p. 33–81.

WECKEL Philippe, «La convention additionelle à l'accord de Schengen», *Revue Générale de Droit International Public*, N° 2, 1991, p. 405–437.

WEIS Paul, «Recent Developments in the Law of Territorial Asylum», *Revue des Droits de l'Homme*, Vol. 1, N° 3, 1968, 15 p.

WEIS Paul, «Le concept de réfugié en droit international», *Journal du Droit International*, N° 1, 1960, p. 928–1001.

WEIS Paul, «Legal Aspects of the Problem of Asylum», Geneva: UNHCR, 1968, 12 p.

WEIS Paul, «The 1967 Protocol Relating to the Status of Refugees and some Questions of the Law of Treaties», *British Yearbook of International Law*, 1967, p. 39–70.

WEIS Paul, «The Draft United Nations Convention on Territorial Asylum», *British Yearbook of International Law*, 1979, p. 151–171.

WEIS Paul, «Legal Aspects of the Convention of 28 July 1951 Relating to the Status of Refugee», *British Yearbook of International Law*, 1953, p. 478–489.

WEIS Paul, «Territorial Asylum», *The Indian Journal of International Law*, Vol.6, N° 2, 1966, p. 173–194.

WEIS Paul, «Human Rights and Refugees», *Israel Yearbook on Human Rights*, Vol. 1, 1971, p. 35–50.

WEIS Paul, «The United Nations Declaration on Territorial Asylum», *The Canadian Yearbook of International Law*, 1969, p. 92–149.

WEIS Paul, «Convention Refugees and de facto Refugees», in Göran Melander and Peter Nobel, ed., *African Refugees and the Law*, Uppsala: Scandinavian Institute of African Studies, 1978, p. 15–22.

WHITAKER Elizabeth M., «The Schengen Agreement and its portent for the freedom of personal movement in Europe», *Georgetown Immigration Law Journal*, Vol. 6, N° 1, 1992, p 191–222.

WIEDERKER Marie-Odile, statement at a seminar on Responsibility for Examining an Asylum Request, Raoul Wallenberg Institute, Lund, 24–26 April 1985, 1986, p. 17–21.

WILLE Petter, «Flyktningebegrepet i FN-konvensjonen om flyktningers stilling av 28. juli 1951» («The Concept of Refugees in the UN Convention on the Status of Refugees), *Lov og Rett*, N° 3, 1989, p. 427–439.

ZOLLER Elisabeth, *Le droit d'asile*, Centre for Studies and Research in International

Law and International Relations of the Hague Academy of International Law, 1989, Dordrecht: Martinus Nijhoff Publishers, 1990, p. 15–61.

ZWAMBORN Marcel, «The Scope for a Refugee Policy of the European Communities as Part of an Overall Human Rights Policy», Utrecht, October 1989, 26 p.

Documents
Conventions and Treaties:
Universal:
- Statute of the Office of the United Nations High Commissioner for Refugees, General Assembly Resolution 428 (V), 14 December 1950.
- Convention relating to the Status of Refugees, 28 July 1951.
- Protocol relating to the Status of Refugees, 31 January 1967.
- Convention for the Repression of the Crime of Genocide, 9 December 1948.
- International Convention on the Elimination of All Forms of Racial Discrimination, 21 December 1965.
- International Convention on the Suppression and Punishment of Apartheid of 1973.
- International Covenant on Economic, Social and Cultural Rights, 16 December 1966.
- Internaional Covenant on Civil and Political Rights, 16 December 1966.
- Geneva Conventions for the protection of victims of war, 12 August 1949 (Convention for the protection of the wounded, and sick; Convention for the protection of wounded, sick and shipwrecked; Convention relative to the treatment of prisoners of war; Conventiuon relative to the protection of civilian persons).
- Additional Protocol to the Geneva Conventions of 1949 Relating to the Protection of Victims of International Armed Conflicts, 8 June 1977.
- International Convention on the Elimination of All Forms of Discrimination Against Women, 18 December 1979
- Convention Against Torture and other forms of Cruel, Inhumane or Degrading Treatment or Punishment, 10 December 1984.
- Convention on the Rights of the Child, 20 November 1989.

Regional:
- European Convention for the Protection of Human Rights and Fundamental Freedoms, 4 November 1950, and the Protocols N° 4 (1963) and N° 7 (1984).
- American Convention on Human Rights, 22 November 1969. («Pact of San José Pact de Costa Rica»)
- African Charter on Human and Peoples' Rights, June 1981.
- OAU Convention governing the specific aspects of refugees problems in Africa, 10 September 1969.
- Treaty on international criminal law, 23 January 1889 (Montevideo).
- Convention on Asylum, 20 February 1928 (Havana).
- Convention on Political Asylum, 26 December 1933 (Montevideo).
- Treaty on international criminal law, 19 March 1940 (Montevideo).

- Convention on Territorial Asylum, 28 March 1954 (Caracas).
- Convention on Diplomatic Asylum, 28 March 1954 (Caracas).
- Inter-American Convention on Extradition, 25 February 1981 (Caracas).
- Treaty of Amsterdam amending the Treaty on European Union, the Treaties establishing the European Communities and certain Related Acts (the Treaty of Amsterdam), 2 October 1997.
- Treaty on European Union (the Maastricht Treaty), 7 February 1992.
- Treaty on European Economic Community (the Treaty of Rome), 25 March 1957.
- Convention applying the Schengen Agreement of 14 June 1985 between the Governments of the States of the Benelux Economic Union, The Federal Republic of Germany and the French Republic, on the Gradual Abolition of Checks at their Common Borders (the Schengen Convention) of 19 June 1990.
- Convention determining the State responsible for examining applications for asylum lodged in one of the Member States of the European Communities and measures for its implementation (the Dublin Convention) of 15 June 1990.

Other instruments and texts relevant to the subject:

Universal:
- Universal Declaration of Human Rights, 10 December 1948.
- United Nations Declaration on Territorial Asylum, 14 December 1967 (General Assembly Resolution 2312 (XXII)).
- Vienna Declaration and Programme of Action, A/CONF.157/23, Vienna, 1992.
- Beijing Declaration and Platform for Action, A/CONF.177/20, Beijing, 1995.

Regional

Council of Europe: Resolutions and Recommendations:
- Final Declaration, Second Summit of Heads of State and Government of the Council of Europe, Strasbourg 10–11 October 1997 (SUM (97)PV 2 prov.))
- Recommendation 1324 (1997) on the Parliamentary Assembly contribution to the Second Summit of Heads of State and Government of the Council of Europe.
- Parliamentary Assembly Recommendation 1278 (1995) on refugees and asylum seekers in central and eastern Europe.
- Parliamentary Assembly Recommendation 1237 (1994) on the situation of asylum seekers whose asylum applications have been rejected.
- Parliamentary Assembly Recommendation 1236 (1994) on the right of asylum.
- Parliamentary Assembly recommendation 1149 (1991) on Europe of 1992 and refugee policies.
- Recommendation 1088 (1988) Parliamentary Assembly on the right to territorial asylum.
- Parliamentary Assembly Recommendation 1031 (1986) on the 24th report on the activities of the Office of the United High Commissioner for Refugees (UNHCR).
- Committee of Ministers Recommendation N° R(94)5 on guidelines to inspire

practices of the member states of the Council of Europe concerning the arrival of asylum seekers at European airports.
- Committee of Ministers Recommendation N° R(84)1 on the protection of persons satisfying the criteria in the Geneva Convention who are not formally recognized as refugees.
- Parliamentary Assembly Recommendation 953 (1982) on the 23rd report on the activities of the Office of the United High Commissioner for Refugees (UNHCR).
- Committee of Ministers Recommendation N° R(81)16 on the harmonization of national procedures on matters of asylum.
- Declaration on territorial asylum, adopted by Committee of Ministers, 18 November 1977.
- Recommendation 817 (1977) Parliamentary Assembly on certain aspects of the right to asylum.
- Recommendation 787 (1976) Parliamentary Assembly on the harmonization of eligibility practice under the 1951 Geneva Convention on the Status of Refugees and the 1967 Protocol.
- Recommendation 773 (1976) Parliamentary Assembly on the situation of de facto refugees.
- Resolution (67)14 Committe of Ministers on asylum to persons in danger of persecution.
- Recommendation 434 (1965) Consultative Assembly on the granting of the right of asylum to European refugees.
- Recommendation 293 (1961) Consultative Assembly on the right of asylum.

Council of Europe: other texts of relevance to the subject:

- Parliamentary Assembly, Committee on Migration, Refugees and Demography: Draft report on the protection and reinforcement of the human rights of refugees and asylum seekers in Europe, AS/PR (1997) 2 rev., 19 February 1997.
- Parliamentary Assembly, Committee on Migration, Refugees and Demography: Preliminary draft report on temporary protection of persons forced to flee their countries, AS/PR (1996) 21, 18 September 1996.
- Parliamentary Assembly: Report on the right of asylum, Doc. 7052, 23 March 1994.
- CAHAR: Guidelines to inspire practice of member states of the Council of Europe concerning the reception of asylum seekers at European airports. Proposal by the Hungarian delegation, CAHAR (93)14, 13 September 1993.
- Parliamentary Assembly: Rapport sur l'Europe de 1992 et les politiques en matière de réfugiés, Doc. 6413, 12 April 1991.
- CAHAR: De facto refugees, CAHAR (90) 3, 3 September 1990.
- CAHAR: Draft Agreement on responsibility for examining asylum requests. Final activity report of the 27 meeting of the CAHAR, CAHAR (88) 9 Final, 25 January 1989.
- CAHAR: First country of asylum. Refugees in orbit. Responsibility for the examination of asylum seekers, CAHAR (86) 1, 17 March 1986.
- CAHAR:Territorial asylum, CAHAR (85) 8, 25 July 1985.

European Communities/ EuropeanUnion:

- European Parliament, Committee on Civil Liberties and Internal Affairs: Working document on the proposal for a joint action concerning temporary protection of displaced persons, Doc. EN/DT/326/326311, 2 Juni 1997.
- Commission of the European Communities: Proposal to the Council for a Joint Action based on Article K.3. 2(b) of the Treaty on Eurpean Union concerning Temporary Protection of dsplaced persons, 5 March 1997.
- European Parliament, Committee on Civil Liberties and Internal Affairs: Report on the functioning and future of Schengen, A4-0014/97, 22 January 1997.
- European Parliament, Committee on Civil Liberties and Internal Affairs: Working dodument, The operation of Schengen: an evaluation, Doc. EN/DT/305/305700, 15 October 1996.
- Council Decision on an alert and emergency procedure for burden-sharing with regard to the admission and residence of displaced persons on a temporary basis, 96/198/JHA, 4 March 1996.
- Council Resolution on burden-sharing with regard to the admission and residence of displaced persons on a temporary basis, 95/C 262/01, 25 September 1995.
- Council Resolution on minimum guarantees for asylum procedures, 20 June 1995.
- Council Conclusions concerning the possible application of Article K. 9 of the Treaty on European Union to asylum policy, 20 June 1994.
- Communication of the Commission to the Council and the European Parliament on immigration and asylum policies, COM(94)23 final, 23 February 1994.
- Council Resolution on certain common guidelines as regards the admission of particularly vulnerable groups of persons from the former Yugoslavia, 1–2 June 1993.
- The Council: Joint Position on the harmonized application of the definition of the term «refugee» in Article 1 of the Geneva Convention of 28 July 1951 relating to the status of refugees (96/196/JHA), 4 March 1996.
- Resolution on manifestly unfounded applications for asylum, adopted by Ministers of the Member States of the European Communities responsible for Immigration, London, 30 November 1992.
- Resolution on a harmonized approach to questions concerning host third countries, adopted by Ministers of the Member States of the European Communities responsible for Immigration, London, 30 November 1992.
- Conclusions on countries in which there is generally no serious risk of persecution, adopted by Ministers of the Member States of the European Communities responsible for Immigration, London, 30 November 1992.
- Report from the Ministers responsible for immigration to the European Council meeting in Maastricht on immigration and asylum policy, SN 4038/91 WGI 930, 3 December 1991.
- Communication of the Commission to the Council and the European Parliament on the right of asylum, SEC(91) 1857 final, 11 October 1991.

Index

Accelerated asylum procedures 224, 275
Agents of persecution,
  see persecution
Asylum/territorial asylum 16, 17, 27, 50, 53, 94, 102, 106, 120, 137, 169–206, 208, 209, 229
  Asylum seeker .16, 26, 27, 71, 79, 93, 112, 175, 186, 188, 192, 212, 224, 230, 233, 240, 245, 256
  Diplomatic Asylum 51, 139–141, 170
  Extra-territorial Asylum 137
  Temporary asylum, see temporary protection
Asylum shopping 243, 253

B-status refugee, see refugee
Benefit of the doubt, see «in dubio pro reo»
Burden of proof 61, 62, 70
Burden sharing 16, 124, 195, 202, 206, 209, 215, 216–219, 229, 261, 278–281

Carrier sanctions 30, 94, 224
Cessation clauses, see Convention relating to the Status of Refugees
Cartagena Declaration 36, 95, 101, 107–109, 117, 128, 149, 150, 165, 194
Centre for Information, Discussion and Exchange on Asylum (CIREA) 187

Chain deportation, see deportation
Change of circumstances 87
Church asylum 17, 138
Collective protection 199
Convention relating to the Status of Refugees (1951 Convention) 13, 30, 35, 43–94, 147
  Cessation clauses 47, 60, 86–89, 191
  Exclusion clauses 47, 89–94, 158
  Geographical limitation 49–51, 238
  Time limitation 47–49
Council of Europe 15, 31, 32, 41, 42, 120–123, 151, 180, 181–186, 195, 205, 206, 227, 229, 232
  CAHAR 120, 121, 237
  Committee of Ministers 42, 122, 123, 151, 182, 232
  European Commission of Human Rights 153–156, 181
  European Court of Human Rights 68, 153–156, 181
  Parliamentary Assembly 31, 42, 85, 108, 120–122, 152, 182–185, 205, 220
Crimes against humanity 84, 90, 91, 177, 209, 210
Customary international law 36, 37, 157–163, 170, 171

«De facto» refugee,
  see refugee
Deportation 153, 230, 245, 260

Diplomatic asylum, see asylum
Displaced persons 22, 96–102, 124, 220
  Internally displaced persons (IDPs) 25, 52, 101, 102, 106
Draft evader 113
Dublin Convention 38, 135, 156, 157, 183, 232, 245, 256, 257, 260
«Dublin/Schengen regime» 234, 235, 253–273, 280

Economic migrant 72
«Ejusdem generis» 75, 81
«En route concept» 238, 242, 244, 245, 246, 278, 282
European Union 14, 27, 50, 65, 66, 119, 123, 124, 128, 156, 157, 184, 186–191, 195, 199–205, 208, 253, 262, 267
  European Council 28, 29
  European Commission 84, 123, 252, 289
  European Parliament 84
European Convention of Human Rights 35, 42, 122, 130, 153–156, 181, 284
Exceptional leave to remain/ exceptional leave to stay 110, 116, 139, 199
Exclusion clauses, see Convention relating to the Status of refugees
Executive Committee of UNHCR, see UNHCR

Fear of persecution, see persecution
First country of asylum 23, 166, 192, 218, 225, 248, 269
«First country of asylum»«safe third country» concept 16, 30, 168, 224, 225, 228, 229–273, 282, 283

Gender related persecution, see persecution
General principles of law 37
Generalized violence 14, 79, 101, 108, 109, 112, 126, 128, 131, 143, 144, 192, 193
Geographical limitation, see Convention relating to the Status of Refugees
Good faith 39
«Good offices» 45, 96–103, 118

Human Rights 32, 35, 36, 43, 67–72, 85, 92, 93, 128, 146, 148, 158, 206, 248, 283
Humanitarian intervention 51, 52

«In dubio pro reo» 61
«In orbit», see refugee
Internal flight 54, 55
International Covenant on Civil and Political Rights 35, 68, 169
International Covenant on Economic, Social and Cultural Rights 35, 71, 222
International solidarity 16, 122, 135, 176, 206, 209, 216–219, 235, 251, 252, 278–282
Irregular movements 239, 240, 241

Large-scale influx, see mass influx
League of Nations .18

Manifestly unfounded 175, 187, 240, 261, 265
Man-made disasters 99, 100, 105

Mass exodus/mass outflow 104, 192, 195
Mass influx 165, 174, 195, 196, 197, 215, 222, 223
Membership of a particular social group, see persecution

Nationality, see persecution
Natural disaster 100, 106, 220
Non-refoulement principle 15, 37, 42, 54, 89, 116, 137, 145, 146–168, 175, 196, 197, 206, 214, 225, 230, 231, 239, 247
    Non-expulsion 163, 164
    Non-extradition 163, 164
    Non-rejection at the border 161–163

OAU Convention 36, 95, 101, 103–107, 108, 109, 117, 128, 149, 165, 178, 194
Opinio juris 37, 42, 160
Organization for Security and Cooperation in Europe (OSCE) 215, 217

Persecution 13, 55–94, 103, 114, 245
    Agents of persecution 65–67
    Gender related persecution 78–85, 112, 113
    Membership of a particular social group (social group) 45, 72, 74–77, 80–85
    Nationality 52, 74, 80
    Political opinion 77, 78
    Race 72, 73
    Religion 73, 74
    Well-founded fear 54, 58–63
Political opinion, see persecution

Principles and purposes of the UN 210
Protected areas 137, 138, 143–146
Protection 23, 31, 32, 40, 43, 93, 102, 106, 118, 129, 136-176, 193, 207, 220, 225, 241
«Protection elsewhere» 229, 241, 242, 246–250, 276, 277
Protocol relating to the Status of Refugees 13, 44, 45, 49

Race, see persecution
Readmission agreements 224, 231, 252, 270–273, 274
refoulement 248
Refugee 229
    B-status refugee 54, 110, 116, 138
    1951 Convention refugee 55, 56, 72–85, 130, 170, 219
    «De facto» refugees 14, 34, 40, 57, 60, 85, 95, 109–124, 138, 202, 212, 219, 221, 248, 260
    «Prima facie» refugee 56, 67, 98, 192
    Quota refugee 45
    Refugee «in orbit» 239, 245, 247, 250, 251, 257, 268, 269, 273, 274, 283
    Refugee «sur place» 53, 54, 113
Refugee status determination procedure 259, 275, 276
Repatriation 137, 167, 212, 213, 223
Resettlement 241
Residence permit on humanitarian grounds/humanitarian reasons 94, 110, 138, 202, 211, 222

Sanctuary 17, 138
«Safe country» concept 246–250
Safe haven 137, 144, 219
«Safe third country» concept, see «first country of asylum»/«safe third country» concept
«Safety and dignity» 167
Schengen Convention 233, 245, 254, 255, 257
Soft law 34, 38, 39, 109, 136, 147, 148, 178, 182
«Sur place», see refugee

Temporary protection 16, 56, 89, 113, 138, 157, 170, 191–206, 209, 218, 220
Time limitation, see Convention relating to the Status of Refugees
«Third country» (of asylum) 231, 235
Tolerated stay 54
Torture
  Torture Convention 35, 148, 156, 159, 222
  UN Committee against Torture 68, 159
Transit 244, 245, 277
Treatment of refugees 120, 132, 206, 209, 221-223
Treaty law 33–36, 157-161
Treaty of Amsterdam 28, 29
Treaty of Maastricht 28, 29, 123, 124, 189, 201

United Nations 20, 25, 52, 171
  Charter of the United Nations 21, 44, 91, 92
  Economic and Social Council (ECOSOC) 21, 24, 25, 34, 40, 99
  General Assembly 21, 25, 34, 38, 39, 40, 95-103, 173
  International Court of Justice 21, 37
  Security Council 21
UNHCR 13, 22, 32, 34, 55, 86, 96-103, 106, 117, 126, 132, 150, 167, 171, 188, 194-199, 215, 226, 240, 263, 264
  Executive Committee of UNHCR 25, 40, 83, 84, 88 97, 98, 108, 109, 251
  UNHCR Handbook 41, 54, 65, 93
  UNHCR mandate 22–25, 32, 40, 96–103, 117, 118, 136, 160
Universal Declaration of Human Rights 35, 40, 44, 68, 71, 133, 134, 171, 172, 173, 222, 225

Visa 30, 93, 225

War crime 84, 90, 91, 144, 177

Well-founded fear, see persecution